United Nations
Department of Economic and Social Development
Transnational Corporations and Management Division

United Nations Library on Transnational Corporations

Volume 3

TRANSNATIONAL CORPORATIONS AND ECONOMIC DEVELOPMENT

Note

The Transnational Corporations and Management Division (formerly the United Nations Centre on Transnational Corporations) of the United Nations Department of Economic and Social Development serves as the focal point within the United Nations Secretariat for all matters related to transnational corporations and acts as secretariat to the Commission on Transnational Corporations, an intergovernmental subsidiary body of the United Nations Economic and Social Council. The objectives of the work programme are to further the understanding of the nature of transnational corporations and of their economic, legal, social and political effects on home and host countries and in international relations, particularly between developed and developing countries; to secure effective international arrangements aimed at enhancing the contribution of transnational corporations to national development goals and world economic growth; and to strengthen the negotiating capacity of host countries, in particular the developing countries, in their dealings with transnational corporations.

General Disclaimer

The designations employed and the presentation of material in this publication do not imply the expression of any opinion whatsoever on the part of the Secretariat of the United Nations concerning the legal status of any country, territory, city or area or of its authorities, or concerning the delimitation of its frontiers or boundaries.

The articles in this series are all reprinted in their original form and country names may not be in accordance with United Nations usage.

The content, views and interpretations are those of the authors and should not be attributed to the United Nations.

United Nations Library on Transnational Corporations

Volume 3

TRANSNATIONAL CORPORATIONS AND ECONOMIC DEVELOPMENT

Edited by Sanjaya Lall

General editor: John H. Dunning

London and New York
published for and on behalf of the United Nations,
Transnational Corporations and Management Division,
Department of Economic and Social Development

First published 1993
by Routledge
11 New Fetter Lane, London EC4P 4EE

Simultaneously published in the USA and Canada
by Routledge
a division of Routledge, Chapman and Hall, Inc.
29 West 35th Street, New York, NY 10001

Typeset by Leaper & Gard Ltd, Bristol, England
Printed and bound in Great Britain by
Mackays of Chatham PLC, Chatham, Kent

British Library Cataloguing in Publication Data

A catalogue reference for this book is available from the British Library.

ISBN 0-415-08536-5 (Vol. 3)
ISBN 0-415-08554-3 (Set A)
ISBN 0-415-08559-4 (All 20 volumes)

*Library of Congress Cataloging in Publication Data
has been applied for.*

ISBN 0-415-08536-5 (Vol. 3)
ISBN 0-415-08554-3 (Set A)
ISBN 0-415-08559-4 (All 20 volumes)

Contents

Preface

The importance of transnational corporations and the globalization of production are now well recognized. Transnational corporations have become central actors of the world economy and, in linking foreign direct investment, trade, technology and finance, they are a driving force of economic growth. Their impact on the economic and social welfare of developed and developing countries is both widespread and critical.

It is one of the functions of the Transnational Corporations and Management Division (formerly the United Nations Centre on Transnational Corporations) – the focal point in the United Nations for all issues relating to transnational corporations – to undertake and promote research on transnational corporations to contribute to a better understanding of those firms and their impact. Over the past thirty years, research on this phenomenon has mushroomed, and hundreds of books and reports, as well as thousands of papers, have been published. It is the principal purpose of this twenty-volume *United Nations Library of Transnational Corporations* to distil, summarize and comment on some of the more influential of those writings on the role of transnational corporations in the world economy. In particular, the contributions in the *United Nations Library* deal with four main issues: the determinants of the global activities of transnational corporations, their organizational structures and strategies, their interactions with the economies and legal systems of the countries in which they operate and the policies that governments pursue towards those corporations. The twenty volumes are intended to cover a wide range of topics that embrace economic, organizational and legal issues.

To accomplish that task, the Centre assembled a distinguished group of editors, who were commissioned to select the seminal contributions to their subject areas published over the past twenty to thirty years. They were also asked to prepare comprehensive bibliographies of writings on their subjects for inclusion in the volumes, and state-of-the-art introductions that summarize the development of their subjects, review the most important current issues and speculate about future work. We hope that the result in each case is a volume that provides a succinct, yet comprehensive, overview of the subject to which it is devoted.

The impact of transnational corporations on economic development has fascinated both researchers and policy-makers since the mid-1960s. In 1973, a group of twenty experts was commissioned by the Economic and Social Council of the United Nations to prepare a report on the impact of transnational corporations on economic development. Subsequently, the United Nations Commission on Transnational Corporations was established and, to assist it, the United Nations Centre on Transnational Corporations was set up.

Since the early 1970s, much has been written on the perceived costs and benefits of foreign direct investment to developing countries. In his introduction to the current volume, Sanjaya Lall, University Lecturer in Development Economics, Institute of Economics and Statistics, and Fellow, Green College, Oxford, and one of the most distinguished and prolific academic researchers and policy advisers on the interaction between the activities of transnational corporations and economic development, reviews both the evolution of scholarly thinking and the changing attitudes of governments towards the contributions of transnational corporations over the past two decades. In particular, he emphasizes the need to take a dynamic view of the role of foreign direct investment in economic development and also cautions against drawing generalized conclusions about the impact of transnational corporations, or of offering simplistic advice to governments of host countries about the appropriate actions towards, or as a consequence of, inbound activities of transnational corporations. So much, he argues, depends on both the characteristics and policies pursued by individual countries, the particular kinds of foreign direct investment being considered and the organizational structure of particular groups of transnational corporations. The extent to which developing countries are generating their own transnational corporations is also of some relevance.

New York, May 1992

Karl P. Sauvant
Chief, Research and
Policy Analysis Branch,
Transnational Corporations
and Management Division

John H. Dunning
General Editor of
United Nations Library on
Transnational Corporations

Acknowledgements

The editors and publishers would like to thank the following publishers and other organisations for permission to reprint copyright material: Allen & Unwin; the American Economic Association; *Industry of Free China*, Council for Economic Planning and Development; *Journal of International Business Studies*, University of South Carolina; Longman Group UK; The Macmillan Press; Pergamon Press; Pinter Publishers; Transaction Publishers, Rutgers University; Unwin Hyman; John Wiley & Sons; World Bank Publications Department.

Acknowledgement is also due to: Basil Blackwell Inc., Basil Blackwell Publishers; Pergamon Press; Unwin Hyman.

Introduction: Transnational Corporations and Economic Development*

Sanjaya Lall

The large literature on transnational corporations (TNCs) and economic development reveals more than a fair share of controversy, but large parts of it have unfortunately been unedifying and unscientific. The original situation, where much was written but little was known about this subject, has only been partly attenuated. Opinions proliferate, but rigorously conducted empirical studies are still relatively scarce. As Richard E. Caves (1982, p. 252) puts it:

> MNEs have encountered hostility and resentment in all countries that host substantial foreign investment, but nowhere more than in LDCs, where they get blamed for the national economy's manifest shortcomings, not to mention the historical sins of colonial domination. Economic analysis has played no great part in resolving disputes between critics and defenders of the MNE's role in development processes. There is little consensus on what institutions and policies most effectively promote the goal of economic development, and writings on the economic role of MNEs have correspondingly run a high ratio of polemic to documented evidence.

The heat of the debate surrounding the role of TNCs in developing countries has, however, subsided considerably in recent years. The closing years of the 1980s have, in fact, witnessed a general warming of attitudes to foreign direct investment, not just in the development literature but also on the part of national governments that were traditionally strongly hostile to TNCs.

There are many explanations for this change: a maturing of the theory of international production, with a better appreciation of the nature and advantages of TNCs; the accumulation of experience of industrialization in the developing world, with some of the exceptionally successful countries drawing heavily on foreign investors, and with many regimes restrictive to

TNCs faring poorly; the growing capability of many developing countries to negotiate with TNCs and, for the more advanced ones, to absorb the leading-edge technologies possessed by TNCs; the slowing down of world economic growth and increasing rate of unemployment in many developing countries; the onset of the debt crisis, with a sharp fall in flows of commercial lending to developing countries; and the speeding up of the process of technological change, with a resulting need of most countries to gain speedy access to modern technologies, services and information networks.

All these developments have coincided with a decline in ideological underpinnings of the more extreme criticisms of TNCs. As radical and dependency analyses have grown unfashionable, and the strategic shifts in most countries in Central and Eastern Europe have gathered pace, there has been a widespread move to greater belief in market efficiency. This move has sometimes been carried to excessive lengths, in that possible deficiencies in free markets (what economists term "market failures") have been glossed over. In the context of TNCs, this has meant, to some analysts, a belief in the absolute virtues of free capital flows, with any interventions regarded as necessarily harmful. Many long-standing concerns about TNC operations have been forgotten by policy makers, some legitimately but others not.

It is not possible to do justice to all these developments in the TNC literature here. The sheer volume of writings on TNCs and development makes comprehensiveness unfeasible; nor is it required. Several issues that this volume is concerned with are being covered in separate volumes in the present series, such as *Technology Transfer*, edited by Edward Chen; *Innovatory Activities*, edited by John Cantwell; *Economic Integration*, edited by Peter Robson; *Industrialization*, edited by Daniel Chudnovsky; *Transfer Pricing and Taxation*, edited by Sylvain Plasschaert; *Market Structure and Industrial Performance*, edited by Richard Newfarmer and Claudio Frischtak; and *Governments and Transnational Corporations*, edited by Theodore Moran. There already exist several useful surveys on the role of TNCs in development: Reuber, *et al.* (1973), Lall and Streeten (1977), Lall (1978) and Hood and Young (1979) of the earlier literature; Caves (1982) of the theory of transnational corporations and their impact on developing countries in the context of this theory; and, more recently, Casson and Pearce (1987), Helleiner (1989), Hill (1990) and Jenkins (1987, 1990). In addition, the United Nations Centre on Transnational Corporations quinquennially publishes useful surveys on issues concerning developing countries (UNCTC, 1988). Cable and Persaud (1987) and UNCTC (1988) contain recent analyses of policy changes in several important host countries.

A full literature survey is thus not attempted here, though the references contain most of the significant contributions in this field. Some of the old debates are touched upon, but accorded less attention because they are inactive, while others are played down because they encroach on other volumes of readings in this series (see below). On the other hand, some issues that are under-represented in the literature are brought out and their significance to the subject is noted.

Analytical Background

Traditional approaches to TNCs were rooted in a framework that treated all foreign capital flows as identical: foreign direct investment was indistinguishable from loans or portfolio investments (MacDougall, 1960). While such analysis yielded some useful insights, much of it was conducted under the highly simplifying assumptions of neoclassical theory (of perfect competition, two factors, identical production functions across countries and the like). The tradition has persisted in the TNC analysis that falls under the aegis of the "pure theory" of trade. Over time, analysts have relaxed some of its unrealistic premises and introduced such imperfections as scale economies, technological leads and lags, intra-firm (intermediate) trade and oligopolistic strategy. However, these approaches remain essentially too abstract for analysing empirically the impact of TNCs on development. They fail to capture the range of market failures that give rise to, and account for the behaviour of TNCs. More importantly, they also fail to confront the market failures that characterize or are faced by developing countries.

At the other end of the ideological spectrum lie radical/dependency approaches to TNCs (for a review, see Jenkins, 1987). The analytical foundations of these approaches are so different from those of mainstream economics that there is often little common ground between them. It does, however, appear that the radical approaches impose their own set of simplifications that greatly reduce their explanatory power (Lall, 1975). In any case, since they assume at the start that TNCs are necessarily exploitative, they leave little scope for investigating their effects on development objectively. Their appeal has, as noted, declined recently, and for practical purposes they no longer figure in serious economic studies of TNCs in development.

The most relevant theoretical basis for analysing foreign direct investment in developing countries originates in Stephen Hymer's (1976) theory of the "monopolistic advantages" (now termed, more correctly, "ownership advantage") of TNCs (see Kindleberger, 1969, for a succinct exposition). In current language, this theory traces the existence of TNCs to market failures in the generation, diffusion and exploitation of such intangible assets as technology, brandnames, marketing or organizational skills (see Caves, 1982, and, for the most comprehensive exposition of an "eclectic theory" which brings together all the determinants of international production, Dunning, 1981, 1988, 1990, and his edited volume *The Theory of the Transnational Corporation* in this series). Those market failures lead to the growth of large firms and oligopolistic market structures in national economies (so creating "ownership advantages"). Those firms may choose to exploit these advantages by direct investment, rather than licensing them to unrelated firms (because of the transnational advantages of internalizing the relevant markets), and the process of internalization may itself generate fresh ownership advantages. They may choose to deploy these advantages in production sites at home, so creating exports, or in specific host countries, so raising international production, because of the cost, marketing or strategic benefits of doing so ("locational advantages"). The final effect on a developing host country arises from the combination of assets that the TNC represents and from its organization of productive activities (including services) across national boundaries.

The evaluation of the impact of TNCs on developing countries requires, however, an understanding, not just of the market failures that give rise to TNCs, but also of the market failures that characterize host economies. The entry of TNCs, with various internalized markets for intangible assets and for several physical (intermediate) products, can powerfully affect the development of markets and economic agents in host countries. It can boost the efficient development of some while retarding that of others, the precise outcome depending on the existing level of development of host country markets, local enterprises and relevant institutional structures. The alternative, or counterfactual situation, of what may have happened in the absence of TNCs, is extremely difficult to gauge, especially as far as non-marginal changes are concerned (Lall and Streeten, 1977). It is not just the paucity of hard data that raises problems, but also the fact that different counterfactual situations may assume different government strategies and differing responses by domestic economic agents (see below).

That problem is inherent to the evaluation of TNCs in development, and exists even when the objective functions of the evaluators are identical. In other words, even if it is agreed, say, that development is to be defined as the growth of per capita incomes in a private enterprise economy, the impact of TNCs may differ because of differing interpretations of development problems and their remedies (if basic value judgements on ownership, distribution or welfare also differ, the variations would obviously be much greater). In the presence of widespread market failures in developing countries, the entry of large enterprises with highly-developed internal markets can have ambiguous economic effects (Encarnation and Wells, 1986). Such entry does not necessarily ensure that host-country markets in general become more efficient; it may only mean that certain imperfect markets improve by becoming integrated into a TNC. Whether or not the economy as a whole benefits depends on the effect on other markets, the nature and extent of spillovers from TNC activity and, also, on measures taken to improve market efficiency by the host government (which may themselves be influenced by the presence of TNCs).

Some of these considerations have been raised in the literature (Streeten, 1974), though not framed in these terms. These will be touched on below. It would be useful, however, to note first some important developments in the empirical setting of TNC operations.

Some Empirical Background

After a drop in foreign-direct-investment flows to the developing world in the early part of the 1980s, the period since 1984 has witnessed a sustained rise. According to recent data published by the United Nations Centre on Transnational Corporations (UNCTC, 1991), investment flows to developing countries have grown by 16 per cent per annum (in current dollars) during 1984–1989, and reached $30 billion in 1989. However, while annual flows have grown by 2.3 times between 1980–1984 ($12.5 billion per annum) and 1988–1989 ($29.2 billion), the share of foreign-direct-investment flows to developing countries has declined from 25.2 per cent to 16.9 per cent in that period. Thus, it is the developed countries that have received an increasing proportion of global investment flows, which rose 3.7 times during the five years 1985–1989, from $53.3 to $196.1 billion, with Japan becoming the second largest investor (after the United Kingdom) and the United States dropping from first to third place.

The distribution of investment flows within the developing world has shown shifts over the 1980s. By the early part of the decade, Latin America, traditionally the largest recipient of foreign direct investment in the developing world, had seen its share drop as its debt problems multiplied. From nearly 65 per cent of foreign-direct-investment flows in 1978–1980, its share dropped to 49 per cent in 1980–1984 and further to 34 per cent by 1988–1989. South and South-East Asia, by contrast, saw its share rise from 23 per cent in 1978–1980 to 37 per cent in 1980–1984 and 52 per cent in 1988–1989. The least developed countries (largely in sub-Saharan Africa), which were always marginal destinations for foreign direct investment, suffered a drop from 1.5 per cent in 1980–1984 to 0.6 per cent in 1988–1989 (UNCTC, 1991). The overall concentration of foreign direct investment remained high over the decade, with the 10 leading recipients (all but China being middle-income countries) accounting for 72 per cent of the total in 1980–1984 and 66 per cent in 1988–1989. Excluding tax havens, those economies (and their share in foreign direct investment to developing countries during 1980–1989) were: Singapore (12 per cent), Brazil (12 per cent), Mexico (11 per cent), China (9 per cent), Hong Kong (7 per cent), Malaysia (6 per cent), Egypt (5 per cent), Argentina (4 per cent), Thailand (3 per cent), Colombia (3 per cent) and Taiwan, Province of China (3 per cent). One noteworthy phenomenon (touched on again below) was the rapid expansion of foreign direct investment from the newly industrializing countries of East Asia (Whitmore *et al.*, 1989).

The nature of international investments has also changed. Banking and other services are attracting larger shares of investment flows, up to 50 per cent of investments by OECD countries (UNCTC, 1988). In manufacturing, the earlier tendency to relocate simple, labour-intensive activities is becoming increasingly the province of developing country enterprises, while developed country TNCs are gradually moving into more complex, technology and scale-intensive activities. The latter investments are more suited to host countries that have well-developed human, physical and technical infrastructures, with an efficient supply and service bases: thus, structural factors are reinforcing macro-economic forces that are leading to a growing concentration of TNCs in better-off host countries, especially in South-East Asia and Mexico.

The switch of host countries to more welcoming postures to foreign investors noted above is thus occurring against a background of shifting resource flows and more demanding investors. It is also taking hold in a period of structural adjustment in a wide spectrum of developing countries. Such adjustments are leading governments to adopt more market and private-sector-oriented policies, with less emphasis on serving highly protected domestic markets and more on setting up competitive activities that can enter export markets. Traditionally, import-substitution policies have served as the main means to attract TNC activity to developing countries, even when the protected activities were inherently inefficient. Economic liberalization, while making TNC entry more welcome and procedures less obstructive, is likely to increase the concentration of investment flows towards countries that offer a large internal market, internationally competitive skills, support systems and infrastructures. Thus, while the quality of direct investment may be improved by structural adjustment, its potential effect on the volume and direction of inflows in the poorer developing economies may be undesirable.

The widespread liberalization of policies towards TNCs need not mean either that the extent of liberalization is uniform, or that large inflows of direct investment have proved necessary for recent economic development. The pace and content of liberalization has differed greatly among countries (UNCTC, 1988), with some major ones remaining relatively restrictive in practice even if they are liberalizing on paper (India and the Republic of Korea may be examples, the former of a continuation of traditional hostility to TNCs, the latter of greater openness, but a strong undercurrent of nationalism). The most sustained liberalization has occurred in the newly industrializing countries of South-East Asia (Indonesia, Malaysia, Thailand) and parts of Latin America.

The experience of the four Asian newly industrializing countries shows that economic success can be combined with high degrees of reliance on TNCs (as in Singapore) or with very low reliance (such as in the Republic of Korea). That experience does not permit a clear judgement to be passed on the benefits of foreign direct investment resulting from broad *strategic* differences on TNCs. What it does suggest is that export-oriented trade strategies – if combined with good macro-economic management, selective measures to promote industrial deepening, heavy investments in human capital and the creation of proficient science and technology networks – can lead to dramatic industrial development with liberal or controlled policies to TNCs. The experience of the Republic of Korea also suggests that a strongly nationalist economic strategy to enter complex areas of industry at world levels of efficiency requires the promotion of very large domestic firms, exceptionally high indigenous expenditures on research and development and significant protection of activities with a dynamic comparative advantage (Lall, 1990; Westphal *et al.*, 1979).

The existing literature does not deal properly with these strategic ramifications of the TNC-development issue. While some relevant questions are tackled when narrower issues are addressed, in particular technology (below), the analysis of larger questions, such as the implications of building up a strong national technological base, or encouraging large national firms to act as replacements for TNCs in complex industries, is practically non-existent (but see Evans, 1979, on Brazil). Yet the evidence suggests that many important questions of policy and analysis with respect to TNCs arise at this level. Much of the literature focuses on the effects of TNCs at the margin, given the broader policy parameters. However, it is one thing to ask whether TNCs are beneficial or not within a given policy framework it is quite another to ask whether or not different strategic frameworks (regarding the building of national capabilities with different degrees of reliance on direct investment) are better or worse for long-term development. Developing countries are concerned with both sets of policy questions, but economic analysts still have some way to go in addressing the second set of questions, concerning what may be called "strategic counterfactuals". It is in evaluating strategic counterfactuals that a knowledge of market failures in developing countries becomes necessary: yet, the analysis of the development of local capabilities and a dynamic comparative advantage in developing countries is still in its infancy.

The interaction between the development of local capabilities and the evolution of inward and outward direct investment has, however, been analysed in a less normative context: the emergence of Third World TNCs. As noted, this has been a notable feature of recent years, especially in East Asia where the largest or second largest investor in every host country is another developing economy (usually Hong Kong, Taiwan, Province of China or the Republic of Korea). Starting with a pathbreaking paper by Lecraw (1977), subsequent explorations of the subject included important studies by Wells (1983) and Lall *et al.* (1983), and papers in Khan (1986) and Kumar and McLeod (1981). The theoretical implications of the transition of countries across different levels of net foreign investment are comprehensively dealt with by Dunning in his analysis of the investment-development cycle (1988, and Chapter 5 of this volume).

The evidence of growing ownership advantages by enterprises in developing countries has prompted much speculation about what such advantages may reside in, relative to established TNCs from developed countries (which had considerable experience in adapting to developing country conditions) and to host-country firms. Two schools of thought (not necessarily contradictory) have emerged. The first, based on the product-cycle approach, treats developing country TNCs as relatively passive recipients of mature technologies and traces their ownership advantages to labour intensity, small-scale operations, lack of differentiation and low overheads (Wells, 1983). The second, derived from the analysis of technological development, looks directly at the process by which enterprises acquire competitive competence (Lall *et al.*, 1983). It suggests that many of the general advantages due to scale and other adaptations should accrue equally to affiliates of developed country TNCs and that, to the extent that advantages of developing country TNCs are technological, they arise from the firm-specific character of technological learning (for a general analysis of technological accumulation and transnational growth, see Cantwell, 1989, 1990). While firm-specific technological learning cannot be expected to yield strong ownership advantages in very simple technologies (where many TNCs from developing countries congregate and where it is likely that advantages reside in other factors like marketing or management; see Chen, 1983), they can provide a plausible explanation of the growth of developing country TNCs in capital, skill and technology-intensive activities. Since such TNCs are much in evidence recently, with a growing presence in developed countries, that tends to support the technology-accumulation interpretation (Cantwell and Tolentino, 1990); their impact is taken up at the end of the fourth section.

Developing country TNCs are part of the large phenomenon of new forms of international involvement (Oman, 1984), which have attracted recent attention. "New forms" reflect many forces (see Chapter 6 of Dunning, 1988): the pace of maturing of various technologies; the growth of specialized intermediaries in technology, finance and other services; technological development in newly industrializing countries; policies of host governments; entry of new investors; and changing risk perceptions in TNC strategies. While it is often noted that "new forms" do not always indicate a shift in the locus of control away from TNCs, it is likely that they generally accompany the acquisition of technological and managerial capabilities by developing countries. The thrust for this acquisition comes, however, from domestic efforts; the international environment for investment and technology transfer operates largely as a permissive factor.

Welfare Impact of Transnational Corporations

The assessment of the costs and benefits of TNCs has, despite the methodological problems mentioned earlier, attracted a large body of analysis. Much of this has been devoted to specific aspects (such as technology, exports, industrial structure and so on). There is, however, a body of statistical analysis relating stocks and/or flows of foreign direct investment to host-country rates of growth. Most of this analysis "has suffered both from the lack of theoretical guidance and in some cases from a surfeit of special pleading by the researchers" (Caves, 1982, p. 275). Its methodological deficiencies render its conclusions suspect, and that literature is not reviewed here (see, however, Caves, 1982, for a brief survey).

Another branch of the literature has dealt with the overall net social welfare effects of TNCs. Given the measurement problems inherent in such social cost–benefit analysis, it is not surprising that this branch is relatively small. The main piece of research of this type on the social costs and benefits of TNCs (Lall and Streeten, 1977) still deserves mention. That study found that a substantial portion of foreign direct investment in sample developing countries (see Chapter 3 below) had negative net social effects on their host economies. The conclusion reached was not, however, that foreign investment was worse than domestic investment, but that the social effects of both depended on the trade regime in which they operated (also see Encarnation and Wells, 1986). Investment in highly protected import-substituting environments generated much lower benefits than those that were undertaken under export-oriented regimes, or those that were exposed to significant foreign competition. That study, however, acknowledged the very considerable problems of evaluating the separate impact of ownership, given the trade regime, primarily because of the difficulties of assessing the precise contribution of TNCs compared to local alternatives.

The trade orientation of TNCs, and of a host country's development strategy, has generally been found to exercise a strong influence on a number of aspects of their impact (mentioned below). While the generalization that export-oriented investment and regimes produce more efficient results probably holds, it should be noted that investment geared to domestic markets, or those afforded protection by governments, may also generate significant benefits. Where protection is given for infant-industry reasons, to allow sufficient time for an investment to become efficient, there is clearly no reason to doubt its desirability (if the discounted present value of net benefits is appropriate). Some apparently inefficient inward-oriented TNC (or local) activities may create large external benefits, e.g., for local suppliers, skills, technology or consumers, just as some export-oriented activities may have negative externalities.

The specific issues that arise for the impact of TNCs on development cover a broad range. These cannot, as noted earlier, be done full justice in this brief review. The following discussion is, therefore, aimed at highlighting the main issues of current interest and those deserving more attention from researchers.

Capital

It was some time ago that economists persuaded developing countries that they should not be concerned with the facts that TNCs "took out more capital than they put in", or relied heavily on local borrowing and retained earnings to finance growth, and that, in a situation without major disruptions (i.e., before the debt crisis), foreign direct investment was more costly than borrowing overseas. The first two were merely inherent features of any investment, with no economic significance as far as the welfare of host countries was concerned. The last was an indication that capital was only part of a larger package of attributes of inward direct investment, and that the rate of interest on capital alone could not capture the cost of buying all the other elements.

The onset of the debt crisis, with a sharp constriction of non-equity flows, greatly enhanced the attractiveness of TNCs as sources of finance *per se*, a role which was fairly minor before 1985 (UNCTC, 1988, p. 138). The fact that TNCs also provided technology and skills, and that profit repatriation was attuned to host country business cycles (unlike fixed-interest debt), added to the perceived benefits of equity inflows by highly indebted countries. Debt-equity conversions were sometimes seen as a major part of a solution to the debt crisis, but careful analysis (Bergsman and Edisis, 1988; UNCTC, 1988) suggests that these did not always result in net new inflows of foreign direct investment, and that they could lead to inflationary problems. While having a potentially beneficial impact, conversions needed to be carefully managed and could only be a small part of the solution to the debt problem; however, such conversions should be seen in a context where foreign-direct-investment flows in general need to be raised to developing countries.

Employment and Training

This set of issues generated by TNCs has received some attention (ILO, 1981, 1984, and UNCTC, 1988). Though TNCs are major direct and indirect employers in the world's market economies, their share of total employment is small, and many of the questions that arise here fall under other issues like choice of technology, impact on local entrepreneurship and linkages (see below). Thus, the analysis of TNC employment issues *per se* has been relatively neglected. The transfer of skills through training is a potentially valuable contribution of TNCs to developing countries (see UNCTC, 1988, pp. 186–7, and the volume of *Human Resources* by Duane Kujawa in this series). However, evidence on the net contribution of TNCs (compared to an alternative situation) in that area is extremely limited. There are two sets of information required, neither of which is easy to collect: first, what are the ownership advantages of TNCs (over local alternatives) in providing employment and training; and second, how does the cross-border nature of TNC activity affect the creation of skills in a particular country (i.e., does a TNC internalize the benefits of training by offering better wages and benefits, or does some of the benefit spill over?). There is a strong presumption that TNCs do provide significant training benefits to developing countries, especially when they enter sophisticated activities, and that spillovers do occur – but this is difficult to evaluate empirically. It is also likely that the host country has to invest heavily in creating skills and efficient labour markets before it can attract high value-added TNC activities (without giving heavy protection). Singapore is the prime example of a successful strategy of this type.

One aspect of TNC employment that has attracted explicit attention has been their location of simple labour-intensive processes in developing countries, which has generated a lot of additional jobs, but perhaps relatively little skill transfer. The phenomenon seems to be past its peak, but a decade ago the "new international division of labour" was much debated, often with undeserved criticism of TNCs (Fröbel *et al.*, 1980). Technological developments (mainly automation) are reducing the pressure for developed country TNCs to relocate those labour-intensive processes that drove the earlier surge (e.g., in electronics assembly), while the structural adjustment that drove others (e.g., in garments and other light consumer goods) is nearly complete. Interestingly, such adjustment is currently being led by developing country TNCs, especially in the Asia–Pacific region (Whitmore *et al.*, 1989), while developed country firms move into more sophisticated activities.

Technology

Technology-related concerns have dominated the literature on TNCs and development. The balance of interest has, however, shifted over time. The earliest literature (and some recent theoretical work) treated TNCs as the major source of modern technology to developing countries (Singer, 1950). The cost of the transfer was then not explicitly considered (relative to other modes of technology transfer), and the appropriateness of the technology was not an issue (presumably technologies were assumed to be completely adaptable, factor markets to be efficient, and TNCs to maximize profits by responding to factor prices and providing appropriate technology). More dynamic issues, relating to the absorption, diffusion and creation of technology within host economies, were also not considered. The simple neoclassical framework used, assuming freely available knowledge that was absorbed instantaneously, excluded such considerations. Empirical studies treated developing countries as passive (and efficient) absorbers of technologies created abroad.

Much of the subsequent analysis was concerned with questioning these assumptions (see Enos, 1989, for a useful survey of the literature on technology transfer). The 1960s and 1970s were replete with critiques of TNCs for charging developing countries too much for technology transfers and providing inappropriate technology. It was always realized that TNCs were a powerful and effective means of transferring new technologies, and that they were often the only sources for very new, innovative technologies. It was argued, however, that the high cost of technology transfer reflected partly the scarcity of the technology (its proprietary nature) and its packaging with other intangible assets, and partly the lack of technical skills on the part of the developing country purchasers. The costs took the form of direct costs (profits, royalties, fees) and indirect ones (restrictive practices on exports, imports, research and development, local diffusion of technology). Market failures in international technology markets (Caves *et al.*, 1983) led some analysts to recommend massive interventions to help host countries (Vaitsos, 1974). Some concern was also expressed that the pace and cost of recent technological development was raising barriers to technology transfers in non-equity forms, thus strengthening the market power of leading TNCs (Ernst and O'Connor, 1989). Recent work on inter-TNC linkages and strategic alliances has added to this concern; a volume in this series (*Cooperative Forms of Activity*, edited by Peter Buckley) contains readings on this issue.

As another volume in this series (*Technology Transfer*, edited by Edward Chen) deals with technology transfer, it is not necessary to review that subject here at any length. Suffice it to say that, while market failures clearly exist in international technology markets, attempts to lower the costs or raise the returns to developing countries by stringent regulations may not be very productive. The direct cost of technology imports may be reduced, but usually at the expense of restricting the inflow of direct investment or high-quality technology in other forms (see Contractor, 1983, for a good theoretical analysis and empirical review, and Desai, 1988, for papers on India, which has one of the most restrictive regimes). As Casson and Pearce (1987, p. 105) note, "there is a certain logic to restrictive business practices" – in essence they tend to reflect the market value of the technologies in question; suppressing one mode of payment can simply lead to its substitution by another. The real issue for developing countries is not so much whether or not to regulate technology negotiations (though they should certainly increase the knowledge of buyers), as how they might build up their domestic technological capabilities to absorb, build and improve upon imported technologies, and so enable them to be more selective in buying foreign technology. The issue of regulating technology transfers as such attracts relatively little notice now, as most developing countries move to more liberal policies on both licensing and direct investment (see Chudnovsky, 1981, and Contractor, 1983, for reviews of relevant policies).

The issue of appropriateness is part of a larger debate on the suitability of modern technologies to developing countries (Stewart, 1977). TNCs attract special attention, as they are the spearheads of modern technology, and their size and marketing strength enable them to overwhelm alternative technologies and create new tastes more readily. The original issue was a static neoclassical one: overly capital-intensive technologies were used in relation to developing country factor endowments. Over time, other concerns were added: the technologies did not create local linkages or build on indigenous skills; they were used to produce inappropriate products; they were rigid and unadaptable to local conditions; and so on.

A number of publications have surveyed the evidence on this issue (see, in particular, Casson and Pearce, 1987; Caves, 1982; Helleiner, 1975; Jenkins, 1990; and Lall, 1978), and have arrived at ambiguous results. Part of the ambiguity lies in the misplaced attribution of blame for inappropriate technologies. Given that the ownership advantage of TNCs lies in the generation and (relatively unadapted) transfer of new and complex technologies, it is natural to find them congregated in activities that demand such technologies. If a developing country requires such technologies to meet the demand for sophisticated products, it seems illogical to blame TNCs for doing so efficiently. A great deal of the criticism attached to TNCs for catering to "luxury" demand seems misplaced, as, more often than not, it is the host country's income distribution which is at fault.

Given the pattern of demand existing in the market, the empirical findings on TNC technical choices and adaptation were also ambiguous. Two sets of questions were raised in that context.

First, do foreign investors adapt their technology to local conditions? The answer was generally "Yes", in one or both of two ways: the initial engineering of a plant (process design, scale, equipment choice) is always geared to the characteristics of each site, regardless of ownership or the nature of technology transfer arrangement. Such adaptation could be substantial (Teece, 1977), and there was no reason to expect TNCs to do it less efficiently than anyone else. Since plant scale is a prime determinant of capital intensity the relative sizes of operations would be a major influence on factor choice: smaller facilities in developing countries would employ less automated and less capital intensive technologies. Once a facility was established (and given the inherent adaptability of the process concerned), further adaptation would occur in those elements of the technology which were relatively cheap and did not affect the basic operating parameters of the core technology. Thus, ancillary activities (like packaging, storage, transport and some machining) may be kept very labour intensive in affiliates as compared to developed countries. Over time, market orientation (export-based activities would tend to keep up with new technologies more than inward-oriented ones), the extent of local competition, factor price changes, the state of the labour market and other factors, would all affect adaptation of existing technologies and the introduction of new technologies to affiliates (Helleiner, 1975). In general, the evidence confirmed that plants in developing countries were less capital-intensive and automated than comparable facilities in developed countries.

The second question was: do TNCs adapt better or worse than local counterparts? Since the above influences affected all firms regardless of ownership, it was not surprising that researchers found that once scale, size, products and markets were controlled, no distinct tendency was found one way or the other. TNCs turned out to be more capital-intensive than local firms in some industries or countries and not in others (Jenkins, 1990; Lall, 1978).

Despite the attention that this set of technology-related questions attracted in the literature, "appropriateness" was not an issue which has greatly exercised policy makers in developing countries. Nor is it an issue that was necessarily central to the long-term developmental effects of technology transfer by TNCs. These effects are really determined by how well the transferred technology is *absorbed, utilized and diffused* in the host economy, and by the contribution it makes to an economy's own *technological capability*, to improve upon the original technology and generate new technology. A body of recent research has established that technological development plays as vital a role in the industrial success of developing countries as it does in developed countries (see Lall, 1990, for a brief review; see also the volume on innovatory activity in this series edited by John Cantwell). Even if developing countries are not on the frontiers of innovation (and some are not even able to utilize very modern technologies), they need to develop new skills, knowledge, institutions and organizational structures to master the technologies they import and to grow efficiently. This entails a process of learning, with risk, uncertainty and cost, and significant scope for supportive policies. Different countries display differing degrees of development of their capabilities to cope with modern technologies, and this turns out to be a major factor affecting their economic success.

The most significant question with respect to TNCs in the technology field (and, indeed, in the whole field of TNCs and development) is: what role do TNCs play in the process of technological development in host developing countries? The answer is, again, somewhat ambiguous (Dunning, 1991). To the extent that technological development consists of mastering the "know-how" (operational procedures) of a given technology, TNCs may be presumed, subject to the impact of the trade and competition regimes, to have a positive effect: they transmit state-of-the art knowledge, and provide the wherewithal to make it operational. Even if foreign skills are needed in initial stages, it is in the TNC's economic interest to develop cheaper local skills to take over all local tasks. It is also in its interest to make the adaptations needed to make the technology function efficiently. And, finally, it is to its own benefit to continually update affiliate's technology as local circumstances dictate, providing it with the fruits of innovations created in developed countries. Moreover, a foreign presence stimulates local competitors to perform more efficiently (see below under "linkages"). Thus, the ownership advantage of TNCs with respect to technology seems to offer significant benefits to countries that wish to apply that technology to production.

However, to the extent that the technological development process involves the growth of deeper indigenous research and innovation ("know-why") capabilities, the benefits of the presence of TNCs are less evident. The very fact that TNCs centralize their innovation in developed countries and have internalized technology markets means that affiliates in developing countries can import all their "know-why" and need to conduct little research and development themselves, beyond that needed for adaptive activity (UNCTC, 1988, p. 181; Dunning, 1991). In some cases, adaptive research and development in foreign affiliates may exceed that in local firms, especially where strong indigenization rules are enforced (as in Indian engineering, Lall, 1985); in others, local firms tend to conduct more research and development (as in Hong Kong, Chen, 1983, or Argentina, Katz, 1984). Not all developing countries can sustain efficient research and development activities; but for the growing number that can, a strong foreign presence may inhibit the development of an indigenous technological base beyond adaptive research. This may happen not just in affiliates but, by raising the cost and risk of local innovative activity, also in competing local firms. The argument applies also to developed countries: where the host country has established technological strengths, TNCs may draw upon them and add to them by setting up local research and development; but where local technology or entrepreneurship are weak, TNCs may contribute little to its development and may even harm it (Cantwell, 1989, 1990). In addition, the impact of a strong TNC presence, with established links with science and technology institutions in advanced countries, may not contribute to infrastructural development in less advanced host countries. A case may thus exist for promoting local technological capabilities by supporting national firms and institutions, and restricting foreign entry, *at certain stages* of development.

An evaluation of this kind can only be based on "strategic counterfactuals", i.e. by comparing countries that have pursued different policies towards TNCs and technological development, rather than by comparing local and foreign firms within a given country. Several country types may be distinguished. Japan and the Republic of Korea are clear examples of coherent and successful technological strategies based on a selective restriction of inward direct investment and developing local "know-why". India is a case of a country which in the 1970s and 1980s, largely excluded foreign TNCs, while practising a policy of high protection, restrictions on domestic private enterprise, conflicting policy objectives, inadequate inflows of foreign technology (in non-equity forms) and an ineffective educational and technology infrastructure. The result has been widespread technical lags and uneven capability development (Lall, 1987). Large Latin American countries, like Brazil, have relied heavily on TNCs in certain industries and excluded them in others. Their technological development seems to have been most rapid where TNCs have been restricted and sufficient skills and institutional support created, but the overall inward orientation of the economy and inadequate skill and institutional development have held back a broadening of the technological base. Singapore has depended most heavily on TNCs, but has intervened actively in the entry process and by improving domestic skills, to induce an upgrading of the industrial structure. Singapore has displayed no ambitions to build up an indigenous technological base, and its indigenous enterprises are the weakest of the four newly industrializing countries; the consequence of its strategy has been a dynamic and efficient industrial structure, but little indigenous "know-why". That may perhaps be a good strategy for a very small economy, but is unlikely to work so well in larger economies.

The lessons of this experience seem to be that a strategy based on restricting foreign entry can be successful *if it is combined with a number of other market-strengthening measures* (export orientation, skill creation, institution building, promotion of large firms and so on). In the absence of such measures, however, keeping TNCs out may be damaging: it would do little for domestic capabilities, and would deprive the economy of the benefit of know-how upgrading and competition that the presence of a TNC involves.

Trade

The promotion of *exports* is a contribution that most developing countries expect from TNCs, and those firms have played a major role in expanding manufactured exports from a number of bases. Helleiner (1973) brought academic attention to bear on the potential of TNCs as "agents of dynamic comparative advantage". The growth of offshore assembly of electronic components and other items requiring cheap semi-skilled labour did contribute significantly to export earnings and employment, but in a small number of countries only (Nayyar, 1978). At the same time, TNCs greatly increased their exports of more complex products from established operations in larger developing countries, reflecting the latter's growth in skills and capabilities as well as low wages. In overall terms, as UNCTC (1988) documents, exports by foreign affiliates rose over time as a percentage of world trade, and often as a share of the host country's total exports (Blomström, 1990). Earlier fears that automation would lead to a loss of developing country competitive advantages were not borne out by the vigorous export performance of foreign affiliates (UNIDO, 1990).

This is not to say, however, that TNCs were the most important agents of the developing countries' dynamic comparative advantage in general. In the East-Asian newly industrializing countries, except for Singapore, local firms accounted for the bulk of export expansion, putting together the package of local and foreign skills needed themselves. In other countries, too, the evidence on the relative export propensities of TNCs versus local firms was mixed (Jenkins, 1990). An important role was played by foreign buyers, especially of simple consumer goods, who took no equity stake in exporting firms (Sharpston, 1975; Keesing, 1983). Moreover, the export marketing function was also increasingly taken over by local firms, especially in the Republic of Korea and Taiwan, Province of China, as they grew in size and sophistication and became TNCs themselves.

There is little doubt that TNCs can make an important net contribution to export promotion when (given conducive policy environments) the host country has a very specific resource (like cheap labour) that can be complemented by elements provided by TNCs, for example, when the marketing of exports requires an established network of vertically integrated facilities across countries, or powerful brand names, or when production involves easily transferred proprietary inputs or knowledge. In other cases, the advantages of TNCs over well-heeled local competitors are far less obvious, since the latter can also put together the required package efficiently. But TNCs retain a strong edge in advanced technologies or in sophisticated international marketing networks (de la Torre, 1974), even where a strong local enterprise sector exists. In the Republic of Korea, for instance, TNC exports are concentrated in offshore assembly operations or some high-technology or brand-intensive products, though local enterprises are constantly encroaching on these fields. For countries with less dynamic indigenous enterprises, TNCs can act as agents of changing comparative advantage, where circumstances are conducive to a transfer and exploitation of their ownership advantages and cross-border coordination of activities. The dynamism of the process depends, nevertheless, on the ability of the host country to continuously upgrade its own input of skills, infrastructure and domestic suppliers; and such an ability can also be exploited by indigenous firms where these are promoted.

The import propensities of TNCs relative to domestic firms has been discussed in the literature (see references in Casson and Pearce, 1987, pp. 106–7), with a general, but not universal, finding that TNCs are more import-intensive. It is not clear, however, that past studies have controlled properly for local supply capacities in the activities concerned. In export activities, where quality, price and delivery are particularly important, import dependence seems to be higher – but no welfare conclusion can be derived from this.

One feature of TNC trade that has attracted considerable scrutiny concerns *intra-firm transactions* between different branches of the same firm. Intra-firm trade is, in fact, a significant and growing proportion of total world trade. The analysis of its pattern (Casson *et al.*, 1986; Casson and Pearce, 1988; Helleiner, 1981; Lall, 1978a; and Peter Gray's volume on international trade in this series) shows that the propensity to internalize physical trade is governed by factors similar to those that lead to the internalization of markets in intangible assets: advanced technology, high sunk costs and the need to assure quality of production or after-sales service. The policy concerns about intra-firm trade arise from the scope it provides for *transfer pricing*. Transfer pricing is dealt with fully in another volume in this series (*Transfer Pricing and Taxation*, edited by Sylvain Plasschaert), so mention need only be made of some important relevant works (Vaitsos, 1974; Lall, 1973; Kopits, 1976; Plasschaert, 1979; and Rugman and Eden, 1985). In the current zeal to attract foreign direct investment, that problem has been relegated to the background by governments of developing countries. In principle, however, it remains an important issue for taxation and control.

Industrial Structure and Linkages

Since foreign-direct-investment flows tend to be dominated by large oligopolistic firms, TNC entry, especially into the small markets of developing countries, raises concerns about their effects on local market structure and competition. As with all discussions of market structure, essentially static concepts of market power are difficult to apply to situations where scale economies abound (and large size is necessary for efficiency). It is not easy, in consequence, to interpret findings that correlate TNC presence with high levels of concentration in the host country over the long term. That subject is, however, also the theme of another volume in this series (*Market Structure and Industrial Performance*, edited by Richard Newfarmer and Claudio Frischtak), and one only needs to mention a few important works (Evans, 1977; Lall, 1979; Newfarmer, 1985; and papers in Dunning, 1985). Useful reviews are also provided by Caves (1982), Casson and Pearce (1987) and Nixson (1984).

Transnational corporations can have many types of linkages with local firms. The most important direct linkages are those established with local suppliers of parts, components and services. Such backward linkages may be regarded as of special significance because they generally involve greater interaction than normal market relations between anonymous buyers and sellers, for example, transfer of information, technology, skills, finance and so on. Such "quasi-vertical integration" is widespread in all intra-industry transactions, in developed as well as developing countries, and can be a valuable source of specialization, diffusion, stability and subcontracting benefits. Some empirical evidence (Lall, 1980; Lim and Pang, 1982; Reuber *et al.*, 1973) suggests that TNCs can be quite active in setting up such linkages when host governments force the pace of indigenization of inputs (generally under import-substituting regimes or when local supply capabilities are highly developed). What the evidence also suggests, however, is that, in an unconstrained environment (with free availability of imports) and weak local capabilities, and especially where export-oriented activities are concerned, TNCs prefer to retain linkages overseas, rather than undertake the extra cost of developing potential local suppliers (Hill, 1985, on the Philippines). One interesting recent feature of linkages is the propensity of TNCs, especially from Japan, to induce their home-country suppliers to follow them in setting up affiliates overseas (UNIDO, 1990). The welfare implications for competing local suppliers is, however, unclear, because they may be displaced rather than being upgraded.

Apart from direct linkages, TNCs can have various indirect linkages with local competitors. Beneficial linkages may include the spillover of skills and efficiency to local firms, partly from externalities created by TNCs (in the form of training and technical efforts which leak out), partly from increasing competitive pressures on local firms in product and factor markets. Evidence suggests that such benefits do exist, and can induce faster structural changes in industries with strong TNC activity (Blomström, 1989). Harmful linkages may arise when the presence of TNCs inhibits entrepreneurial or technological development in local competitors (as noted above), or induces them to adopt socially undesirable practices like distorting consumption patterns by powerful marketing (this is argued, for instance, by Langdon, 1981, for Kenya). The crowding out or suppression of local entrepreneurs from complex areas of industrial activity is a real danger in developing countries, because a strong TNC presence can prevent the high learning costs from being borne by inexperienced entrants (Dunning, 1991; Evans, 1979). The economic division of labour between TNCs and local firms that emerges may, in other words, become fixed and static if imposed in early stages of development, and negative spillovers may overshadow positive ones (for theoretical treatments, see Buckley and Casson, 1989; and Grossman, 1984). The negative effects of TNCs on consumption patterns are less obvious, because such patterns are influenced by a variety of other mechanisms apart from local marketing by TNCs (UNCTC, 1988, pp. 222–25). The process of taste transfer is being speeded by technological changes in information, entertainment, transport and so on, and that sort of criticism of TNCs is less common now.

Other Impacts

Concern has been expressed about other possible effects of TNCs on developing countries, including in the areas of culture, politics, women, food security, environment, regional integration and industrial location. Some of these issues (reviewed in UNCTC, 1988) are of real significance to developing host countries and will assume greater significance in the future (e.g., environment). The existing literature does not, however, seem to contain much rigorous analysis and data on the impact of TNCs in those areas, and methodological problems are rife. Governments and analysts would benefit from more, and better disciplined, research in this area. A stimulating theoretical analysis of the socio-cultural impact of TNCs (Buckley and Casson, 1989, and in this volume) shows one line along which work may proceed.

Summary and Conclusions

To conclude this review of the impacts of TNCs on development, it may be useful to make some general points:

- The overall impact of TNCs is very difficult to assess, partly because of the complexity of issues involved and the paucity of data, and partly because of conceptual problems in defining strategic counterfactuals. It is clear, nevertheless, that plausible counterfactuals will depend crucially on the *level of development already achieved* in the relevant country. That would depend, in turn, on the stage of development of indigenous skills and capabilities, infrastructure and institutions and the policy orientation and administrative efficiency of the government. The realistic alternative to TNCs in the least developed countries may not be a competitive private sector, while in some middle-income countries it may be feasible to conceive of strategies to promote indigenous enterprise in demanding areas by restricting TNC entry. At even higher levels of development, when indigenous enterprise, capabilities and institutions are on a par with other industrialized countries, there would appear to be little need to restrain the flow of international investment, though particular technological objectives may still call for other forms of intervention (as occurs sometimes in Europe, Japan or the United States).
- Given the strategic counterfactuals, the impact of TNC investment depends, as with other investment, on the incentive and capability structures within which they exist. The incentive structures that are most conducive to efficiency are those associated with stable macro-economic regimes, export-oriented trade strategies, liberal internal competition policies and relatively open policies to international flows of services and knowledge. Such structures are not, however, necessarily the result of *laissez-faire* policies: export orientation may go together with high levels

of intervention in trade (to protect infant industries), resource allocation and industrial structure. The capability structures that enhance investment efficiency are those that provide high quality skills (appropriate to the pace and direction of development of the country), a supplier network that permits specialization and cost competitiveness and a suitable physical, scientific and institutional infrastructure (Porter, 1990). To realize the dynamic benefits of TNC entry into continuously upgraded manufacturing and service activities, it is vital for the host country to invest in improving all its capabilities. TNCs themselves can contribute to building some capabilities, but they cannot be expected to upgrade the basic structure within which they have to operate. Their specific contribution can thus be much greater when the recipient's absorptive capabilities are rising autonomously.

- Given the incentive and capability structures of the host economy, and considering only marginal changes in foreign direct investment (rather than strategic counterfactuals), it would appear that TNCs *generally offer net benefits* to host developing countries. Their behaviour does not differ significantly from that of comparable local firms, but they possess certain ownership and internalization advantages over local counterparts. If the host country can induce these advantages to be transferred and deployed by TNCs, it is likely to benefit from the presence of TNCs. Exceptions to that generalization are nevertheless possible, when TNCs engage in undesirable practices like tax evasion (e.g., by transfer pricing) or predatory behaviour to local competition, or where they give inadequate attention to potential local suppliers, do not strike up links with local technological institutions, invest too little in local research and development, or fail (for strategic reasons) to exploit the export competitiveness of their affiliates. These apart, it is also important to note that there may be *trade-offs between the different advantages* offered by TNCs, e.g., local linkages versus exports, local research and development versus immediate application of new technology, and so on. The net effects of TNCs then depend on the specific trade-offs chosen by host countries.

- There may be grounds to expect different strategies and welfare effects from TNCs of different origins. Firms from some countries favour "classic" foreign direct investment (majority or wholly foreign-owned ventures), while others are more amenable to joint ventures or selling technologies to unrelated firms. Some TNCs are very export-oriented because they are specialized in serving world markets with products that are becoming uncompetitive at home or because they have global networks of supply to exploit locational and internalization advantages; others are more geared to serving domestic markets, and so on. These differences are generally traceable to technological and structural characteristics of their home countries, though over time the differences may be disappearing as firms interact in a common arena. The growth of *developing country TNCs* has created expectations that they would offer special benefits in terms of appropriate technology, management and skills, greater sharing of their advantages, more local sourcing and better corporate behaviour (as well as the socio-political benefits of enhanced South–South cooperation). There may well be some such benefits, and a great deal of foreign direct investment from the newly industrializing countries of East Asia is currently very export-oriented (as their economies adjust to rising costs). The composition of their TNCs is, however, likely to change over time, and it is not clear that their more high-technology firms would be any different from TNCs from developed countries.

- Finally, the critical issues of whether *TNCs as a whole* contribute to technology, skills, efficiency or exports in host developing countries ultimately depend on the strategic counterfactuals. The fact that this is largely an area of ignorance is perhaps a reflection on how narrowly TNC research has been defined, and how market failures in host countries have been relatively neglected.

Unresolved Issues

This brings to a close this introductory review of the impact of TNCs on developing host countries. The review has not been, and was not intended to be, a comprehensive literature survey. Selectivity has been exercised in mentioning issues that are of most concern at this time. Various methodological and empirical questions have been raised, and it has been noted that many of the traditional debates in the field are now of largely historical interest.

The large questions that remain unresolved have to do with what has been termed the "strategic counterfactuals" – what may happen if a different broad strategy to TNCs were adopted. At the margin, given their strategy, TNCs are rather similar in behaviour to large local firms, but have much to offer in terms of their ownership advantages: with sensible trade and industrial policies, therefore, their effects are likely, on balance, to be beneficial. When non-marginal differences are considered, however, their effects may be more ambiguous. Much depends on an economy's initial and evolving conditions. A strategy of selectivity restricting TNC entry may provide a period of protection to capability-building, if domestic market failures are efficiently tackled, skills promoted and local enterprise encouraged. TNCs can then be selected according to the dynamic, rather than the static comparative advantages of domestic firms. A strategy of constricting TNCs' entry may, on the other hand, turn out to be economically costly if local enterprises and capabilities are not developed and if corrective policies are not taken in hand. A choice between these alternatives is often one of degree, but recent experience suggests that in practice there can be very real differences in the strategies pursued.

In analytical terms, what is lacking is a comprehensive theory of development that takes existing market failures into account and suggests practical remedies for these structural problems. Existing theories are often too strongly rooted in equilibrium systems where market failures are absent or trivial, and tend to end up with simple solutions (liberalize and "get prices right"). A proper consideration of TNCs in development, in other words, requires a more complex framework for analysing the development process itself, with a larger role for market imperfections and their correction. Once the strategic issues are decided, questions of the specific impact of TNCs seem to be easier to answer. Some important questions still remain on this level, of course, e.g., the scope for effective and productive bargaining between TNCs and host countries an old problem, but one that is likely to remain, see Part IV of this volume), the impact of current changes in technology (Ernst and O'Connor, 1989), the growth of strategic alliances among TNCs (Moody, 1990), and the effects of the evolution of market economies in Central and Eastern Europe on investment flows to the Third World. These issues will continue to stimulate research in this area, and much attention will focus on means to stimulate investment flows to the least developed countries.

The most interesting issues for future research seem the following five:

- The impact of TNCs on indigenous entrepreneurship, technological capabilities and export competitiveness, *if different strategies on trade, capability building and foreign entry were adopted by the host government.* That research would call for careful comparisons of the experience of different countries, or different sectors within a country subjected to different strategies.
- The *impact of current technological changes* and *TNC responses* on the access of developing countries to new technology, both by foreign direct investment and by other channels.
- The requirement for *stimulating efficient TNC activity* in the least developed countries, which are increasingly marginalized in the global foreign direct investment scene (that would cover capabilities, as well as incentive structures).
- The recent evolution of *developing country TNCs*, and the prospects for increasing foreign-direct-investment flows among developing countries.
- The relationship between foreign direct investment in services and economic development, in particular services (such as transport, communication and marketing) related to industrialization.

In some respects, the subject of TNCs in development is perhaps less exciting than it once was. Recent development experience, a disillusionment with interventionist policies, growing government sophistication and adverse international economic circumstances, have combined to produce a much more favourable, and less controversial, environment for foreign-direct-investment flows. The maturing of the literature on TNCs in development reflects that shift. That maturity is to be welcomed, since many of the heated debates of the past were arid and irrelevant. It does not, however, signify that all issues have been resolved and that the broad parameters for future empirical research are given. This review has argued that that is not the case: some basic questions remain, and deserve probing in the future.

Note

*I am grateful for helpful comments and advice from John Dunning, Karl P. Sauvant, Michael Mortimore and Miroslav N. Jovanović.

Bibliography

Bergsman, Joel and Wayne Edisis, "Debt-equity swaps and foreign direct investment in Latin America" (Washington, D.C., International Finance Corporation, Discussion Paper No. 2, 1988), mimeo.

Blomström, Magnus, *Foreign Investment and Spillovers* (London, Routledge, 1989).

——, *Transnational Corporations and Manufacturing Exports from Developing Countries* (New York, United Nations Centre on Transnational Corporations, 1990).

Buckley, Peter J. and Mark Casson, "Multinational enterprises in less-developed countries: cultural and economic interactions" (Reading, University of Reading Discussion Papers in International Investment and Business Studies, No. 126, 1989), mimeo.

Cable, Vincent and Bishnodat Persaud, eds., *Developing with Foreign Investment* (Beckenham, Croom Helm, 1987).

Cantwell, John, *Technological Innovation and the Multinational Corporation* (Oxford, Basil Blackwell, 1989).

——, "The technological competence theory of international production and its implications" (Reading, University of Reading Discussion Papers in International Investment and Business, No. 149, 1990), mimeo.

Cantwell, John and Paz Estrella Tolentino, "Technological accumulation and third world multinationals" (Reading, University of Reading Discussion Papers in International Investment and Business, No. 139, 1990), mimeo.

Casson, Mark, *et al.*, *Multinationals and World Trade: Vertical Integration and the Division of Labour in World Industries* (London, Allen and Unwin, 1986).

Casson, Mark and Robert Pearce, "Multinational enterprises in LDCs", in Norman Gemmell, ed., *Surveys in Development Economics* (Oxford, Basil Blackwell, 1987), pp. 90–132.

——, "Intra-firm trade and the developing countries", in D. Greenway, ed., *Economic Development and International Trade* (London, Macmillan, 1988), pp. 132–156.

Caves, Richard E., *Multinational Enterprise and Economic Analysis* (Cambridge, Cambridge University Press, 1982).

Caves, Richard E., Harold Crookel and Peter Killing, "The imperfect market for technology licences", *Oxford Bulletin of Economics and Statistics*, 43 (1983), pp. 249–267.

Chen, Edward K.Y., *Multinational Corporations, Technology and Employment* (London, Macmillan, 1983).

Chudnovsky, Daniel, "Regulating technology imports in some developing countries", *Trade and Development*, 3 (1981), pp. 133–150.

Contractor, Farok J., "Technology importation policies in developing countries", *The Journal of Developing Areas*, 17 (July 1983), pp. 499–520.

de la Torre, José, "Foreign investment and export dependency", *Economic Development and Cultural Change*, 23 (1974), pp. 135–150.

Desai, Ashok, *Technology Absorption in Indian Industry* (Delhi, Wiley Eastern, 1988).

Dunning, John H., *International Production and the Multinational Enterprise* (London, Allen and Unwin, 1981).

——, *Explaining International Production* (London, Unwin Hyman, 1988).

——, "The eclectic paradigm of international production: a personal perspective", in Robert Sugden and Christopher Pitelis, eds., *The Nature of the Transnational Firm* (London, Routledge, 1990), pp. 117–136.

——, "Multinational enterprises and the globalization of innovatory capacity" (Reading, University of Reading, 1991).

Encarnation, Dennis J. and Louis T. Wells Jr., "Evaluating foreign investment", in Theodore Moran, ed., *Investing in Development: New Roles for Foreign Capital?* (Washington, D.C., Overseas Development Council, 1986), pp. 61–86.

Enos, John L., "Transfer of technology", *Asian-Pacific Economic Literature*, 3 (March 1989), pp. 3–37.

Ernst, Dieter and John O'Connor, *Technology and Global Competition: The Challenge Ahead for Newly Industrializing Economies* (Paris, OECD, 1989).

Evans, Peter B., "Direct investment and industrial concentration", *Journal of Development Studies*, 13 (1977), pp. 373–385.

——, *Dependent Development: The Alliance of Multinational State and Local Capital in Brazil* (Princeton, Princeton University Press, 1979).

Fröbel, Folker, Jürgen Heinrichs and Otto Kreye, *The New International Divison of Labour* (London, Cambridge University Press, 1980).

Grossman, Gene, "International trade, foreign investment, and the formation of the entrepreneurial class", *American Economic Review*, 74 (1984), pp. 605–614.

Helleiner, Gerald K., "Manufactured exports from less-developed countries and multinational firms", *The Economic Journal*, 3 (March, 1973), pp. 21–47.

——, "The role of multinational corporations in less developed countries' trade in technology", *World Development*, 3 (1975), pp. 161–189.

——, *Intra-firm Trade and Developing Countries* (London, Macmillan, 1981).

——, "Transnational corporations and direct foreign investment", in Hollis B. Chenery and T.B. Srinivasan, eds., *Handbook of Development Economics* (Amsterdam, Elsevier Science Publishers, 1989), pp. 1442–1480.

Hill, Hal, "Subcontracting, technological diffusion and the development of small enterprise in Philippine manufacturing", *Journal of Developing Areas*, 19 (1985), pp. 245–261.

——, "Foreign investment and East Asian economic development", *Asian-Pacific Economic Literature*, 4 (September 1990), pp. 21–58.

Hood, Neil M. and Stephen Y. Young, *The Economics of Multinational Enterprise* (London, Longman, 1979).

Hymer, Stephen H., *The International Operation of National Firms: A Study of Direct Foreign Investment* (Cambridge, Mass., MIT Press, 1976).

ILO, *Employment Effects of Multinational Enterprises in Developing Countries* (Geneva, International Labour Office, 1981).

——, *Technology Choice and Employment Generation by Multinational Enterprises in Developing Countires* (Geneva, International Labour Office, 1984).

Jenkins, Rhys, *Transnational Corporations and Uneven Development* (London, Methuen, 1987).

——, "Comparing foreign subsidiaries and local firms in LDCs: theoretical issues and empirical evidence", *Journal of Development Studies*, 26 (January 1990), pp. 205–228.

Katz, Jorge M., "Domestic technological innovations and dynamic comparative advantage", *Journal of Development Economics*, 16 (1984), pp. 13–38.

Keesing, Donald B., "Linking up to distant markets: south to north exports of manufactured consumer goods", *American Economic Review, Papers and Proceedings*, 73 (May 1983), pp. 338–342.

Khan, Kushi M., ed., *Multinationals of the South* (London, Macmillan, 1986).

Kindleberger, Charles P., *Amerian Business Abroad* (New Haven, Yale University Press, 1969).

Kopits, George F., "Intra-firm royalties crossing borders and transfer-pricing behaviour", *Economic Journal*, 86 (1976), pp. 781–805.

Kumar, Krishna and Maxwell G. McLeod, eds., *Multinationals from Developing Countries* (Lexington, D.C. Heath, 1981).

Lall, Sanjaya, "Transfer pricing by multinational manufacturing firms", *Oxford Bulletin of Economics and Statistics*, 35 (August 1973), pp. 173–193.

——, "Is 'dependence' a useful concept in analysing underdevelopment?", *World Development*, 3 (November–December 1975), pp. 799–810.

——, "Transnational, domestic enterprises and industrial structure in host LDCs: a survey", *Oxford Economic Papers*, 30 (1978), pp. 217–248.

——, "The pattern of intra-firm exports by U.S. multinationals", *Oxford Bulletin of Economics and Statistics*, 42 (1978a), pp. 201–222.

——, "Multinationals and market structure in an open developing economy: the case of Malaysia", *Weltwirtschaftliches Archiv*, 115, 1979), pp. 325–348.

——, "Vertical interfirm linkages in LDCs: an empirical study", *Oxford Bulletin of Economics and Statistics*, 42 (1980), pp. 203–282.

——, *Multinationals, Technology and Exports* (London, Macmillan, 1985).

——, *Learning to Industrialize* (London, Macmillan, 1987).

——, *Building Industrial Competitiveness in Developing Countries* (Paris, OECD, 1990).

Lall, Sanjaya and Paul Streeten, *Foreign Investment, Transnationals and Developing Countries* (London, Macmillan, 1977).

Lall, Sanjaya, in collaboration with Edward K.Y. Chen, Jorge M. Katz, Bernardo Kosacoff and Annibal Villela, *The New Multinationals: The Spread of Third World Enterprises* (Chichester, John Wiley and Sons, 1983).

Langdon, Stephen, *Multinational Corporations in the Political Economy of Kenya* (London, Macmillan, 1981).

Lecraw, Donald T., "Direct investment by firms from less developed countries", *Oxford Economic Papers*, 29 (1977), pp. 442–457.

Lim, Linda Y.C. and Eng Fong Pang, "Vertical linkages and multinational enterprises in developing countries", *World Development,* 10 (1982), pp. 585–595.

MacDougall, George D.A., "The benefits and costs of private investment from abroad: a theoretical approach", *Economic Record,* 35 (March 1960), pp. 13–35.

Mody, Ashoka, "Learning through alliances" (Washington, D.C., World Bank Industry and Energy Department, 1990), mimeo.

Nayyar, Deepak, "Transnational corporations and manufactured exports from poor countries", *The Economic Journal,* 88 (1978), pp. 59–84.

Newfarmer, Richard S., "International industrial organization and development: a survey", in Richard S. Newfarmer, ed., *Profits, Progress and Poverty* (Notre Dame, University of Notre Dame Press, 1985), pp. 13–62.

Nixson, Frederick I., "Business behaviour in the private sector", in Colin H. Kirkpatrick, Nick Lee and Frederick Nixson, eds., *Industrial Structure and Policy in Less Developed Countries* (London, Allen and Unwin, 1984), pp. 86–149.

Oman, Charles, *New Forms of International Investment in Developing Countries* (Paris, OECD, 1984).

Plasschaert, Sylvain R.F., *Transfer Pricing and Multinational Corporations* (Farnborough, Saxon House, 1979).

Porter, Michael E., *The Competitive Advantage of Nations* (New York: Free Press, 1990).

Reuber, Grant L. *et al., Private Foreign Investment in Development* (Oxford, Clarendon Press, 1973).

Rugman, Alan M. and Lorraine Eden, *Multinationals and Transfer Pricing* (Beckenham, Croom Helm, 1985).

Sharpston, Michael, "International subcontracting", *Oxford Economic Papers,* 27 (1975), pp. 94–135.

Singer, Hans W., "The distribution of gains between investing and borrowing countries", *American Economic Review,* 40 (1950), pp. 473–485.

Stewart, Frances, *Technology and Underdevelopment* (London, Macmillan, 977).

Streeten, Paul P., "The theory of development policy", in John H. Dunning, ed., *Economic Analysis and the Multinational Enterprise* (London, Allen and Unwin, 1974), pp. 252–279.

Teece, David J., "Technology transfer by multinational firms: the resource cost of transferring technological know how", *The Economic Journal,* 87 (1977), pp. 242–261.

UNCTC, *Transnational Corporations in World Development: Trends and Prospects* (United Nations publication, Sales No. E.88.II.A.7).

——, "Recent developments related to transnational corporations and international economic relations: the triad in foreign direct investment", E/C.10/ 1991/2.

UNIDO, *Foreign Direct Investment Flows to Developing Countries: Recent Trends, Major Determinants and Policy Implications* (Vienna, United Nations Industrial Development Organization, 1990).

Vaitsos, Constantine V., *Intercountry Income Distribution and Transnational Enterprises* (Oxford, Clarendon Press, 1974).

Wells, Jr., Louis T., *Third World Multinationals* (Cambridge, Mass., MIT Press, 1983).

Westphal, Larry E., Yung W. Rhee and Gary Pursell, "Foreign influences on Korean industrial development", *Oxford Bulletin of Economics and Statistics,* 41 (November 1979), pp. 359–388.

Whitmore, Katherine, Sanjaya Lall and Jung-Taik Hyun, "Foreign direct investment from the newly industrialized economies" (Washington, D.C., World Bank Industry and Energy Department Working Paper, Industry Series Paper No. 22, 1989), mimeo.

PART ONE: Welfare of Host Developing Countries

The first part of this selection deals with general issues relating to TNCs and development, with more specific studies taken up later in Part Three. The impact of TNCs is, as noted in the general introduction, extremely difficult to assess in quantitative terms; and even qualitative evaluations are hemmed in by qualifications and simplifying assumptions. Attempts have been made to relate foreign-direct-investment flows and stocks to rates of growth, but those econometric exercises fail to address the real economic issues raised by TNCs, and have not been included in this selection.

It is interesting, in tracing how the development literature treated foreign investment inflows, to look at H. Singer's (1950) classic article on "the distribution of gains" (Chapter 1). The concern, in those early days of industrialization, was with the overwhelmingly primary product orientation of foreign capital: the enclaves set up to extract natural resources for export had minimal linkages with the rest of the host economy, generated few externalities and tied the developing world to a static pattern of specialization (which, according to Singer, also ran a high risk of suffering declining terms of trade). In his view, industrialization had to lead to structural transformation of developing countries, a proposition that most developing countries accepted enthusiastically, and which later research confirmed as an empirical pattern. Singer was, nevertheless, well aware of the need to promote education, infrastructure and technological development to launch the process of industrialization.

Singer saw foreign direct investors as the prime movers in the industrialization process. Their main contribution would be the inflow and reinvestment of capital: physical investment was the key to sustained development, and it was assumed that the necessary skills and institutions would rise *pari passu* with physical capacity. Experience has revealed many flaws in this simple view, but it is useful to look back at the reasoning which guided governments, and the expectations they had of TNCs, in the first flush of modern development policy. The incentive regime under which investments were made turned out to have a profound impact on the economic value of the investment. The capacity of host countries to absorb and build upon imported technologies differed enormously, and building physical capacity was often wasteful. Ultimately, foreign investors played the lead role that Singer envisaged for them in only a very few countries.

The following two chapters, extracted from books by Sanjaya Lall and Paul Streeten (1977) and N. Hood and S. Young (1979) provide fairly comprehensive surveys of the analytical considerations and empirical findings on TNCs in developing countries. While these writings are now well over a decade old, the analysis and evidence are still relevant in many ways, and there is a systematic consideration of the theory and evidence. What has changed is the early concern, strongly expressed in Lall and Streeten, with the social and distortionary impact of TNCs on poor countries. The literature is, as suggested in the general introduction, far less worried now about the appropriateness of products and technologies transferred by TNCs, and more by the conditions under which new technologies are effectively utilized. Issues of domestic technological and entrepreneurial development are mentioned in those works, but not fully developed.

The chapter by Peter Buckley and Mark Casson addresses some aspects of those questions. While it does not tackle empirically the effects of foreign presence on domestic entrepreneurial development, it poses some important questions that much of the economics literature overlooks. Long-term economic development depends ultimately on the growth of domestic entrepreneurship, with sweeping changes in attitudes, beliefs, laws and institutions underlying such growth. Many least developed countries, particularly in sub-Saharan Africa, have not experienced those changes, and their entrepreneurship remains at a low level, unable to cope with the needs of modern technologies. Partly as a consequence of that, foreign direct investment cannot play the positive role that it does in more advanced economies. Though TNC entry can catalyse the development of high-level entrepreneurship, there is a simultaneous risk of socio-cultural disruption, as the traditional patterns struggle to adjust to the sudden introduction of modern values and entrepreneurship. The chapter by Buckley and Casson covers broader issues than the effects of TNCs on developing countries, but is stimulating and highly relevant to current concerns.

1

The Distribution of Gains between Investing and Borrowing Countries[1]*

H.W. Singer

*Source: *American Economic Review*, 40, (1950), pp. 473–485.

International trade is of very considerable importance to underdeveloped countries, and the benefits which they derive from trade and any variations in their trade affect their national incomes very deeply. The opposite view, which is frequent among economists, namely, that trade is less important to the underdeveloped countries than it is to industrialized countries, may be said to derive from a logical confusion—very easy to slip into—between the absolute amount of foreign trade which is known to be an increasing function of national income, and the ratio of foreign trade to national income. Foreign trade tends to be proportionately most important when incomes are lowest. Secondly, fluctuations in the volume and value of foreign trade tend to be proportionately more violent in that of under-developed countries and therefore *a fortiori* also more important in relation to national income. Thirdly, and *a fortissimo*, fluctuations in foreign trade tend to be immensely more important for underdeveloped countries in relation to that small margin of income over subsistence needs which forms the source of capital formation, for which they often depend on export surpluses over consumption goods required from abroad.

In addition to the local confusion mentioned above, the great import-ance of foreign trade to underdeveloped countries may also have been obscured by a second factor; namely, by the great discrepancy in the productivity of labor in the underdeveloped countries as between the industries and occupations catering for export and those catering for domestic production. The export industries in underdeveloped countries, whether they be metal mines, plantations, etc., are often highly capital-intensive industries supported by a great deal of imported foreign tech-nology. By contrast, production for domestic use, specially of food and clothing, is often of a very primitive subsistence nature. Thus the economy of the underdeveloped countries often presents the spectacle of a dualistic economic structure: a high productivity sector producing for export coexisting with a low productivity sector producing for the domestic market. Hence employment statistics in underdeveloped countries do not adequately reflect the importance of foreign trade, since the productivity of each person employed in the export sector tends to be a multiple of that of each person employed in the domestic sector. Since, however, employment statistics for underdeveloped countries are notoriously easier to compile than national income statistics, it is again easy to slip, from the fact that the proportion of persons employed in export trade is often lower in underdeveloped countries than in industrialized countries, to the conclusion that foreign trade is less important to them. This conclusion is fallacious, since it implicitly assumes rough equivalence of productivity in the export and domestic sectors. This equivalence may be safely assumed in the industrialized countries but not in the underdeveloped countries.

A third factor which has contributed to the view that foreign trade is unimportant in underdeveloped countries is the indisputable fact that in many underdeveloped countries there are large self-contained groups which are outside the monetary economy altogether and are therefore not affected by any changes in foreign trade. In industrialized countries, by contrast, it is true that repercussions from changes in foreign trade are more widely spread; but they are also more thinly spread.[2]

The previously mentioned fact, namely, the higher productivity of the foreign trade sector in underdeveloped countries might, at first sight, be considered as a cogent argument in favor of the view that foreign trade has been particularly beneficial to underdeveloped countries in raising their general standards of productivity, changing their economies in the direction of a monetary economy, and spreading knowledge of more capital-intensive methods of production and modern technology. That, however, is much less clearly established than might be thought. The question of ownership as well as of opportunity costs enters at this point. The productive facilities for producing export goods in underdeveloped countries are often foreign owned as a result of previous investment in these countries. Again we must beware of hasty conclusions. Our first reaction would be to argue that this fact further enhances the importance and benefits of trade to underdeveloped countries since trade has also led to foreign investment in those countries and has promoted capital formation with its cumulative and multiplier effects. This is also how the matter is looked at in the economic textbooks—certainly those written by non-socialist economists of the industrialized countries. That view, however, has never been really accepted by the more articulate economists in the underdeveloped countries themselves, not to mention popular opinion in those countries; and it seems to the present writer that there is much more in their view than is allowed for by the economic textbooks.

Can it be possible that we economists have become slaves to the geographers? Could it not be that in many cases the productive facilities for export from underdeveloped countries, which were so largely a result of foreign investment, never became a part of the internal economic structure of those underdeveloped countries themselves, except in the purely geographical and physical sense? Economically speaking, they were really an outpost of the economies of the more developed investing countries. The main secondary multiplier effects, which the textbooks tell us to expect from investment, took place not where the investment was physically or geographically located but (to the extent that the results of these investments returned directly home) they took place where the investment came from.[3] I would suggest that if the proper economic test of investment is the multiplier effect in the form of cumulative additions to income, employment, capital, technical knowledge, and growth of external economies, then a good deal of the investment in underdeveloped countries which we used to consider as "foreign" should in fact be considered as domestic investment on the part of the industrialized countries.

Where the purpose and effect of the investments was to open up new sources of food for the people and for the machines of industrialized countries, we have strictly domestic investment in the relevant economic sense, although for reasons of physical geography, climate, etc., it had to be made overseas. Thus the fact that the opening up of underdeveloped countries for trade has led to or been made possible by foreign investment in those countries does not seem a generally valid proof that this combination has been of particular benefit to those countries. The very differential in productivity between the export sectors and the domestic sectors of the underdeveloped countries, which was previously mentioned as an indication of the importance of foreign trade to underdeveloped countries, is also itself an indication that the more productive export sectors—often foreign owned—have not become a real part of the economies of underdeveloped countries.

We may go even further. If we apply the principle of opportunity costs to the development of nations, the import of capital into underdeveloped countries for the purpose of making them into providers of food and raw materials for the industrialized countries may have been not only rather ineffective in giving them the normal benefits of investment and trade but may have been positively harmful. The tea plantations of Ceylon, the oil wells of Iran, the copper mines of Chile, and the cocoa industry of the Gold Coast may all be more productive than domestic agriculture in these countries; but they may well be less productive than domestic industries in those countries which might have developed if those countries had not become specialized to the degree in which they now are to the export of food and raw materials, thus providing the means of producing manufactured goods elsewhere with superior efficiency. Admittedly, it is a matter of speculation whether in the absence of such highly specialised "export" development, any other kind of development would have taken its place. But the possibility cannot be assumed away. Could it be that the export development has absorbed what little entrepreneurial initiative and domestic investment there was, and even tempted domestic savings abroad? We must compare, not what is with what was, but what is with what would have been otherwise—a tantalizingly inconclusive business. All we can say is that the process of traditional investment taken by itself seems to have been insufficient to initiate domestic development, unless it appeared in the form of migration of persons.

The principle of specialization along the lines of static comparative advantages has never been generally accepted in the underdeveloped countries, and not even generally intellectually accepted in the industrialized countries themselves. Again it is difficult not to feel that there is more to be said on the subject than most of the textbooks will admit. In the economic life of a country and in its economic history, a most important element is the mechanism by which "one thing leads to another," and the most important contribution of an industry is not its immediate product (as is perforce assumed by economists and statisticians) and not even its effects on other industries and immediate social benefits (thus far economists have been led by Marshall and Pigou to go) but perhaps even further its effect on the general level of education, skill, way of life, inventiveness, habits, store of technology, creation of new demand, etc. And this is perhaps precisely the reason why manufacturing industries are so universally desired by underdeveloped countries; namely, that they provide the growing points for increased technical knowledge, urban education, the dynamism and resilience that goes with urban civilization, as well as the direct Marshallian external economies. No doubt under different circumstances commerce, farming, and plantation agriculture have proved capable of being such "growing points," but manufacturing industry is unmatched in our present age.

By specializing on exports of food and raw materials and thus making the underdeveloped countries further contribute to the concentration of industry in the already industrialized countries, foreign trade and the foreign investment which went with it may have spread present static benefits fairly over both. It may have had very different effects if we think of it not from the point of view of static comparative advantages but of the flow of history of a country. Of this latter school of thought the "infant" argument for protection is but a sickly and often illegitimate offspring.

To summarize, then, the position reached thus far, the specialization of underdeveloped countries on export of food and raw materials to industrialized countries, largely as a result of investment by the latter, has been unfortunate for the underdeveloped countries for two reasons: (*a*) because it removed most of the secondary and cumulative effects of investment from the country in which the investment took place to the investing country; and (*b*) because it diverted the underdeveloped countries into types of activity offering less scope for technical progress, internal and external economies taken by themselves, and withheld from the course of their economic history a central factor of dynamic radiation which has revolutionized society in the industrialized countries. But there is a third factor of perhaps even greater importance which has reduced the benefits to underdeveloped countries of foreign trade-*cum*-investment based on export specialization on food and raw materials. This third factor relates to terms of trade.

It is a matter of historical fact that ever since the seventies the trend of prices has been heavily against sellers of food and raw materials and in favor of the sellers of manufactured articles. The statistics are open to doubt and to objection in detail, but the general story which they tell is unmistakable.[4] What is the meaning of these changing price relations?

The possibility that these changing price relations simply reflect relative changes in the real costs of the manufactured exports of the industrialized countries to those of the food and primary materials of the underdeveloped countries can be dismissed. All the evidence is that productivity has increased if anything less fast in the production of food and raw materials, even in the industrialized countries[5] but most certainly in the underdeveloped countries, than has productivity in the manufacturing industries of the industrialized countries. The possibility that changing price relations could merely reflect relative trends in productivity may be considered as disposed of by the very fact that standards of living in industrialized countries (largely governed by productivity in manufacturing industries) have risen demonstrably faster than standards of living in underdeveloped countries (generally governed by productivity in agriculture and primary production) over the last sixty or seventy years. However important foreign trade may be to underdeveloped countries, if deteriorated terms of trade (from the point of view of the underdeveloped countries) reflected relative trends of productivity, this could most assuredly not have failed to show in relative levels of internal real incomes as well.

Dismissing, then, changes in productivity as a governing factor in changing terms of trade, the following explanation presents itself: the fruits of technical progress may be distributed either to producers (in the form of rising incomes) or to consumers (in the form of lower prices). In the case of manufactured commodities produced in more developed countries, the former method, i.e., distribution to producers through higher incomes, was much more important relatively to the second method, while the second method prevailed more in the case of food and raw material production in the underdeveloped countries. Generalizing, we may say that technical progress in manufacturing industries showed in a rise in incomes while technical progress in the production of food and raw materials in underdeveloped countries showed in a fall in prices. Now, in the general case, there is no reason why one or the other method should be generally preferable. There may, indeed, be different employment, monetary, or distributive effects of the two methods; but this is not a matter which concerns us in the present argument where we are not concerned with internal income distribution. In a closed economy the general body of producers and the general body of consumers can be considered as identical, and the two methods of distributing the fruits of technical progress appear merely as two formally different ways of increasing real incomes.

When we consider foreign trade, however, the position is fundamentally changed. The producers and the consumers can no longer be considered as the same body of people. The producers are at home; the consumers are abroad. Rising incomes of home producers to the extent that they are in excess of increased productivity are an absolute burden on the foreign consumer. Even if the rise in the income of home producers is offset by increases in productivity so that prices remain constant or even fall by less than the gain in productivity, this is still a relative burden on foreign consumers, in the sense that they lose part or all of the potential fruits of technical progress in the form of lower prices. On the other hand, where the fruits of technical progress are passed on by reduced prices, the foreign consumer benefits alongside with the home consumer. Nor can it be said, in view of the notorious inelasticity of demand for primary commodities, that the fall in their relative prices has been compensated by its total revenue effects.

Other factors have also contributed to the falling long-term trend of prices of primary products in terms of manufactures, apart from the absence of pressure of producers for higher incomes. Technical progress, while it operates unequivocally in favor of manufactures—since the rise in real incomes generates a more than proportionate increase in the demand for manufactures—has not the same effect on the demand for food and raw materials. In the case of food, demand is not very sensitive to rises in real income, and in the case of raw materials, technical progress in manufacturing actually largely consists of a reduction in the amount of raw materials used per unit of output, which may compensate or even overcompensate the increase in the volume of manufacturing output. This lack of an automatic multiplication in demand, coupled with the low price elasticity of demand for both raw materials and food, results in large price falls, not only cyclical but also structural.

Thus it may be said that foreign investment of the traditional type which sought its repayment in the direct stimulation of exports of primary commodities either to the investing country directly or indirectly through multilateral relations, had not only its beneficial cumulative effects in the investing country, but the people of the latter, in their capacity as consumers, also enjoyed the fruits of technical progress in the manufacture of primary commodities thus stimulated, and at the same time in their capacity as producers also enjoyed the fruits of technical progress in the production of manufactured commodities. The industrialized countries have had the best of both worlds, both as consumers of primary commodities and as producers of manufactured articles, whereas the underdeveloped countries had the worst of both worlds, as consumers of manufactures and as producers of raw materials. This perhaps is the legitimate germ of truth in the charge that foreign investment of the traditional type formed part of a system of "economic imperialism" and of "exploitation."

Even if we disregard the theory of deliberately sinister machinations, there may be legitimate grounds in the arguments set out above on which it could be maintained that the benefits of foreign trade and investment have not been equally shared between the two groups of countries. The capital-exporting countries have received their repayment many times over in the following five forms: (*a*) possibility of building up exports of manufactures and thus transferring their population from low-productivity occupations to high-productivity occupations; (*b*) enjoyment of the internal economies of expanded manufacturing industries; (*c*) enjoyment of the general dynamic impulse radiating from industries in a progressive society; (*d*) enjoyment of the fruits of technical progress in primary production as main consumers of primary commodities; (*e*) enjoyment of a contribution from foreign consumers of manufactured articles, representing as it were their contribution to the rising incomes of the producers of manufactured articles.

By contrast, what the underdeveloped countries have to show cannot compare with this formidable list of benefits derived by the industrialized countries from the traditional trading-*cum*-investment system. Perhaps the widespread though inarticulate feeling in the underdeveloped countries that the dice have been loaded against them was not so devoid of foundation after all as the pure theory of exchange might have led one to believe.

It is, of course, true that there are transfer difficulties on the part of the underdeveloped countries which are avoided by production for export directly to the investing countries, but the above analysis may perhaps make a contribution to understanding why this traditional investment system broke down so rapidly and so irreparably in 1929 and 1930. The industrialized countries had already received real repayment from their foreign investments in the five forms described above, and in these ways they may have collected a pretty good return on their investments. When on top of the returns received in those five forms they also tried to "get their money back," they may perhaps have been asking (in the economic, though not in the legal, sense) for double payment; they may have been trying to get a quart out of a pint bottle.

There is a fairly widespread impression that this traditional trend towards deteriorating price relations for primary producers has been sharply reversed since prewar days, although this impression is not as strong now as it was in the middle of 1948. Even if we take that point of time, which represents the peak of postwar primary commodity prices up till now, a detailed analysis does not bear out the impression that terms of trade have significantly improved in favor of the underdeveloped countries since prewar days.[6]

It may be suggested that the impression that price relations have sharply improved for primary producers can be attributed partly to the abnormal composition of primary commodity imports into the U.S. where coffee plays a predominating part (coffee prices have increased particularly heavily in the immediate postwar period), and also specially to the wide-spread idea that foreign trade between underdeveloped countries and industrialized countries is an exchange of the primary commodities of the former for the capital goods of the latter. In fact, among the imports of the underdeveloped countries capital goods do not generally form the largest category, mainly because the import of capital goods from abroad requires a great deal of complementary domestic investment in those countries for which the domestic finance does not exist or is not mobilized.

The major proportion of the imports of the underdeveloped countries is in fact made up of manufactured food (especially in overpopulated under-developed countries), textile manufactures, and manufactured consumer goods. The prices of the type of food imported by the underdeveloped countries, and particularly the prices of textile manufactures, have risen so heavily in the immediate postwar period that any advantage which the underdeveloped countries might have enjoyed in the postwar period from favorable prices realized on primary commodities and low prices of capital goods has been wiped out.

A further factor which has contributed to the impression that relative price trends have turned sharply in favor of primary producers since the war is the deterioration in British terms of trade and the publicity which this deterioration has received because of the strategic importance of the British balance of payments in the network of world trade. It should, however, not be forgotten that the changes in British postwar terms of trade do not merely represent *ceteris paribus* price changes but reflect considerable quantum changes; namely, an increase in the quantity exported and a decrease in the quantity imported. It may be suggested, perhaps, that these quantum changes rather than underlying price changes account for the adverse trend before devaluation of British terms of trade. Unless it is to be assumed that the elasticity of demand for British exports is infinite, it is obvious that an expansion in the volume of total exports of manufactured goods by almost 100 per cent will be reflected in lower unit prices for British exports; conversely, the reduction in the quantity of British imports is also reflected in higher prices paid than would otherwise have been the case, partly as a reflection of the diminishing bargaining

strength of Britain in consequence of lower imports and partly as a necessary political concession to primary producers to enable them to maintain
their incomes in the face of lower quantities sold. The supposition that the
changed quantity relations in British trade (as well as deliberate colonial
development policies) are largely responsible for the adverse trend in
British terms of trade rather than price changes in world markets is greatly
strengthened by the fact that other Western European exporters of manufactured goods did not only fail to experience any deterioration in their
terms of trade, but on the contrary showed improved terms of trade.[7] The
effect of quantum changes on British terms of trade is of course difficult to
disentangle statistically. It is more in the nature of a gain missed through
inability of exploiting the postwar sellers' market price-wise to the full. It is
surely a remarkable fact that in a world hungry for capital goods, and with
her two most important direct industrial competitors eliminated, England
should have experienced adverse terms of trade in the years 1945 to 1948.

At this point it might be worth noting the curious ambivalence which
price relations in foreign trade play for the underdeveloped countries.
Good prices for their primary commodities, specially if coupled with a rise
in quantities sold, as they are in a boom, give to the underdeveloped
countries the necessary means for importing capital goods and financing
their own industrial development; yet at the same time they take away the
incentive to do so, and investment, both foreign and domestic, is directed
into an expansion of primary commodity production, thus leaving no room
for the domestic investment which is the required complement of any
import of capital goods. Conversely, when the prices and sales of primary
commodities fall off, the desire for industrialization is suddenly sharpened.
Yet, at the same time, the means for carrying it out are sharply reduced.
Here again it seems that the underdeveloped countries are in danger of
falling between two stools: failing to industrialize in a boom because things
are as good as they are, and failing to industrialize in a slump because
things are as bad as they are.[8] It is no doubt true that failure to utilize high
boom exports proceeds more determinedly for capital formation because of
purely temporary price relations shows a deplorable lack of foresight, but
this is hardly very apposite criticism of those underdeveloped countries
which rely mainly on private development. All private activity tends to be
governed by the price relations of the day.

If our view is accepted (namely, that the traditional type of foreign
investment as it was known prior to 1929 was "foreign" only in the geographical sense and not in the relevant economic sense) does it then follow
that foreign investment has failed to fulfill one of the functions traditionally
ascribed to it (and hoped for from it for the future); i.e., to spread industrialization more widely and more evenly throughout the world? It would
be premature to jump to this conclusion. What has been maintained in the
preceding part of this argument is that past foreign investment, and the

type of foreign trade which went with it, failed to spread industrialization to the countries in which the investment took place. It may be, however, that for a full understanding of the process we have to consider not merely the investing and the invested countries but a third group of countries as well.

It is an interesting speculation that European investment overseas was the instrument by which industrialization was brought to North America. Roughly speaking, the supplies of food and raw materials pouring into Europe as the result of the investment-*cum*-trade system and the favorable terms of trade engendered by this system enabled Europe to feed, clothe, educate, train, and equip large numbers of emigrants sent overseas, principally to the United States and Canada. Thus the benefits to the investing countries of Europe arising out of the system described above were in turn passed on to the United States—the converse of the Marshall Plan—and were the main foundation of the enormous capital formation the result of which is now to be observed in North America. This "macroeconomic" analysis is, of course, in no way contradicted by the fact that the individual migrant was motivated by the prospect of raising his standards of living by the transfer.

Attention may be drawn to the interesting statistical computation of Corrado Gini that even the enormous capital stock characteristic of the United States economy is not more than the equivalent of the burden in consumption goods and in such services as health, education, and other provision for the immigrants—a burden which the United States was enabled to save by shifting it to the European mother countries of the immigrants. Perhaps in the final result it may be said that the ultimate benefits of the traditional investment-*cum*-trade system were not with the investing countries of Europe but with the new industrial countries of North America.[9]

If this analysis is correct, the industrialization of North America was made possible by the combination of migration and the opening up of underdeveloped overseas countries through European investment and trade. To that extent, Point Four and technical assistance on the part of the United States would be a gesture of historical justice and return of benefits received in the past.

It may be useful, rather than end on a wild historical speculation, to summarize the type of economic measures and economic policies which would result from the analysis presented in this paper. This first conclusion would be that in the interest of the underdeveloped countries, of world national income, and perhaps ultimately of the industrialized countries themselves, the purposes of foreign investment and foreign trade ought perhaps to be redefined as producing gradual changes in the structure of comparative advantages and of the comparative endowment of the different countries rather than to develop a world trading system based on existing comparative advantages and existing distribution of endowments.

This perhaps is the real significance of the present movement towards giving technical assistance to underdeveloped countries not necessarily linked with actual trade or investment. The emphasis on technical assistance may be interpreted as a recognition that the present structure of comparative advantages and endowments is not such that it should be considered as a permanent basis for a future international division of labor.

Insofar as the underdeveloped countries continue to be the source of food and primary materials and insofar as trade, investment, and technical assistance are working in that direction by expanding primary production, the main requirement of underdeveloped countries would seem to be to provide for some method of income absorption to ensure that the results of technical progress are retained in the underdeveloped countries in a manner analogous to what occurs in the industrialized countries. Perhaps the most important measure required in this field is the reinvestment of profits in the underdeveloped countries themselves, or else the absorption of profits by fiscal measures and their utilization for the finance of economic development, and the absorption of rising productivity in primary production in rising real wages and other real incomes, provided that the increment is utilized for an increase in domestic savings and the growth of markets of a kind suitable for the development of domestic industries. Perhaps this last argument, namely, the necessity of some form of domestic absorption of the fruits of technical progress in primary production, provides the rationale for the concern which the underdeveloped countries show for the introduction of progressive social legislation. Higher standards of wages and social welfare, however, are not a highly commendable cure for bad terms of trade, except where the increment leads to domestic savings and investment. Where higher wages and social services are prematurely introduced and indiscriminately applied to export and domestic industries, they may in the end turn out a retarding factor in economic development and undermine the international bargaining strength of the primary producers. Absorption of the fruits of technical progress in primary production is not enough; what is wanted is absorption for reinvestment.

Finally, the argument put forward in this paper would point the lesson that a flow of international investment into the underdeveloped countries will contribute to their economic development only if it is absorbed into their economic system; i.e., if a good deal of complementary domestic investment is generated and the requisite domestic resources are found.

Notes

1. The author wishes to acknowledge help and advice received from many friends and colleagues; in particular Mr. Henry G. Aubrey, Dr. Harold Barger, of

the National Bureau of Economic Research, Dr. Roberto de Oliveira Campos, of the Brazilian Delegation to the United Nations, Dr. A. G. B. Fisher, of the International Monetary Fund, Professor W. Arthur Lewis, of the University of Manchester (England), and Mr. James Kenny. He also had the inestimable advantage of a discussion of the subject matter of this paper in the Graduate Seminar at Harvard University, with Professors Haberler, Harris, and others participating.

2. A more statistical factor might be mentioned. Some underdeveloped countries—Iran would be an illustration—exclude important parts of their exports and imports from their foreign trade statistics insofar as the transactions of foreign companies operating in the underdeveloped country are concerned. This is a tangible recognition of the fact that these pieces of foreign investments and their doings are not an integral part of the underdeveloped economy.

3. Often underdeveloped countries had the chance, by the judicious use of royalties or other income from foreign investment, to use them for the transformation of their internal economic structure—a chance more often missed than caught by the forelock!

4. Reference may be made here to the publication by the Economic Affairs Department of the United Nations on "Relative Prices of Exports and Imports of Under-developed Countries."

5. According to U.S. data of the WPA research project, output per wage earner in a sample of 54 manufacturing industries increased by 57 per cent during the twenty years, 1919–39; over the same period, agriculture increased only by 23 per cent, anthracite coal mining by 15 per cent, and bituminous coal mining by 35 per cent. In the various fields of mineral mining, however, progress was as fast as in manufacturing. According to data of the National Bureau of Economic Research, the rate of increase in output per worker was 1.8 per cent p.a. in manufacturing industries (1899–1939) but only 1.6 per cent in agriculture (1890–1940) and in mining, excluding petroleum (1902–39). In petroleum production, however, it was faster than in manufacturing.

6. For details see the above mentioned study of "Relative Prices of Exports and Imports of Under-developed Countries" (Economic Affairs Department of the United Nations).

7. *Economic Survey of Europe in 1948* (United Nations, Department of Economic Affairs), pp. 93–106, especially 97, 98 and 99.

8. This ambivalence of changing terms of trade has also been stressed in a different context by Professor Lloyd Metzler in his important article on "Tariffs, Terms of Trade and Distribution of National Income," in the *Journal of Political Economy*, February, 1949.

9. In more recent years, specially since 1924, U.S. capital accumulation had of course become quite independent from the original stimulus supplied by immigration, and proceeded without any visible check in spite of a heavy reduction in immigration. The argument put forward here is meant as a historical explanation rather than an analysis of the present sources of capital investment.

2

TNCs and Welfare of Host Countries: Analytical Considerations*

S. Lall and P. Streeten

*Source: S. Lall and P. Streeten, *Foreign Investment, Transnationals and Developing Countries* (London, Macmillan, 1977), pp. 53–80, 235–239.

Provision of Capital

The world's largest enterprises can command enormous financial resources for investment, both internally and by tapping various external capital markets and financial institutions. Not only do TNCs have access to finance: they often have *privileged* access, and can obtain funds on better terms than other firms (certainly as compared with firms from LDCs, most of which cannot on their own raise long-term funds in international markets at all). Furthermore, with the expansion of transnational banking into several LDCs, TNCs which have long-established links with the parent banks can extend these links to their subsidiaries, and enable them to raise credit on favourable terms.

Besides the benefits that TNCs can offer in terms of *direct* provision of capital, they can also stimulate it *indirectly* in three ways. First, a transnational investor wanting to set up an exceptionally large plant may invite other TNCs to contribute to its financing (and to share in the risks). The incidence of such multinational consortia has risen quite noticeably in recent years, especially in Eastern Europe and the Middle East, and in industries with scale economies and stable technologies. Secondly, the free entry of private capital may stimulate, indeed sometimes may be a condition for, the flow of official aid from the home countries of the TNCs (as well as from international aid agencies). Thirdly, foreign firms may mobilise local savings, which would otherwise remain idle or be used in less productive activities, by offering attractive investment opportunities on domestic capital markets.

As against these benefits that TNCs can offer in terms of filling the savings and foreign exchange 'gaps' in LDCs, we can set several *costs*.

(a) Direct private investment is a relatively expensive way to acquire foreign capital, and investment by the large transnationals tends to be more expensive than investment by smaller firms. There is little doubt that the rate of profit of TNCs is significantly higher than the long-term rate of interest in international capital markets and that TNCs are more profitable than other firms;[1] our own studies confirm that host economies do not gain much financial benefit from foreign direct investment, and would be seen to gain even less if hidden remittances in the form of transfer pricing were fully known. Two points must, however, be noted. First, the main advantages offered by TNCs are supposed to be not finance, but technology, marketing and superior management, and these are presumably reflected in the higher cost of the finance (whether or not the host LDC receives genuine 'welfare' gains from the other advantages is another matter, and must be judged on different grounds from case to case). Secondly, aid and foreign borrowing are not generally substitutable for foreign direct investment by an LDC; they are, if anything, complementary. On the other hand, the host country can always divert foreign exchange from other uses if extra aid is not available. The proper economic calculation would be to compare the cost of servicing TNC investment with the opportunity cost of providing the capital domestically plus the cost of buying the other components of the TNC package. This is on the assumptions, of which neither may be correct, that the 'other' components are wanted and are for sale at acceptable prices. The assessment would depend on the particular circumstances.

(b) The actual inflow of capital provided by the TNC may not be very large. We noted in Chapter 2 [Lall and Streeten, 1977] that US parent TNCs as a whole provided only 12 per cent of the total value of expenditures on capital investment and profit remittances in 1966–70, the remainder coming from *locally earned and reinvested profits* and *local savings.* As far as reinvested profits go, the amount of the investment may legitimately be considered as a foreign-exchange inflow as long as the funds could have been repatriated by the foreign firm. Though many critics of TNCs, especially in Latin America, complain that this somehow represents a misuse of local resources to finance foreign profit-bearing investments, the reasoning is invalid – at least, so long as one accepts the legitimacy of profit. A more valid criticism may be that the profits earned are 'too high', because of the market power of large TNCs; but this is irrelevant to the above argument, which is concerned not with the level of profits but, apparently, with the ethics of the private-enterprise system.

As far as the use of local savings is concerned, we must distinguish between local equity (which earns profits) and local borrowing (which earns interest). Local equity shareholders get the same return on their capital as do foreign shareholders in the TNC (unless transfer pricing is used against the former so as to remit profits clandestinely to the foreign parent), and there is little ground for objecting to TNCs raising local capital in this form, as long as the investment as such is considered desirable. On the contrary, since the TNC usually has sources of market power beyond the reach of local firms, such financing, if the TNC can be persuaded or obliged to accept it, is a good way of capturing a part of its rents domestically.

Local financing in the form of loans is different, for two reasons: (i) it raises the rate of profit on foreign capital which is 'geared' with domestic loans,[2] and so diverts domestic savings from other uses only to benefit the foreign investor; and (ii) it may lead to foreign subsidiaries being preferred as clients by financial institutions, by virtue of being part of transnational businesses, and so to local firms having less credit than they otherwise would. The first may be regarded as socially undesirable, as long as the funds would have been used equally productively elsewhere in the economy. Several governments in LDCs seem to take this condition for granted, and restrict the amount of long-term loans that foreign firms can raise locally.[3] If their assumption is reasonable, it follows that capital should, as far as possible without harming present and future relationships with TNCs, be provided to them in the form of equity rather than loans. The second point, concerning the status of foreign subsidiaries as privileged borrowers, is often mentioned in the literature but is difficult to verify empirically. Our own sample data (see Chapter 6 [Lall and Streeten, 1977]) do not indicate that foreign firms gear themselves more highly than domestic ones, though this does not, of course, establish that they are not favoured borrowers. If it *were* the case that TNCs were given preference – and this seems likely on *a priori* grounds – it could lead to a socially un-desirable pattern of lending, and there would be a strong case for the re-direction of credit to help deserving local entrepreneurs.

(c) The capital contribution of a TNC may be in the form of machinery or capitalised intangibles (know-how, goodwill, and so on) rather than cash. The valuation of such contributions is difficult, and may be quite arbitrary. Thus, in order to raise its equity share in an investment, the TNC may assign a high value to, say, used machinery or a brand-name, the value of which most LDC governments normally would not check closely. Furthermore, a domestic technology buyer or shareholder may knowingly collaborate in the overvaluation of equipment and intangibles so as to by-pass official control of profit and royalty payments.[4] This raises issues of transfer pricing, which we shall discuss later.

Organisation and Management

In the previous chapter [Lall and Streeten, 1977] we described the evol-ution of the organisational structure of TNCs, and the possible advantages that this might confer upon them. The growth of international activities across diverse ranges of products, the need to control a large number of units in a flexible yet cohesive manner, and the emergence of a 'global' view of business have necessitated major evolutions in the managerial and organisational practices of TNCs. The tendency has been, though it is by no means universal, to centralise a number of crucial functions and to delegate authority on more routine ones, reinforcing the structure with sophisticated communication systems, procedures and manuals, to ensure compliance with general policies.[5]

The *benefits* to host countries of the managerial superiority of TNCs are of three types.

(a) Managerial efficiency in operations, arising from better training, higher standards of recruitment, faster communications with the parent company and the world as a whole, and a more dynamic outlook generally.

(b) Entrepreneurial ability in seeking out investment opportunities, organising suppliers and markets, and perhaps developing new technologies to suit particular conditions.

(c) Externalities arising from training received by employees (technical, executive, accounting, and so on) who later leave the firm, and the demonstration effect on competing local firms, suppliers and even government officials who come into contact with the practices adopted by TNCs.

These benefits presumably show up in lower costs and prices, better investments, and a general improvement in managerial standards in the host country. Two qualifications may be noted. First, the sheer size and growth of TNCs is sometimes taken as evidence of their superior efficiency in operations. If this is not interpreted as a mere tautology – success defines efficiency – there is room for doubt whether the practices of TNCs are in fact more efficient than those of smaller firms, and whether their size does not, after a certain level, tend to act as a defence against threats from smaller but more efficient rivals. There is certainly some evidence (references are given in the notes to Chapter 2 [Lall and Streeten, 1977]) that large firms are less productive of innovations per unit of R & D expenditure than smaller firms are, and the same may be true of routine management, though evidence for or against this is hard to find.[6] Second, much of the benefit of training locals in the practices of TNCs may not lead to external benefits in LDCs, because these practices may be irrelevant, even alien, to the normal methods of business operation there. In such a case, departing employees may worsen the effective standards of management in the host country, by importing practices suitable to very large, complex and impersonal institutions into small, personal and culturally different ones.

Such qualifications apart, the tightly controlled and hierarchial structure of TNCs may entail more important *costs* to host LDCs. The first may be broadly labelled the *dependence and subordination* which this structure imposes on subsidiaries in a worldwide transnational system. The centralisation of authority and crucial decisions in the head offices of TNCs, which, as we noted in the previous chapter [Lall and Streeten, 1977], are staffed by the nationals of the home countries of these companies,[7] leads to a sort of imperialist system in the organisation, with the head office dictating to the 'colonies', the subsidiaries, the rules, the actions and the values to be followed. The most vivid description of this is by Hymer, who writes,

> It is not technology which creates inequality; rather, it is *organisation* that imposes a ritual judicial asymmetry on the use of intrinsically symmetrical means of communication and arbitrarily creates unequal capacities to initiate and terminate exchange, to store and retrieve information, and to determine that extent of the exchange and the terms of the discussion ... [The result is that] a regime of multinational corporations would offer under-developed countries neither national independence nor equality.... It would turn underdeveloped economies into branch-plant countries, not only with reference to their economic functions but throughout the whole gamut of social, political and cultural roles.[8]

Two points are immediately obvious about Hymer's argument. First, the conventional welfare paradigm has been totally rejected. The scope of inquiry stretches far beyond the narrowly economic, and value judgements (about independence, autonomy, dignity, equality and subordination) are introduced which have no role in the conventional scheme. Second, the 'alternative situation' implicitly considered is not of a marginal change in foreign investments – in that case, the social, political and cultural factors would hardly change – but of a radical change in all the external relations of LDCs, with TNCs being a leading, but not the only, representation of these relations. Neither of these points is, as such, a criticism of the substance of Hymer's argument.

We have little to say on the non-economic aspects of the case: it is incontestable that TNCs are among the most powerful external forces affecting social and cultural attitudes in LDCs[9] and that they directly or indirectly influence political currents in host countries (we discuss this later); whether this is a 'good thing' or not is a matter of preference. As for the economic aspects, while it is plain that the growth of TNCs has an effect on the technological, consumption and other patterns of host countries, and that this has several undesirable features, it is not clear that it is *organisation* that is the main causal element, with the others being merely passive. It may be argued that the hierarchical form which the organisation takes is a product of growth compelled by technological factors or by oligopolistic competition more generally. The sort of inequality and loss of autonomy which Hymer is attacking is inherent in the entire structure of international economic relationships between developed and less-developed areas,[10] and there is little analytical purpose served by selecting one manifestation.

The second type of cost arises from the *financial practices* which a tightly-knit organisational structure facilitates. An important facet of the international growth of firms has been that a number of transactions between different countries now take place between units of the same firms. These cover sales of technology and services as well as of commodities of all kinds, and the valuation placed on these, particularly the last, has given rise to the well-known problem of *transfer pricing.*[11]

The problem arises from the fact that transfer prices, being under the control of the firm concerned, can be put at levels which differ from prices which would obtain in 'arm's-length' transactions, and so can be manipulated to shift profits clandestinely from one area of operations to another. If the different units of a TNC behaved like independent firms, clearly the problem would not arise. However, given the growing extent of intra-firm trade,[12] it is the *centralisation of authority* and the growth of a *global business strategy* that creates fears on the part of governments (both host and home) that they are losing legitimate tax revenue.

We must be careful not to exaggerate. There are indications that different TNCs have different policies with regard to transfer pricing, and a prominent business-school text points out that many firms are losing 'millions of dollars' through 'sub-optimal' use of the various financial devices open to them.[13] On the other hand, the very process of organisational rationalisation and increasing intra-firm trade that accompanies transnational growth (and, of course, the advice tendered by business specialists) tends to increase the ability of TNCs to handle complex international pricing strategies, and the increasing concern expressed by governments about the regulation of transfer-pricing practices shows that the problem is acutely felt.[14] The examples of flexibility of pricing manipulations mentioned in Chapter 2 [Lall and Streeten, 1977], the evidence on transfer pricing in Colombia presented in Chapter 7 [Lall and Streeten, 1977], and the existence of several thriving tax havens[15] should warn us against treating the phenomenon lightly.

The *inducements* to TNCs to use transfer pricing have been amply discussed in the literature,[16] and here we need mention them only briefly. They may be grouped under two headings. Those that arise from the desire (directly) to *increase global post-tax profits* are: international differences in tax and tariff rates, multiple exchange rates, quantitative restrictions on profit remission, existence of local shareholders, exchange-rate instability, and the overstating of apparent costs as a means to obtain higher protection against imports. Those that arise from the need to *reduce risk and uncertainty* over the long term are: present or anticipated balance-of-payments difficulties, political threats to profit repatriation (or to survival) in a particular country, trade-union pressures, and the risk of attracting competition from other (mainly transnational) firms. In general, it seems plausible to argue, as Lall (1973) has done, that many LDCs, with their combination of exchange problems, pressures for local shareholding, political risks and tendencies to socialism, will offer substantial incentives to TNCs to keep a 'low profit profile' and so use transfer pricing against them. The incidence may differ from country to country (those with the political machinery to implement an all-out capitalist strategy may feel more secure) and from industry to industry (low-technology industries with standardised inputs being less vulnerable), but the danger is certainly present and cannot be ignored.

These are the external factors which may cause a firm to use transfer prices to move profits out of a host country. Actual transfer-pricing policies may be affected not only by these, but also by *constraints* which are set by external (checks by tax and customs authorities) and internal (the need to monitor and control subsidiaries) factors. Firms make a great deal of the fact that, because of external checks, they are unable to manipulate transfer prices, and it is certainly true that, with a growing awareness of the problem, several governments have tightened their procedures for regulating intra-firm transactions. The following points should, however, be noted.

(a) The monitoring of prices charged on intra-firm transactions is a difficult, complex and expensive task with which most administrations in LDCs are ill-equipped to deal.[17] Furthermore, the two sets of authorities which are normally concerned with these prices may act in conflicting ways: customs authorities want to set high prices on imports to increase tariff revenue, while tax authorities want the opposite, to increase taxable profits.

(b) While there are serious administrative problems in checking whether firms are charging correct market prices, there are far more difficult problems which arise when the goods are *specific* to the firm and *do not have* market (or comparable arm's-length) prices. Many of the commodities exchanged in intra-firm trade are of this type, and there are severe practical as well as theoretical problems in deciding what a correct reference price should be. The greatest difficulty arises in allocating such fixed costs as R & D, administration and marketing expenses incurred by the parent company to individual items produced by it and 'sold' to affiliates. For research-based TNCs this involves determining not only how fixed costs of successful as well as unsuccessful innovations should be spread over particular items, but also what a 'fair' reward is for risk in doing research and what it is 'fair' to charge subsidiaries in countries which do not benefit from major areas of its research. Clearly there cannot be a *correct* solution (in the absence of actual competitive arm's-length prices); any price set within a range is bound to be arbitrary. In such a situation, it will not be costs that determine price but 'what the market will bear – and this will be determined by the bargaining strength of the parties involved (in this case the TNC and the governments of host and home countries).[18] It is likely, however, that, given this indeterminacy and the relative administrative weakness of host governments in LDCs, the transfer-pricing tool will be used more to the advantage of the sophisticated TNCs than to that of the host LDCs. It is also likely that the incidence of transfer pricing will be higher the more highly technological the industry and the more firm-specific the goods involved; the fact that the bulk of the evidence comes from the pharmaceutical industry tends to support this hypothesis (see Chapter 8 [Lall and Streeten, 1977]).

(c) Most of the official action taken recently to regulate transfer pricing has in fact occurred in the developed countries, despite the publicity which has been given in the literature to attempts by the Andean Pact. The US government, under section 482 of its Internal Revenue Code, is probably the most rigorous and experienced in dealing with this problem;[19] it uses three methods for determining arm's-length prices, the actual outcome in most cases being determined by a negotiation (bargain) between the company and the authorities. Its example is being followed by many European countries,[20] which are also setting up procedures for international exchange of price data on TNC trade. The Andean Group's attempts, while yielding valuable fiscal benefits, are still not very comprehensive; other developing countries have still to make a start in dealing with transfer pricing.[21] If it is the case that official checks evolve faster and more stringently in the developed world, the effect would be to *tilt the balance further against the less-developed countries*, with the fiscal authorities of the former gaining at the expense of the latter.[22]

The costs to host LDCs from transfer pricing accrue not only to the authorities which lose tax revenue (net of any gains made in tariffs), but also to local shareholders who lose part of their legitimate profits, workers who lose if low declared profits retard wage increases, and consumers who pay higher prices if TNCs are able to obtain greater protection and charge higher prices.

The internal constraints to transfer pricing arise from the need to exercise proper financial control over subsidiaries and to offer proper incentives to the management of subsidiaries which might otherwise be required to show low profits or losses. While it may be true that some firms operating internationally do find these constraints important (thus the variety of practice noted above), it is difficult to believe that, with a centralisation of pricing decision-making, sophisticated accounting and communication techniques, and the ease of keeping different accounts for different purposes, they will continue to be important for the majority of TNCs. Certainly the evidence on financial manipulations (referred to elsewhere in this book) does not indicate that such constraints are by themselves very binding.

The final cost of the managerial and entrepreneurial superiority of TNCs is the *suppression of domestic entrepreneurship.* It is often argued[23] that unrestricted entry of TNCs into an underdeveloped economy with a weak national entrepreneurial class will cause all the dynamic sectors of industry to be taken over by the transnationals, with the domestically owned industrial sector relegated to subsidiary role of the provider of ancillary inputs. There is certainly good reason to expect this. Even a developed economy with strong entrepreneurial resources (for instance, Canada) can find it difficult to prevent the leadership in the main branches of industry from passing to foreign TNCs; a backward economy with far weaker defences faces a much greater threat.

There may be two reasons for regarding this as a cost. First, on 'purely' economic grounds, the domination of an economy (or of many of its leading industries) by TNCs may be *economically detrimental* to the long-run development of the host country (taking 'development' now to stand simply for the growth of GNP at market prices) on three counts.

(a) It may lead to a lower rate of accumulation domestically because a proportion of the profits is repatriated rather than invested locally. This would be the case, however, only if local investors earned the same rate of profit as foreign ones (essentially if they have the same technology and managerial skills), if they did not also send part of their profits abroad, and if conditions in the host economy (politically as well as economically) were such that the foreign investor chose to repatriate rather than enlarge his investments.

(b) Similarly, it may lead to higher (open or hidden) charges for technology or other services, a greater incidence of undesirable practices such as transfer pricing and export restrictions, or a lower degree of national control over monetary and fiscal policy. Again, the final economic cost of this depends upon whether the technology or other services would have been available in the alternative situation, whether affiliates were in fact charged more than unrelated buyers of technology, and whether a relatively 'open' economy (with respect to exchange rates, capital flows, and so on) is not more efficient than one which is more insulated from international market forces.[24]

(c) Its effect on the market structure may be to induce a very high degree of oligopolistic concentration, and so to impose the costs of diminished price competition, excessive product differentiation, possible cartelisation, and so on. This assumes that a nationally owned industrial structure would be different, and that domestic oligopolists would behave differently.[25]

On 'purely' economic grounds, therefore, there are clearly a number of potential costs of foreign domination, but it is difficult to assess how important these may be without specifying a number of conditions – about various political and economic factors affecting foreign investment, about the availability of technology, about the capabilities of domestic entre-preneurs and the efficacy of national policies which go against 'free' market forces, about alternative market structures during industrial development, and so on which are in practice almost impossible to assess. Several of these points are touched upon elsewhere, so we shall not labour them here.

The second reason for regarding domination by TNCs as a cost is based upon 'non-economic' considerations. Such considerations may be grouped into four views, ranging from that of mild nationalism to that of radical socialism: first, national ownership of means of production may be regarded as desirable *per se*; second, foreign ownership may impose costs in social, political and cultural terms; third, it may distort the pattern of development, inhibit local technology and primarily serve to enrich a small section of the population; and, fourth, it may block the road to socialist reforms in the future.[26] The first represents an undercurrent of feeling contained in much of the criticism of TNCs, especially in the 'American Challenge' sort of reaction which was popular in Europe in the 1960s. The second is common in many developing countries, but in a 'pure' form (i.e. without other ideological connotations) is perhaps best seen in the Canadian resentment of US transnationals. The third is the sort of mixture of socialism and nationalism which many Latin American writers of the 'structuralist' and 'dependence' schools display, while the fourth is expli-citly Marxist.

It is difficult to separate the 'economic' arguments from the 'non-economic' ones, and we do not wish to draw a very firm distinction or to suggest that one is more legitimate or objective than the other (thus the inverted commas). Indeed, we ourselves introduce, as we noted before, explicitly 'non-economic' judgements into our discussion of welfare effects. The foregoing analysis is mainly intended to illustrate, once more, how differences in assessment of the virtues of national enterprise reflect differ-ences in interpretation of (and gaps in) information, differences in value judgements, and differences in the desired 'alternative situations' with which the actual one is compared.

Technology

The 'transfer of technology' has now become perhaps the predominant issue around which discussions of TNCs and their dealings with developing countries revolve.[27] Indeed, concern with the control and regulation of TNCs as a whole seems to have become increasingly subsumed under a consideration of policies for transferring technology on terms favourable to the receiving developing countries, and under conditions that are in some sense appropriate to their social and economic needs. It is not difficult to understand why. 'Technology', defined widely to mean the human ability to handle the means of production, and 'innovation', the production of new technology, are the lifeblood of economic growth, accumulation, trade and even changes in the organisation of social relations and the relations of production. In this general sense, the transfer of the ability to produce most efficiently is held to be the key to progress in the poor countries, and is the attribute which they demand most from TNCs.[28]

While in this very general sense technology is certainly a vital component of economic progress, it has, however, come to be increasingly recognised that the *particular form* that technology takes at a given time and in a given context is heavily influenced by the socio-economic environment for which it is produced. It cannot, in other words, simply be assumed to be a neutral factor which has to be transferred wholesale to completely different environments 'to raise productivity' and 'welfare'.[29] An evaluation of the real welfare effects of technology transferred by TNCs must be based upon an understanding of the context in which TNCs produce their technology, the market and institutions which govern the transfer of this technology to LDCs, and the social and economic effects of the transfer.

We have already described the main elements of the context in developed countries in which the bulk of modern technology is produced. Let us reiterate the main points. The production of new technology (as measured by the distribution of R & D expenditures or patents taken out) is very highly concentrated among the most advanced capitalist countries, and within these among a few leading (mostly transnational) firms. With the growing oligopolistic nature of manufacturing industry, in 'low' as well as 'high' technology sectors, a great deal of technological innovation (directed at the *rich* markets which account for the bulk of sales, and based on competitive and cost pressures in *developed* countries) is aimed not at discovering new processes and products, but at product differentiation. The balance between 'real' technological advance and 'marketing-oriented' innovation varies from one industry to another, depending upon the scientific base of the industry, the stage of maturity of the ruling technology, the stability of the oligopoly, and the nature of the market, with some sectors (such as computers) being heavily science and 'real'-technology based, and so spending relatively little on marketing innovation,[30] and others (such as processed foods) being heavily market based, with relatively little 'real' innovation and a stable and widely diffused technology.[31] While it obviously is difficult to draw a firm line between the two sorts of innovation, the distinction between them is widely recognised, and it is vital for our purposes to bear it in mind.

The most important force behind the transnational growth of the leading oligopolistic firms has been the possession of a 'package' or combination of these technological and marketing advantages and the pressure to capitalise on these in larger markets. Within the present structure of manufacturing industry (and growing more so over time), the production of new technology is in many industries inextricably linked with, and dependent upon, the process of product differentiation and the use of a highly sophisticated, widespread and effective marketing structure. Technological innovation could not survive without marketing, and marketing would not succeed without a constant stream of new or differentiated products. Thus, only a part of what is normally termed 'innovation' goes towards the production of genuinely new processes and products ('raising the productive forces' in Marxist terms, in order to raise the rate of surplus value); the rest is broadly defensive and marketing-oriented (for 'realising' surplus value in the process of capitalist competition).

This is the background to the production of the technology which is relevant to our discussion. Let us now briefly examine the nature of the market (and supporting institutions) and the socio-economic context of recipient LDCs, in order to assess its welfare effects.

Technology Markets and Institutions

The technology 'market' has several peculiarities which distinguish it from a normally functioning market for commodities.[32] These peculiarities arise from the fact that it deals with knowledge, which, once produced, costs little at the margin to sell (in unlimited quantities), yet can be very expensive to produce and commercialise, and, mostly because of this, is extremely concentrated in its ownership. Since private production of marketable knowledge must earn a suitable reward for effort and risk, the intrinsically social (or 'public-good') nature of the product must be counterbalanced by secrecy and legal rights (both of which have limited durations) and by its embodiment in a suitably marketed branded commodity (which may have a fairly long remunerative life). And since the buyer of knowledge is, especially when he buys the whole 'package' of direct investment by a TNC, very imperfectly informed of what he is buying, the usual assumption of an 'informed buyer' acting in a competitive market does not hold.

If we add to this the consideration that LDCs have little capacity to 'go it alone' in many fields of advanced technology and that they often lack even the information or the ability to shop around for alternative technologies and sources of supply, it is easy to see why 'The situation is quite different from that of an "equilibrium price" reached in a competitive market. It is more like that of a bilateral monopoly or oligopoly where bargaining theory applies',[33] a situation where, we may add, the developing countries often find themselves at a grave disadvantage. If we disregard for the moment questions of appropriateness and concentrate on the direct financial costs of buying technology in this market, the following points may be made about technology transfers through TNCs.

First there are several *sources of technology* besides large transnational companies – from consultants who have no interest in directly owning and running manufacturing enterprises, and smaller firms which may license the technology or undertake direct investments, to official and international agencies which can provide technical assistance without charge or for a small fee, and enterprises from socialist countries. The relative importance of TNCs in this spectrum depends on how technology-intensive an industry is, how rapidly the technology is changing, and how far the commercialis-ation of technology needs organisational and marketing know-how (and export markets). Clearly, the more advanced and dynamic the technology, and the more difficult its commercialisation, the greater the hold of TNCs.

Second, within the sector of the market dominated by TNCs (which in fact comprises the main part of technology transfers in manufacturing), there are *several ways* in which technology can be bought: ranging from the outright purchase of a design or patent, via several intermediate arrange-ments requiring technical collaboration and/or equity participation by the TNC, to direct investment in a wholly-owned subsidiary.[34] The choice of form is strongly influenced by the policy of the host government, but it depends also upon the sophistication and secrecy of the technology, the monopoly power and corporate policy of the seller, the absorptive capacity of the buyer, and the need for continuous and close co-operation to keep abreast of latest developments.[35] A powerful TNC in a high-technology sector will usually demand – and get – high equity participation or complete ownership in a subsidiary; a TNC in a low-technology sector facing a capable recipient may well sell a licence or settle for a minority position.[36]

Third, the *price set* will depend greatly on the form of transfer chosen and the bargaining skills of the parties. A wholly-owned subsidiary may not pay royalties or technical fees separately, since the benefits of technology accrue, in any case, to the parent, in the form of dividends; if it does pay royalties, the purpose would be to minimise tax payments in home or host countries. As the percentage of equity held by the TNC declines, the price charged rises, so that the local partner pays proportionately for the benefit he receives in the form of higher profits; at the other end, in the case of an outright sale, the TNC gets all its returns from royalties unless it can realise profits from charging high prices for selling machinery, intermediates and services to accompany the technology.[37] The importance of *bargaining* can hardly be over-stressed. The acceptable price to the seller may lie between the marginal cost of transferring the technology (which would be very low or nil unless the future threat to markets were also included) and the price which would compensate it for the alternative of direct investment (which would be higher, since the TNC would profit from a package of several 'advantages' not just superior technology) if this were feasible, or a price which would drive the buyer to other sources of technology. The price to the buyer, correspondingly, may be between zero and the net (after allowance for profit) discounted stream of benefits it expects from the new technology, or the net cost of finding alternative sources of technology (including, at the extreme, the cost of developing the technology locally). The range within which bargaining can occur may be fairly wide, especially where the technology is scarce and the different parties have differing assessments of values and alternatives.

Fourth, the *conditions attached* to the transfer of technology, reflecting to some extent elements of the sale (such as future threat to export markets) which cannot be readily included in the price, can substantially modify the benefits that are transferred with the technology.[38] These conditions may restrict the freedom of the licensee to buy and sell commodities related to the technology transferred, and may sometimes stipulate how the benefits of future technological advances by the licensee are to be exploited, how the contracts are to be terminated and where disputes are to be arbitrated. A great deal of the current argument about 'international codes of conduct' for technology transfer revolves around the legitimacy of these restrictions, but there seems to be emerging agreement that they should be minimised and strictly regulated.

Finally, the institution of the *patent system*, as embodied in the Paris Convention and national laws, has come in for a great deal of criticism in recent years,[39] and it seems likely that, under the initiative of UNCTAD, many developing countries will modify their laws on patenting and tighten up their administration of them. The main arguments of the critics have been that, while the granting of patent protection by LDCs to TNCs which produce innovations mainly for the developed world does not offer any significant benefits, either in terms of stimulating R & D or in terms of promoting foreign capital and technology inflows, it does entail some significant costs: since the great majority of patents taken out are foreign and are not used for production within the country, the effect is to block the domestic market from cheaper imports and to prevent domestic firms from using the patented (or relevant competitive) technology. Furthermore, the sale of patented technology is often hemmed in by restrictive clauses and backed by the sale of intermediate and capital goods on which transfer pricing can be used.

It *is* widely accepted that patents granted by LDCs do not significantly stimulate innovation, and that the existence of patent protection does not, except indirectly as a sign of goodwill towards private enterprise, by itself attract foreign capital.[40] As for the costs, there is certainly *some* truth in the allegations noted above. However, we should be careful in interpreting the evidence. As Penrose (1973) points out, a number of the abuses may be found in technology transfers even in the absence of patents: there may be good economic reason for not using patents for production in particular LDCs, so that 'non-use' is not really an abuse of patent protection; other abuses (such as restrictive clauses) may well accompany the sale of non-patented technology (this is noted for India in Chapter 7 [Lall and Streeten, 1977]); and alternative imports or technology may simply not be available, so that it would be unfair to blame patents for the high price of technology.

There are other reasons for not putting too great an emphasis on the role of the patent system in the transfer of manufacturing technology as a whole.[41] With the growing importance of unpatented know-how in the application of new technology, with rising minimum scales of production and with the growing importance of marketing *vis-à-vis* technology in securing the market power of the leading oligopolistic firms, *patents have become relatively insignificant for a number of important transnational industries*, especially the engineering, electrical, food-processing and transport industries. The main sector for which they continue to be important, and which, consequently, is in the forefront of all battles to protect and extend patent protection, is fine chemicals – in particular, pharmaceuticals. Here the innovation is relatively easy to copy without recourse to un-patented know-how and there are sources of cheap imports from non-patent-observing countries such as Italy (though Italy seems to be in the process of adopting EEC patent laws). The bulk of evidence on patent 'abuse' thus comes from the drug industry and it is here that LDCs can gain most by opting out of seriously modifying the system (with a qualification about possible loss of exports). The evidence thus far is more indicative than definitive, and it may well be that patents remain significant for innovations by small firms in other sectors of developed countries; however, as far as LDCs are concerned, it seems fair to say that the main reforms should concentrate on minimising the costs of the patent system in a few selected sectors where patent-generated monopoly has significant independent effects.[42]

What, then, are the costs and benefits of buying technology from TNCs? The *benefits* arise from the fact that TNCs are the main producers, and in many cases the only ones, of technology in manufacturing; that direct investment by them may prove the fastest and most efficient way of getting access to the latest technology; and that they are able to provide the whole package which can enable the transfer and successful commercial appli-cation of technology. The *costs* arise because the rents TNCs can realise by virtue of their monopolistic power may be excessive in relation to the technological benefit received by the host LDC. In the case of a wholly-owned subsidiary, the host economy pays not just for the technology but also for the whole combination of 'advantages' which constitute the TNC's market power. In the case of a licensing agreement, the host economy may not pay for the whole package, but then it may not receive the latest technology, and/or it may, because of its weak bargaining position, pay too much (directly or indirectly) for the technology received, and suffer from restrictive practices. Moreover, because of administrative weaknesses, an LDC may 'over-import' technology, i.e. let several firms buy similar technology from different sources, or allow TNCs to enter sectors where domestic technology is quite adequate, and where the advantage of the foreign investors lies in their marketing superiority. We return to these problems in Part III of this book [Lall and Streeten, 1977], where we discuss policy issues.

Appropriateness of Technology

The above discussion has assumed a situation where the technology supplied is 'appropriate' to the needs of the host economy; let us now assume that the cost is suitable and concentrate on the much more difficult problem of appropriateness.[43] It is here that we again come up squarely against problems of defining 'welfare'.

The question of appropriateness has two aspects: as regards the products which are made with the technology transferred, and as regards the use of factors of production. Let us start with the *appropriateness of products*. We saw in the last chapter [Lall and Streeten, 1977], that the rise of TNCs is, in many industries (clearly in consumption goods, but also in others whose product can be used only in certain consumer industries), crucially dependent upon their ability to produce a sophisticated, highly differentiated and heavily promoted, constantly changing and well-packaged range of commodities. This is not an attribute that is, in some sense, 'added on' to their technological or managerial advantages: it is the *very essence* of the oligopolistic competition and technological progress which are the basis of transnational expansion.

It is this tendency that is partly responsible for the excessive sophistication and over-elaboration of many products and processes and their inappropriateness for LDCs. True, part of the explanation must be found in the fact that these products have been developed in high-income, high-savings, high-investment-per-worker countries, where consumer demand is sophisticated and capital per worker is plentiful. But this is not the whole story. Companies in search of profits should not find it difficult to invent and develop cheap, mass-produced products, appropriate to the lower incomes of the masses in the poor countries. But if imitation is easy, as it is in the case of simple products and processes, and the advantage soon lost, the incentive is lacking. It is therefore in the nature of the TNC that its products and processes should be excessively sophisticated in relation to the needs of the LDCs and in relation to the chances of a favourable bargain.

What are the welfare implications of having TNC technology which has evolved in this oligopolistic structure? The conventional paradigm would tell us that – barring problems arising from income distribution, which it is for the government to resolve on 'political' grounds anyway – it is good because it 'fulfills preferences' and 'widens the range of choice'. We would argue, on the other hand, that the fulfilment of preferences expressed in the markets is not the final criterion of welfare, certainly not in extremely poor countries, and that the use of scarce resources for the production of goods which are over-differentiated, over-packaged, over-promoted, over-specified and within the reach of only a small elite, or, if bought by the poor, at the expense of more essential products, is not conducive to 'national welfare'. This is not to say that all TNC technology is unnecessary in LDCs – clearly that would be absurd. But the free import of foreign capital and of the sort of technology many TNCs excel in would reproduce the pattern of the developed countries and would be undesirable. In other words, a definition of welfare based on meeting *basic social needs* would lead to a *fairly small proportion of TNC technology being regarded as beneficial.* We cannot provide *a priori* rules for judging what is, or is not, beneficial (the evaluation must vary according to the needs and circumstances of each country) but we can make a clear break from the logic which leads to the *a priori* conclusion that the free flow of investment and technology always tends to maximise welfare (unless government policy is wrong).

The issue of *appropriateness of factor use* is related to, but not identical with, the previous problem. It arises from the fact that TNCs transfer to LDCs technology which is excessively capital-intensive in relation to their factor endowments, and so cause: (a) an aggravation of employment problems; (b) a worsening of income inequalities; (c) distorting influences on technology used by other industrial firms; and (d) a bias in production towards the sort of high-income, sophisticated and differentiated products for which the technology has been developed. While the evidence on the precise extent of adaptability of modern technology and the actual adaptation of existing techniques to the labour-surplus situation of LDCs by foreign firms is far from complete, and to some extent conflicting,[44] the following conclusions may be drawn from the literature.

(a) As far as *adaptability* goes, much of modern 'high' technology cannot be changed to suit LDCs' endowments: the demands of precision, continuity, scale and complexity are too great. However, some 'low' technologies (for instance, in simple industries such as textiles) and 'peripheral' or 'ancillary' technology (for instance, transport or handling) are more adaptable. The scope of adaptability can be extended, but the cost, in terms of R & D and organisational requirements, may be quite high.

(b) As far as *adaptation* of foreign technology goes, the bulk of *basic or 'core' production technology* transferred by TNCs, both directly and by licensing, is not adapted in any significant way to low-wage conditions, though some *scaling down* of technology seems to be undertaken to adjust to smaller runs that would be appropriate in developed countries. There is evidence, however, that even a given 'core' technology can, with some adaptation, be used more intensively so as to yield higher output and/or employ more labour, and the peripheral or ancillary technologies are often adapted to more labour-intensive methods.

(c) As far as the *comparative performance* of TNCs and local or other foreign firms is concerned, the results are unclear and the method of comparison rather shaky.[45] There is not enough evidence to conclude that, compared with other firms, TNCs *as such* use more capital-intensive technology in relevant industries (though they may well be concentrated in capital-intensive industries); if anything, the evidence suggests that TNCs are *more able to adapt* given basic technologies to suit factor endowments in LDCs, especially when put under competitive pressure.

Several reasons have been advanced for the lack of any major modification of transferred technology.[46] Besides the obvious one that a range of technologies appropriate to LDCs simply does not exist in several high-technology industries, they are: inappropriate prices for labour and capital (relatively over-pricing the former); low labour productivity; lack of competition; scale requirements; skewed ('dependent') patterns of consumption favouring modern products; the danger of having technologies 'stolen' if they are too simple; lack of local adaptive R & D; the threat of labour problems; and the greater adaptability of capital-intensive plants to fluctuations in demand.[47]

In general it may be argued that, given the potentially high costs of adaptation, the reason why TNCs make so little effort to change their core technologies is precisely that *it is on the basis of the advantages of possessing these technologies that they have become transnational.* The very essence of profiting from international operations lies in the ability to apply a given package to different areas with as little costly adaptation as possible. In many important ways, therefore, the transmission of 'unsuitable' technology to produce 'inappropriate' products is the main driving force of transnational investment. And, as long as TNCs are increasingly the dominant form of production in the developed capitalist world, it is difficult to see how *any* mode of technology transfer can provide an 'appropriate' technology for LDCs that are (however imperfectly) integrated into the capitalist system. As Frances Stewart (1974) has argued, once the pattern of demand is given – and the pattern of industrial demand in LDCs is largely determined by the progress of technology in the developed world – the sort of technology needed is also defined. The advance of the capitalist mode of production in LDCs, if one likes to think in these terms, takes place via its most developed technological forms in the capitalist world; and, in so far as this is true, there is little scope for 'intermediate' technology in much of manufacturing industry (though the system *will* transfer the labour-intensive parts of complex technologies to low-wage areas). Thus, the 'costs' of TNC expansion, in this sense, are not due to inaction or intent on the part of TNCs and technology buyers; they are a reflection of a wider phenomenon.

Other Effects

The integration of LDCs into an international framework of technology transfer where there is negligible autonomous R & D conducted has far-reaching consequences for *science and research* in these countries.[48] The attitudes of subservient dependence it creates may inhibit the capacity to do even relatively minor adaptive research, or to put into industrial application processes which *have* been developed locally.[49] At a more basic level, it may bias the whole science and education policy towards over-theoretical or irrelevant curricula, and so prevent even preliminary moves towards technological 'independence'. Furthermore, the small R & D establishments which some TNCs maintain in industrially advanced LDCs may serve, among other purposes (mainly marketing innovation), as antennae to pick up and transmit abroad research done locally.[50]

Defenders of TNCs argue that notions of technological 'independence' are unrealistic and obsolete today, and that LDCs should not waste valuable resources in duplicating the enormous investments in R & D undertaken by developed countries. This is certainly valid for that part of complex, modern technology which is necessary for the well-being of LDCs,[51] but it leaves out two important points. First, as noted above, a large part of the actual process of innovation is not geared to meeting the social needs of LDCs, and, if it is to be replaced by more appropriate products and processes, may have to be replaced by indigenous technology. Second, unless one believes that countries which are at present underdeveloped will *never* make important technological contributions, there is a strong case for initiating policies which counter some of the more damaging effects of technological dependence. This is one field where 'learning by doing' and, more important, by making mistakes, is absolutely vital, and a passive acceptance of the *status quo* can prevent LDCs from ever undertaking the cost and effort of this process.

On the benefit side, the integration of LDCs into a worldwide structure of production by TNCs, with only that sort of technology being transferred to them which, given their labour and skill endowments, fits in with global cost-minimisation of these companies, may lead to an *expansion of exports* of compensated ('sourcing' exports, as distinct from the TNC-related exports mentioned in the following section) which would otherwise be available.[52] While there are clear advantages, in terms of foreign exchange, tax revenue and employment, that host countries can receive from 'sourcing' investments and technology, it has been noted that these benefits are not very large[53] and may be unstable over a long period. The ample opportunities that exist for transfer pricing, the use of relatively skilled labour, competition between LDCs for such investments, the 'footloose' nature of these facilities, the limited externalities that result, and their sensitivity to tax concessions, wage rates and labour conditions (they are extremely allergic to unionisation), may all reduce the final gain to the host economy.[54] On the other hand, some countries, such as Mexico,[55] that (for geographical and political reasons) have been successful in attracting a large quantity of sourcing investment, have managed to expand exports and employment on this basis for a long period (albeit at the cost of substantial foreign domination of industry, and of the types of distortion noted previously).

There are now signs that many LDCs are eager to break into this game, and it is likely that the next phase of TNC expansion into the Third World will have sourcing investment as a major component. If this occurs, TNCs may themselves act as pressure groups in favour of trade liberalisation (for the relevant manufactured products) in their developed home countries, as they have done in the past in the USA with respect to the tariff provisions for 'offshore' processing.[56] This may be counted as an important benefit to LDCs which share in this boom, to be offset against the costs of greater absorption into the TNC ambit.

Marketing

While recent theories of direct foreign investment, trade in differentiated products and technological innovation have placed enormous emphasis on the role of marketing, there is a curious, and unfortunate, lack of empirical studies concerning the effects of the marketing practices of TNCs on less-developed host countries. The scattered evidence that exists[57] does, however, confirm that the advertising, promotion and product-differentiation practices of TNCs do serve to influence market demand strongly and create barriers to entry for smaller and less effective marketers. This is, of course, hardly a startling proposition. Few people doubt that 'advertising pays': business firms themselves attach crucial importance to marketing, and the literature on industrial organisation stresses the interrelationships of promotion, product differentiation, concentration, entry barriers and profitability.

In the context of TNC operations in LDCs, two additional points may be noted: first, there tends to be a strong prejudice in favour of foreign products and brand names, a legacy of the colonial experience and a hall-mark of the socio-cultural 'dependence' that characterises most elites in developing capitalist countries; and, second, there is a considerable 'spill-over' effect of the promotional efforts of TNCs in the developed world, so that many leading brands are well known even before TNCs launch marketing drives in particular LDCs.[58] Both these factors serve to strengthen greatly the marketing power of foreign firms in LDCs.

There are two sorts of *benefits* that host LDCs may derive from the marketing skills of TNCs. First, as regards the *internal* marketing and distribution networks, the skills of foreign firms may bring about improvements in, for instance, storage and transport arrangements, leading, where this is relevant, to longer life, better quality, improved delivery and lower prices of products; closer co-ordination of supply and design with the particular specifications of products demanded, which is an important benefit in selling capital and intermediate goods to other manufacturers;[59] better information about products to consumers in general; and the provision of a wider range of products, with accompanying progress in methods of retailing, market research, and in realising the economies of large-scale distribution networks.

Second, on the *external* side, manufactured exports may be greatly increased by using the worldwide marketing outlets, skill and reputation of TNCs. The benefits to exports are, again, of two sorts: (a) the buying and retailing of relatively simple 'traditional' products which are labour-intensive in their production,[60] and (b) the marketing of sophisticated, product-differentiated, brand-name goods where heavy promotional expenditures are required.[61] (We do not include 'sourcing' exports of components – considered in the last section – here, since these are based not on the marketing skills involved in selling them abroad, but on the transfer of labour-intensive parts of complex technologies. However, many of the considerations noted for 'sourcing' also apply here.)

There are also *costs* of submitting to the powerful marketing practices of TNCs. The *internal* costs are of two types. First, there are some relatively less important ones to be set against the benefits noted above: the benefits of improved marketing may not show up in lower prices to the consumer (or may show up temporarily while local competition lasts) and may add only to the profits of the TNCs; franchising and exclusive-dealership practices by TNCs, often used for well-known branded products, may strengthen their market power but not help consumers; their advertising and promotion tactics may, similarly, increase the degree of monopoly, facilitate takeovers and add to marketing costs.

Second, at a more fundamental level, there are the social costs which arise from the product differentiation and proliferation, need and taste creation and elite consumption that are inherent in the marketing practices of TNCs.[62] Unless one held to the traditional paradigm so firmly that one regarded all market preferences as autonomous and social welfare as defined by their fulfilment, it would be very difficult to accept the obvious effects of TNCs in this regard as beneficial to poor societies where even the most essential human needs are not met. On the contrary, it can be persuasively argued that all such promotional practices which add to the unnecessary characteristics ('necessity' being defined by reference to essential human needs) of products and create demand for them are *wasteful and undesirable* – the more so if they further raise barriers to the entry of domestic firms, lead to greater concentration and induce similar marketing expenditures by local firms.

As with most such arguments, there arises the problem of *attribution*. Is the 'blame' for excessive promotion to be attached only to TNCs, or is it inherent in the nature of modern capitalist enterprise? On the one hand, it is clear that local firms and importers advertise and differentiate. On the other, it is also clear that TNCs, being the most powerful and dynamic elements in the growth of private enterprise, in some sense lead and shape the pattern of oligopolistic marketing behaviour. Thus, while it would be illegitimate to 'blame' TNCs as such, it would also be illegitimate to regard them as passively reacting to forces beyond their control. How costs are attributed depends largely on how the 'alternative situation' is defined; no definitive answer is possible.

As far as *exports* are concerned, it is certainly true that TNCs possess advantages in marketing certain manufactures in world markets. Three qualifications may, however, be noted. First, these exports are still a very small proportion of manufactured exports for those LDCs, such as India, that are not strongly dominated by TNCs, and that have recently managed, by the efforts of domestic firms, to achieve impressive gains in these exports.[63] Second, comparative analyses of the actual export performances of foreign and domestic firms do not support a *general* presumption that the former are better at exporting than the latter are.[64] TNCs perform better than local firms in some countries and not in others; sufficient evidence does not yet exist to explain why, though the incidence of restrictive clauses as regards exports in technology transfers and the growing importance of global planning by TNCs[65] may provide part of the explanation. Third, TNCs appear to be particularly reluctant to invest heavily in export-oriented facilities in LDCs where there are signs of political hostility or instability, labour pressures, or strong moves towards local participation (though they are willing to take greater risks in import-substituting investments, which do not pose the same problems for long-term global planning). Thus, LDCs which desire large doses of export-oriented investments from abroad may well have to curtail union power and curb nationalist (or socialist) policies, and (often by political repression) toe a strict line which appeals to TNCs.

Bargaining and Political Power

As far as *bargaining* is concerned, it is generally considered that TNCs, with their command over resources, markets and technology, their ability to manipulate prices and their possession of bargaining skills, are able to extract more concessions from host governments than small foreign or local firms can do. Three qualifying factors should be mentioned: first, bargaining strength would vary from industry to industry, depending upon the scarcity of the technology, the TNCs' hold upon markets, and the scale of investments required; second, it would depend upon the timing of the bargain, since the TNC would be in a weaker position once its investment had been made or once a competing TNC had entered the area; and, third, it would depend upon the political orientation of the government and the strength of the domestic industrialist class (for instance, TNCs with joint ventures with local firms may be in a stronger position in some countries than those with wholly-owned subsidiaries).

In general, however, it is probably true that TNCs have a bargaining position superior to that of other firms, and that their superiority is increasing with their growing economic power in the developed world. It is probably also true that LDC governments with vast, inefficient and corruptible administrations (and conflicting objectives to achieve), are not able to make the best use of the power they do have – though they seem to be 'learning by doing'. (These issues will be considered in Part III [Lall and Streeten, 1977].) The bargaining power of TNCs may be regarded as a social *cost* to host LDCs if (a) it leads to the latter's share of net benefits being smaller than it would be with another form of investment; (b) it leads to a higher rate of protection and so raises domestic prices and distorts the industrial structure in general; (c) it is accompanied by un-ethical practices, such as bribery by the firms or by political pressures by home governments of TNCs (via aid, trade and military channels); (d) it pre-empts investment opportunities which would otherwise have been exploited by local firms; or (e) it causes the host government to adopt broad economic and political policies which it would not otherwise have chosen to adopt. On the other hand, it may be regarded as a *benefit* if: (a) it forces the government to adopt more rational economic policies (though the criteria of 'rationality' are open to debate); (b) it introduces more competition into protected markets; or (c) TNCs are less prone to unethical practices than local firms are.

As far as *political power* is concerned, the issues are far more contro-versial and ideological. There are two sorts of problems that arise. The first derives from the *theory of the state* which is explicitly or implicitly employed. Most economists of the conventional welfare school assume, as we noted previously, that the state is the 'repository of the national interest' and is able freely to pursue policies which it regards as being conducive to 'national welfare'.[66] In extreme cases the state is (implicitly) taken to be above all group or class interests, to perceive conflicts and inequities as they arise and to deal with them justly and wisely. A more realistic stand is taken by those who, while holding the state to be the ultimate repository of national interest, admit that it is open to pressures, intimidation or favouritism,[67] and so may, for some periods, pursue policies which promote sectional rather than 'social' interests. We then find a range of theories from those that treat states as predominantly elitist[68] to explicitly Marxist ones that treat political power essentially as a crystallisation of class forces concerned to maintain the capitalist system of property relations.[69] The relations between TNCs and political power in host countries can be, and evidently are, interpreted very differently according to the theory used: the differences lie not so much in the evidence as in the assumptions.

The second problem derives from the *welfare assessment* of the interaction of governments and TNCs. Even if everyone accepted that governments attempt variously to nationalise, restrict, control, regulate or encourage TNCs, and that TNCs, in their turn, attempt variously to bribe, threaten, persuade or co-operate with governments, there would be considerable disagreement about what the 'proper role' of governments is. The 'optimum' may range from a fully-integrated capitalist system with a minimum of ('economically irrational' or 'misguided') nationalist intervention by governments, to relatively autarkic LDCs pursuing 'genuine' development along socialist lines; similarly, the 'proper role' for government would then range from simply providing the basic legal, political and infrastructural framework, and appropriate macro-economic policies, for untrammelled free enterprise, to completely owning the means of production and tightly controlling TNCs when dealings with them become necessary for LDCs. The significance of what Myrdal termed the 'political element' in economic prescriptions can hardly be overstressed.

Concluding Note

It should be obvious why we have not attempted to synthesise the preceding arguments to arrive at a new evaluation of the welfare effects of TNCs on LDCs. Instead of trying to pass 'objective' judgement in this extremely controversial issue, we have tried to show, with reference to the main 'advantages' which are claimed for TNCs, how little we actually know and why there may be valid grounds for dispute about the normative interpretation of what we do. It is far from evident what TNCs actually do as regards transfer pricing, technology adaptation or political manoeuvring, for instance. It is even less evident what would happen to domestic enterprise, productivity, technology and consumption if TNCs were absent. But it is entirely open to question how we should normatively assess the contribution of their various possible effects, and whether we should attribute them to particular firms, to TNCs as a whole or to the workings of the capitalist system, of which TNCs are the leading force.

This chapter has concentrated on the actual (i.e. large and oligopolistic) character of TNCs, both for the sake of realism and in order to deal with issues which arouse most concern in the Third World today. In the next chapter we shall deal briefly with more traditional treatments of foreign investment, which are derived from 'pure' theory and do not specifically take the peculiarities of TNCs, as opposed to capital inflows in general, into account.

Notes

1. For US evidence, see Horst (1975) and research by Vaupel mentioned in Dunning (1973).
2. As long as the rate of profit is higher than the rate of interest. See Chapter 6 [Lall and Streeten, 1977] for more information on gearing.
3. However, this in turn raises the problem about how to distinguish between short- and long-term borrowing when short-term loans are 'rolled over' from year to year. Most governments allow TNCs free access to commercial bank 'short-term' borrowing for purposes of inventory financing; such loans can easily be rolled over and extended to long-term uses, but the net contribution is bound to be fairly marginal.
4. This is noted for India by Carlsen and Neerso (1973) and for Colombia by Vaitsos (1974b).
5. See Brooke and Remmers (1970), Stopford and Wells (1972), Vernon (1971) and Barnet and Müller (1974).
6. There is, however, some evidence from Asia and Latin America that certain kinds of local firms are just as efficient as US TNC subsidiaries. See Negandhi and Prasad (1975).
7. Though the actual nationality of the particular people involved is less significant than the division of authority and status among the constituent units of the TNC (i.e. its *structure*).
8. Hymer (1972), pp. 126, 129.
9. For a colourful account, see Barnet and Müller (1974).
10. This is the burden of the argument of the *dependencia* school as well as of that of the neo-Marxists (though not of the palaeo-Marxists). For references and critiques, see Philip O'Brien (1975) and Lall (1975c).
11. See Lall (1973), Vaitsos (1974b), US Tariff Commission (1973), Hanson (1975), Robbins and Stobaugh (1974) and Brooke and Remmers (1970). Some indirect evidence on export pricing is produced by Müller and Morgenstern (1974) for Latin America, but their case is not conclusively established, because of the lack of direct price data.
12. Estimates by Lall (1973) indicate that roughly one-fourth to one-third of total manufactured trade among *developed* countries was intra-firm by 1970, with its share of total trade growing over time. Its share in LDCs' trade of manufactures as a whole was smaller; but, for Mexico and Brazil, two countries relatively well integrated into the TNC framework, had reached 80 per cent of total exports of foreign affiliates by 1972 (see Newfarmer and Mueller, 1975).
13. On different attitudes and internal constraints to transfer-price manipulations, see Shulman (1969) and Verlage (1975). On the use of 'optimal' financial policies, see Robbins and Stobaugh (1974).

14. See UN (1974), the main text and the 'Technical Papers' on taxation.

15. See Fleck and Mahfouz (1974).

16. On the theoretical aspects, see Horst (1971); on the implications for LDCs, see Lall (1973) and Vaitsos (1974b); on financial strategy, see Robbins and Stobaugh (1974); on taxation, see Musgrave (1974); and, on managerial and legal aspects, see Verlage (1975).

17. For instance, the 1971 Indian Government study shows that, around 1969–70, each 'examiner' in the port of Bombay had to handle over 26,000 shipping bills, and each 'appraiser' nearly 8000 original valuations and 66,000 rechecks of shipping bills annually. This study notes several difficulties in the adequate control of import–export prices and points out how these lead to a loss of foreign exchange.

18. See Verlage (1975) for a discussion of how several governments of developed countries attempt to deal with these problems.

19. See Keegan (1969) and Verlage (1975).

20. But less rigorously; as the US Tariff Commission (1973, p. 133) remarks with some sarcasm, 'Perhaps surprisingly, European government and EC officials remain rather calm over the issue of the MNC's tax behavior.... The chief strategy of tax minimization by multinational companies is manipulation of transfer prices.'

21. Some African countries, such as Kenya and Tanzania (and some others, but precise information is not to hand) employ a Swiss firm, the General Superintendence Company, to check prices and shipments on trade, but it is not clear how effective this is as a means of controlling transfer pricing on firm-specific products.

22. If, on the other hand, the realisation of taxes via the assignation of transfer prices becomes a point of inter-government conflict, it might well be the TNCs that suffer from effective overall taxes that are higher than nominal ones. This may, in turn, provoke retaliatory state action of the type discussed by Bergsten (1974).

23. See, among many others, Hirschman (1969) and the *dependencia* writers mentioned above. This argument may, of course, be extended to other sources of TNC superiority, such as technology or marketing, but, for ease of exposition, we shall deal with it here.

24. For instance, it is widely accepted that hedging and speculative action by US TNCs so exacerbated pressures on the dollar in the early 1970s that a devaluation became necessary. This may, however, have been a 'good thing' in so far as it forced the authorities to adopt a more sensible, if less popular, economic policy.

25. While there is good reason for thinking that oligopolistic competition among private firms in LDCs would,in the long run, take the same form as seen in developed countries, it likely that the entry of TNCs significantly speeds up the process of oligopolisation in developing host countries. For evidence from Mexico and Brazil, see Newfarmer and Mueller (1975), and on Central America see Willmore (1976).

26. For examples of the four approaches, see Servan-Schreiber (1968), Levitt (1970), Newfarmer and Mueller (1975) and Frank (1969), respectively.

27. See the document on this subject submitted by the UNCTAD secretariat to UNCTAD IV in Nairobi (UNCTAD, 1976).

28. For general discussions, see references mentioned in the discussion of technology in the previous chapters [Lall and Streeten, 1977]. On the implications of transfer of technology for LDCs, see Streeten (1972), Stewart (1974), Helleiner (1975), Morawetz (1974), Pavitt (1971), Vaitsos (various dates), Reuber *et al.* (1973), Griffin (1974), Chudson and Wells (1974) and the numerous references given there.

29. A number of proponents of free capital flows continue to regard technology as a neutral factor (for example, Johnson, 1970 and 1975, and Kindleberger,

(1969). Their analysis is based upon a logical application of the neoclassical welfare paradigm outlined above in which value judgements about 'appropriateness' are not allowed; see Lall (1976b).

30. For an analysis of the interaction of technological and marketing factors in securing market power in the US computer industry, see Brock (1975).

31. See Horst (1974a).

32. See Streeten (1972), Vaitsos (1974b) and Johnson (1970).

33. Streeten (1972), p. 227.

34. See Wilkins (1974), Stopford and Wells (1972) and Helleiner (1975).

35. A TNC which against its preference accepts a minority position may well transmit technology of older vintage than it would to a wholly-owned subsidiary.

36. Given a relatively free hand, however, even a TNC in a low-technology but high-marketing sector may prefer wholly-owned subsidiaries if it is in the process of reorganisation or rationalisation of its product lines (see Franko, 1971). In the context of LDCs, where most countries now demand local participation (usually over 50 per cent) as a precondition for TNC entry, these considerations become irrelevant: it is only the TNC in a strong bargaining position, offering high technology or (increasingly) export markets, that can demand high equity participation. See Chapter 2 above [Lall and Streeten, 1977].

37. See the section on transfer pricing above [Lall and Streeten, 1977].

38. See various studies by UNCTAD under the titles *An International Code of Conduct on Transfer of Technology* and *Restrictive Businesss Practices*; Vaitsos (1974b); Peter O'Brien (1975); and the discussion on exports in Chapter 7 below [Lall and Streeten, 1977].

39. See Penrose (1973), UN (1964), UNCTAD (1974), Vaitsos (1973, 1976), Grundmann (1976) and Greer (1973) and references there.

40. This may be especially significant for TNC investments in export-oriented industries, which seem to require a more congenial environment than do import-substituting industries. There are some indications, from Latin American evidence, that strong patent protection encourages export performance by pharmaceutical TNCs. See Mundowsky and Sell (1976).

41. See Lall (1976a) and Taylor and Silberston (1973).

42. Vaitsos (1976) presents an analysis of the main reforms needed and the difficulties in achieving them.

43. We cannot cover this subject in depth here, but see Helleiner (1975), Morawetz (1974), and Stewart (1974) for fuller discussions and references.

44. See Helleiner (1975), Agarwal (1976), Wells (1973), White (1976), Pack (1976), Bhalla (1975), Courtney and Leipziger (1975), Reuber (1973), Vaitsos (1974a), Willmore (1976), Morawetz (1974) Mason (1973), Stewart (1974), Morley and Smith (1974) and Stobaugh (1974), as well as some indirect evidence adduced in Chapter 6 [Lall and Streeten, 1977].

45. See Chapter 6 [Lall and Streeten, 1977].

46. See Helleiner (1975), Streeten (1972) and UNCTAD (1976).

47. This greater adaptability arises from the possibility that 'It may be easier and cheaper to alter the number of shifts or the machine speed in an automated plant, in response to fluctuations in demand, than to hire and train, or lay off employees in a labour-intensive one' (Helleiner, 1975, p. 169).

48. See Cooper (1974) and Sunkel (1971).

49. For an interesting example of how technological 'dependence' may afflict even public enterprises, see Aurora and Morehouse (1972), who cite the case of a public-sector firm in India that refused to use domestic in preference to imported (from Eastern Europe rather than a TNC) technology for producing small tractors. For other examples of biases against local technology in India, see Kidron (1965);

and, for a discussion of how the Chinese have managed to promote local technology, see Ishikawa (1976).

50. See Reuber *et al.* (1973) and, on pharmaceuticals, Lall (1975b).

51. For instance, a number of capital-goods industries and export industries that compete with those of advanced countries.

52. See Helleiner (1973, 1975), Sharpston (1975), UNCTAD (1975), US Tariff Commission (1970) and Finger (1975).

53. As Streeten (1973) has argued about sourcing investments, 'Specialisation between countries is not by commodities according to factor endowments, but by factors of production: the poor countries specialising in low-skilled labour, leaving the rewards for capital, management and know-how to the foreign owners of these scarce but internationally mobile factors. The situation is equivalent to one in which *labour itself* rather than the *product of labor* is exported' (pp. 5–6).

54. See Nayyar (1975).

55. See Newfarmer and Mueller (1975) and König (1975).

56. Helleiner (1975b).

57. See, for instance, Barnet and Müller (1974), Ledogar (1975) on food and drugs, Lall (1975b) on drugs, Langdon (1974) on soap, and *The New Internationalist* (1975) on baby foods.

58. This may account for the fact that, for our sample firms (Chapter 6 [Lall and Streeten, 1977]), no significant difference between the advertising expenditures of TNCs and those of non-TNCs was found in Colombia. It should be noted, of course, that advertising expenses on their own are only a part of what is broadly defined as 'marketing'; various other types of promotion and product differentiation are part of the cost of production and are impossible to assess separately.

59. On this aspect of marketing see, for instance, Lonsdale (1966).

60. Such as footwear, clothing or sports goods; see Helleiner (1973, 1975) and Sharpston (1975). This is more the province of large buying companies than of transnational manufacturers proper (see Hone, 1974).

61. Such as some processed food products, televisions, automobiles, cameras and tobacco. See de la Torre (1974) for a study of some Latin American countries, and Frankena (1973) on India.

62. See Ledogar (1975).

63. See Nayyar (1975).

64. See Cohen (1975) and Chapter 7 below [Lall and Streeten, 1977].

65. See Chapter 7 below [Lall and Streeten, 1977].

66. For a 'liberal' critique see Rowley and Peacock (1975), Kindleberger (1969), Reuber *et al.* (1973) and Lal (1975) may be taken as examples of this school in the area of foreign investment in LDCs.

67. Behrman (1974) and Goodsell (1974) provide good illustrations.

68. Streeten (1971), or Bell's chapter on the 'The Political Framework' in Chenery *et al.* (1974).

69. See Poulantzas (various dates) Murray (1971), Alavi (1972) and the survey by Gold *et al.* (1975), as well as various *dependencia* writers, such as dos Santos (1970).

References

Agarwal, J.P. (1976), 'Factor Proportions in Foreign and Domestic Firms in Indian Manufacturing', *Economic Journal*, pp. 589–94.

Alavi, H. (1972), 'The State in Post-Colonial Societies: Pakistan and Bangladesh',

New Left Review, no. 74, pp. 59–81.

Aurora, G.S. and Morehouse, W. (1972), 'Dilemma of Technological Choice: The Case of the Small Tractor', *Economic and Political Weekly*, pp. 1633–44.

Barnet, R.J. and Müller, R. (1974), *Global Reach: The Power of the Multinational Corporations* (New York: Simon and Schuster).

Behrman, J. (1974), 'Actors and Factors and Policy Decisions on Foreign Direct Investment', *World Development*, Aug. pp. 1–14.

Bergsten, F. (1974), 'Coming Investment Wars?', *Foreign Affairs*, October, pp. 135–52.

Bhalla, A.S. (ed.) (1975), *Technology and Employment in Industry* (Geneva: International Labour Office).

Brock, G.W. (1975), *The US Computer Industry, A Study of Market Power* (Cambridge, Mass.: Ballinger).

Brooke, M.Z. and Remmers, H.L. (1970), *The Strategy of Multinational Enterprise* (London: Longman).

Carlsen, J. and Neerso, P. (1973), *Transfer of Technology to India* (Copenhagen: Institute for Development Research), mimeo.

Chenery, H., Ahluwalia, M.S., Bell, C.L.G., Duloy, J.H. and Jolly, R. (1974), *Redistribution with Growth* (London: Oxford University Press).

Chudson, W.A. and Wells, L.T. (1974), *The Acquisition of Technology from Multinational Corporations by Developing Countries* (New York: United Nations, ST/ECA/12).

Cohen, B. (1975), *Multinational Firms and Asian Exports* (New Haven, Conn.: Yale University Press.

Cooper, C. (1974), 'Science Policy and Technological Changes in Underdeveloped Economies', *World Development*, Mar. pp. 55–64.

Courtney, W.H. and Leipziger, D.M. (1975), 'Multinational Corporations in Less-Developed Countries: The Choice of Technology', *Oxford Bulletin of Economics and Statistics*, Nov. pp. 297–304.

de la Torre, J. (1974), 'Foreign Investment and Export Dependency', *Economic Development and Cultural Change*, Oct. pp. 133–50.

dos Santos, T. (1970), 'The Structure of Dependence', *American Economic Review*, pp. 231–6.

Dunning, J.H. (1973), 'The Determinants of International Production', *Oxford Economic Papers*, pp. 289–336.

Finger, J.H. (1975), 'Tariff Provisions for Offshore Assembly and the Exports of Developing Countries', *Economic Journal*, pp. 365–511.

Fleck, F.H. and Mahfouz, R. (1974), 'The Multinational Corporation: Tax Avoidance and Profit Manipulation via Subsidiaries and Tax Havens', *Schweizerische Zeitschriff für Velkwirtschaft und Statistik*, June. pp. 145–60.

Frank, A.G. (1969), *Capitalism and Underdevelopment in Latin America* (New York: Monthly Review Press).

Frankena, M. (1973), 'Marketing Characteristics and Prices of Exports of Engineering Goods from India', *Oxford Economic Papers*, pp. 123–32.

Franko, L.G. (1971), *Joint Venture Survival in Multinational Corporations* (New York: Praeger).

Gold, D., Lo, C.Y.H. and Wright, E.O. (1975), 'Recent Developments in Marxist Theories of the Capitalist State', *Monthly Review*, Oct. pp. 29–43, and Nov. pp. 36–51.

Goodsell, C.T. (1974), *American Corporations and Peruvian Politics* (Cambridge, Mass.: Harvard University Press).

Greer, D.F. (1973), 'The Case Against Patent Systems in Less-Developed Countries', *Jornal of International Law and Economics*, pp. 223–66.

Griffin, K.B. (1974), 'The International Transmission of Inequality', *World Development,* Apr. pp. 3–16.
Grundmann, H.E. (1976), 'Foreign Patent Monopolies in Developing Countires: An Empirical Analysis', *Journal of Development Studies,* Jan. pp. 186–96.
Hanson, J.S. (1975), 'Transfer Pricing in the Multinational Corporation: A Critical Appraisal', *World Development,* Nov.–Dec. pp. 857–66.
Helleiner, G.K. (1973) 'Manufactured Exports from Less Developed Countries and Multinational Firms', *Economic Journal,* Mar. pp. 21–47.
Helleiner, G.K. (1975), 'Transnational Enterprise, Manufactured Exports and Employment in Less Developed Countries', paper prepared for the World Employment Conference (Geneva: International Labour Office), mimeo.
Hirschman, A.O. (1969), 'How to Divest in Latin America and Why'. Princeton Essays in International Finance, No. 76.
Hone, A. (1974), 'Multinational Corporations and Multinational Buying Groups: Their Impact on the Growth of Asia's Export of Manufactures', *World Development,* Feb. pp. 145–50.
Horst, T. (1971), 'The Theory of the Multinational Firm: Optimal Behaviour under Different Tariff and Tax Rates', *Journal of Political Economy,* pp. 1059–72.
Horst, T. (1974a), *At Home Abroad: A Study of the Domestic and Foreign Operations of the American Food-Processing Industry* (Cambridge, Mass.: Ballinger).
Horst, T. (1975), 'American Investments Abroad and Domestic Market Power', (Washington, D.C.: Brookings Institution), mimeo.
Hymer, S. (1972), 'The Multinational Corporation and the Law of Uneven Development', in J. Bhagwati (ed.) *Economics and the World Order* (New York: Macmillan).
Ishikawa, S. (1976), 'The Chinese Method of Technological Development', *The Developing Economies,* Dec. pp. 430–58.
Johnson, H.G. (1970), 'The Efficiency and Welfare Implications of the International Corporation', in C.P. Kindleberger (ed.), *The International Corporation* (Cambrdige, Mass.: MIT Press).
Johnson, H.G. (1975), *Technology and Economic Interdependence* (London: Macmillan).
Keegan, W.J. (1969), 'Multinational Pricing: How Far is Arm's Length?', *Columbia Journal of World Business,* May–June pp. 57–66.
Kidron, M. (1965), *Foreign Investments in India* (London: Oxford University Press).
Kindleberger, C.P. (1969), *American Business Abroad: Six Lectures on Direct Investment* (New Haven: Yale University Press).
König, W. (1975), 'Towards an Evaluation of International Subcontracting Activities in Developing Countries' (Washington, D.C.: UNECLA (Economic Commission for Latin America), mimeo.
Lal, D. (1975), *Appraising Foreign Investment in Developing Countries* (London: Heinemann).
Lall, S. (1973), 'Transfer Pricing in Multinational Manufacturing Firms', *Oxford Bulletin of Economics and Statistics,* pp. 173–95.
Lall, S. (1975b) in collaboration with the UNCTAD Secretariat, 'Major Issues in Transfer of Technology to Developing Countries: A Case Study of the Pharmaceutical Industry' (Geneva: UNCTAD, TD/B/C.6/4).
Lall, S. (1975c), 'Is "Dependence" a Useful Concept in Analysing Underdevelopment?', *World Development,* Nov.–Dec. pp. 799–810.
Lall, S. (1976a) 'The Patent System and the Transfer of Technology to Less-Developed Countries', *Journal of World Trade Law,* Jan.–Feb. pp. 1–16.

Lall, S. (1976b), 'Conflicts of Concepts: Welfare Economics and Development', *World Development*, Mar. pp. 181–95.

Lall, S. and Streeten, P. (1977), *Foreign Investment, Transnationals and Developing Countries* (London: Macmillan).

Langdon, S. (1974), 'Multinational Corporations, Taste Transfer and Under-development: A Case Study of Kenya' (Institute of Development Studies, University of Sussex), mimeo.

Ledogar, R.J. (1975), *Hungry for Profit: US Food and Drug Multinationals in Latin America* (New York: IDOC/North America).

Levitt, K. (1970), *Silent Surrender* (Toronto: Macmillan).

Lonsdale, J.E. (1966), *Selling to Industry* (London: Business Publications).

Mason, R.H. (1973), 'Some Observations on the Choice of Technology by Multi-national Firms in Developing Countries', *Review of Economics and Statistics*, pp. 349–55.

Morawetz, D. (1974), 'Employment Implications of Industrialisation in Developing Countries: A Survey', *Economic Journal*, pp. 491–542.

Morley, S.A. and Smith, G.W. (1974), 'The Choice of Technology: Multinational Firms in Brazil', Rice University Program in Development Studies, Paper no. 58 (mimeo).

Müller, R. and Morgenstern, R.D. (1974), 'Multinational Corporations and Balance of Payments Impact in LDCs: An Econometric Analysis of Export Pricing Behaviour', *Kyklos*, pp. 304–21.

Mundowsky, M. and Sell, A. (1976), 'Auswirkungen unterschiedlicher Patent-systeme auf die wirtschaftliche Entwicklung von Entwicklungslandem: Gine empirische Untersuchung am Beispiel der pharmazeutischen Industrie in Lateinamerika', University of Kiel, Discussion Papers of the Institut für Wirtschaftspolitik, no. 1 (mineo).

Murray, R. (1971), 'The Internalisation of Capital and the Nation State', *New Left Review*, May–June, pp. 84–109. Reprinted in H. Radice (ed.), *International Firms and Modern Imperialism* (Harmondsworth, Middx: Penguin, 1975).

Musgrave, P.B. (1974), 'International Tax Differentials for Multinational Corpor-ations. Equity and Efficiency Considerations, in UN Department of Economic and Social Affairs', *The Impact of Multinational Corporations on Development and on International Relations, Technical Papers, Taxation* (New York: United Nations, ST.ESA/M0.

Nayyar, D. (1975), 'The Impact of Transnational Corporations on Exports of Manufactures from Developing Countries' (Geneva: UNCTAD), mimeo.

Negandhi, A. and Prasad, B. (1975), *Frightening Angels: A Study of US Multi-nationals in Developing Countries* (Kent, Ohio: Kent State University Press).

New Internationalist, The (1975), 'Kicking the Bottle' Mar. pp. 13–15.

Newfarmer, R.S. and Mueller, W.F. (1975), 'Multinational Corporations in Brazil and Mexico: Structural Sources of Economic and Non-Economic Market Power', Report to the Subcommittee on Multinational Corporations of the Committee on Foreign Relations, US Senate (Washington, DC: US Govern-ment).

O'Brien, Peter (1975), 'Foreign Technology and Industrialisation: The Case of Spain', *Journal of World Trade Law*, pp. 525–52.

O'Brien, Philip (1975), 'A Critique of Latin American Theories of Dependency', in I. Oxaal *et al.*, *'Beyond the Sociology of Development'* (London: Routledge and Kegan Paul).

Pack, H. (1976), 'The Substitution of Labour for Capital in Kenyan Manufacturing', *Economic Journal*, pp. 45–48.

Pavitt, K. (1971), 'The Multinational Enterprise and the Transfer of Technology', in

J.H. Dunning (ed.), *The Multinational Enterprise* (London: Allen and Unwin).

Penrose, E.T. (1973), 'International Patenting and Developing Countries', *Economic Journal*, pp. 768–86.

Poulantzas, N. (1973a), *Politial Power and Social Classes* (London: New Left Books).

Poulantzas, N. (1973b), 'Marxism and Social Classes' *New Left Review, no. 78.*

Poulantzas, N. [n.d.] *Classes in Contemproary Capitalism* (London: New Left Books).

Reuber, G.L. with Crookel, H., Emerson, M., and Gallais-Hammonno, G. (1973), *Private Foreign Investment in Development* (Oxford: Clarendon Press, for the OECD Development Centre).

Robbins, S.M. and Stobaugh, R.B. (1974), *Money in the Multinational Enterprise: A Study in Financial Policy* (New York: Basic Books).

Rowley, C.K. and Peacock, A.T. (1975), *Welfare Economics: A Liberal Restatement* (London: Martin Robertson).

Servan-Schreiber, J.J. (1968), *The American Challenge* (London: Hamish Hamilton).

Sharpston, M. (1975), 'International Sub-Contracting', *Oxford Economic Papers*, pp. 94–135.

Schulman, J.S. (1969), 'Transfer Pricing in the Multinational Firm', *European Business*, Jan. pp. 46–54.

Stewart, F. (1974), 'Technology and Employment in LDCs', *World Development*, Mar. pp. 17–46.

Stobaugh, R.B. (1974), 'A Summary and Assessment of Research Findings on US International Transactions Involving Technology Transfers', in National Science Foundation, *The Effects of International Transfers of Technology on the US Economy* (Washington, D.C.: US Government).

Stopford, L.M. and Wells, L.T. (1972), *Managing the Multinational Enterprise: Organization of the Firm and Ownership of the Subsidiaries* (New York: Basic Books).

Streeten, P.P. (1971), 'Costs and Benefits of Multinational Enterprises in Less-Developed Countries', in J.H. Dunning (ed.), *The Multinational Enterprise* (London: Allen and Unwin). Reprinted in *The Frontiers of Development Studies* (London: Macmillan, 1972).

Streeten, P.P. (1972), 'Technology Gaps between Rich and Poor Nations', *Scottish Journal of Politial Economy*, pp. 213–30. Reprinted in *The Frontiers of Development Studies* (London: Macmillan, 1972).

Streeten, P.P. (1973), 'The Multinational Enterprise and the Theory of Development Policy', *World Development*, Oct. pp. 1–14.

Sunkel, O. (1971), 'Underdevelopment, the Transfer of Science and Technology, and the Latin American University', *Human Relations*, February, pp. 1–18.

Taylor, C.T. and Silberston, Z.A. (1973), *The Economic Impact of the Patent System* (London: Cambridge University Press).

UN (1964), *The Role of Patents in the Transfer of Technology to Developing Countries* (New York: United Nations).

UN (1974), *The Impact of Multinational Corporations on Development and on International Relations* (New York: United Nations).

UNCTAD (1974), *The Role of the Patent System in the Transfer of Technology to Developing Countries* (Geneva: United Nations Conference on Trade and Development, TD/B/AC11/19), and Addendum on Laws of Selected Countries.

UNCTAD (1975), *International Subcontracting Arrangements in Electronics between Developed Market-Economy Countries and Developing Countries* (New

York: United Nations, TD/B/C.2/144/Supp.1.)

UNCTAD (1976), *Transfer of Technology* (Nairobi: United Nations Conference on Trade and Development, TD/190).

US Tariff Commission (1970), *Economic Factors Affecting the Use of Items 807.00 and 806.30 of the Tariff Schedules of the United States* (Washington D.C.: US Government).

US Tariff Commission (1973), *Implications of Multinational Firms for World Trade and Investment and for US Trade and Labor* (Washington, D.C.: US Government).

Vaitsos, C.K. (1971), 'The Process of Commercialisation of Technology in the Andean Pact', (Lima) mimeo.

Vaitsos, C.V. (1973), 'Patents Revisited: Their Function in Developing Countries', in C. Cooper (ed.), *Science, Technology and Development* (London: Frank Cass).

Vaitsos, C.V. (1974a), 'Policies on Foreign Direct Investment and Economic Development in Latin America', Institute of Development Studies, University of Sussex, Communication no. 106.

Vaitsos, C.V. (1974b), *Intercountry Income Distribution and Transnational Enterprises* (Oxford: Clarendon Press).

Vaitsos, C.V. (1975), 'Power, Knowledge and Development Policy: Relations beteen Transnational Enterprises and Developing Countries', in G.K. Helleiner (ed.), *A World Divided: The Less Developed Countries in the World Economy* (London: Cambridge University Press).

Vaitsos, C.V. (1976), 'The Revision of the International Patent System: Legal Considerations for a Third World Position', *World Development*, Feb. pp. 85–102.

Verlage, H.C. (1975), *Transfer Pricing for Multinational Enterprises* (Rotterdam: Rotterdam University Press).

Vernon, R. (1971), *Sovereignty at Bay: The Multinational Spread of US Enterprises* (New York: Basic Books).

Wells, L.T. (1973), 'Economic Man and Engineering Man: Choice of Technology in a Low Wage Country', *Public Policy*, Summer, pp. 319–42.

White, L.J. (1976), 'Appropriate Factor Proportions for Manufacturing in Less Developed Countries: A Survey of the Evidence'. (Princeton Woodrow Wilson School, Research Program in Development Studies).

Wilkins, M. (1974), 'The Role of Private Business in the International Diffisuion of Technology'. *Journal of Economic History*, pp. 1166–88.

Willmore, L. (1976), 'Direct Foreign Investment in Central American Manufacturing', *World Development*, June pp. 499–578.

3

TNCs and Economic Developments in Host Countries: Empirical Results*

N. Hood and S. Young

*Source: N. Hood and S. Young, *The Economics of Multinational Enterprise* (London, Longman, 1979), pp. 198–223, 227–228, 383–384.

In presenting the empirical evidence a distinction is made between: resource transfer effects; balance of payments impact; competitive and anti-competitive effects; and sovereignty and autonomy costs. In addition some consideration is given to various studies which attempt to measure the aggregate impact of foreign direct investment. Most of the evidence relates to the LDCs, but where possible developed country examples are also quoted.

Resource Transfer Effects

Capital

In the early post-war period capital was stressed as the key factor in development. Foreign direct investment was therefore seen as a source of funds which supplemented domestic savings, and which might relieve foreign exchange shortages. In fact the contribution of foreign capital to worldwide capital formation has been small, e.g. during the 1960s foreign direct investment in Latin America represented at most 4–5 per cent of total capital formation. This does not appear to have mattered greatly, however, since the evidence of the last twenty years has been that capital has been less scarce than expected. This was firstly because the level of domestic savings was quite high in some LDCs; secondly because more foreign aid (as well as foreign investment) became available, and thirdly, because the capital/output ratio turned out to be lower than development models had postulated. In the 1960s the share of gross investment in the GNP of LDCs was almost 20 per cent and the share of savings in GNP over 15 per cent.[1] A deficiency of savings has seemed only to be an acute problem at the very early stage of the development process. Once LDCs have achieved a certain measure of growth, they appear to be able to develop their own indigenous means of mobilising savings.

A more significant problem would arise if it could be shown that MNEs have drawn on these local savings and deprived indigenous firms of funds. Certainly foreign affiliates have been shown to generate a large proportion of their capital requirements locally: in the period 1966–72, for example, finance from the parent corporations represented only about one-fifth of total funds employed by US affiliates in all developing countries.[2] The remainder came from depreciation provisions, other foreign funds raised in third countries, retained earnings, and locally-raised loans and equity (although arguably the reinvested profits should be considered as a foreign exchange inflow since the funds could have been repatriated by the affiliate). However, there have been no systematic attempts to test whether foreign firms enjoy preferential treatment from host country financial institutions when borrowing locally or whether in the process local firms are starved of funds. Where foreign firms do use local savings, moreover, a distinction should be made between equity financing and borrowing. The former is obviously preferred from a host country viewpoint since local equity shareholders receive the same return on their investment as do foreign investors. The limited evidence on this issue relating to a number of LDCs suggests that foreign affiliates do not have a significantly different financing pattern (borrowing v. equity finance) than do domestic firms.[3]

Technology

Recent theoretical developments, backed up by empirical evidence, have shown that it is chiefly the technological application of factors and production such as capital and not merely their existence which produces economic growth. That is, quality matters more than quantity. Econometric studies relating to some industrialised countries during the period 1950–62 indicated that between 60 and 85 per cent of measured economic growth resulted from increased output per unit of input (factor productivity): only the remaining 15–40 per cent was attributable to increases in inputs of labour, capital and land.[4]

It is this technology component which MNEs are pre-eminent in providing to host countries. There are admittedly fears in recipient states about technological dependence on the countries and corporations providing the know-how, but technological dependence *per se* is not particularly important. As has been argued, host country research and development should not be encouraged if the economy was likely to grow faster or more efficiently by borrowing technology and using the freed resources in other ways. In other words comparative advantage in the production of technology should be pursued like any other comparative advantage. What is more relevant is, firstly, the appropriateness of the technology obtained, and, secondly, the costs of the technology received, since it is these factors which will determine whether or not the recognised association between technology and economic growth is actually translated into net benefits at the host country level.

Appropriateness of Transferred Technology

In this instance, an appropriate technology for the LDCs is taken to be one in which factor substitution takes place to reflect differing factor avail- abilities (i.e. labour abundance). It is easy to quote individual examples where technologies have or have not been adapted to take account of different circumstances in the LDCs. Thus adaptation of existing tech- nology in India enabled buffalo milk to be used instead of cow's milk as the basis for powdered baby food. Again, a Japanese glass manufacturer set up a subsidiary in India that is half the size of the parent firm but employs three times as many workers. In Kenya, on the other hand, criticism has been directed at the fact that imported corrugated iron sheets are used instead of local materials such as timber and bamboo for roofing. And in Brazil, a tyre plant was said to be a virtual copy of a factory in the home country, while a tractor manufacturer was reported as claiming to ignore labour cost differentials entirely when choosing machinery.[5]

The broader empirical studies which have been undertaken have produced conflicting results. This is partly a reflection of the methodology of the studies themselves, but also indicates that the actual practices employed by foreign-owned firms in the application of technology are quite complex. Mason found that indigenous firms and US-owned MNEs in the Philippines and Mexico did not have significantly different amounts of plant and machinery per factory worker.[6] But such results could be interpreted either as implying adaptation by the MNEs or that local firms copied the unadapted technology of the MNEs through a 'demonstration effect'. In another study, Reuber found that about 30 per cent of a sample of 78 MNEs drawn from a range of industries and countries adapted their technology in some way when moving into the LDCs.[7] While other findings do not necessarily support this result in terms of the degree of adaptability, they do confirm that the situation may differ widely across industries and countries. Courtney and Leipziger, for example, found that in six of eleven industries studied, technology differed between affiliates in developed and less-developed countries, but not systematically in a more labour-using or capital-using way; in the other five industries technology did not differ significantly.[8] A further piece of research, using data relating to Ghana, revealed that MNEs used plant and machinery embodying different factor proportions from those in domestic industries; but whether or not the multinational firms used more capital-intensive or labour-intensive methods varied from industry to industry.[9]

The explanation for adaptation or lack of adaptation is the critical element for policy, but on this issue evidence is piecemeal. Most of the results quoted above would not support the argument of a lack of choice of technology. Moreover the evidence of Forsyth and Solomon conflicts with the hypothesis and limited evidence that MNEs use more capital-intensive methods because of shortages of skilled labour in the LDCs. It has been found that the degree of adaptation of MNEs to local factor costs and availability was partly a function of competitive pressures. Where product differentiation and the degree of market power was high, adaptation was low. There is other evidence of factor price distortions in many developing countries, wages paid being higher than the marginal social cost of labour and capital being under-priced as a result of credit subsidisation and interest-rate ceilings.[10] The position is thus complex, but in trying to develop policy implications it is worth quoting from the results of a recent study by Morley and Smith relating to Brazil: '. . . the evidence suggests that the choice of technique is not so limited as it is often portrayed to be and that the failure of firms to adapt may well be the result of their limited search in a permissive environment rather than technical factors'. Therefore '. . . if LDCs want multinationals to employ more labour-intensive methods, they should be prepared to reduce the permissiveness of the environment. This means allowing greater competition from imports and avoiding "overkill" in granting favors to attract foreign firms'.[11] Furthermore, because of prestige factors LDCs may sometimes insist on developing industries that are capital intensive by their nature, and also resist the importation of 'outdated' or second-hand equipment when, in fact, the latter could permit a more efficient use of local resources.

What is encouraging is that some major MNEs are now consciously attempting to introduce appropriate technologies for the developing countries: Ford's low cost 'modern model T' (Fiera), for example, is designed to be manufactured in small job shops where brake presses and simple welding jigs are to be used instead of the stamping dies and automated equipment operated in the United States. If this production technology is successful in the first plant in the Philippines, Ford plan to introduce it throughout the Asia-Pacific region.[12] Assuming this turns out to be satisfactory, it may well stimulate other MNEs to think rather more seriously than they may have done in the past about the possibilities of adapting technologies in their Third World locations.

Cost of transferred technology

This issue is closely linked to that of the balance of payments and transfer pricing, and some of the evidence relating to the overpricing of imports where technology transfer is involved will be presented in that context. Basically, the alleged problems associated with the transfer of technology are, firstly, that the royalties and licence fees charged by MNEs are too high; secondly, that tie-in clauses in technology contracts require the licensee to purchase capital equipment and intermediate parts from the parent company, when such items could have been obtained more economically from elsewhere; and thirdly, that technology contracts frequently incorporate export prohibition clauses, limited the sale of goods using this imported technology to the receiving country. The level of royalties and licence fees cannot really be adjudged empirically because of the lack of any objective method of pricing technology. What can be assumed is that where royalty payments etc. are settled through bargaining, the agreement reached will depend a great deal on the relative negotiating strengths of the parties involved. In the industrialised countries, firms which are potential licensees will often be large and sophisticated, and moreover specialised government agencies may sometimes exist (e.g. MITI and JETRO in Japan), to undertake or assist with the negotiations. Developing countries may be at a disadvantage because of a lack of the necessary bargaining skills at both firm and government levels.

Regarding tie-in and export-restrictive clauses there is a certain amount of evidence mainly relating to some Latin American countries. In an investigation of 250 contracts for technology transfer in Bolivia, Colombia, Ecuador and Peru, it was found that 81 per cent of the contracts prohibited exports totally and a further 5 per cent incorporated some restrictive clauses on exports.[13] These figures refer to all firms making technology contracts, including wholly-owned foreign affiliates, joint ventures and indigenous firms. Where Andean-owned firms alone are considered, 92 per cent of the contracts prohibited the exportation of goods produced with foreign technology. For three of these same countries – Bolivia, Ecuador and Peru – two thirds of the contracts for which information was available (136) included tie-in clauses. The most important tie-in arrangement was the requirement to purchase materials from the technology supplier. Some of the contracts also made such tied purchase conditional on a maximum price being paid for the goods purchased. Other contracts, in addition, prohibited, limited and controlled the use of local materials. It is difficult to interpret the implications of these restrictive arrangements, but certainly they do seem to present fairly formidable obstacles to the entry of LDCs into world trade in manufactures. That such restrictive practices may seriously affect the net benefits available to host countries from technology transfer is also evidenced by action taken in the United Nations. Thus in 1975 a 'Code of Conduct for the Transfer of Technology' was formulated with 40 restrictive business practices in technology transfer being prohibited. To give one example from this code, technology suppliers would not be able to limit exports of licensees' products. These control aspects of technology transfer will be considered further in Chapter 6 [Hood and Young, 1979]. It should be noted in conclusion that with the attention being given to these issues in the last few years, host country governments and indigenous firms must now be fully aware of the problems associated with technology contracts. It may thus be assumed that host countries and firms will be commensurately more careful when negotiating terms and conditions.

Employment

The importance of employment creation in the LDCs as an objective of economic development has already been noted. In general, however, the contribution of the industrial sector to employment growth has been disappointing.[14] To take an example from Brazil, while gross value added in manufacturing increased at an annual rate of 6.5 per cent during the 1960s decade, numbers of employees in manufacturing increased annually by only 1.1 per cent; in India the equivalent figures were 5.9 and 3.8 per cent; and in Nigeria 14.1 and 5.7 per cent.

By virtue of their very existence in host nations, MNEs clearly make some contribution to increasing the level of employment. Considering the *direct* impact on employment in developing countries, the United Nations estimated that MNEs had created 2 million jobs by 1970. This represents roughly 0.2 per cent of the total active population of the LDCs, and compares with an unemployment total of about 50 million.[15]

These comparisons are not very meaningful, and what is required is some assessment of whether the MNEs' contribution to employment is greater or smaller than it might have been. This will depend partly on the *choice of techniques* and partly on the *composition of output.*

The discussion above on the *choice of technology* implied that criticisms of MNEs for using capital-intensive techniques (and thereby minimising employment creation) may not be valid in many instances or at least that the responsibility often rests with the developing countries themselves. In some industries MNEs have a greater absorptive capacity for unskilled labour than indigenous firms. On the other hand, there have been studies looking at the macro-employment implications of adopting particular technology policies, which have indicated considerable potential for increasing jobs. While not merely referring to MNE-created employment, it was calculated that a ten-year 'technology freeze' policy in Puerto Rico could have increased 1963 employment from the actual figure of 600,000 to 1 million jobs, if the level of industrial output had not been affected.[16] But the latter is a heroic proviso, and in general there are serious problems associated with these types of studies.

Equally important in respect of employment creation is the *composition of output.* The most significant issue related to the relative merits of import-substituting and manufactured export-promotion policies. The evidence is fairly clear, namely that labour abundant countries are likely to create more employment by following an outward-looking than an inward-looking strategy. In a study relating to Korea, Westphal and Kim concluded that the employment-generation effect of export expansion achieved during the 1960s was far greater than would have been attained from an equivalent amount of import substitution.[17] Again, Sheahan in research on Mexico found that the mix of industrial goods exported in the

Table 1 Sources of inputs for MNE affiliates in developing countries, by type of investment (1972)

	Type of investment	
	(% of total value of inputs)	
Sources of inputs	*Local market orientation*	*Export orientation*
Indigenous local firms	52.4	27.8
Locally-based foreign subsidiaries	7.4	9.3
Parent company	28.2	50.8
Parent company suppliers	2.6	8.4
Other	9.4	3.7

Source: Reuber *et al.*, 1973.

1960s used 16–20 per cent more labour per unit of output than industrial import substitutes.[18] Multinationals are, of course, strongly represented in both import and export sectors in the LDCs. These results, therefore, primarily reflect the fact that while import substitutes may be produced by MNE affiliates using either capital-intensive or labour-intensive methods, the new phenomenon of manufactured exports from the LDCs is almost exclusively based on the utilisation of cheap labour by multinational firms.

Apart from the direct employment effects of MNEs there is also the *indirect* impact to be taken into consideration. There may be various indirect employment effects, arising from the competition of MNEs with local firms and from the use of the earnings resulting from their operations. In the present context, however, the employment effects of the purchase of intermediate goods are most relevant. One study found that linkages between the activities of MNE affiliates oriented towards local markets were considerably higher than in export-oriented affiliates (Table 1). In this work relating to foreign investment in developing countries, it was established that MNE affiliates engaged in import substitution activities obtained about 60 per cent of their inputs from locally-based firms. On the other hand, export-oriented affiliates derived nearly 60 per cent of inputs from their parent companies or suppliers of the parent companies located abroad.

Although it is the kind of result that might be expected *a priori*, the evidence is not completely unanimous on this. What is fairly clear is that in general MNEs have a tendency to import more than local firms, as borne out by studies relating to both developed and developing countries. This conclusion is relevant, of course, not only to the indirect employment effects of MNEs but also to the balance of payments impact.

Balance of Payments Impact

Trade Effects

The evolving views with regard to the impact of trade on economic development were discussed in the theoretical section of this chapter, and some of the evidence relating to the relative merits of import substitution and export promotion policies has been presented from an employment viewpoint. The balance of payments impact flows directly from this and therefore little extra needs to be said. The general view on import substitution policies in the LDCs is that the industries concerned 'have been employing too capital intensive a technology, operating on too small a scale, and earning their countries too little in terms of income, foreign exchange or employment'.[19] Nor have such policies reduced the dependence of the countries concerned on foreign countries and foreign firms. The aim of this section is thus to focus on the role of the MNEs in the export of manufactured goods from the LDCs. With the renewed emphasis on the importance of trade (exports) in development, this is bound to become an increasingly important issue for the developing countries.

Table 2 shows the growing importance of manufacturing exports to some LDCs during the 1960s. The data also reveal that a very small

Table 2 Manufactured and total exports from selected LDCs

Country	Value of manufacturing exports (1969, $ million)	Rate of growth per annum (%)	
		Manufacturing exports (1962–1969)	Total exports (1960–1970)
Hong Kong	1484	20.1	13.8
Taiwan	570	36.5	24.2
India	547	6.1	3.9
Mexico	380	19.8	6.2
South Korea	365	77.1	38.2
Brazil	244	16.2	8.0
Argentina	208	11.7	5.0
Pakistan	197	23.7	6.3
Philippines	138	10.2	6.6
Iran	133	8.7	10.9
Malaysia	130	18.0	3.6
Nigeria	38	18.1	10.1
UAR	33	4.8	3.0
Colombia	26	19.6	4.8
Chile	23	8.4	9.2
Indonesia	20	21.3	3.9

Source: Helleiner, 1973.

Table 3 Share of MNEs* in the exports of manufactures from selected LDCs (circa 1972)

Hong Kong	Taiwan	South Korea	India	Singapore	Brazil	Mexico	Argentina	Pakistan	Colombia
10%	At least 20%	15%	5%	Nearly 70%	43%	25–30%	At least 30%	5–10%	30% or more

*Excludes multinational buying groups, e.g. Montgomery Ward and Sears-Roebuck of the USA and Marks and Spencer of the UK, which are important outlets for manufactured exports from Hong Kong, South Korea and Taiwan.

Source: Nayyar, 1978.

number of countries account for a very high proportion of total LDC manufactured exports. By 1973, in fact, ten countries – Hong Kong, South Korea, Mexico, Brazil, India, Singapore, Malaysia, Argentina, Pakistan and Columbia – were responsible for 78 per cent of exports of manufactures.[20] Multinational firms have obviously played an important part in determining the rates of growth and the country-concentration of manufactured exports, but figures are not readily available on the subject. One estimate of the MNEs' share of exports of manufactures from various countries is shown in Table 3.

Unlike the position for foreign investment overall, non-US MNEs are about as important as US MNEs in this trade. Japanese companies are particularly prominent within the group of non-US multinationals, with a large proportion of investments being directed towards the small Asian economies in order to utilise the supplies of unskilled labour and low wage rates. Regarding European MNEs, it is possible to cite examples of companies which have moved part of their production to the LDCs for the purpose of exporting: Volkswagen in Brazil and Rollei in Singapore are examples, and companies such as Philips, Olivetti and Dunlop also have export-oriented manufacturing facilities in Third World locations. In general, however, European firms have been much less active in this field and most of their investments in developing countries have been concerned with import substituting activities.

Most of this export expansion is associated with MNE manufacture of simple labour-intensive products, and with the establishment of labour-intensive processes for manufacturing or assembling components. Thus, clothing, leather luggage and baseballs are sewn together in Mexico, the West Indies and S.E. Asia for Japanese and US firms; and a wide range of automobile parts and accessories are produced in numerous LDCs, e.g. radio circuits and antennae, piston rings and cylinder linings in Taiwan, autolamps in Mexico, diesel engines and braking equipment in India, etc.

The electronics industry, nevertheless, is still by far the most important, with the semiconductor sector being particularly significant.

The Case of Semiconductors[21]

This industry came into being in the early 1950s. It was initially dominated by the USA with three firms, Texas Instruments, Fairchild and Motorola in the forefront, although subsequently European companies such as Philips and Japanese firms, including Hitachi and Toshiba, have become increasingly competitive. Semiconductors are produced by a three-stage process. The first two stages involve complex, delicate operations and as a rule take place in the advanced countries. The third stage, consisting of assembly and testing, is labour-intensive, tedious and repetitive; this operation has generally been located in the LDCs in the so-called 'offshore locations' (although in some cases testing represents a fourth stage which is undertaken back in the developed countries). With extremely rapid technological change in the industry and product life exceptionally short, cost reduction is crucial; hence the moves to exploit lower labour costs by offshore assembly in the Far East, Mexico, the West Indies, and elsewhere. To take an example of only one company – Fairchild – affiliates were located in five different countries (see Table 4), the primary aim of this diverse locational pattern being to minimise risks. In spite of the vast distances involved, it is profitable for firms such as Fairchild to airfreight components to the Far East or Mexico for assembly, then perhaps to airfreight them back to an advanced country (possibly in Europe) for testing, prior to final sales. As Table 4 indicates, Fairchild employed nearly 6,500 people in offshore locations in 1970; but in fact some of the electronics companies now employ as many as 15,000 workers in these Far Eastern and Central American countries.

Problems and Potential in Export-oriented Assembly Industries in the LDCs

For some countries, thus, exports of manufactures have become very important to the economy. In Mexico, for example, 152 factories employing 21,000 people had been established alongside the border by the early 1970s; and in Taiwan 120 companies had built plants in the Free Trade Zone.[22] But this growth is not without its problems, of which the following should be noted:

(i) A major reason for the growth of offshore assembly is related to the condition of Sections 806.30 and 807 of the Tariff Schedule of the USA.[23] Under the terms of these, goods can be exported from the USA for assembly abroad and then returned to the USA at highly favourable tariff rates. Essentially, import duties are levied only on the value added abroad. Inevitably, therefore, with the majority of inputs

Table 4 The offshore locations of Fairchild

Location	Number of employees	Year established
Hong Kong	2,000	1961
Korea	2,000	1964
Singapore	1,500	1968
Okinawa	200	1970
Mexican Border	500	1969
Mexico City	150	1968

Source: Chang, 1971.

being imported and the majority of output exported, linkages with the host economy are minimal. This is accentuated by the fact that these export industries may be located in specially established export processing zones or free trade zones which are classic enclaves, e.g. in 1965 the Mexican Government began the so-called Border Industrialisation Program establishing a 2000-mile long free trade zone to attract the foreign assembly firms.

(ii) The advantages to host economies are also reduced by the substantial financial concessions offered to foreign investors. A good deal of the value added in the countries concerned may represent tax haven profits for use as a cash revenue for the MNEs' world-wide investment programmes. Where such large-scale incentives are used to attract MNEs there are always dangers of 'competitive bidding' by LDCs, as between, say, Taiwan, Hong Kong, South Korea and Singapore.

(iii) Apart from the special incentives, for countries to be suitable locations, political stability, low labour costs and/or limited distance and a docile labour force are important factors. Table 5 presents some comparisons of US and foreign labour costs prepared by the US Tariff Commission relating to the year 1970.

Much lower labour costs are inevitably required in the Far East to offset distance factors in comparison with Mexico. However, such wage differentials may only be transient, which raises considerable doubts as to the long-term position. The requirement of political stability means that the risks of nationalisation are reduced to a minimum, but as already shown, some companies also follow a policy of geographical diversification and multi-sourcing to offset the impact of any political or other disruptions. Finally a docile labour force permits employment to be cut back during recessions and removes the possibility of industrial disputes.

(iv) The range of products is still narrow, and is changing rapidly due to the speed of technological advance in industries such as electronics. The

Table 5   Average hourly earnings including supplementary compensation (consumer electronics products, 1970)

Country	Average hourly earnings* ($)		Ratio of US to foreign hourly earnings
	Foreign	USA	
Taiwan	0.14	2.56	18.2
Hong Kong	0.27	3.13	11.8
Mexico	0.53	2.31	4.4
Japan	0.58	1.60	2.8
Canada	3.50	3.85	1.1

*for equivalent products.

Source: US Tariff Commission, 1973.

countries concerned must clearly hope that assembly operations will evolve towards integrated production but the prospects for this may not be too hopeful. An associated point is that the simplicity of operations located in the LDCs does nothing to improve standards of skill among the labour force. It should be pointed out that, given these problems, some countries and notably South Korea are trying to make efforts to 'persuade' the companies to establish higher value added processes locally.

(v) In the home countries, particularly the USA, trade unions have begun to campaign against firms setting up 'runaway plants' in offshore locations.

It is therefore important to keep the issue of manufactured exports from the LDCs very firmly in perspective. Although trade is again seeming to act as an 'engine of growth', the rapid expansion of these exports is no measure of the benefits derived by the countries concerned. Nor does it indicate the foreign exchange gains because of the low value added locally. Moreover, while MNE-derived exports of manufactures from the LDCs seem likely to continue to expand fairly rapidly, the trade is still small in relation to exports from multinational firms in the developed countries: in 1970, US MNEs accounted for 11 per cent of total manufactured exports from the LDCs, but 21 per cent of exports of manufactures from OECD countries.[24] Finally, LDC manufactured exports are concentrated in a narrow range of countries and products. The work of Lall and Streeten (relating to a sample of firms in Jamaica, Kenya, India, Colombia and Malaysia, none of which were engaged in processing components) revealed that 'trans-nationality does not appear to have been an important aid to exporting'.[25]

Other Balance of Payments Issues

Of all the potential problems posed by MNEs, *transfer pricing* probably arouses the strongest emotions (see also Chapter 3 pp. 120–3 [Hood and Young, 1979] on this topic). There is, however, a dearth of empirical evidence available on the issue. A major reason for this is that at the micro-level, transfer pricing is difficult to detect, given present disclosure requirements in company accounts, inter-country differences in company laws and so on. A certain amount of information has been made available from individual company studies, and it was such an investigation by the British Monopolies Commission that brought to light the excessive prices charged for drugs in the UK by Hoffmann-La Roche, the Swiss pharmaceutical firm. According to the company itself, transfer prices were determined by 'what is reasonable for tax purposes.'[26] The drugs in question were purchased by the UK affiliate from the group at £370 and £922 per kilo respectively, whereas the same goods were available on the open market at £9 and £20 per kilo. This was in spite of the fact that in the UK as in most other countries, transfer prices are required at least in principle to conform to an arm's length standard. This arm's length price is supposedly determined by reference either to market prices or to some mark-up on prime costs or mark-down on the ultimate selling price.

One of the most well-known pieces of work relates to transfer pricing in Colombia.[27] This study was undertaken by the Colombian government to establish the extent of overpricing of imports and to reduce its incidence by legal action. For the period 1967–70 it was estimated that import prices for pharmaceuticals were 87 per cent greater than the world price; for 1968 the extent of overpricing was 155 per cent. Through government action, annual savings of $3.3 million were achieved, out of an import bill of $15 million. The principal determinant of these practices was probably the quantitative ceiling imposed on profit repatriation by the Colombian government. The extent of overpricing for some other imported products was: rubber 44 per cent, chemicals 25 per cent, and electrical components 54 per cent. Furthermore, studies on other Latin American countries quoted by Vaitsos show generally similar patterns of overpricing; and the same author has linked overpricing with the restrictive clauses which may be contained in contracts for the transfer of technology.[28]

With respect to the impact of taxation on transfer pricing, the US Treasury Department in 1973 published data relating to 871 cases, which they had investigated. The aim was to establish the extent to which US parent MNEs reallocated foreign source income to avoid taxation. It was estimated that reallocations were made in more than one half of the cases examined and that for merchandise trade alone the reallocations deviated from arm's-length prices by $312.5 million.[29] The reallocations were approximations and a significant proportion of the cases, could be contested by the firms. On the other hand, the figures could represent an understatement in that only a limited number of firms were investigated.

Various authors have attempted to estimate the extent of discretionary transfer pricing schemes indirectly using statistical methods. Müller and Morgenstern, for example, undertook a study of merchandise exports from companies (chiefly affiliates) in ten Latin American countries.[30] It was estimated that intra-firm exports within Latin America were significantly underpriced for tax reasons, whereas this did not apply to exports for the rest of the world. But, the results are ambiguous at best. The most interesting work is that of Kopits which relates not to the effects of transfer pricing on the prices of tangible goods, but to the use of transfer prices to manipulate intra-firm royalties and licence fees. The latter may be an important means of repatriating profits, thereby influencing the revenues and balance of payments of host countries. Kopits undertook a study on a sample of US MNEs, using 1968 data, to investigate the impact of host country tax rates on intra-firm royalty payments. The results indicated that nearly one quarter of total royalty remittances represented overpricing of intra-firm technology imports by MNEs prompted by tax considerations. In the developed countries overpricing was most prevalent in France, Germany and the UK, amounting to between 30 and 50 per cent of each country's total royalties. In the LDCs the highest incidence of overpricing was found in India and the Philippines. When the overpricing was expressed in terms of tax revenue or foreign exchange losses, it was estimated that host governments lost $38 million in 1968 (a figure which would rise to $60 m. if the total universe and not merely a sample of US firms was taken into consideration). Two thirds of this consisted of British and German losses, derived from the tax-induced substitution of royalties for dividends by the US companies concerned. It was concluded 'that it would be in the interests of certain high-tax industrialised host countries, especially Germany and the United Kingdom, and to a lesser degree Canada and France, if they could adopt and enforce transfer-pricing rules, which led to the use of standard royalties in intra-firm intangible transactions'.[31]

That the potential losses for host countries are very significant has been indicated by some theoretical work based on the value of intra-firm trade by US MNEs and the level of declared earnings.[32] It was estimated that a 12 per cent change in transfer prices on intra-firm trade in 1970 would have equalled the total of interest and dividends earned by US MNE affiliates abroad; an 18 per cent change in prices would have been equivalent to total earnings abroad (interest, dividends, royalties and management fees). The implication is that foreign exchange losses from transfer pricing may be more important than the costs to the host country balance of payments of dividend repatriation, etc.

An associated issue is that of *monetary speculation* by MNEs, since transfer pricing is the major instrument by which large shifts of funds can

Table 6 Net 1966 earnings and capital inflows of affiliates of US MNEs located in developing countries ($ million)

Year of affiliation	Affiliates in Latin America		Affiliates in other developing countries	
	Net earnings	Net capital inflows	Net earnings	Net capital inflows
1964–66	42	218	5	264
1961–63	26	56	67	50
1958–60	86	70	162	45
1957 and earlier	1,037	−69	1,600	57
Total	1,191	275	1,834	416

Source: Adapted from Vernon, 1972.

take place and one that the monetary authorities may be unable to counter. The topic became news with a statement from the Governor of the Bank of England at a conference in 1973 that 'transfers of liquid balances by multinational companies did account for an important part of the transfers which eventually led to the floating of the £, the devaluation of the $, the floating of the yen and the situation of widespread floating in which we now find ourselves'.[33] While this is no doubt a factual statement, no further published details exist. It is possible that MNEs cause monetary crises. If fears of a currency depreciation exist, MNEs acting *individually* may transfer funds into strong currencies to avoid losses. The sum of these individual actions could be enough to produce a 'self-prophesying' impact. The relevance of transfer pricing emerges because national governments are implementing an array of severely constricting controls in an attempt to prevent the overt shifting of funds.

Although transfer pricing effects are potentially more important to host countries, nevertheless *dividend repatriation* and other remittances from overseas affiliates to the parent company are also significant from a balance of payments viewpoint. The classic example which is quoted is that relating to General-Motors Holden's Ltd. in Australia (the subsidiary of General Motors Corporation of Detroit). Although the comparisons are not terribly meaningful, it appeared that in the one year, 1953–54, profits of the Australian subsidiary amounted to 14 per cent of sales, 24 per cent of funds employed, 39 per cent of shareholders' funds (net worth) and 560 per cent of GM's original investment. Dividends paid to the parent company out of these profits amounted to 260 per cent of the original investment and about 8 per cent of Australian export earnings for the year. The implication being drawn was that MNEs required to make only a small initial capital investment in host countries; through re-investment of profits locally, the affiliate could expand rapidly and after a time create balance of payments difficulties by substantial dividend payments to the parent company.

It is obviously true that the balance between capital inflows and the outflows of dividends etc. for any individual subsidiary will change over time. As the rather dated but still interesting results of Table 6 show, most recently established affiliates are responsible for the largest capital inflows, and the older affiliates for the bulk of the earnings (earnings are used as a surrogate for remittances).

Even so, it is not correct to interpret this as meaning that older established subsidiaries constitute a net drain on the balance of payments position of the LDCs. The crucial question is what would have happened in the absence of the foreign investment. Such an economic drain would exist only if domestic output could have replaced the foreign investment, without any further resource cost to the host country.

Aggregate Balance of Payments and Income Effects

The review of the empirical evidence relating to the effects of MNEs on host countries is not yet complete. No consideration has been given to the competitive and sovereignty effects of multinational operations. It is nevertheless a convenient point to stop and try to assess how the costs and benefits of MNE activities net out overall. One major study which has attempted to do this is that by Streeten and Lall relating to 159 companies in 6 developing countries.[34] Some of these results have already been quoted but the research is much wider than perhaps has been indicated hitherto, extending to a comparison of the performance of these 159 companies over 5–7 years in the late 1960s with various alternative possibilities such as: (i) importing the products and (ii) 'most likely' local replacement, where an estimate was made of the likelihood of firms having or being able to obtain the technology to replace the output of the foreign affiliate.[35]

In terms of overall balance of payments effects, it was found that for all countries except Kenya the net impact was negative. The average effects for the various states expressed as a percentage of sales were: Kenya +2.7%; Jamaica −25.5%; India −11.7%; Iran −55.0%; Colombia −35.3%; and Malaysia −37.6%. The nature of the effects in terms of the ownership of the firms is given in Table 7. Very few individual firms recorded positive balance of payments effects – only 11 out of 133 foreign-controlled companies and 3 out of 26 locally-controlled firms – while for 34 firms the negative effect was in excedss of 50 per cent of sales.

In order to identify the causes of these adverse results, it is necessary to look in greater detail at the component balance of payments items. In the

Table 7 Relationship between ownership and balance of payments effects

Classification of firms	Total no.	Total with negative balance of payments effects	Total with negative effects worse than 50% of sales
Foreign controlled*	133	122	30
Locally controlled	26	23	4
All firms	159	145	34

*Wholly and majority foreign owned subsidiaries, plus 24 firms with minority foreign ownership.

Source: Lall and Streeten, 1977.

first place, the *export performance* of firms in the sample was poor: 35 and 40 per cent of both foreign and locally-controlled firms did not export anything and the median firm exported only 15–19 per cent of its sales. As was suggested earlier, this indicates that the sample mainly contains firms which were engaged in import substitution activities; and indeed exports from the companies in India seemed to be largely a function of government coercion. A second component in the balance of payments is the *net capital inflow*. This comprises the total amount of capital (equity, long-term loans and retained earnings out of foreign profits) brought in from abroad less profits and interest returned abroad. Such figures are not so meaningful in that they do not indicate the total capital contribution of a firm over its life, but the results indicated that the vast majority of firms had a small positive net inflow. Of more interest is the net financial effect which is defined as the capital inflow minus royalties, profits, interest and technical payments. The results here revealed that of the 147 firms with foreign capital only 49 recorded a positive financial effect and as Streeten and Lall comment: 'On the whole the sample foreign firms do seem to be "taking out more than they are putting in" during the period studied'.[36]

A third element in the balance of payments is *import dependence.* This is important because the greater the reliance on imports of components, etc., the smaller is the linkage of the industry to the local economy and the greater is the direct foreign exchange cost. Moreover, the greater the reliance of foreign-controlled firms on imports, the larger is the scope for transfer pricing. The study shows that over half of the total number of firms in the sample imported goods worth over 30 per cent of their sales, and nearly two thirds of firms imported over 20 per cent of the value of their sales. While there is sizeable variation across countries, there is little difference between foreign and locally controlled firms.

As has been noted at various points, results such as these, while interesting, do not tell the whole story. They do not show, for example, what would have happened had the foreign investment not occurred. In addition, they do not reveal the indirect effects of the investment on the balance of payments via domestic sales and the use of local resources. Such issues pose major methodological problems and, in the event, Lall and Streeten ignore many of the latter effects – usually termed 'externalities'. To give one instance, some of the sample firms were market leaders in their respective industries which may have had effects on price levels, advertising tactics and so forth, but these were not quantified. Bearing this in mind, the procedure followed was to calculate the net effects of the sample firms on national income and then to compare the results with the alternative of local replacement. Of the 159 firms, it was estimated that the net income effect (as a percentage of sales) was positive to 97 companies and negative for 62 companies. There was not much variation between foreign and locally-controlled firms, but sizeable differences between countries; for Kenyan firms, the average net income effect was 12.7 per cent for sales; for Jamaican firms 7.0 per cent; Indian 1.3 per cent; Iranian 5.6 per cent; Colombian −1.5 per cent; and Malaysian firms −4.5 per cent. To quote the authors: 'the most important finding of these exercises, if we accept the premises of the analysis, is that *a very large proportion of manufacturing investments in the sample are undesirable from the point of view of social welfare* ... This finding serves to confirm for foreign investments what has been observed more generally for import-substituting industrialisation policies in a number of developing countries'.[37]

There are clearly enormous difficulties in making meaningful comparisons of actual foreign investments with their 'most likely' local replacements. The procedure followed was to estimate for each sample firm the possibility of replacing foreign technology either with existing local technology or with the purchase abroad of easily available technology. It was assumed that 30 per cent of the total number of firms with foreign equity were totally replaceable by local firms; another one half of firms seemed to be replaceable to the extent of 20–30 per cent of their production, the complexity or non-availability of technology preventing the remainder of their output from being replaced; the final 20 per cent of firms were assumed not to be replaceable at all.[38] The results of these estimates suggested that of the 147 firms with foreign capital, 55 had negative income effects when a comparison was made with the alternative of local replacement. These estimates are extremely tentative, omitting such important factors as transfer pricing, economies of scale, bargaining efficiency and exports when comparing the actual with the alternative situation. Nevertheless, the analysis at least suggests that within the LDCs a significant number of foreign affiliates are yielding negative net social income effects. It was concluded, as a consequence, that projects should be evaluated individually, with host governments being advised to negotiate the best deal possible for themselves in each case.[39]

Competitive and Anti-competitive Effects

It was noted in the study above that competitive effects were specifically excluded from the analysis. Yet there is evidence that depending upon circumstances the impact of MNEs on competition and efficiency may be very significant. One case often quoted is that of the automobile industry in Latin America: in Chile in 1963–64, 22 firms, most of them MNEs, were assessing less than 8000 vehicles in total, which meant an annual production run of 400 cars per plant.[40] It may be argued that the MNEs were merely reacting to government import substitution policies and tariff barriers, but a more plausible explanation is that of 'oligopolistic reaction'. Thus all the major manufacturers have established affiliates or licensees to prevent other firms gaining a position of advantage in each market. This inefficient industrial structure was not unique to Chile as Table 8 shows. The effect of low volume production has been to produce very high cost output. In Brazil unit costs were 35 per cent greater than in the multinationals' home countries, but this rose to a figure of 164 per cent in Chile where even by 1972 output per firm was still as low as 3,290 units.

Other evidence for Latin America indicates that MNEs are most common in highly concentrated industries. In Chile, for example, 1970 data show that 50 per cent of a sample of foreign-owned subsidiaries had a monopoly or duopoly position and a further one third occupied leadership roles in oligopoly markets.[41] What is particularly important is to assess whether or not such market structures are associated with restrictive business practices and excess profits. On this issue, some research has been undertaken on behalf of a US Senate Sub-Committee into the position in Brazil and Mexico.[42] Once again it was revealed that market concentration was particularly high in the industries where MNEs were most prominent; and statistical analysis confirmed the expectation that the profitability of affiliates was closely and positively related to this degree of market concentration, as well as to the relative market position of individual firms and barriers to entry.

The powerful market position of MNEs in Brazil and Mexico is very revealing. In Mexico, for instance, one half of the largest 300 manufacturing firms were MNE affiliates in 1972.[43] In markets of very high concentration, where the top four plants controlled over three quarters of production, MNEs produced 71 per cent of sales. Similarly in Brazil, American and other foreign firms accounted for 147 of the 300 largest manufacturing enterprises and 59 of the 100 largest. Again, in those industries where MNEs were dominant, the combined market share held by the top four plants averaged 54 per cent, compared with 39 per cent in industries dominated by Brazilian-owned firms. The two countries are indeed close reflections of each other in terms of the structural sources of MNE power. In both cases the share of total output controlled by foreign

Table 8 No. of firms, output per firm and production costs in the Latin American motor industry

	No. of firms (1972)	Output per firm* (1972)	Index of production costs† (1970)
Argentina	10	26,859	195
Brazil	10	60,947	135
Chile	8	3,290	264
Colombia	3	8,005	194
Mexico	9	25,530	153
Peru	5	4,759	164
Uruguay	13	491	n.a.
Venezuela	15	5,876	145

*Number of vehicles
†Country of origin = 100

Source: Jenkins, 1976.

firms has been rising rapidly: in Mexico, MNEs increased their share of total market sales from 20 per cent in 1962 to 28 per cent in 1970; in Brazil US subsidiaries alone produced 20 per cent of manufacturing sales in 1970, an increase from 13 per cent in 1966. What is also interesting is that growth by acquisition was an important means of expansion: in the 1971–72 period, three-quarters of the affiliates established in Mexico represented take-overs of going concerns; and n Brazil one quarter of all growth in US firms' assets in the years 1960–1972 was due to acquisitions.

The principal conclusion reached by Newfarmer and Mueller, the authors of this study, was that the progressive industrial denationalisation (the share of host country industry and resources owned by MNEs) witnessed in Brazil and Mexico, has had the effect of diminishing the economic sovereignty of both countries. It was considered that MNEs in these countries possessed enormous economic power which could be misused from the viewpoint of the host nation, but in addition they held considerable potential non-economic power. To quote the authors: 'Since the extensive concentration of foreign holdings in a market results in a few firms making pivotal economic decisions, the structural possibility of joint action for economic and non-economic objectives is always present.[44]

In the developed countries too there is a certain amount of evidence to show that when MNEs have a dominant position in markets, they may use their oligopolistic power in adverse ways. The behaviour of the oil companies, for example, has been a source of irritation to various host countries at different times. To give a different example, early in 1978 United Brands, the world's largest grower and supplier of bananas, was found guilty and fined by the European Court of Justice on three counts of abusing a dominant market position in the EEC. The corporation was convicted of various restrictive practices including the charging of different prices in different EEC markets and refusing to supply particular distributors.

More generally, some evidence was presented in Chapter 3 (pp. 124–7) [Hood and Young, 1979] on the impact of MNE activities on industry performance in various developed host countries. From a negative viewpoint, there is some evidence that MNEs may compound problems of industry fragmentation, as in the case of the Latin American automobile industry quoted earlier; but equally, a study of the Australian chemical industry revealed that some MNEs, even with tariff protection, installed smaller scale, near optimum-size plant which meant little if any excess capacity.[45] In any event, fragmentation and excess capacity is only likely to be a problem in small, relatively isolated developed countries and not, say, in Western Europe. MNEs may also be able to create additional barriers to entry to host industries through the exploitation of scale economies and their product differentiation, marketing and technological advantages. On the other hand, there are a number of instances quoted where MNE entry has broken down the monopoly position of an established firm in the host country, and even the potential entry of a multinational firm may constrain excess monopoly profits. Furthermore, there may be favourable effects on the competitive position because MNEs are likely to be less collusive than indigenous oligopolists. Overall UK experience has been that US subsidiaries have provided increased competition for established dominant firms and stimulated an increasing awareness of the role of R & D and productive management. One specific study relating to the pharmaceutical industry in the UK indicated that American competition in the market stimulated British companies to undertake high quality research and to perform competitively within a wide range of new drug technologies.[46] Competition from US multinationals has also encouraged European firms to merge into more viable economic units in some cases. Although the domestic computer industry in the EEC is still in a transient state, the formation of ICL in the UK and of CH-Honeywell Bull in France are examples of different responses to multinational competition.

This is not to say that the conduct of MNEs will always have a positive effect on competitiveness. Various restrictive practices employed by multinational firms have anti-competitive effects (see the discussion in Chapter 3 [Hood and Young, 1979]). One of the most frequently quoted of these is the operation of restrictive export franchises, deriving from the common MNE practice of allocating various markets globally. Secondly, the pricing of intra-firm transactions at other than arm's length prices and international price discrimination policies represent further restrictive practices. Thirdly, excessive product differentiation not only raises entry barriers but also entails a waste of resources. It is interesting that such practices do not simply adversely affect the *competitive* position in host countries. In all cases the practices other harmful effects, as, for example, manipulative transfer pricing and export restrictions, may create balance of payments difficulties.

A great deal of literature has emerged relating to the impact of the MNE on labour relations, but the area is very short of systematic research. In addition, most discussions relate to developed rather than less developed countries. There are a number of *a priori* reasons for expecting multinational companies to have more unsettled labour relations than domestic firms. In the first place, ultimate decision-making resides abroad, which may produce a range of effects – from increasing employee hostility in the host country, to increasing the possibilities of misunderstanding at a management level; and secondly, different industrial relations procedures and practices may exacerbate conflict. One measure of the impact of MNEs on labour relations will obviously be the *incidence of industrial disputes*, although absenteeism and labour turnover may be more revealing indicators of dissatisfaction. In spite of the *a priori* expectations, evidence for the UK has indicated that foreign-owned firms may have fewer labour disputes than domestic firms, especially after allowing for differences in industry mix.[47] Other research, moreover, based on a sample of foreign-owned companies operating in the USA, found no difference between the strike propensity of these as compared with indigenous firms.[48] Even so, in both cases, there did appear to be some differences in the character of the disputes.

Although in total the dispute record of MNE affiliates may not be any worse than domestic firms, there are numerous examples of issues within the categories noted which have caused difficulties. In respect of the multinational status of such firms, one significant issue concerns the use of withdrawal threats as a bargaining weapon. All of the US automobile companies in the UK have used this threat from time to time, so much so that it has become totally counterproductive. But similar threats have been made in other countries. Ford, for example stated in 1973 that the refusal of unions to relax strict rules on overtime scheduling might force them to shun Belgium for future expansion. Other allegations against MNEs regarding the role of the parent company in negotiations and so on are difficult to substantiate.

Turning to differences in industrial relations traditions and procedures, there is obviously an inclination for an incoming MNE to try to amend the host country system in the light of its own experience. This is particularly so where practices are pursued which the MNE considered to be detrimental to productivity. Union recognition policy is one area of industrial relations that has brought conflict. In Singapore and Malaysia, unions seem to have experienced recognition problems in recent years at the electronic plants of companies such as Texas Instruments, Hewlett-Packard and Motorola. Similar problems have arisen with IBM and Esso in Holland, and with Kodak, Heinz and IBM in the UK. Aside from union recognition policy, factors such as differences in the nature and duration of agreements, plant personnel practices and the level of negotiations may all create difficulties in management/union relations. Given the dearth of hard evidence, there is still great uncertainty over the extent to which MNEs do or do not try to conform to the national conditions as they find them, or whether in fact they should. Chrysler in the UK, for example, which had a notoriously bad labour relations reputation during the early 1970s, nevertheless attempted to make numerous innovations which were in the interests of higher productivity, had they been negotiated and implemented satisfactorily.

With a dispute record no worse than indigenous firms and generally greater productivity, MNE affiliates may appear to have a favourable impact on host economies. More important issues, however, may concern levels of wages and conditions in MNEs, and the impact these have upon remuneration levels and labour availability for domestic firms; research on these topics is still very scanty.

Sovereignty and Autonomy Effects

It is difficult to establish criteria for judging the impact of the MNE on national sovereignty or autonomy, and the mere assumption that loss of sovereignty entails a cost involves a value judgement. There is the general point that greater foreign investment will increase the difficulties of host governments in pursuing independent policies, and some of the *dependencia* type of issues arising will be discussed in Chapter 8 [Hood and Young, 1979]. The problems arise essentially because of differences between the objective of the multinational firm and the objectives of the host government. To make only one point, the MNE may be pursuing some global objective, such as profit maximisation. In the pursuit of this it is likely to set particular, but not necessarily similar, objectives for each of its affiliates, e.g. an affiliate in Brazil may be set a profit objective related to securing a certain share of the Brazilian market, but the latter may conflict with government objectives relating to increasing exports to neighbouring Latin American countries and elsewhere.

It may be argued from this that the greater the degree of autonomy delegated by the parent to the affiliate (and thus the greater the responsibility of the affiliate for setting its own objectives), the lower will be the sovereignty costs to the host government. As a consequence of this view most empirical research in the area has centred round the autonomy/ centralisation issue. Autonomy may be assumed to be greater when affiliates have authority which extends beyond short-run operational decisions, that is, are more than mere 'branch plants'. In research on US investment in Scotland, it was established that one third of all firms had no marketing responsibilities for the output they produced.[49] Also – of particular relevance to the technological dependence debate – only one quarter of firms had a significant research and development department in Scotland. Bearing in mind earlier comments on the need to pursue research comparative advantage, nevertheless, this means that a very high proportion of firms are completely tied to the innovative progress of their parent companies. Similar results were obtained in some early research relating to the R & D performance of non-resident owned firms in Canada; although it should be noted that some recent work has thrown doubt on these results, indicating that in a good number of industries there is not much difference between R & D expenditures of foreign-owned as compared with Canadian-owned companies.[50] Another issue which is pertinent to the question of host country sovereignty is that of export restrictions on affiliates. Several empirical studies have shown that parent MNEs impose strict control over the countries to which their affiliates may or may not export.

For the host country, the aim is clearly to try to maximise the net benefits from foreign direct investment. The importance of these and other costs therefore depends upon the extent to which host governments can control the multinational firm. This is the topic of the following chapter, but in the present context it is worth noting that the size, centralised control and possibly global perspective of multinational firms gives them a certain countervailing power *vis-à-vis* national governments which is not possessed by domestic firms. While it will be shown that host governments, even less developed host governments, are far from helpless in their dealings with MNEs, the power of these firms undoubtedly entails a sovereignty loss for the recipient state.

Final Remarks

In the theoretical section of this chapter it was indicated that no clear-cut conclusion could be reached on the issue of whether or not MNEs bring positive net benefits to host states. The empirical evidence presented essentially bears out this point. The limited empirical work which has been undertaken to estimate the *aggregate* effects of MNE operations suggests that the overall impact is usually positive on national income, jobs and government revenues. Even so, the balance between positive and negative effects seems to be fairly close in numerous instances, with many foreign firms producing a negative income effect when consideration is given to what might have happened in the absence of the foreign investment. Major doubts have been raised about the impact of direct foreign investment on the balance of payments positions of host countries, derived particularly from the payment of royalties, interest charges and dividends and from the uncertain effects of transfer pricing. And there are certain other areas where MNE activity always imposes a cost on the recipient state, principal among these being the cost associated with loss of sovereignty. On the other hand, it has been suggested that in some instances host country policies themselves are to blame for adverse effects, as, for example, when MNEs are 'encouraged' to introduce capital intensive technologies by tax and other incentives. These conclusions thus mean that better host country policies towards foreign direct investment (on issues such as incentives) are a prerequisite for increasing the net benefits attained, quite apart from any controls imposed on the incoming multinationals *per se.*

One issue which has only been touched upon in this chapter concerns the relative impact on host nations of inward direct investment from different source countries and the relative impact of different types of investment (as between import-substitution and export-base types, for example). Regarding the varying forms of investment, it is possible that export-platform type investments may offer greater potential net benefits. But these have not been realised in many instances because of the concessions granted to multinational firms, and the fact that such investments provide few linkages with the rest of the economy. This conclusion is also relevant to the impact of MNEs from different source countries given that, for instance, much of Japanese investment falls into the resource-based and export-platform categories. Apart from this, there is some evidence available that foreign direct investment from less developed home countries may be particularly beneficial to recipient states. LDC multinational firms are insignificant in terms of size and numbers, of course, but they may be expected to increase as the economies of their countries develop. A study of LDC MNEs in Thailand indicated that the sample of firms tended to use labour-intensive technology which was suitable for small-scale production; they were more likely than with other MNEs or domestic Thai firms to buy their machinery locally; they tended to repatriate less of their profits than did other foreign firms; and since they used standard technology, their royalty payments were lower than other MNEs on average.[51] At least in the case of the Thai economy, therefore, LDC multinationals offered significant benefits without many of the costs associated with other inward direct investment.

No comment has yet been made on certain other alleged quasi-economic effects of MNEs such as the impact on income distribution, and on consumption patterns. Derived from the evidence presented on the capital intensity of incoming foreign investment and the use made by foreign firms of domestic savings, it would be expected that MNEs would have an adverse effect on income distribution in host nations. The problem would be exacerbated if chronic unemployment existed in the recipient country, since capital intensive foreign investment could bid up wages for skilled domestic workers who were in short supply, leaving the overall employment situation unchanged. What information there is indicates that other factors in the host country must have a greater influence on the level of income distribution than foreign investment. Thus in research relating to six developing countries with deteriorating income distribution during the 1960s (Panama, Korea, Brazil, India, Mexico and Venezuela), various patterns of foreign investment existed: Panama and Venezuela were among the highest recipients of direct investment from abroad, Korea and India were among the lowest, and Brazil and Mexico were in the middle.[52] Therefore the theoretical conclusion of adverse income distribution effects associated with foreign direct investment has not yet been validated empirically.

Radical economists have emphasised the role of MNEs in transferring the consumption patterns of advanced capitalist countries to under-developed countries, thereby extending consumerist capitalism. This topic is associated with that of technology transfer as discussed earlier, with the effect possibly being to increase import propensities in host countries, to adversely influence income distribution and generally to maintain a 'dependency' relationship between home and host nations. Little quantitative information exists on this issue. Although there has been some attempt to relate levels of consumerism (as measured by the consumption of expensive consumer durables such as cars and television sets), there is to date inadequate evidence to back up the contentions which have been postulated. But as with the income distribution issue, testing is no easy matter given the difficulty of isolating the impact of foreign investment from that of other factors, and it would be wrong to be over-complacent.

Overall, no clear generalisations are possible either in regard to the impact of MNEs on *national income* in developing host countries or in respect of the effects on *other development goals*. In turn, this conclusion indicates serious limitations in existing knowledge concerning the impact of direct foreign investment on economic development. As in the previous section, the empirical results reviewed here have very largely referred to the LDCs. That the impact of MNEs on host developed countries is more favourable is generally accepted.

Further Reading

1. The classic MacDougall article is an essential starting point: G. D. A. MacDougall, 'The benefits and costs of private investment from abroad: a theoretical approach', 1960, reprinted in J. H. Dunning (ed.), *International Investment*, Harmondsworth: Penguin Books, 1972, pp. 129–58. It is useful to refer to this source for the article since a number of other relevant theoretical papers are included, e.g. A. E. Jasay, 'The social choice between home and overseas

investment', pp. 117–28, and M. C. Kemp, 'The benefits and costs of private investment from abroad: comment', pp. 159–62.

2. There are no general references which completely cover the second part of the theoretical section. The distinction between resource transfer effects, trade and balance of payments effects, etc. was made by Streeten and two articles by this author are worth reading: P. Streeten, 'Costs and benefits of multinational enterprises in less-developed countries' in J. H. Dunning (ed.), *The Multinational Enterprise*, London: George Allen and Unwin, 1971; P. Streeten, 'The theory of development policy' in J. H. Dunning (ed.), *Economic Analysis and the Multinational Enterprise*, London: George Allen and Unwin, 1974, pp. 252–79.

3. On specific topics the following papers should be consulted:

MNE's and exports of manufactures from developing countries – G. K. Helleiner, 'Manufactured exports from less developed countries and multinational firms', *Economic Journal*, 83, 1973, pp. 21–47; D. Nayyar, 'Transnational corporations and manufactured exports from poor countries', *Economic Journal*, 88, 1978, pp. 59–84.

MNEs and transfer pricing – S. Lall, 'Transfer pricing by multinational manufacturing firms', *Oxford Bulletin of Economics and Statistics*, **35**, 1973, pp. 173–95; G. F. Kopits, 'Intra-firm royalties crossing frontiers and transfer-pricing behaviour', *Economic Journal*, 86, 1976, pp. 781–805.

MNEs and technology transfer – S. A. Morley and G. W. Smith, 'Limited search and the technology choices of multinational firms in Brazil', *Quarterly Journal of Economics*, XCI, 1977, pp. 263–87; C. V. Vaitos, 'The process of commercialization of technology in the Andean Pact', in H. Radice (ed.), *International Firms and Modern Imperialism*, Harmondsworth: Penguin Books, 1975, pp. 183–214.

4. The excellent study of Lall and Streeten relating to the impact of MNEs on six developing countries is summarised in: S. Lall and P. Streeten, *Foreign Investment, Transnationals and Developing Countries*, London: Macmillan, 1977, Part II and particularly Ch. 7, 8 and 9.

Notes

1. Streeten, 1974.
2. Bergsten, 1976.
3. Lall and Streeten, 1977.
4. Denison, 1967.
5. Morley and Smith, 1977.
6. Mason, 1971.
7. Reuber *et al.*, 1973.
8. Courtney and Leipziger, 1974.
9. Forsyth and Solomon, 1977.
10. Morawetz, 1974.
11. Morley and Smith, 1977, p. 287.
12. Quoted in Bergsten, 1976, p. 32.
13. Vaitsos, 1975.
14. Morawetz, 1974.
15. Sabolo, 1975.
16. Weisskoff *et al.*, 1973.
17. Westphal and Kim, 1973.

18. Sheahan, 1971.

19. Helleiner, 1973.

20. Nayyar, 1978.

21. Chang, 1971.

22. Murray, 1972. The points noted in the section following broadly follow Murray.

23. Almost every industrial country has now such a provision in its tariff, whereby domestic components may be sent out of the country for processing and/or assembly and then returned, with the tariff being assessed only on value added abroad. See Finger, 1975, 1976.

24. Nayyar, 1978.

25. Lall and Streeten, 1977, p. 135. See also reference 58 in Chapter 4 [Hood and Young, 1979].

26. Monopolies Commission, 1973.

27. Quoted in Lall, 1973.

28. Vaitsos, 1975.

29. For other transactions, the estimated deviations from arm's-length prices were as follows: sale of intangibles, $52.4 m; loans, $75.9 m; sale of services, $127.0 m; and other transactions, $94.1 m. See Kopits, 1976b.

30. Müller and Morgenstern, 1974.

31. Kopits, 1976a, p. 802.

32. Lall, 1973.

33. Opening address by the Governor of the Bank of England, Lord O'Brien, at a Colloquium at the University of Nottingham in April, 1973.

34. The results are summarised in Lall and Streeten, 1977.

35. A third alternative considered was that of 'financial replacement'. Here the estimates were based on the assumption that the foreign capital was obtained in portfolio form, but that the technology and thus the input requirements of the local firm would remain the same as those of the foreign firm.

36. Lall and Streeten, 1977, p. 142.

37. Ibid., p. 173.

38. The question as to what would have happened in the absence of the foreign direct investment is crucial. It is arguable that if local entrepreneurs could have undertaken the investment because technology was available, they would have done so. If they did not undertake the investment, then it is questionable if it is valid to assume that the MNE investment is replaceable.

39. While not reported here, another important study was that undertaken by Bos, Sanders and Secchi (1974) into the overall impact of foreign direct investment in India, the Philippines, Ghana, Guatemala and Argentina. The effects of foreign direct investment on national income and on government revenues were found to be positive in all cases, but the impact on the balance of payments was always negative. The actual size of the positive and negative effects varied widely as in the Lall and Streeten study, the inference again being that host-country policies can have a marked effect on the outcome. Unlike Lall and Streeten, the Bos *et al.* study did not seek to compare the results of foreign direct investment with the likely results of alternatives available to the host nation.

40. L. L. Johnson, 1967.

41. Vaitsos, 1975, p. 209.

42. Connor and Mueller, 1977.

43. Newfarmer and Mueller, 1975.

44. Ibid., p. 152.

45. This section draws extensively on Parry, 1977.

46. Lake, 1976.

47. Gennard and Steuer, 1971.
48. Jedel and Kujawa, 1976.
49. Hood and Young, 1976.
50. Hewitt, 1977.
51. Lecraw, 1977.
52. Bergsten, 1976, pp. 40–42.

References

Bergsten, C. F. (1976), 'An Analysis of the US Foreign Direct Investment Policy and Economic Development', AID Discussion Paper, no. 36, Nov.
Bos, H. C., Sanders, M. and Secchi, C. (1974), *Private Foreign Investment in Developing Countries*, Boston: D. Reidel.
Chang, Y. S. (1971), *The Transfer of Technology, Economics of Offshore Assembly, the Case of the Semicondutor Industry*, New York: UNITAR.
Connor, J. H. and Mueller, W. F. (1977), *Market Power and Profitability of Multinational Coporations in Brazil and Mexico*, Report to the Subcommittee on Foreign Economic Policy of the Committee on Foreign Relations, United States Senate, Washington: US Government Printing Office, April.
Courtney, W. H. and Leipziger, D. M. (1974), *Multinational Corporations in LDCs: The Choice of Technology*, Washington: USAID, Oct.
Denison, E. (1967), *Why Growth Rates Differ*, Washington: Brookings Institution.
Finger, J. H. (1975), 'Tariff provisions for offshore assembly and the exports of developing countries', *Economic Journal*, 85, pp. 365–71.
Finger, J. H. (1976), 'Trade and domestic effects of the offshore assembly provision in the US tariff', *American Economic Review*, 66, pp. 598–611.
Forsyth, D. J. C. and Solomon, R. F. (1977), 'Choice of technology and nationality of ownership in manufacturing in a developing country', *Oxford Economic Papers*, 29, no. 2, July, pp. 258–82.
Gennard, J. and Steuer, M. D. (1971), 'The industrial relations of foreign-owned subsidiaries in the United Kingdom', *British Journal of Industrial Relations*, 9, pp. 143–59.
Helleiner, G. K. (1973), 'Manufactured exports from less developed countries and multinational firms', *Economic Journal*, 83, pp. 21–47.
Hewitt, G. K. (1977), 'The Effect of Foreign Ownership on Self-Financed Research and Development in Canada's Manufacturing Industries – a cross-sectional study', Working Paper no. 1977–3, Concordia University, Department of Economics, Montreal.
Hood, N. and Young, S. (1976), 'US investment in Scotland: aspects of the branch factory syndrome', *Scottish Journal of Political Economy*, 23, pp. 279–94.
Hood, N. and Young, S. (1979), *The Economics of Multinational Enterprise*, London: Longman.
Jedel, M. J. and Kujawa, D. (1976), 'Management and Employment Practices of Foreign Direct Investors in the United States', Georgia State University, March.
Johnson, L. L. (1967), 'Problems of import substitution: the Chilean automobile industry', *Economic Development and Cultural Change*, 15, pp. 202–16.
Kopits, G. F. (1976a), 'Problems of import substitution: the Chilean automobile industry', *Economic Development and Cultural Change*, 15, pp. 202–16.
Kopits, G. F. (1976a), 'Intra-firm royalties crossing frontiers and transfer pricing behaviour', *Economic Journal*, 86, pp. 781–805.
Kopits, G. F. (1976b), 'Taxation and multinational firm behaviour: a critical survey', *International Monetary Fund Staff Papers*, 23, no. 3. Nov. pp. 624–73.
Lake, A. W. (1976), 'Foreign Competition and UK Pharmaceutical Industry', Working

Paper no. 155, New York: National Bureau of Economic Research, Nov.

Lall, S. (1973), 'Transfer pricing by multinational manufacturing firms', *Oxford Bulletin of Economics and Statistics*, 35, pp. 173–95.

Lall, S. and Streeten, P. (1977), *Foreign Investment, Transnationals and Developing Countries*, London: Macmillan.

Lecraw, D. (1977), 'Direct investment by firms from less developed countries', *Oxford Economic Papers*, 29, no. 3, pp. 442–57.

Mason, R. H. (1971), *The Transfer of Technology and the Factor Proportions Problem: The Philippines and Mexico*, New York: UNITAR.

Monopolies Commission (1973), 'Chlordiazepoxide and Diazepam', London: HMSO.

Morawetz, D. (1974), 'Employment implications of industrialisation in developing countries', *Economic Journal*, 84, pp. 491–542.

Morley, S. A. and Smith, G. W. (1977), 'Limited search and the technology choices of multinational firms in Brazil', *Quarterly Journal of Economics*, XCI, pp. 263–87.

Müller, R. and Morgenstern, R. D. (1974), 'Multinational corporations and balance of payments impacts in LDCs: an econometric analysis of export pricing behaviour', *Kyklos*, 27, Fasc. 2, pp. 304–21.

Murray, R. (1972), 'Underdevelopment, international firms and the international division of labour', in *Towards a New World Economy*, Papers and Proceedings of the 5th European Conference of the Society for International Development, Rotterdam: Rotterdam U.P., pp. 159–247.

Nayyar, D. (1978) 'Transnational corporations and manufactured exports from poor countries', *Economic Journal*, 88, pp. 59–84.

Newfarmer, R. S. and Mueller, W. F. (1975), *Multinational Corporations in Brazil and Mexico: Structural Sources of Economic and Non-Economic Power*, report prepared for the Subcommittee on Multinational Corporations of the Senate Foreign Relations Committee, Washington: US Government Printing Office, Aug.

Parry, T. G. (1977), 'Trade and non-trade performance of US manufacturing industry: revealed comparative advantage', *Manchester School of Economic and Social Studies*, 43, June pp. 158–72.

Reuber, G. L. *et al.* (1973), *Private Foreign Investment in Development*, Oxford: Clarendon Press.

Sabolo, Y. (1975), 'Employment and unemployment, 1960–1990', *International Labour Review*, Dec.

Sheahan, J. (1971), 'Trade and Employment: Industrial Exports Compared to Import Substitution in Mexico', Williamstown, Mass: Williams College Center for Development Economics, Research Memorandum 43.

Streeten, P. (1974), 'The theory of development policy', in Dunning, J. H. (ed.), *Economic Analysis and the Multinational Enterprise*, London: George Allen and Unwin, pp. 252–79.

Vaitsos, C. V. (1975), 'The process of commercialization of technology in the Andean Pact' (1971), in Radice, H. (ed.), *International Firms and Modern Imperialism*, Harmondsworth: Penguin Books, pp. 183–214.

Weisskoff, R., with Levy, R., Nisonoff, L. and Wolff, E. (1973), 'A Multi-Sector Simulation Model of Employment, Growth and Income Distribution in Puerto Rico: A re-evaluation of "Successful" Development Strategy', mimeo, New Haven, Conn.: Yale Economic Growth Center.

Westphal, L. E. and Kim, K. S. (1973), 'Industrial Policy and Development in Korea', mimeo, Washington: Development Research Center, International Bank for Reconstruction and Development.

4

Multinational Enterprises in Less-developed Countries: Cultural and Economic Interactions*

Peter J. Buckley and Mark Casson

*Source: University of Reading, Discussion Papers in International Investment and Business Studies, Series B, No. 126, January 1989.

1. Introduction

This paper analyses the operations of multinational enterprises (MNEs) in less developed countries (LDCs) in terms of the interplay between two types of culture. The MNE, it is claimed, personifies the highly entrepreneurial culture of the source country, whilst the LDC personifies the less entrepreneurial culture of the typical social group in the host country. This view places MNE–LDC relations in an appropriate historical perspective. It is the entrepreneurial culture of the source country which explains why in the past that country had the economic dynamism to become a developed country (DC). Conversely, the limited entrepreneurial culture of the host country explains why it has been so economically static that it has remained an LDC. The current problems perceived by MNEs in operating in certain LDCs – and also the problems perceived by these LDCs with the operation of foreign MNEs – reflect the difficulties of attempting to bridge this cultural gap.

The concept of entrepreneurial culture is, of course, related to the concept of 'modernisation' which appears in the sociology of development (Eisenstadt, 1973; Herskovits, 1961; Inkeles and Smith, 1974). There are important differences, however. The concept of entrepreneurial culture derives from economic theories of the entrepreneur (Hayek, 1937; Kirzner, 1973; Knight, 1921; Schumpeter, 1934) which identify specific functions such as arbitrage, risk-bearing and innovation needed for economic development. It describes the cultural values which stimulate the emergence of individual personalities capable of performing these functions competently. Modernisation, on the other hand, typically begins with a wide range of attitudes associated with Western industrial societies, and examines how far these attitudes have permeated LDCs. Entrepreneurial theory suggests that not only are some 'modern' attitudes irrelevant to economic development, but others are actually inimical to it. Emphasis on entrepreneurial culture does not therefore imply a trite endorsement of 'modern' values. Entrepreneurial theory has been applied to development issues by a number of previous writers – Hagen (1962), Hoselitz (1961), Kilby (1971) and McClelland and Winter (1969), for example – but along rather different lines.

Countries classified as LDCs form an extremely heterogeneous group. Indeed, differences between the poorest and the wealthiest LDCs are in some respects greater than between the wealthiest LDCs and many DCs. This paper is concerned principally with the poorest and most persistently underdeveloped LDCs – such as some countries of sub-Saharan Africa. Since these countries are, generally speaking, the ones with the lowest MNE involvement, it may be asked why a focus on these countries is appropriate. One reason is that this low involvement itself merits explanation, since the continuing confinement of these countries to the periphery of the world economy is of considerable policy interest (Wallerstein, 1979). By examining the difficulties encountered by the small number of MNEs that actually invest in these countries, the lack of interest of the majority can be explained in terms of their rational perception of the size of the problem. The second reason is that the starker contrast between wealthy DCs and the poorest LDCs reveals cultural influences in a sharper relief.

Levels of development can vary not only across LDCs but also across regions within any one of them. This point is fully recognised by the analysis in this paper, which emphasises that regional differences in development are endemic in DCs as well (Berger and Piore, 1980). The difference between urban (especially metropolitan) and rural areas is fundamental in this respect. Indeed the analysis below suggests that many international differences in levels of development can be ascribed to differences in the relative influence of urban as opposed to rural culture.

Multinationals differ too; in the present context, differences between source countries are likely to be most significant because these affect the national culture upon which the headquarters of the firm draws. There can also be differences between firms from the same country due, for example, to the religious affiliations of the founders, or the impact of the size of the firm on its organisation and leadership style. Due to limited space, however, this paper abstracts from such considerations by working with the concept of a representative MNE.

Section 2 delineates the main areas in which conventional economic theory appears to be deficient in explaining MNE behaviour in LDCs. The 'residual' phenomena which remain unexplained by economic factors, it is suggested, may be explicable by cultural factors instead. The analytical core of the paper comprises sections 3–7. These sections consider in detail the interaction between geographical and cultural factors in the process of development. Section 3 identifies three conditions for successful economic development; one is geographical – entrepôt potential – and two are cultural – a scientific outlook, and a commitment to voluntary methods of social and economic coordination. Sections 4–6 elaborate on each of these factors in turn, generating a check-list of country characteristics relevant to economic development. Section 7 draws on the core analysis to expound an evolutionary model of world development, which focuses on the dynamics of the linkages between DCs and LDCs, as mediated by MNEs. Section 8 returns to the key issues identified in section 2. It explains how difficulties faced by some LDCs in learning new technologies originate in specific cultural factors, and argues that these same cultural factors explain other phenomena too. Attention is drawn to the weaknesses as well as the strengths of contemporary entrepreneurial cultures, and it is suggested that some of the cultural values transmitted by MNEs to LDCs hinder rather than help the process of development. Section 9 concludes the paper with suggestions for further research.

2. Key Issues

Any analysis of multinational operations in LDCs must address a number of key stylised facts. Some of these facts are readily explained by conventional economic theory (see, for example, Casson and Pearce, 1987), but others are not. The facts that conventional theory can explain include

(1) *The limited scale and disappointing economic performance of import-substituting manufacturing investments in LDCs.* This is partly attributable to inappropriate LDC trade policies. By protecting relatively small domestic markets for finished manufactures, LDC governments have encouraged the proliferation of downstream assembly-type operations of less than efficient scale. It is only the ability to charge monopoly prices well above world export prices that has encouraged MNEs to continue operating in these protected markets.

(2) *The increase in foreign divestments since the oil price shocks of the mid-1970s* is partly explained by the reduction in real consumer incomes in oil-exporting LDCs, which has reduced local demand for relatively sophisticated MNE-produced goods. The threat of blocked profit repatriations from countries with balance of payments difficulties has also encouraged a preemptive liquidation of foreign investments by MNEs.

(3) *The recent poor performance of resource-based investments in Africa and Latin America* is partly explained by another consequence of the oil price shocks – namely the recession in Western heavy industries – and by the continuing protection of domestic agriculture in industrial societies. It is also due partly to the development of new mineral deposits in the Asia–Pacific region. Finally, the emergence of synthetic substitutes has reduced the long-term demand for certain minerals (although the price

advantage of oil-based substitutes has declined).

(4) *The use of capital-intensive technologies by MNEs in labour-abundant LDCs* can be explained partly by the cost of adapting to local conditions a technology originally developed for use in Western locations. It can also be explained by the importance of mechanisation in meeting quality standards in export markets – and in home markets dominated by wealthy consumers (in countries with a highly-skewed distribution of income). The distortion of factor prices in LDC markets through minimum wage legislation, capital subsidies, etc. may also be significant.

Some of the salient points which existing theory cannot easily explain are:

(5) *The failure of technology transfer to generate sustained innovative capability in LDC industries.* The much slower rate at which foreign technologies are assimilated by the poorest LDCs compared to newly industrialising countries such as Korea, or successfully industrialised countries such as Japan, suggests that cultural factors may inhibit the acquisition of scientific ideas and Western working practices.

(6) *The confinement of modern industry to 'enclaves', and in particular the failure of foreign investors to develop backward linkages with indigenous suppliers.* Where resource-based investments are concerned, there may be limited opportunities for backward linkages in any case. Even in developed countries, furthermore, large scale investments often fail to develop a local supply base; the disciplined routine of work in large plants seems to inhibit the 'incubation' of entrepreneurial skills in the local workforce. Nevertheless, the frequent claim by MNE managers of medium-size manufacturing operations that the quality of local supplies is persistently deficient suggests that there may be a systematic failure in LDCs to appreciate the importance of component quality and of precision work in manufacturing industries.

(7) *Poor internal relations, both between headquarters and subsidiary, and between management and labour within the foreign subsidiary.* Conflicts between different groups within the firm over the distribution of profit, the level of investment, and so on, are common in any business activity, and there may be special reasons – such as the high risks perceived by foreign investors and their consequently short-term perspective on cash flow – why these conflicts may be particularly acute in respect of LDC operations. Nevertheless, it is also possible that the failure to resolve these conflicts effectively is due to frequent misunderstandings caused by cross-cultural barriers to communication.

(8) *The tendency for industrialisation through foreign technology to precipitate the disintegration of traditional social groups within the host economy.* All innovation does, of course, involve 'creative destruction', but the social groups of developing countries seem to be much more vulnerable in this respect than do equivalent social groups in the developed world.

It is worth noting that even the 'successful' explanations in (1)–(4) involve only the most proximate causes of the effects involved. Thus in respect of (1), for example, it is possible to ask the more fundamental question of why so many LDC governments opted for protectionism in the first place. Were they susceptible to economic analysis supporting import-substitution because they were predisposed to break economic as well as social and political ties with their colonial powers in order to bolster independence? It seems that – in this case at least – the more fundamental are the questions asked, and the further back the quest for explanations goes, the more likely are cultural factors to become significant.

A good theory often has the capacity to explain more than was originally asked of it, and it is claimed that this is also true of the analysis presented here. The theory can explain not only contemporary differences between DCs and LDCs, but also certain aspects of the historical process of indus-trialisation in countries which have become DCs. Thus the vulnerability of traditional social groups, for example, noted above, applies also to the social groups which became extinct a century or more ago during the industrialisation of DCs. There is insufficient space in the present paper, however, to document all the relevant facts, let alone substantiate the claim of the theory to explain them.

3. The Process of Development

A necessary condition for development in any locality is that there are resources with a potential for exploitation. Conventional economic theory tends to underestimate the obstacles that lie in the path of realising this potential, however. Working with traditional concepts of resource endow-ment – land, labour and capital – cross-section regressions using the total factor productivity approach have only limited success in explaining inter-national differences in material economic performance (as measured by *per capita* GNP) (Pack, 1987). Some countries clearly underperform by failing to realise their potential, and the question is why this should be so (Leibenstein, 1978).

Differences in education and training are commonly cited as a possible explanation, and the analysis presented here is generally consistent with this view. It goes beyond it, however, in recognising that education takes place largely outside formal institutions. Early education, in particular, is effected through family influence, peer group pressure within the local community, and so on. To benefit fully from formal education it may be necessary for people to 'unlearn' beliefs from their informal education. But if the conflict between the two sets of beliefs is acute then psychological obstacles to unlearning may arise. Measures of educational input based on gross expenditure fail to capture these important factors. The analysis in this paper helps to identify those aspects of the formal curriculum which are crucial in supporting economic development. It also identifies those elements of general culture which prepare people to benefit from such education.

Two main obstacles to the efficient use of national resources can be identified. The first is geographical: the inability to effect a division of labour due to obstacles to transportation. In this context, it is argued below that the presence of a potential entrepôt centre is crucial in facilitating the development of a region. The second is the absence of an entrepreneurial culture. An entrepreneurial culture provides an economy with flexibility – in particular, the structural flexibility to cope with changes in the division of labour. These changes may be progressive changes stemming from essentially autonomous technological innovations, or defensive changes made in response to resource depletion or various environmental disturbances.

An entrepreneurial culture has two main aspects: the technical and the moral (see Table 1). The technical aspect stimulates the study of natural laws through experimentation, and the assimilation of technologies developed by other cultures too. It also develops judgemental skills in decision-making – skills that are particularly important in simplifying complex situations without unduly distorting perceptions of them (Casson, 1988b).

Entrepreneurial opportunities are usually best exploited through contracts, organisation-building, and other forms of association. The moral aspect involves a grasp of the principles involved in voluntary associations of this kind. These principles include commitments to honesty, stewardship, and other values that underpin contractual arrangements of both a formal and informal nature. They also include a concept of group mission which is needed to mitigate agency problems in large organisations. A willingness to trust people other than kin is also important. Finally, there must be no rigid attachments to specific occupational roles or places of residence which can inhibit social or geographical mobility at times when structural adjustments are required.

It is worth stressing the diversity of the elements embraced by this moral aspect. Some of these elements have recently been eroded within Western industrial societies (Hirsch, 1977). These societies – notably the US – have developed an extreme competitive individualism, in which levels of trust are inefficiently low. The level of trust required for successful voluntary association is more likely to be present in countries with sophisticated traditional cultures that have recently been modernised – such as Japan.

It is useful to distinguish between high-level entrepreneurship, as exemplified by Schumpeter's heroic vision of system-wide innovation, and low-level entrepreneurship of the kind undertaken by petty traders in small market towns, which can be analysed using the Austrian concepts of arbitrage and market process. High-level entrepreneurship generally requires all the elements of entrepreneurial culture itemised in Table 1, whilst low-level entrepreneurship requires only some – it depends principally

Table 1 Factors in the long-run economic success of a nation

I. Geographical factors that influence entrepôt potential

   A Location near to major long-distance freight transport routes.
   B Natural harbour with inland river system.
   C Extensive coastline.
   D Land and climate suitable for an agriculture with potential for local downstream processing.
   E Mineral deposits and energy resources.

II Entrepreneurial culture

   Technical aspects
   A Scientific attitude, including a systems view.
   B Judgemental skills, including
       (i)   ability to simplify
       (ii) self-confidence
       (iii) detached perception of risk
       (iv) understanding of delegation

   Moral aspects
   C Voluntarism and toleration.
   D Association with trust, including
       (i)   general commitment to principles of honesty, stewardship, etc.
       (ii) sense of corporate mission
       (iii) versatile personal bonding (friendship not confined to kin)
       (iv) weak attachments to specific locations, roles, etc.
   E High norms in respect of effort, quality of work, accumulation of wealth, social distinction, etc.

---

on good judgement, and to some extent on the absence of atachments that impede mobility. It is this contrast between high-level and low-level entrepreneurship – rather than the presence or absence of entre-preneurships – which seems to be important in explaining the difference between DCs and LDCs. In other words, it is a relative and not an absolute difference with which the analysis is concerned.

Geographical and cultural factors are linked because the geography of a territory can influence the kind of culture that emerges within it. This is because geographical impediments to communication reduce personal mobility and partition a country into small isolated social groups. Internal coordination within these groups tends to rely on primitive mechanisms of reciprocity etc. which depend crucially on stability of membership (Casson, 1988a,b). As explained below, the cultures of these groups are likely to emphasise conformity and coercion rather than individuality and choice, and so inhibit spontaneous entrepreneurial activity.

Good communications, on the other hand, provide opportunities for appropriating gains from interregional trade. Groups that inhabit areas with good communications will tend to prosper, provided their leaders adopt a tolerant attitude toward entrepreneurial middlemen who promote trade. Groups which develop an entrepreneurial culture will tend to expand the geographical scope of their operations (through commercially-inspired voyages of discovery, and so on). Technological advances in transportation will be encouraged because their liberal policies permit the appropriation of material rewards by inventors and innovators. Geographical expansion eventually brings these groups into contact with isolated groups who occupy resource-rich locations. These locations would be inaccessible without the transportation technology, the entrepreneurial group can, if its leaders wish, subdue the isolated groups by military means. Different entrepreneurial groups may become rivals in preempting opportunities for the exploitation of overseas resources. This may lead to military conflict between the groups, or to a compromise solution where each group maintains its own economic empire and political sphere of influence.

The creation of a transport infrastructure within these hitherto isolated territories not only gives access to resources (and incidentally improves imperial defence); it also tends to undermine the viability of indigenous cultures. Ease of transportation promotes personal mobility and so destroys the stability of membership on which the local groups' methods of internal coordination depend. The confrontation between MNEs and LDCs can be understood as one aspect of this final phase in which the technologies of the entrepreneurial societies are transferred to the regions occupied by the hitherto isolated social groups. To fully understand the nature of this confrontation, however, it is necessary to study in detail the various aspects of the process of development outlined above.

4. Geographical Determinants of Entrepôt Potential

A division of labour creates a system of functionally specialised elements. The elements which constitute the system have complementary roles. The division of labour is normally effected over space. Different activities are concentrated at different locations and are connected by intermediate product flows. A large system typically comprises interrelated subsystems, and usually the subsystems themselves can be further decomposed.

System operation over space depends on ease of transportation, and in this context the existence of low-cost facilities for the bulk movement in intermediate products is crucial.

Water transport has significant cost advantages for the bulk movement of freight, and this implies that a good river system and a long coastline (in relation to land area) is an advantage. These conditions are most likely to be satisfied by an island or peninsula with low-lying terrain. Water transport is, however, vulnerable through icing, flooding, etc., and so geological features that facilitate road and rail construction are also useful.

Good transportation expands the area of the market for the final output of each process. It permits a much finer division of labour because economies of scale in individual plants can be exploited more effectively. In general, steady expansion of the market permits the evolution of system structure. The horizontal division of labour expands to proliferate varieties of final product whilst the vertical division of labour extends to generate a larger number of increasingly simple (and hence more easily mechanised and automated) stages of production.

The development of a region depends not only on the progress of its internal division of labour, but also on its ability to participate in a wider division of labour beyond its boundaries. The external division of labour (as traditional trade theory emphasises) allows the region to specialise in those activities which make the most intensive use of the resources with which it is relatively best endowed.

The interface between the internal and external division of labour is typically an entrepôt centre. Whether or not a region includes a location with entrepôt potential will exert a significant influence on its development (Hodges, 1988). The general advantages of water-transport, noted earlier, are reflected in the fact that the cost of long-distance bulk transportation is normally lowest by sea. This means that port facilities are normally necessary for successful entrepôt operation. Since ships afford significant economies of scale in their construction and operation a successful port must be designed to handle large sea-going (and ocean-going) vessels.

A port located close to major international and intercontinental shipping routes may become an important node on a global network of trade. Port activities will comprise both the transhipment of bulk consignments on connecting trunk routes and also 'break bulk' and 'make bulk' operations geared to local feeder services. In this context, the location of the port on the estuary of an extensive river system is advantageous. A centre of transhipment and consolidation is, moreover, a natural place at which to carry out processing activities. Handling costs are reduced because goods can be unloaded directly into the processing facility from the feeder systems, and then later loaded directly from the processing facility onto the trunk system (or *vice versa*).

The need for processing exported goods depends upon the type of agricultural and mineral production undertaken in the hinterland of the port. In the pre-industrial phase of port development, agricultural processing is likely to be particularly significant. Now crops such as corn and barley offer relatively limited opportunities for downstream processing before consumption – baking and brewing being respectively the main activities concerned – whilst rice feeds into even fewer activities. Animal production, by contrast, generates dairy products, meat and hides, while hides, in turn, feed into the leather and clothing sequence. Sheep are particularly prolific in generating forward linkages, as their wool feeds into the textile sequence. The textile sequence is simple to mechanise and has the capacity to produce a wide range of differentiated fashion products. (Cotton feeds into a similar sequence, but unlike sheep does not generate meat and hides as well.) The potential for forward linkages varies dramatically, therefore, from rice growing at one extreme to sheep farming on the other.

The location of the processing at the port depends, of course, on it being cheaper to locate the processing in the exporting rather than the importing country. This requirement is generally satisfied by both agricultural and mineral products. The perishability of agricultural products means that processing is usually done as close to the source as possible. Mineral products, though durable, lose weight during processing, and so to minimise transport costs it is usually efficient to process close to the source as well.

Mineral processing is, however, energy intensive, and energy sources, such as fossil fuels, are often even more expensive to transport than mineral ores themselves. The absence of local energy resources can there-fore lead to the relocation of processing away from the exporting country. Mineral processing can also generate hazardous byproducts. Access to a coastline near the port where such byproducts can be dumped is important, therefore, if minerals are to be processed before export.

Whilst the processing of imported products is likely to be of much less economic significance, for reasons implicit in the discussion above, there are a few exceptions. Imports from an LDC, for example, may well arrive in a raw state, because of the lack of suitable energy supplies or labour skills in the exporting country. Furthermore, the more sophisticated are consumer tastes in the importing country, the more extensive is the processing that is likely to be required. Thus the greater the gap in develop-ment between the exporting and importing country, the more likely it is that the amount of value-added in import-processing will be significant.

The agglomeration of activities within a port provides an opportunity for exploiting economies of scale in the provision of defence, law and order, drainage and sewage systems, and so on. It also provides a large local market which promotes the development of highly specialised services – not only commercial services, but also consumer services – of the kind that could never be provided in country areas with dispersed populations. (Such economies of urbanisation can, of course, be provided without a port, and many countries do, in fact, contain inland administrative capitals which support such services. The viability of such capitals often depends, however, on cross-subsidisation from tax revenues generated at an entrepôt centre, and the social benefits derived from them may therefore be imputed to entrepôt activity.)

It is sometimes claimed that, contrary to the argument above, entrepôts devoted to the bulk export of agricultural products and raw materials are inherently enclavistic. The crucial question here is how fast the linkages between the entrepôt and the village communities of the hinterland develop. In the history of western DCs provincial agricultural marketing and light manufacturing have grown up in medium-sized towns whose merchants intermediate between the village and the entrepôt. Even in LDCs with limited rural transport infrastructure, the tentacles of trade can extend to the village in respect of livestock farming because livestock can be driven to market over distances that are prohibitive so far as the carriage of crops is concerned. It is, therefore, only if rural culture is strongly opposed to merchant activity that the entrepôt is likely to remain an enclave indefinitely.

The conditions most favourable to industrialisation, it may be concluded, are the existence of a natural harbour close to major shipping routes, good internal communications between the port and its hinterland, livestock farming in the hinterland, abundant endowments of both minerals and primary energy sources, and a coastline suitable for the disposal of pollutants. These considerations alone go some way towards explaining both the early industrialisation of temperate-climate, mineral-rich island countries with coastal deposits of fossil fuels, and good inland river systems, such as the United Kingdom, and their relative decline once their minerals and fossil fuels have been depleted and their comparative advantage in livestock farming has been undermined by the development of overseas territories.

5. Scientific Outlook and Systems Thinking

A territory with entrepôt potential can find its development inhibited by an unsuitable culture. Cultural constraints inhibit entrepreneurship both directly, by discouraging individual initiative, and indirectly by encouraging political leaders to distort incentives and over-regulate the economy.

In some societies, the absence of a scientific outlook may well be a problem. Western analysts studying LDCs typically perceive this problem as resulting from the absence of any Renaissance or Enlightenment. The society has not gone through an intellectual revolution in which a mystical view of the world gives way to a more realistic one. The society still relies on anthropomorphic explanations of natural processes, interprets unusual but scientifically explicable events as omens and perceives its real-world environment as the centre of a metaphysical cosmos. This emphasis on things as symbols of something beyond inhibits recognition of things as they really are. It discourages the understanding of nature in terms of mechanism and system interdependency.

A realistic systems view of nature does, however, raise philosophical problems of its own, which can be resolved in various ways. A major difficulty is that if man himself, as a part of nature, is pure mechanism, then choice and moral responsibility become simply an illusion caused by lack of self-knowledge. Western liberal thought resolves this problem through Cartesian dualism, in which the moral world of intentional action coexists alongside the physical world of mechanism.

The scientific outlook does not imply, as is sometimes suggested, a completely secular view of the world. Western Christian thought has also embraced dualism by redefining the role of God as the creator and architect of a self-contained universe, rather than as a supernatural force intervening directly through everyday events. The view that man is fashioned in the image of God encourages the idea that man too has creative abilities. Rejection of the view that the earth is the centre of the universe diminishes man's stature and raises that of nature, encouraging the idea that nature is worthy of serious investigation. Man's contact with God can no longer reasonably be maintained through sacrifices offered in anticipation of favours, but it can be sustained in other ways, such as an appreciation of the elegance and simplicity of physical laws which express this design. Man's creative abilities can be used to explore this design through observation and experiment.

The systems view of nature translates readily into a systems view of production. Production involves a system created by man and superimposed on the system of nature, with which it interacts. A systems view of production involves awareness of the principle of the division of labour – in particular, the importance of decomposing complex tasks into simple ones and allocating resources between these tasks according to comparative advantage. The systems view also emphasises that the strong complementarities between different elements of the system make it vulnerable to the failure of any single element and so create a strong demand for quality control.

The close connection between religious beliefs and attitudes to nature means that in countries where mysticism or superstition prevail, a scientific outlook and systems thinking are unlikely to develop. The concept of harnessing nature to control the future is absolute folly to people who believe that the future is already pre-ordained, or is in the personal hands of powerful and arbitrary gods. As a consequence, their ability to assimilate technological know-how will be very low. Awareness of how local operations fit into a global division of labour will be minimal. For example, the idea that system complementarities necessitate continuity of operation, rigorous punctuality, etc., will be quite alien to local operatives. Appreciation of the importance of quality control in the manufacture of components and intermediate products will be missing too.

6. Competitive Individualism *versus* Voluntary Association

The development of a scientific attitude in the West was associated with the rise of individualism. The idea that people are intelligent and purposeful was applied democratically. Intelligence was not something confined to a traditional elite, but a feature of every mature adult. Emphasis on intelligence led to demands for reasoned arguments rather than appeal to traditional authority or divine revelation for the legitimation of moral objectives.

Individualism asserts that each person is the best judge of how his own interests are served. He can deal with other individuals as equals, and use his intelligence to safeguard his own interests in his dealings with them. Interference in other people's affairs on paternalistic grounds is unacceptable. Individualism claims that everyone is capable of forming judgements on wider issues too. Since different people have different experiences, no one can assume that their own opinion is necessarily correct, and so toleration of other people's views is required. Differences of opinion over collective activity need to be resolved peacefully, and so in political life commitment to the democratic process is regarded as more important than approval of the outcome of the process.

Four aspects of individualism are worthy of special mention. The first is the alienability of property, which helps to promote markets in both products and labour. The demystification of the world through the emergence of a scientific outlook undermines the view that people impart something of themselves to the things they produce. It breaks the anthropomorphic link between production and use. As the product of labour becomes depersonalised and objectified, it becomes acceptable to alienate it for use by others. Conversely, it becomes acceptable to claim ownership over things one did not produce. So far as natural resources are concerned, they no longer need to be held in common by the territorial group. They can be privately appropriated, giving the owner an incentive to manage them properly and avoid excessive depletion.

The second aspect is freedom of entry (and of exit) which allows individuals to switch between trading partners and between markets without the permission of established authority. Such freedom also implies freedom from statutory regulation of entry too.

Thirdly, respect for contract, and a right of recourse to an independent judiciary for the resolution of contractual disputes, are aspects of individualism which are important in reducing transaction costs.

Finally, an individualist appreciates that multilateral trade is most easily established through separately negotiated bilateral trades in which goods are bought and sold using a medium of exchange. He recognises that currency is useful as a specialised medium of exchange, and that the most convenient currency is the debt of a reputable debtor such as the sovereign or the state. Individualism is therefore tolerant of debt and of the personality cult that surrounds notes and coin that carry the head of the sovereign. It imposes obligations on the debtor, however, to live up to his reputation through self-restraint; in particular he must not debase the currency through over-issue.

A major cultural weakness of LDCs seems to be a lack of individualistic thinking. In the extreme case of a primitive rural economy, the link between production and consumption remains unbroken: individuals consume what they themselves produce, and thereby forego the gains from trade. In so far as there is a division of labour, it is confined to within a social group. Different activities are coordinated both by relations of reciprocity between individual members and by members' common sense of obligation to the leader. These mechanisms are most effective within small, stable and compact groups, such as the extended family or the village community. In such groups members regularly expect to encounter one another again, offenders quickly acquire a reputation for bad behaviour and can be easily punished by the leader and, indeed, by other members of the group.

A major defect of such coordination mechanisms is they depend crucially on stability of membership. If it becomes easy for members to quit, then reputations become less valuable, and punishment is easier to evade. Moreover, conditions of geographical isolation, which tend to promote stability of membership, also mean that the threat of expulsion from the group can be very severe. This allows a leader to acquire enormous power over individual members, provided he can 'divide' the members against each other or otherwise prevent them joining forces to overthrow him. Thus while isolation may help to promote close emotional ties between the followers, the leader may be feared rather than respected or loved.

Individualism has its own problems, however in coordinating the activities of groups. Because individualism promotes inter-group mobility, it not only undermines the 'despotic' solution to intra-group coordination but also the internal reputation mechanism too. A purely competitive form of individualism, which encourages individuals to join teams purely for the material benefits, offers no effective substitute for primitive reciprocity.

When followers' efforts can be easily monitored by the leader there is little problem for competitive individualism, because the material rewards of each member can be linked to his individual performance. When effort becomes difficult to monitor, however, material incentives have to be related to team output, and when the team is large a share of the team bonus may be insufficient to prevent team members slacking. Unless there is a shared sense of corporate mission, individuals are likely to put too little effort into team activity. The leader cannot trust his followers not to slack. If the leader cannot be trusted either then the followers may not respond to his incentives anyway, because they believe he will default on the agreement if he can get away with it.

Another problem of individualism is that the inalienability of the individual's right to quit may induce higher rates of intra-group mobility than are compatible with efficiency. Successful teamwork often requires members to accumulate on-the-job experience in learning to anticipate each other's actions; unrestricted freedom to enter and exit can allow transitory members who lack this experience to profit at the expense of their colleagues.

Widening the range of an individual's legitimate commitments from mere respect for property and contract to generate trust by instilling a sense of corporate mission significantly modifies the moral basis of individualism. The resulting philosophy is essentially one of voluntary association. This philosophy retains many of the attributes of competitive individualism, but emphasises that the contract of group membership involves acceptance of discipline imposed by the leader. Freedom exists principally in choosing between alternative group commitments, rather than in maintaining full discretion within the chosen group. It also emphasises that commitment to a group is a source of emotional satisfaction, and that more commitment rather than less may make people better off. It does not attempt to repudiate the 'minimal commitment' of competitive individualism but rather to augment this commitment with others.

Widening the range of commitments creates the possibility of moral conflicts. To a heavily committed individual, indeed, it is the resolution of moral dilemmas that often appears to be the essence of choice. Experience in coping with moral dilemmas of this kind may well improve general decision-making skills.

The global organisation of production implemented by sophisticated MNEs depends crucially upon such commitments to mitigate what would otherwise be insuperable agency problems. However intense the competition between MNEs, within each MNE cooperation between the parent and each subsidiary needs to be maintained at a high level. A clear group mission, articulated by a charismatic business leader who makes an effective role model, can be crucial in this respect.

It is therefore worth noting that the kind of individualism harnessed by the successful MNE is very different from the culture of unrestrained self-assertion – or even exhibitionism – which can be found in many societies, including LDCs. The extrovert 'individualism' of adolescent males, for example, has little connection with the mature individualism of the successful entrepreneur. People who exhibit no self-restraint cannot normally be trusted, and so make poor business risks for financiers, and bad employees. The observation, often heard, that there is 'too much individualism' rather than too little in LDCs, confuses exhibitionism with the mature individualism described above. It is not too much individualism that is the problem, but too little individualism of the appropriate kind.

7. Geographical and Cultural Aspects of a Global Trading System

The preceding analysis suggests that the differences between developed countries (DCs) and LDCs lie not only in resource endowments but in the fact that the territories of the former embrace potential entrepôt centres and that cultural obstacles to the realisation of this potential are relatively weak. An LDC is likely to be a country that has no entrepôt potential, and poor internal communications which make it unlikely to develop an indigenous entrepreneurial culture. A DC, on the other hand, is a country with both entrepôt potential and an entrepreneurial culture.

A country that has entrepôt potential but lacks an indigenous entrepreneurial culture is likely to find that, in the course of time, entrepôt operations emerge under the ownership and control of foreign entrepreneurs based in DCs. These entrepreneurs have the system thinking needed to recognise the entrepôt potential, and are likely to control established international transport and distribution systems into which the new operations can be integrated. The external commercial relations of these countries may become heavily dependent upon an international trading system governed by the requirements of DC markets, and controlled by DC interests, whilst profits generated by entrepôt operations may be repatriated too.

Within any given historical epoch, the process of development begins with the countries that later emerge as the DC investors in LDCs. These countries may subsequently go into decline, but this process of decline is not considered here – it is treated as a separate issue, involving the transition from one historical epoch to another (cf. Wiener, 1981).

In modelling the process of development in global terms, the advantages of water transport over land-based transport – emphasised earlier – play an important role. These advantages mean that maritime trade between entrepôt centres in different countries is likely to be of much greater significance for each country than inland trade between the entrepôt and its remoter hinterland. The fortunes of individual countries are therefore closely linked to their place within the world trading system. Another consequence of the dominance of maritime trade is that even DCs may experience a degree of dualism in their development, between the entrepôt centre on the one hand, and the remoter hinterland on the other. A somewhat ironic corollary of this is that the most unfortunate LDCs, which have no valuable resources and no entrepôt potential, may be the only countries not to experience dualism, purely because they have no development either.

A typical sequence of global development is shown in Figures 1 and 2. There are two phases. The first involves the rise of DCs prompted by the development of trade between them. The second involves the emergence of LDCs and their own subsequent development.

In the first phase (see Figure 1) it is assumed that there are two potential DCs, A and B, each of which is initially segmented into isolated social groups which control particular resources (see sector (a)). Resource endowments are denoted by circles, with large endowments that have foreign trade potential (because, for example, the output is nonperishable and has a high value per unit weight) being denoted by two concentric circles. Each square box encloses a group of people who share a common culture and reside close to a given resource endowment.

Both countries have a natural harbour which forms a potential entrepôt centre. The resources all lie in a hinterland which can be accessed given suitable investment in transport infrastructure. The harbour represents a potential entrepôt centre, and is denoted by a white triangle. It is assumed that in each country the indigenous culture around the major resource is reasonably progressive, so that this potential can be realised. A line of communication is established between the groups controlling the major resource of each country, and two-way trade develops through the entrepôt ports. Realisation of the entrepôt potential is indicated by the switch from the white triangle to the black one in sector (b).

The trade flow intensifies communications between the two countries, leading to cultural homogenisation. This is illustrated by the fact that the two countries now lie within the same box – at least so far as the entrepôt centres and the export-oriented hinterlands are concerned. This culture differs from the cultures of the isolated groups in the less promising hinterlands. The trading system strengthens the progressive element in the indigenous culture of the export-oriented hinterland by giving greater emphasis to the individual's right to hold property and his ability to fend for himself in the negotiation of trades. Competition between the port and the hinterland for employees also stimulates a friendlier and less autocratic style of leadership within social groups. This new commercial culture is distinguished from the culture of the isolated groups by the use of a dashed line in the figure.

As each entrepôt centre develops, the advantages of utilising more fully its indivisible facilities – notably the port – encourage the generation of additional feeder traffic by investment in transport links with the less-promising areas of hinterland (see sector (c)). The entrepôt now handles not only additional export traffic, but also inter-regional traffic between different parts of the hinterland. In other words, the entrepôt becomes a hub for domestic freight transport too. Each country becomes homogenised around the commercial culture as a result. This stage of evolution may well be protracted. Many so-called developed countries still contain isolated rural areas where the commercial culture has made limited inroads.

Before this stage has been completed, the fourth stage may begin. This involves processing exports at the port, in order to reduce the bulk and increase the value of long-distance cargo. Downstream processing of this

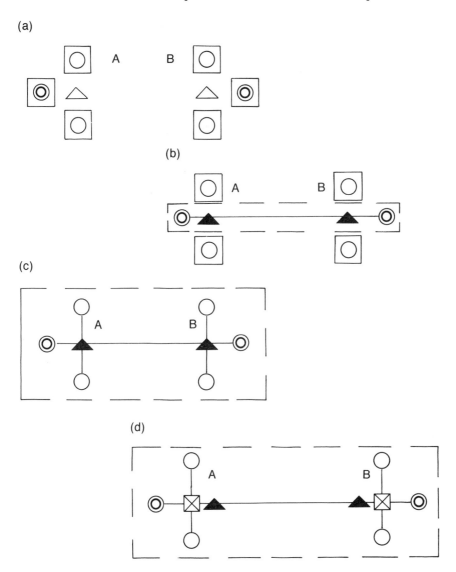

Figure 1

Note: For explanation of symbols, see text.

kind is illustrated in the figure by a cross within a square (see sector (d)). Industrialisation around the port will have further cultural consequences, but these are not considered here.

The second phase of the development sequence begins when one of the developed countries, say A, makes contact with an LDC, C. C is still in the

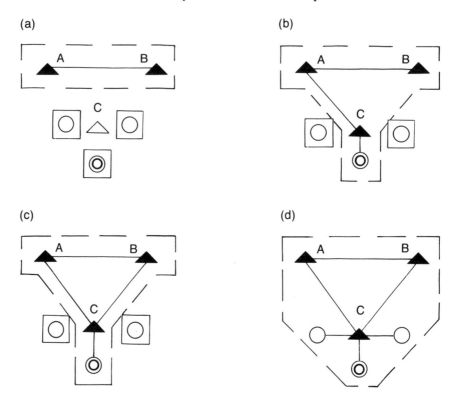

Figure 2

situation that A was in at the beginning of the first phase, but with this difference – that C remains undeveloped partly because it has a less progressive culture. Its initial state is illustrated in sector (a) of Figure 1. The figure has been simplified by omitting the domestic trade flows within countries A and B.

If A discovered C before B does, A may attempt to monopolise trade with C, so that all trade between B and C has to be routed *via* A. Colonial occupation or control of international shipping lanes may be used to enforce the exclusion of B. So far as C is concerned, it is faced with the impact *via* A, of an established commercial culture which has evolved over a long time from roots which are, in any case, more progressive. This opens up a wide cultural gap within C between the highly commercial imported culture of the entrepôt centre on the one hand and the less-promising areas of hinterland on the other. This is illustrated in sector (c). Cultural dualism impedes the final stage of development, shown in sector (d), where linkages are established with the remaining hinterland. Downstream processing around the entrepôt centre may also develop in this final stage, but this is not shown in the figure.

Two main social groups are available to bridge this cultural gap. One is the resident expatriates, who may have moved abroad originally as employees of the MNE or the DC government. The other is the group of indigenous individuals – merchants and other educated people drawn mainly from the middle and upper ranks of the host society – who are quick to take advantage of the profit opportunities from cultural brokerage. They are willing to learn the language and customs, and adopt the style of dress, of the DC – and perhaps send their children to be educated there as well – in order to consolidate their position. The size of these two groups, and their ability to combine forces where necessary, is crucial in determining the spread of entrepôt influence within the DC.

The analysis suggests that while the process of development in an LDC is similar in outline to that previously followed by an established DC, there are three important differences, which arise chiefly because the LDC is a latecomer to development.

First, the reason why it is a latecomer is partly that it has an unprogressive culture. There may be considerable resistance to the development of entrepôt activity, and indigenous entrepreneurs may be so slow off the mark that foreigners dominate the operations. There may even be political support for a policy of closing the harbour to foreign merchants.

Secondly, if the entrepôt centre is opened up under colonial rule, foreign merchants may enjoy significant market power. Thus few of the gains of trade that accrued to the developed country in the early stages of its own development may accrue to the LDC as it passes through a similar stage itself.

Thirdly, the LDC is confronted with a very sophisticated trading system organised by developed country trade, and with a matching culture very much at variance with its own. Thus, although superficially it might seem that an LDC should be able to catch up quickly with developed countries, its vulnerability to the exercise of market power and the magnitude of the cultural gap may well cause discrepancies in the level of development to persist for a very long time.

8. Cultural Aspects of MNE Operations

The MNE is the major institution through which both the technology and the entrepreneurial culture of the DC is transferred to the LDC economy. The largest and most sophisticated MNEs are based in DCs; they utilise advanced technologies to operate internationally rationalised production systems. Systems thinking is highly developed in the headquarters of these firms. Strategic attitudes to competition are also well developed because of continuing oligopolistic rivalry between MNEs in major DC markets.

The analysis in this paper shows that there are substantial cultural barriers to disseminating attitudes of this kind to indigenous managers, and to their subordinates, in LDCs. One obvious way of educating local employees is to send out managers from headquarters on short term overseas appointments. This may encounter difficulties if the location is sufficiently unattractive to Western eyes that managers resist reassignment to the extent that they prefer to resign instead. In any case, these managers may have difficulties communicating with their subordinates, so while headquarters-subsidiary relations may be good, internal relations within the subsidiary may be poor. In some cases resident expatriates may be employed instead, though there is a risk that they will be out of touch with the more sophisticated ideas developed at headquarters.

An alternative is to hire locally and send recruits to headquarters for extensive training before they return to the subsidiary. Training is, however, likely to be difficult – even at headquarters – unless the local recruits already have some Western-style education, which may well mean that indigenous recruitment is confined to a small social elite. This strategy is inappropriate, moreover, when establishing a new subsidiary; managers will normally have to be sent out from headquarters to organise recruitment, and they can only be replaced when the flow of trained recruits has come on-stream.

Cross-cultural barriers also explain why spill-overs from MNE operations in LDCs are so limited. The capacity of indigenous competitors to imitate – let alone adapt or improve upon – imported technologies is limited by their lack of a scientific outlook. Similarly, the inability of local firms to emerge as subcontractors competing against imported component supplies stems from their failure to appreciate the importance of precision and punctuality – an importance that is so transparent once a systems view of production is adopted.

This is not to deny that profit-oriented indigenous innovation will occur. It will proceed slowly, however – because, for example, the nature of the innovation may have to be explained with the aid of an expensive foreign-run 'demonstration' plant, as the basic scientific logic cannot be assimilated. Cautious indigenous businessmen may wait for an indigenous innovator to operate successfully before committing themselves. Unfortunately, if the indigenous innovator does not understand the logic of the situation, he may be unable to improvise solutions to unforeseen difficulties, and so the innovation may gain an undeserved reputation for being unworkable.

When significant spill-overs do occur, and agglomerations of local industries begin to develop, the effect on the cultural life of the indigenous communities can be devastating. The development of urban areas in which MNE activities are concentrated draws labour away from the rural areas. The migration of rural labour is a selective process. Younger and more entrepreneurial workers are attracted to the towns, leaving the least entrepreneurial workers, and the immigrants' aged dependants, behind. Although rural incomes may be partially sustained by intra-family remittances from the towns, the loss of the more productive and entrepreneurial individuals may well harden the conservative and inward-looking attitudes of those that are left behind. Faced with rising out-migration, the reputation mechanisms that coordinate the activities of rural communities are undermined. Rural economic performance declines, and the dualistic structure of the economy is reinforced.

Meanwhile, cut off from their traditional life-style, new urban workers tend to consume a higher proportion of the convenience products and sophisticated durables marketed by the MNEs. Some of these products are promoted using advertising strongly influenced by Western-style competitive individualism. Instead of creating an urban culture based upon voluntary association, which could lead in the long run to a lively entrepreneurial society, commercial media tend to promote attitudes of unrestrained self-assertion which are inimical both to industrial discipline and to honest business practices.

The social disruption caused by MNE activities does not end here, however. The tradition of subservience to despotic authority, sustained in isolated communities, can sometimes be usefully exploited by MNEs searching for cheap unskilled labour that is easily disciplined by intimidation. Women and children accustomed to absolute paternal authority may become useful factory or plantation employees, for example. Once the women acquire a measure of economic independence, however, the economic basis for paternal authority is undermined, and attempts to sustain it through religious teaching may only be able to slow the trend rather than reverse it. As a result, the whole fabric of traditional family organisation may be thrown into disarray.

Another form of disruption is to encourage mass immigration of refugees or landless peasants from other areas in order to depress wages in the locality of the subsidiary. Besides redistributing income away from labour, this strategy carries major problems of cultural integration within the local community, which may spill over into violence, particularly where the immigrants are readily recognised by their language, style of dress, or physical characteristics.

Finally, there is the political disruption which may result from the fragmentation of political alliances which occurs when some local leaders opt for cooperation with foreign interests whilst others oppose it. Both groups may be forced into extreme positions – one as 'lackeys' of the foreign power and the other as intransigent fundamentalists favouring isolation. This fragmentation of the polity may enable the foreign power to 'divide and rule' the country.

This rather negative view of the social consequences of the MNE may be countered by many instances in which MNEs have attempted to become good corporate citizens of the host country. The difficulty here is that many LDCs – particularly former colonies – are in fact agglomerations of different tribes and castes, and that the concept of a good citizen with which the MNE conforms is merely the view held by the social group that is currently in power. Thus in a country with a long history of internal divisions, being officially recognised as a good citizen may require covert discrimination against rival indigenous groups.

Situations of this kind pose various dilemmas for the MNE. In a country, for example, where the religion of the dominant group stresses paternal authority, should contracts for the employment of married women be negotiated through their husbands, so that women in effect become wage-slaves? Is obstructing the economic liberation of women a satisfactory price to pay for being a good corporate citizen and maintaining the economic basis of traditional family life?

In many recently-independent LDCs political power changes frequently, often in response to military initiatives. Should the MNE favour political stability and, if so, use its economic influence on the military to secure the kind of stable regime most acceptable to the liberal Western conscience? If the MNE remains aloof, and instability continues, it is likely to be confronted with a series of corrupt demands for payments to government officials, as the holders of influential offices attempt to make their fortunes before they are deposed in the next change of government. Should the MNE jeopardise the interests, not only of its shareholders, but also of its indigenous employees by refusing to make payments, or should it respect 'local culture' and support the bribery endorsed by the 'unofficial constitution'?

The way managers resolve these moral issues will be determined by the MNE's own corporate culture, which will in turn reflect, at least in part, the national culture of the DC in which it is headquartered. In this respect the balance between the philosophies of competitive individualism and voluntary association in the source country culture will be a critical factor in determining how far broad moral concerns dominate the pursuit of shareholder's short-term interests.

9. Conclusion

Previous economic literature on MNEs in LDCs has tended to concentrate on issues of market power and the choice of contractual arrangements (for example, Lall and Streeten, 1977; Calvet and Naim, 1981). The integration of cultural issues into an economic analysis of the subject reflects the authors' belief that economic factors such as these cannot entirely explain the relevant phenomena. This paper has not proved that cultural factors must be taken into account. It is always possible that some new and more sophisticated economic explanation of these phenomena could be contrived instead. Putting this unlikely possibility to one side, however, this paper has taken a step towards analysing the way that cultural factors in economic development impact upon, and are modified by, the MNE.

A great deal of further work needs to be done before the hypotheses advanced in this paper can be properly tested. The full extent of the cultural differences among LDCs and among the DC countries in which MNEs are based, needs to be recognised. The performance of a given MNE in a given LDC is likely to be governed by (a) the degree of entrepreneurship in the culture of the firm, (b) the degree of entrepreneurship in the culture of the host country, and (c) an 'interaction' or 'coupling' term which captures the overall degree of similarity between the cultures, recognising that culture is a multi-faceted phenomenon.

To apply this method it is necessary to profile the cultures of both the entities involved. It may require in-depth interviews with many people to establish profiles which can make any claim to objectivity. Complete objectivity can never be achieved, of course, in any study of cultural phenomena because of the distortion created by the culture-specific prejudices of the observer. Nevertheless, it is unnecessary to go to the other extreme and adopt an entirely relativistic view. Different observers may still be able to agree on some things, even if they cannot agree on everything.

Cultures contain a certain amount of inertia because of the way they are transmitted between generations through family upbringing. Nevertheless, the advent of public education and mass media communications has the potential to accelerate cultural change. The trend towards greater rapidity of cultural change does, indeed, give a sense of urgency to understanding the mechanisms, and the economic effects, involved.

Economic changes can themselves precipitate cultural change, because they affect the shared experiences of members of a society. The increasing interdependence within the world economy is, in fact, another reason why the process of cultural change may have speeded up. This paper has, unfortunately, treated culture as though it were an exogenous parameter rather than an endogenous variable. A full study of cultural factors would, however, involve a dynamic analysis containing feedback loops of a kind far too complex to be considered here.

Even in its present state, though, the theory provides some simple predictions about comparative economic development. It suggests, for example, that small island economies which enjoy a sophisticated cultural legacy may be better equipped to develop than mainly land-locked countries whose cultural traditions are derived almost exclusively from small isolated rural communities. The entrepôt potential and cultural legacy of Hong Kong, Singapore and Taiwan, say, may therefore explain why they have been able to industrialise and develop indigenous business services so much faster than many sub-Saharan African economies. This is quite consistent with the view that outward-looking trade policies have also promoted their development. It underlines, however, the earlier suggestion that trade policy itself may, in the long run, be culturally specific. Imposing outward-looking trade policies on a less entrepreneurial country in Africa is unlikely to have the same dramatic result as has the voluntary adoption of such policies in S.E. Asian NICs.

Finally, it should be noted that recognition of cultural factors has significant welfare implications. The emotional benefits that individuals derive from group affiliation are commonly omitted from the preference structures assumed in conventional social cost-benefit analysis of foreign investment. The cultural specificity of the policy-maker's own attitudes are also ignored, although these attitudes are crucial in validating the highly materialistic individual preferences assumed in conventional policy analysis. On a more specific level, the failure of conventional analysis to recognise the important economic function of culture in reducing transaction costs, means that conventional analysis has overlooked the significant material as well as emotional costs that cultural disintegration poses on many sectors of the economy. A number of judgements about the net benefits of foreign investment derived from conventional analysis will have to be carefully reconsidered in the light of this cultural analysis.

Acknowledgements

Previous versions were given at the EIBA Conference, Antwerp, December 1987, the Department of Economics seminar at the University of Surrey, October 1988, the ESRC Development Economics Study Group, London, March 1989, and the Annual Conference of the UK Chapter of the Academy of International Business, Bath, April 1989. The authors would like to thank all those who have commented on the paper, particularly V.N. Balasubramanyam, John Dunning, Geoffrey Jones, Homi Katrak, Colin Kirkpatrick, Don Lecraw, Matthew McQueen, Hafiz Mirza, M.M.Z. Njolwa, Klaus Weiermair and Mo Yamin.

References

Berger, S. and M.J. Piore (1980) *Dualism and Discontinuity in Industrial Societies,* Cambridge: Cambridge University Press.
Calvet, A.L. and M. Naim (1981) The Multinational Firm in Less Developed Countries: A Markets and Hierarchies Approach, Barcelona, Spain: Paper presented at AIB/EIBA Conference.
Casson, M.C. (1988a) The Theory of International Business as a Unified Social Science, *University of Reading Discussion Papers in International Investment and Business Studies,* Series B. No. 123.

Casson, M.C. (1988b) Entrepreneurial Culture as a Competitive Advantage, *University of Reading Discussion Papers in International Investment and Business Studies*, Series B. No. 124.

Casson, M.C. and R.D. Pearce (1987) Multinational Enterprises in LDCs, in N. Gemmell (ed.) *Surveys in Development Economics*, Oxford: Blackwell, 90–132.

Eisenstadt, S.N. (1973) *Tradition, Change, Modernity*, New York: Wiley.

Hagen, E.E. (1962) *On the Theory of Social Change: How Economic Growth Begins*, Homewood, Illinois: Dorsey Press.

Hayek, F.A. von (1937) Economics and Knowledge, *Economica* (New Series), 4, 33–54, reprinted in F.A. von Hayek, *Individualism and Economic Order*, London: Routledge and Kegan Paul, 1949.

Herskovits, M.J. (1961) Economic Change and Cultual Dynamics, in R. Braibanti and J.J. Spengler (eds), *Tradition, Values, and Socio-Economic Development*, Durham, N.C.: Duke University Press, 114–38.

Hirsch, F. (1977) *Social Limits to Growth*, London: Routledge and Kegan Paul.

Hodges, R. (1988) *Primitive and Peasant Markets*, Oxford: Blackwell.

Hoselitz, B.F. (1961) Tradition and Economic Growth, in R. Braibanti and J.J. Spengler (eds) *Tradition, Values, and Socio-economic Development*, Durham, N.C.: Duke University Press, 83–113.

Inkeles, A. and D.H. Smith (1974) *Becoming Modern: Individual Change in Six Developing Countries*, London: Heinemann.

Kilby, P. (1971) Hunting the Heffalump, in P. Kilby (ed) *Entrepreneurship and Economic Development*, New York: Free Press, 1–40.

Kirzner, I.M. (1973) *Competition and Entrepreneurship*, Chicago: University of Chicago Press.

Knight, F.H. (1921) *Risk Uncertainty and Profit* (ed. G.J. Stigler) Chicago: University of Chicago Press.

Lall, S. and P. Streeten (1977) *Foreign Investment, Transnationals and Developing Countries*, London: Macmillan.

Leff, N.H. (1978) Industrial Organisation and Entrepreneurship in the Developing Countries: The Economic Groups, *Economic Development and Cultural Change*, 26, 661–75.

Leibenstein, H. (1978) *General X-efficiency Theory and Economic Development*, New York: Oxford University Press.

McClelland, D.C. and D.G. Winter (1969) *Motivating Economic Achievement*, New York: Free Press.

Pack, H. (1987) *Productivity, Technology and Economic Development*, New York: Oxford University Press.

Schumpeter, J.A. (1934) *The Theory of Economic Development* (trans. R. Opie) Cambridge, Mass: Harvard University Press.

Wallerstein, I. (1979) *The Capitalist World-Economy*, Cambridge: Cambridge University Press.

Wiener, M.J. (1981) *English Culture and the Decline of the Industrial Spirit*, Cambridge: Cambridge University Press.

PART TWO: New Developments

The foreign-direct-investment scene is constantly evolving. New investors emerge, and their rise poses challenges to prevailing theories of the ownership advantages of TNCs. The forms of the contractual relationship involved in the transfer of capital, technology and skills change, sometimes superficially and, at other times, in significant ways. The activities in which TNCs are predominant shift as technologies change, and technological needs force TNCs to enter into new forms of alliances with each other. This part of the readings deals with some of those new developments.

The chapter by John Dunning provides a valuable analytical framework for viewing the broad phenomenon of the rise and fall of nations as international investors. Drawing on his eclectic paradigm of international production, Dunning argues that ownership, location and internalization factors are systematically related to a country's level of development, as well as to its economic strategies, political and cultural factors. Evidence is drawn from a range of developing and developed countries to support the hypothesis of a cycle in which countries start as low recipients and exporters of capital, evolve into net recipients, then start to export their own investment and, finally, end up in some kind of balance, with thoroughly internationalized industrial structures. In the developing world, Dunning singles out the newly industrializing countries of East Asia as the only ones currently heading towards economically rational specialization in international production.

Charles Oman's analysis of "new forms" of foreign direct investment deals with a variety of contractual arrangements that have proliferated as alternatives to the classic forms of majority or wholly-owned foreign direct investments. To the extent that those new forms are genuine alternatives to classic TNC participation, they are of great interest to developing countries seeking to build up their national capabilities and indigenous enterprises. The debt crisis and its aftermath have reversed, to some extent, the swing from old to new forms, but underlying structural changes in technology, the rise of new competitors and intermediaries, and perceptions of risk, all continue to make new forms attractive in many activities. Oman's analysis is very much in line with Dunning's eclectic paradigm, and his empirical analysis of different industries and countries is instructive. His warnings on some of the risks associated with the new forms are salutary.

One "new form" of foreign direct investment that has been much mentioned in the context of the debt crisis is the swapping of debt for equity. The chapter by Bergsman and Edisis explores whether swaps represent net new capital inflows or simply the switching of the form of investment, as well as raising some other important issues in the handling of debt equity swaps. They conclude that well-designed and administered swap programmes can attract new net foreign direct investment to indebted countries, which can be direct to priority areas. Swaps can only be a partial solution to the debt problem, but they carry additional benefits: foreign direct investment brings new technology and skills, and the Latin American experience suggests that the investors drawn in by swaps are largely export-oriented.

The chapter by Louis Wells returns to the subject of Third World TNCs, a topic in which he has done much of the pioneering research. The selected article focuses on the similarities and differences between Third World and developed country TNCs, drawing on his original work which suggests that the former tend to be in low-cost manufacture of more standardized products or those in which trade name plays a lesser role. He notes, however, that Third World firms are learning to differentiate their products and to innovate. The main area in which the two kinds of TNCs compete directly is in mature technologies, but it is also in those areas that they can collaborate most fruitfully.

The Wells interpretation of the growth of Third World TNC activity has considerable weight. As noted in the general introduction earlier, however, it is based on a particular reading of how the ownership advantages of TNCs from developing countries arise. A different reading, based on the learning process undergone by enterprises in developing countries, could lead to another interpretation of the similarities and differences between developing and developed country TNCs. While the Wells thesis retains validity for a significant proportion of Third World TNCs, the alternative may provide a better explanation of the new wave of such TNCs that are concentrated in complex, high-skill industries and focused on developed country destinations.

5

The Investment Development Cycle and Third World Multinationals*

J.H. Dunning

*Source: J.H. Dunning, *Explaining International Production* (London, Unwin Hyman, 1988), pp. 140–168.

Introduction

Data now emerging on the growth and pattern of outward direct investment by several Third World countries enable us to examine more closely the relevance and validity of the eclectic paradigm of international production – and, more specifically, the investment development cycle – as an explanation of this phenomenon.[1] Although the published statistics are still too inadequate to allow any econometric testing, we have a much better appreciation of the character of Third World investment than we did when the idea of the cycle was first mooted in 1979 at a Conference of Third World multinationals held at the East–West Cultural Learning Institute in Honolulu.[2] At the same time, since that date, there have been several modifications and extensions of the theory of international production (and those of its near relation, the theory of the multinational enterprise),[3] some of which have paid particular attention both to the new international investment arena (Giddy and Young, 1983), and to new forms of international involvement (Oman, 1984).

This chapter begins with an amplification of some aspects of the Mark 2 version of the eclectic paradigm set out in Chapter 2 of this book [*Explaining International Production*; hereafter *EIP*]. It then seeks to apply the paradigm to explain not only the existing international investment position of Third World countries, but how this has evolved over the last decade or so. There is also an attempt to compare the pattern of outward direct investment of the leading capital exporters; for, as we shall describe, there are as many differences in these patterns among countries *within* the Third World as there are between developed and developing countries. Arguing that the level and pattern of international production, like trade, both influences and is influenced by country specific ESP characteristics (see Koopman and Montias, 1971, and Chapter 1 [*EIP*]), a 'stages' approach to economic development is adopted:[4] as countries pass from one stage to another not only does the role of inward and outward direct investment change, but so does the character and composition of such investment. Political factors are also seen to be crucial (Schneider and Frey, 1985).

Some Theoretical Issues

Chapter 2 [*EIP*] has explained how our current thinking on the determinants of foreign production draws upon two strands of economic theory: the theory of international resource allocation and the theory of economic organization based upon the distribution of factor endowments.[5] Between them, we believe that these theories help to explain the origin of the ownership, location and internalization (*OLI*) advantages created or expected by firms, and the strategic management of them. It is, for example, widely accepted that an MNE's choice of location for exploiting its advantages will be influenced by the distribution of immobile resources and by non-market forces which are country specific; but, in explaining the *origin* of some kinds of competitive advantages, these considerations may be no less relevant. Why do some countries innovate more than others (Ergas, 1984 [*sic*]); and why does the pattern of innovation differ between countries (Davidson, 1976)? Why do countries generate different production technologies, management capabilities and entrepreneurial initiatives? Why do the extent and form of product differentiation differ across national boundaries? Why do some countries excel at some kinds of research and development activities relative to others? For the kind of intangible assets which become the proprietary right of the firms, but which, to be produced in the first case, need a certain legal, technological and entrepreneurial environment which is country specific, then this model holds good. Within both the developed and developing worlds, the patterns of inward and outward direct investment – like those of trade – do differ between countries. So does the product composition of the world's largest companies (Dunning and Pearce, 1985). So also do the patterns of international patenting, licensing and technology transfer (Pavitt, 1987; Cantwell, 1985).

   To this extent, then, international production combines the export of intermediate products, requiring inputs in which the home country is relatively well endowed, with the use of resources in which the host country is relatively well endowed. But if this were all there was to it, we would not need a separate theory of international production: an extension of international trade theory to incorporate trade in intermediate products, allowing for the mobility of at least some resources would be sufficient. On the other hand, attempts to explain patterns and levels of international production without taking into account the distribution of country specific endowments is like throwing the baby out with the bath water.[6] Clearly, such endowments are relevant to most resource-based investment, and also (if one allows for non-market forces, e.g. import controls, taxes and subsidies, commercial policy, etc.) some export substituting investment as well. It is likely to be most relevant in explaining North–South, South–North and South–South international trade and production. We would also argue – and Chapter 7 [*EIP*] takes this point up in more detail – that, as with trade, firms will normally first engage in international production to take advantage of the differences in the international disposition of resource endowments. Hence, one would expect the early overseas ventures of developing countries to be at least partly explainable by a factor endowment type model.

The failure of the factor endowment approach to explain completely, or in some cases even partially, international production arises simply because it is predicated on the existence of perfect markets, for both final and inter-mediate goods. In neoclassical trade theory, this leads to all sorts of un-realistic assumptions, e.g. atomistic competition, equality of product functions, the absence of risk and uncertainty, and implicitly at least, that technology is a free and instantaneously transferable good between firm and countries. Since 1950, economists have been grappling to incorporate market imperfections into trade theory but, in the main, their attention has been directed to final rather than intermediate goods markets. Because of this, they have paid little attention to the organization of production and transactions across, or indeed within, national boundaries,[7] the implicit assumption being that this question is irrelevant to an understanding of the 'where' of economic activity. In situations involving some locational choice between producing intermediate products at home or overseas this is assumed to influence the export versus licensing decision of a foreign firm, rather than export versus foreign production.[8]

This peculiar lack of concern with ownership or governance questions in trade theory that has spread to some writers, notably Kojima (1978, 1982), who derive their models of direct foreign investment from neoclassical trade theory, we suggest arises because such theory – again implicitly rather than explicitly – assumes that all firms are single-activity or product firms. The effect on trade patterns of the vertical integration or horizontal diversi-fication of firms is not discussed in the literature. Since the option of internalizing domestic markets for intermediate products or buying inputs and selling outputs in the open market within a country has not interested trade economists, it is hardly surprising that they have been little concerned with issues of international production. Yet, as Casson (1987) has shown, the unique characteristic of the MNE is that it is both multi-activity and engages in the internal transfer of intermediate products across national boundaries. In other words, it produces at different points of the value-added chain and in different countries. Since firms which produce at more than one point on the chain necessarily engage in intra-firm rather than, or in addition to, inter-firm transactions, and are multi-activity, this implies the existence of some kind of market failure, in the sense that, whether within or between countries, firms are motivated to replace the market as a transaction agent. When these activities are undertaken across national boundaries, then there is international market failure. *It is the difference between domestic and international market failure that distinguishes the multinational from the uninational multi-activity firm.*[9] It is the failure of the market to organize a satisfactory deal between potential contractors and contractees of intermediate products that explains why one or the other should choose the hierarchical rather than the market route for exploiting different factor endowment situations.

Several types of market failure are identified in the literature (Casson, 1979, 1985, 1987). In an assessment of Stephen Hymer's contribution to the theory of MNE, Dunning and Rugman (1985) distinguished between structural and transactional market failure. The former, which Hymer tended to emphasize, gives rise to monopoly rents arising from an imperfect market structure among the constituent firms which, by passing the external market can be captured, and sometimes increased and captured by the internalizing firm.

The second type of market failure arises from the ability of arm's length transactions to perform efficiently. This might happen for three reasons. the first, and perhaps the most important when considering the differences between international and domestic market failure, is the additional risk and uncertainty associated with cross-border transactions. The MNE, if nothing else, engages in foreign production to counteract environment volatility (Kogut, 1983). Such risks are particularly noteworthy in raw materials and high-technology industries that typically incur high development cost; where there is a danger of disruption of supplies; where there is a likelihood of property rights being dissipated or abused by foreign licensees; and where the threat of the pre-emption of markets or sources of supplies, or an improvement in the competitive position by rival oligopolists, will encourage a follow-my-leader strategy by firms (Vernon, 1983).

The second reason for transactional market failure is that the market cannot take account of the benefits and costs associated with a particular transaction between buyers and sellers which accrue to one or another of the parties, but which are external to that transaction. Where products are normally supplied jointly with others, or are derived from a common input or set of inputs, then there may be good reason why the different stages of the value-added chain should be co-ordinated within the same firms. Cross-border transactions may give rise to additional advantages of common governance such as those which exploit the imperfections of international capital and exchange markets (Aliber, 1971) and different national fiscal policies.

The third cause of transactional market failure arises wherever the market is insufficiently large to enable firms to capture economies of size, scope and co-ordination, while facing an infinitely elastic demand curve. Such economies may be in production or in purchasing, marketing, research and development, finance, organization and so on; they are essentially those which are external to a particular activity, but internal to the total activities of a firm.

These and other market failures cause enterprises, be they uninational or multinational, to diversify their value-adding activities vertically, horizontally or laterally. They do it partly to reduce the transaction costs of using markets and to exploit the transactional benefits of hierarchies, and partly to ensure that they gain the maximum economic rent (discounted for risk) from the asset advantage they possess. Again, we repeat: the only difference between the actions of multinational and uninational firms in this respect is the added dimension of market failure when a particular transaction is concluded across the exchanges. Moreover, market failure may vary according to the attributes of the parties engaging in the exchange; here too, country-specific factors may enter the equation.[10] Returning again to our parallel between a firm engaged in international trade and another in international production, it is quite possible that while both may engage in *exactly* the same value-added activities, the former does so within a single country and exports its final product, whereas the latter undertakes at least part of its value adding activities outside its national boundaries. This it will do because of the advantages offered by a foreign, *vis-à-vis* domestic location.

Earlier, we suggested that at least some of the endogenous advantages offered by different locations are likely to be based upon the distribution of country specific variables; others, however, will have to do with market failure which, itself, may be country specific. Let us offer two examples: the first is transfer pricing and the second the diversification of the investment portfolio.

If it is in the best interest of MNEs to allocate revenues or costs arising from the activities in one country to those in another so as to reduce its global tax burden, and/or protect itself against foreign exchange *et al.* risks, then differences in corporation taxes between countries, and the risk attached to holding assets in different currencies, may occasion firms to counter such market failure[11] by under- or overpricing on intra-firm transactions, the use of leads and lags of payment and so on. Clearly the more countries in which MNEs operate, the more these country-specific market failures are likely to affect trans-border resource allocation. Second, due to country-specific risks, a firm's decision of where to engage in value added activities may well be related to the structure of its existing investment portfolio (Rugman, 1979). Given the same opportunity to make gross profits, then one MNE or group of MNEs might view the advantages of a particular location differently than another MNE or group or, for that matter, a uninational firm. Other examples of firms being influenced in their choice of location by country-specific market failure are set out by Kogut (1983).

There are other ways in which market failure might affect the activities of MNEs. So far we have asserted that firms internalize markets to reduce transaction costs, including risks. We have suggested this has a locational dimension. At the same time, the replacement of market transactions by hierarchical fiat may be undertaken to steal a march on competitors or to protect an existing market position. The intention to capitalize on the internalization of external economies by co-ordinating complementary value-added activities is one example. As a firm widens its territorial horizons, it may well be able to exploit advances in information and communication technology better than its uninational competitors. At the same time, transactional competitive advantages may be difficult, if not impossible, to buy or sell on the open market, simply because their economic rent is related to the way in which resources are allocated rather than in the possession of resources *per se*.[12]

We have suggested that the O advantages arising from the efficient co-ordination of complementary assets are likely to assume greater importance as a firm's foreign commitments increase; they are also related to the technical characteristics of the products produced, and particularly the extent to which it is profitable to engage in the specialization of economic activities along the value-added chain or between different value-added chains. The literature suggests that there are certain types of production which lend themselves to an international division of labour and others which do not (Casson *et al.*, 1985). Similarly, there are some activities which require closer locational linkages than others. Obviously, the greater the economies of scale or scope, and the less the need for activities to be spatially linked, the less concentrated, yet the more specialized, production in a particular location is likely to be.[13] This is the case, for example, in much of the North–South vertical production and some North–North horizontal production in specialized products. Usually, apart from resource-based investment and that involving high transfer (e.g. transport) costs, investment based upon this kind of ownership advantage is geared to supplying products with a high-income elasticity of demand.

So far we have not mentioned the economic environment in which international production takes place. The literature is full of illustrations of how country-specific factors influence the generation of O advantages of firms, the location in which production takes place using these advantages as inputs and the extent to which value added activities are undertaken by the same firm (Dunning, 1981b). The next section will discuss these from the perspective of Third World MNEs. We have already identified the role of resource endowments in the creation and use of the first two advantages.

As regards the third, three factors are of crucial importance: the first is the level of economic development, as typified, for example, by the educational, legal, technological and commercial infrastructure within which both foreign and domestic firms have to operate; the second is the structure of the economy, i.e. what types of economic activity are best suited to its resource patterns and size; and the third is the role of national governments in fashioning political and economic systems, attitudes, entrepreneurship and business strategy.[14]

Again, we shall confine ourselves to three illustrations. The first is the attitude of governments towards being involved in the international economy. The less restrictions are placed on trade and commerce, then *ceteris paribus*, the more firms will locate their production units according to the dictates of comparative production and transaction costs. But it is also the case that the fewer the restrictions on the movements of goods and services, the more MNEs can benefit from other forms of international market failure, e.g. those arising from economies of scale, externalities and risk. For example, as Chapter 11 will show [*EIP*], without regional economic integration in Europe, the easing of trade restrictions within Latin America and the establishment of export processing zones in several Asian countries, much rationalized and export-led manufacturing investment by MNEs would not have taken place. Neither, indeed, would a good deal of international contracting of materials and parts by multinational and other firms have been feasible.

The second illustration concerns the effect which government policy may have on the establishment of domestic linkages by foreign affiliates, and the forms of such linkages. This might be partly affected by inducements to source locally, but no less so by the ability and willingness of governments to influence the supply capabilities of its own firms: for example, by the improvement of training, technological and industrial programmes; by fiscal incentives and by encouraging the appropriate kind of market structure (UNCTC, 1981).

The third example relates to the role of government in affecting the pattern and pace of commercial innovation. Here its influence ranges from its funding and regulation of education – particularly higher educational – programmes and facilities to its subsidization of research and development, its direct intervention in many high-technology sectors (e.g. aerospace, communications and industrial electronics) and its attitudes towards co-operative agreements aimed at increasing the innovatory competitiveness of its own companies.

Let us now conclude this general review of the determinants of international production. The unique characteristic of such production is that it marries the trans-border dimension of value added activities of firms with the common governance of those activities. While the former draws upon the economics of spatial distribution of immobile resources and market structures to explain the location of production independently of its owner-ship, the market-failure theory helps explain the ownership of activity independent of its location. The blending of the two suggests that market imperfections specific to the transaction of intermediate or final goods across national boundaries, together with the desire of firms to locate the production of different stages of the value added chain in different countries, should be the core ingredients of any generalized paradigm of international production. The precise character and pattern of that pro-duction will depend on the configuration of ownership and internalization advantages of firms and the locational advantages of countries; and these, in turn, reflect not only the nature of the activities undertaken, and the countries in which they are undertaken, but also the attributes of firms themselves *vis-à-vis* their competitors which will determine their strategy in international markets.

One aspect of the eclectic paradigm which is especially interesting is how far these determinants, and the balance between the factor endowments and market failure explanations, are related to the developmental stage of a country and its strategy for development, and how these in turn influence its degree and form of international economic involvement. We have suggested – and we shall take up this point in more detail in Chapter 7 [*EIP*] – that there are parallels between the internalization of production and that of trade. At first, trade tends to occur between nations with markedly different patterns of resource endowments;[15] later, depending on the manner and the speed at which a country develops relative to others, trade is likely to be increasingly between countries with similar or converging patterns of resource endowments. In such cases, while some trade may continue to be based on factor endowment differences and/or differentiated tastes, part will require a 'market failure' type of explanation.

On the other hand, while trade (in its entirety) is always balanced (or nearly balanced), international production need not be. Indeed, such production is based on the transfer of intermediate products like tech-nology that require resources with which developed countries are compara-tively well endowed or are best exploited by large and diversified MNEs.[16] One would expect there to be more concentration among the suppliers than recipients of foreign direct investment and that MNEs would originate mainly from industrialized countries. The facts uphold both these prop-ositions.[17]

Some Data on Third World Outward Direct Investment

We now turn to consider the relevance of the investment development cycle to our understanding of outward direct investment by developing countries. First, some facts. Table 1 shows our best estimate of the stock of foreign direct investment originating from developing countries in 1983. Omitting those investments (mainly from Panama, The Netherlands Antilles and Bermuda) which are part of tax minimization or related programmes, or represent intermediate investments by MNEs (mainly from developed countries) and also those financed by oil money from the Middle East – which are more properly described as portfolio rather than direct investments – we arrive at a figure of around $15 billion. This represents a fifteen-fold increase since 1960 – a rate of increase about two and a half times that of its counterpart from the developed countries. The data were derived from a variety of sources and represent the author's best guess of the stock of foreign direct investment by selected developing countries at the end of 1982. The main sources were: for direct investment flows, *IMF Balance of Payments Yearbook* (various issues), supplemented by data on direct investment income from the same source; data supplied from government departments or agencies and the individual developing countries; and estimates by researchers working in the field, notably those contained in Lall (1983), UNCTC (1983b) and ESCAP/UNCTC (1985b). In general, the data on the leading outward investors from Latin America and Asia enable us to make a reasonable estimate of their direct investment stake; those from African countries are pitifully inadequate. We have tried to separate oil and tax haven related investments from the rest (mainly using data on inward investment published by the developed countries). We have not, however, been able to identify separately non-productive (e.g. property) investments; nor those which are genuinely from firms indigenous (cf. subsidiaries of foreign investors) to the home countries.

Although many developing countries have some direct investment in neighbouring territories, only about a dozen have so far emerged as investors of international significance. These include Singapore, Hong Kong, South Korea, Taiwan, the Philippines, India and Malaysia in Asia; Brazil, Mexico, Chile, Colombia, Venezuela in Latin America; the oil states in the Middle East and Nigeria in Africa. Officially published data on the activities of their MNEs remain limited; but several studies now being conducted by economists from developing countries are providing us with valuable new insights.[18] From these it is clear that not only is the real value of outward investment increasing, but that it is increasing faster than inward investment. Some further macro-statistical data drawn from a variety of sources are set out in Tables 2 and 3.

While it is not our purpose to describe the nature and character of the investment by Third World MNEs in detail, some features do throw interesting light on the theoretical perceptions set out previously. First, consider the geographical orientation of the investment. This seems to be of five kinds, excluding tax havens and 'convenience' or 'intermediate' investment.[19] The first, and most important, is in neighbouring and/or

Table 1 Estimates of total stock of foreign direct investment by selected developing countries, 1982 ($ million)

Asia and Pacific[1]		Africa[1]	
Hong Kong	2,500–3,000	Algeria	25–30
India	150–200	Cameroons	35–50
Indonesia	100–150	Gabon	80–100
Korea	250–300	Kenya	50–75
Malaysia	200–250	Seychelles	25–35
Papua New Guinea	20–25	Swaziland	35–40
Philippines	150–200	Senegal	8–10
Singapore	1,500–1,750	Tunisia	50–75
Taiwan	300–325	Zimbabwe	100–150
Thailand	75–100		
Unclassified	750–1,000	Unclassified	1,200–1,500[2]
Total	5,995–7,300	Total	1,608–2,065
Latin America[1]		*Middle East*[1]	
Argentina	750–1,000	Egypt	75–100
Brazil	1,250–1,500	Israel	120–150
Chile	75–100	Kuwait	200–250
Colombia	250–300	Libya	100–120
Costa Rica	20–25	Unclassified	300–500
Jamaica	400–450	Total	795–1,120
Mexico	350–400		
Venezuela	300–350	Oil investments[3]	4,000–5,000
Uruguay	50–75		
Unclassified	750–1,000	Other[4]	12,500–15,000
Total	4,195–5,205	Total	29,093–34,570

Notes:
[1] Other than oil investments.
[2] Of which direct investment in the UK in 1981 was $1 billion.
[3] Mainly from Middle East, Indonesia, Nigeria and Venezuela.
[4] Netherland Antilles, Panama, Bermuda, Liberia, E.G. tax havens and shipping investments; and mainly invested in the US.

ethnically related territories,[20] and is usually in sales and marketing, and downstream import-substituting manufacturing ventures. Between 1965 and 1978, for example, 99 per cent of Argentinian investment was in other Latin American countries; the corresponding proportions for Chile and Colombia, for approximately the same period, were 95 per cent and 52 per cent respectively. (UNCTC, 1983b). Similarly, most direct capital investments made by Asian MNEs is elsewhere in Asia. For the four Asian NICs in 1980 it was 71 per cent and for India in 1982 it was 47 per cent.

The second kind of Third World investment is that made in developed countries either to gain access to export markets or to acquire particular skills and/or technologies and sometimes to make their international presence known. It is difficult to put a value on these upstream investments but they are known to be quite important in the case of the Asian NICs (15 per cent of total foreign investment in 1980) and some Middle Eastern firms.[21]

The third kind of investment – which is mainly in the construction sector – is chiefly directed to the Middle East where, as part of a resource transferring package, the investing companies usually provide labour as well.[22] Here the best examples are Korean, Philippine and Turkish construction companies in the Middle East. A fourth type of investment, designed to obtain or protect the supply of raw materials for domestic manufacture, is by its nature, directed to the countries in which these materials are located. More often than not they are outside the region in which the home country is situated.[23] A fifth type of investment, more accurately described as 'flight capital', is usually made in adjacent territories or developed economies perceived to be politically and economically stable.[24]

The industrial composition of Third World MNE activity is mixed; at the same time, it strongly reflects the country-specific characteristics (including stage of development) of home and recipient countries. Here, there is evidence both to support the contention of Wells (1983) that the *O* advantages of Third World MNEs tend to be in sectors using mature or standardized technology and management skills – and most of this investment is of a South–South variety[25] – and also that of Lall (1983), who points to some foreign activity by Hong Kong, Singaporean, Taiwan and Korean MNEs being fairly sophisticated and in advanced technological sectors, e.g. pharmaceuticals and electronics. In both cases – but especially the latter – investment by local firms tends to follow investment in the same sectors by foreign firms. This then becomes disseminated, adapted and scaled down, and either the subsidiaries or their local competitors re-export intermediate products via foreign direct investment.[26] Indeed, the majority of both Hong Kong and Singaporean outward investment is by expatriate firms (Lall, 1983). In this way, there is a kind of entrepôt trade in intermediate products.[27]

At the same time, there is another type of investment arising from the possession of *O* advantages that are entirely indigenously generated. These are usually based on natural resources and include Indian shrimp canners, Argentinian meat packing firms, Hong Kong and Thai textile manufacturers, Philippine timber companies, Malaysian rubber companies, Brazilian coffee processing firms, Taiwanese pulp and paper producers and so on; but occasionally, they relate to the development of specialized and, usually, individualistic skills and technologies in manufacturing. By contrast, Third World MNEs do not normally expect to generate the brand-name and trade-mark loyalties associated with MNEs supplying consumer goods from the wealthier nations.[28] These investments are sometimes

Table 2 Outward direct investment by selected developing countries, 1970–85 (millions of SDRs)

	1970	1971	1972	1973	1974	1975	1976	1977	1978	1979	1980	1981	1982	1983	1984	1985
Africa																
Cameroons	na	na	na	3	neg	2	7	4	5	-2	-6	neg	4	5	10	na
Gabon	na	na	na	na	na	6	33	17	neg	5	6	6	4	5	3	na
Kenya	na	na	na	na	na	1	4	2	2	5	1	2	3	4	3	10
Senegal	neg	neg	2	neg	3	-6	neg	2	na	na	na	na	na	na	na	na
Seychelles	na	na	na	na	na	na	na	2	2	2	3	6	4	3	4	na
Zimbabwe	na	na	na	na	na	na	na	7	3	6	17	4	14	6	10	na
Asia and Pacific																
China, People's Rep. of	na	na	na	na	na	na	na	na	na	na	na	na	40	87	131	619
Korea, Rep. of	35	na	26	61	-75	3	5	18	22	15	10	36	133	118	36	33
Papua New Guinea	na	na	na	na	na	na	na	2	4	3	12	1	2	1	2	na
Philippines	4	5	8	1	neg	1	5	15	24	97	170	60	160	134	na	na
Singapore	na	na	na	na	na	na	na	na	na	125	70	26	193	47	86	75
Taiwan	1	1	4	3	7	2	4	14	5	9	42	11	12	11	na	na
Thailand	na	na	na	na	na	na	na	na	5	3	2	2	2	1	1	1
Latin America																
Argentina	na	na	na	na	na	na	na	-1	-19	-45	-85	-91	-26	2	na	na
Brazil	14	1	25	31	49	92	158	125	100	151	284	177	336	171	42	78
Chile	na	na	na	na	na	na	na	4	3	9	33	18	15	37	11	2
Colombia	4	3	1	1	5	4	10	18	38	23	109	53	29	105	20	na
Costa Rica	na	na	na	na	na	na	na	na	1	1	3	3	2	5	4	5
Venezuela	na	na	na	na	na	na	22	96	na	na	na	na	4	na	6	na
Middle East																
Algeria	2	1	2	1	neg	28	3	5	na	12	26	12	10	14	14	2
Egypt	na	na	na	na	na	na	na	6	16	4	5	5	8	18	16	na
Israel	1	4	4	na	na	na	6	5	5	1	na	76	38	106	22	57
Kuwait	na	na	na	na	na	na	95	45	76	-146	313	-128	98	225	92	56
Libya	neg	2	1	1	1	1	1	1	na	16	36	21	17	na	na	na

Table 3 Changing intensity of outward flows of foreign direct investment from selected Asian and Latin American countries, 1967–83

| | Asian countries[1] | | |
| | Average annual flow ($ millions) | | Relative intensity: |
Time	Outward (a)	Inward (b)	(a/b) (%)
1967–9	21.2	207.3	10.2
1970–2	64.3	596.5	13.0
1973–5	118.5	893.6	13.3
1976–8	197.8	984.9	20.1
1979–80	272.3	726.4	37.5
	Latin American countries[2]		
	Average annual flow ($ millions)		Relative intensity:
Time	Outward (a)	Inward (b)	(a/b) (%)
1967–9	0.8	103.5	0.8
1970–2	6.4	225.0	2.9
1973–5	30.3	569.8	5.3
1976–8	73.5	778.5	9.4
1979–80	134.3	889.8	15.1
1981–3	142.2	1,194.5	11.9

Notes:
[1] These include Korea, Singapore, Malaysia, India, Philippines, Hong Kong and Taiwan.
[2] These include Brazil and Colombia.

Source: United Nations Centre on Transnational Corporations, New York (various reports on Foreign Direct Investment); *IMF Balance of Payments Yearbook.*

preceded by, or associated with, those to promote exports; their role is not so much to add value in the host country as to protect and expand production capacity in the home country. Finally there is investment, mainly undertaken by State owned MNEs, to secure raw materials abroad. These include the large Latin American state oil companies, the Korean publicly owned Pohang Iron and Steel Company and India's Hydrocarbons India Private Ltd., a subsidiary of the State Oil and Natural Gas Commission.

Third, it would seem that, apart from the enterprises just identified, and a few service sector MNEs in the construction, banking and hotel industries, most foreign firms from the Third World are fairly small in size, and their investments are confined to a limited number of foreign countries. Occasionally, home governments assist these operations by loans or tax incentives. Many prefer to be involved in joint ventures,[29] both to limit their capital commitments and to obtain know-how, managerial and organizational skills or access to markets of their foreign partner(s). Most too are greenfield investments, except those from the wealthier Middle Eastern and Asian countries whose main objective is to buy into sectors which might earn a good rate of return (e.g. hotels) and/or provide some of the know-how for their domestic operations (e.g. petrochemicals and electronics engineering). Few, it appears, have been prompted abroad to diversify their risks (Shieve and Hsueh), but some have sought to protect themselves against an uncertain political future in their home economies as, for example, in the case of Hong Kong, Argentina and Taiwan.

The Investment Development Cycle Revisited

A basic proposition of the investment development cycle is that as countries develop, their international direct investment position moves through a variety of stages. The speed and direction of this movement will depend on the structure of their indigenous resource endowments – including cultural endowments; their interactions with the rest of the world economy – e.g. their trading position, the extent of their ethnic communities abroad, etc.; the size of the local market; their political and economic systems; the extent and form of government intervention or influence; and the nature of the markets for the kind of transactions their own companies wish to engage in with foreign entities.[30] Given these and the management strategies of both foreign and home country firms, countries will pass through four, and possibly five,[31] stages.

At very low levels of income (i.e. gross national product (GNP) per head), countries attract little or no inward direct investment as neither domestic markets nor resources offer opportunities for corporate profits; neither do indigenous firms possess the necessary competitive advantages for outward investment. As income and domestic demand rise, and local resource capabilities improve through education and training and by provision of more infrastructure, inward investment may become commercially viable. Depending on the value of the contextual variables mentioned above, inward investment will be largely confined to import substitution or resource-based activities; some vertically integrated manufacturing investment might take place in industrialized economies with cheap but well-motivated labour. As in stage one, there is unlikely to be much outward investment since indigenous enterprises will not have generated sufficient O advantages of their own to overcome the initial barriers to foreign production. However, it is possible there may be a limited amount of MNE activity, particularly that geared to (1) the exploitation of resource endowments in neighbouring territories, (2) based on an adaptation of the O advantages of subsidiaries of foreign MNEs, and (3) that designed to buy an entry into a foreign market, for example, preparatory to manufacturing investment or to acquire technology and/or managerial resources.

The third stage is the most interesting one, and the one through which most developing countries considered in this chapter are now passing. During this stage one of two things is likely to happen, depending on whether the government chooses to participate in the international specialization of trade and production, or pursue a strategy of economic sufficiency. If the latter, then indigenous firms will tend to take over from foreign affiliates, as the latter's tutorial role is completed (Kojima, 1978), though there may remain some inward investment based on O advantages which their owners cannot or are unwilling to transfer through the market. Outward investment is likely to remain insignificant as governments prefer their own firms to produce at home; however, where the domestic economic or political environment is unfavourable, firms might still seek opportunities abroad. The recent spate of outward investment by Indian firms is an example of this.

At the other extreme, as illustrated by the city-state economies like Hong Kong and Singapore, a strategy of export-led growth tends to make for international specialization, which may spill over from trade to production, whenever it creates country-specific O advantages in innovatory activities. The other side of such a strategy is that it usually welcomes inward direct investment, in as much as it helps make better use of indigenous resources, in which the country has (or is likely to have) a comparative advantage. Inward investment then complements the L advantages offered by the immobile resources of the recipient country, while outward investment compensates for the location disadvantages of the home country. The net result is (or should be) a more wealth creating economic structure through international specialization.

During this third stage of the development cycle, inward investment is likely to change in character as it starts to become more influenced by the global goals of the MNEs and the likely gains of co-ordinated production. *Inter alia*, this will result in a growing propensity of MNEs to engage in intra-firm transactions, to centralize sourcing and marketing and financial decisions and to prefer a full ownership of their subsidiaries.

As and when countries develop, and depending on the nature of their resource endowments, they may eventually reach the fourth stage, at which point they become net outward investors. This may occur because the real costs of indigenous immobile resources become less favourable than those offered by other countries and/or because their comparative advantages become increasingly concentrated in the production of intermediate products such as management and organizational skills, advanced technology, information, etc., which are easily transferable abroad. The United Kingdom and the United States typified this stage in the 1950s and 1960s, and Japan, West Germany and Sweden are in it today. Because of the convergence of income levels and resource structures between the most advanced industrialized economies in the 1970s and early 1980s, the number of net outward investors increased from seven in the 1969–75 period to twelve in 1975–83.

Clearly not all countries can be in stage four of the investment development cycle at the same time, as the stock of world-wide outward direct investment must equal that of inward direct investment. This requires one or two possible modifications to the cycle as a predictive concept. One is to look at economic development in relative terms, postulating, for example, that countries whose GNP per capita is above average and increasing the most rapidly are those most likely to be improving their net outward investment position. The second is to introduce a fifth stage of the development cycle which suggests a reconvergence of outward and inward investment flows, due to the growth of intra-industry rationalized direct investment, which, itself, is based not primarily on factor endowments but on the advantages of co-ordinating international production and internalizing cross-border markets.

As regards the former, there is some evidence to suggest that those advanced countries that have most improved their economic performance, and particularly their technological competitiveness in recent years, are also those which have most strengthened their net outward investment position. The rise of both Japan and West Germany as outward investors and the resurgence of inward investment in the United States are cases in point.[32] But unfortunately, it is not as simple as that. Some countries have increased their outward direct investment because their locational advantages are declining. A lot of activity by Swedish, British and Canadian MNEs has been of this kind and, in the developing world, by Indian MNEs as well. In such cases increased outward investments reflect high real domestic costs (or lack of economic dynamism) rather than improved O advantages of MNE firms from those countries. What is most likely is that countries go through cycles of changing L and O advantages and that,[33] according to their capacity to innovate and/or the value of their real exchange rate,[34] their net outward direct investment position is likely to fluctuate relative to their major competitors.

It might further be postulated that as the economic characteristics of industrialized economies converge, so will their international investment positions. In such a situation one would expect there to be a good deal of cross-hauling of production in similar industries, and particularly in those dominated by MNEs, pursuing global or regionally integrated strategies. One would also expect MNE activity to be increasingly motivated by market-failure-considerations, especially those designed to protect market share positions among international oligopolists (Vernon, 1983) and which tend to be firm or industry rather than country specific in kind.

Some Earlier Findings

Let us now look further into the investment patterns of LDCs in order to examine the hypothesis suggested in the previous paragraph. The gist of our argument is contained in three sets of hypotheses:

(1) As a country develops, its international investment position changes from it being solely an importer of direct investment capital to it becoming an exporter, and eventually, depending on the conditions set out in (2), a net exporter of capital.
(2) The nature of the relationship between the development of a country (as measured in terms of output per head) and its outward direct investment will critically depend on (a) the amount, quality and composition of its factor endowments, (b) its political and economic system and, in particular, the role non-market forces play in influencing resource allocation and (c) the extent and form of its economic, political and cultural interface with other countries.
(3) The sectoral distribution of outward investment will also vary according to the factors identified in (2).

To examine these propositions, we earlier classified countries into eight groups according to their income levels. Our main empirical findings were as follows:

(a) Gross outward investment was strongly associated with the stock of human capital and research and development expenditure, with any substantial amounts of outward investment being restricted to countries whose most educated and trained workers account for 10 per cent or more of the population and whose R&D expenditure as a per cent of gross national output is normally 1.6 or above.[35]
(b) There is some suggestion that outward investment per capita is greater in industrialized than resource rich countries, but apart from this, in the lower income countries, the possession of natural resources is positively associated with outward investment.
(c) It seems that there is a generally positive association between average earnings and outward direct investment; but a generally negative association between growth in industrial output and such flows, at least for the most developed countries. For most of the other locational variables, the association is in the reverse direction to what one might expect, but we believe this primarily reflects their 'pull' on inward investment rather than their 'push' to outward investment.[36]
(d) There is some reason to suppose that above average outward investment is associated with the degree of international market failure, but the relationship is not a significant one.
(e) There is no clear association between population size and the

propensity to engage in outward investment: looking at individual data, of the 12 countries with an average outward investment of more than $10 per capita, five had populations of more than 50 million and five of less than 22 million.

Later data for the years 1979–83 confirm these statements, but within this period, rather more definite trends have emerged which enable us to be a little more specific in identifying the extent and pattern of the outward direct investment by developing countries. We are also in a slightly better position to study the relationship between the propensity of countries to invest abroad and the value of certain explanatory variables over time. The following paragraphs first examine the statistical relationships between the foreign direct capital state of 25 developing countries in 1982 and a group of explanatory variables, most of which were used in our previous study (Dunning, 1981 [*sic*], p. 124 ff.). Second, with respect to time-series data (which are very fragmentary), we concentrate on just four of the leading outward developing country investors, which regularly supply data to the IMF; and see how their investment positions have changed over the last two decades or so. We also examine some of the differences in the extent and form of investment between the countries. The countries chosen are Brazil, Colombia, South Korea and the Philippines.

The Statistical Results

Cross-sectional Data

Table 4 sets out some details of the outward direct investment position of some 25 developing countries at the end of 1982. First taking a cross-sectional approach, the data strongly suggests a positive association between both outward direct investment and GNP per capita; and also between the former and certain structural variables – notably educational provision at a secondary and tertiary level, the structure of employment, urbanization and trade intensity.

In subjecting these data to more rigorous statistical testing, we first calculated a series of linear bivariate and multiple regression equations. A selection of these, set out in Table 5, reveal that only the extent to which a country engages in international trade (INT) is consistently and significantly related to outward direct investment; indeed several variables, including GNP per head, appear to be negatively correlated with outward investment (see, for example, Equation 2.6). Trade intensity also explained by far the greater proportion of variations in outward investment, as demonstrated, for example, by the very high R^2 in Equation 2.1.

We next expressed the *dependent* variable in logarithmic form. Here the hypothesis is that there is some reason to suppose that the outward invest-

Table 4 Some economic characteristics of developing countries which are outward direct investors

Foreign direct capital stake in 1982	GNP per capita (1982) (GNP)	Per cent educated pop. (1981) (EDUC)	Per cent emp. in ind. & services (1980) (INDSE)	Trade intensity (1982) (INT)	Urbaniz- ation index (1982) (UR)
1 Over $30 per capita (Singapore, Hong Kong, Kuwait, Libya, Israel)	275.3	39.2	93.4	81.1	86.0
2 $10–29 per capita (Argentina, Taiwan, Malaysia, Brazil, Colombia)	17.5	31.6	70.2	22.4	65.4
3 $5–9 per capita (Costa Rica, Algeria, Chile, Korea, Papua New Guinea)	8.8	30.3	62.2	30.0	49.6
4 $2–4 per capita (Philippines, Kenya, Cameroons, Egypt)	2.6	24.6	35.8	19.5	33.8
5 Under $2 per capita (Thailand, Senegal, Tunisia, Togo, Indonesia, India)	1.1	16.9	34.3	32.5	28.7

Note: Column 2: Per cent educated population = number enrolled in secondary school as per cent of age group + number enrolled in higher education as per cent of population 20–24 divided by 2. — Column 3: Per cent of labour force employed in industry and services (i.e. non-agricultural activities). — Column 4: Value of exports plus imports of goods, divided by 2 as per cent of GNP. — Column 5: Urban population as per cent of total population. For further details see The World Bank [1984, p. 282].

ment stake might increase at a faster rate as a country moved to its more advanced stages of development. In fact as Table 6 shows, the significance of the explanatory variables changes quite significantly. All the independent variables now become positively related to outward direct investment, with trade intensity, industrial structure (INDSE), the extent of urbanization (UR), each being statistically significant in, at least, some equations. Again however, trade intensity (INT) is consistently the most significant explanatory variable.

Converting both dependent and independent variables to logarithmic form affects the results even more dramatically. Now, GNP per head

Table 5 Linear regression equations between outward direct investment stake and selected economic variables (all variables expressed in non-log form)

Equation	Constant	GNP	EDUC	INDSE	INT	UR	R^2	DW	N
2.1	−96.5	–	–	–	2.17 (9.64)[2]	–	0.80	1.38	23
2.2	−144	–	–	–	1.95 (8.39)[2]	1.20 (2.12)[1]	0.84	1.52	22
2.3	−156	−0.00589 (−1.40)	–	–	2.03 (8.66)[2]	1.63 (2.58)[1]	0.85	1.78	21
2.4	−146	−0.00550 (−1.17)	−1.04 (−0.57)	1.74 (1.67)	2.05 (8.01)[2]	–	0.83	1.60	20
2.5	−150	−0.00552 (−1.25)	–	−0.45 (−0.36)	2.03 (8.48)[2]	2.00 (1.64)	0.85	1.80	20
2.6	−144	−0.00583 (−1.29)	−0.97 (−0.55)	−0.03 (−0.02)	2.01 (8.10)[2]	1.99 (1.60)	0.85	1.68	19

Notes: For details of variables and sources of data in Tables 5 to 7, see Table 4.
[1]Significant at the 5 per cent level.
[2]Significant at the 1 per cent level.

becomes consistently the most significant explanatory variable (*inter alia* this reflects the huge dispersion of outward investments per capita from $350 in the case of Singapore to $0.4 in the case of India),[37] while all other variables apart from our measure of human capital, that is, educational intensity (EDUC), are significant in at least some equations. Of these other variables, trade intensity is the most consistently significant, but even its effects are swamped by the GNP variable. As Table 7 indicates, a bivariate linear regression between GNP per head and outward direct investment per head gives an R^2 of 0.75.

It should be noted that several of the explanatory variables (e.g. educational intensity, urbanization and GNP per head) are strongly correlated with each other; and indeed are often used as proxies for economic development. This, however, is not the case with two other variables viz. economic structure and trade intensity, which are the least correlated with each other and the other independent variables.

An econometric exercise on these data suggests the most significant of the five variables considered are GNP per capita and the urbanization index. More fragmentary evidence from other developing countries points to the same conclusions. Exceptions include some countries undergoing difficult economic conditions, for example Argentina, while in India, as we have suggested, constraints on domestic economic expansion have driven Indian firms abroad. But overall, the degree and pattern of industrialization and the development strategy pursued by host governments are among the more important structural variables influencing Third World MNE activities.[38]

Table 6 Semi-log regression equations between outward direct investment stake and selected economic variables (dependent variable expressed in log form; independent variable in non-log form)

Equation	Constant	GNP	EDUC	INDSE	INT	UR	R^2	DW	N
3.1	−0.531	–	–	0.0244 $(6.48)^2$	–	–	0.65	1.72	23
3.2	−0.399	0.00005 (1.65)	–	0.0197 $(4.30)^2$	–	–	0.69	1.86	22
3.3	−0.587	–	–	0.0187 $(5.84)^2$	0.00539 $(4.12)^2$	–	0.80	1.57	22
3.4	−0.508	0.00003 (1.17)	–	0.0164 $(4.40)^2$	0.00303 $(3.78)^2$	–	0.81	1.67	21
3.5	−0.378	0.00004 (1.45)	–	0.00491 $(3.64)^2$	–	0.0158 $(4.35)^2$	0.81	2.04	21
3.6	−0.328	0.00006 $(2.33)^1$	0.0217 $(2.84)^2$	–	0.00620 $(4.06)^2$	–	0.74	2.03	21
3.7	−0.517	0.00003 (1.15)	0.00153 (0.16)	0.0158 $(2.80)^1$	0.00507 $(3.66)^2$	–	0.81	1.70	20
3.8	−0.576	–	0.00047 (0.05)	0.0108 (1.35)	0.00520 $(3.82)^2$	0.00864 (1.24)	0.81	1.68	20
3.9	−0.510	0.00003 (1.11)	0.00183 (0.19)	0.00840 (1.01)	0.00490 $(3.55)^2$	0.00829 (1.20)	0.83	1.84	19

Time Series Data

The time series data, based on investment flows and set out in Table 8, are more inconclusive. Partly this is because investment flows are likely to be 'lumpier' than the other data. Moreover, one would expect considerable lags between, for example, an improvement in education and/or R&D and outward investment. Finally, not all the data are published annually. While there is some suggestion that the propensity to engage in outward direct investment goes hand in hand with a more educated population, and with more trade it would be difficult to read much into the data.

Implications for Understanding Third World MNEs

What are the implications of these data for our understanding of the recent emergence of Third World MNEs? Basically, they suggest that as far as their propensity to be outward direct investors is concerned, developing countries (about which there are data available) may be classified into three main groups. Group 1 consists of the wealthier and city-state economies of Hong Kong and Singapore.[39] These are typified by (1) the small size of their domestic market, (2) their adherence to a market-oriented system, within the framework of a well-defined industrial economic and technological

Table 7 Log-linear regression equations between outward direct investment stake and selected economic variables (all variables expressed in log form)

Equation	Constant	GNP	EDUC	INDSE	INT	UR	R^2	DW	N
4.1	−4.02	1.54 $(8.26)^2$	−	−	−	−	0.75	1.86	23
4.2	−4.41	1.35 $(6.72)^2$	−	−	0.573 (1.97)	−	0.79	1.45	22
4.3	−4.63	1.01 $(2.91)^2$	−	−	0.702 $(2.29)^1$	0.671 (1.22)	0.80	1.65	21
4.4	−4.50	−	0.253 (0.48)	−	1.18 $(3.91)^1$	1.81 $(3.57)^2$	0.72	1.73	21
4.5	−4.35	−	0.135 (0.17)	2.05 $(2.53)^1$	1.11 $(3.23)^1$	−	0.66	1.35	21
4.6	−4.62	1.01 $(2.75)^1$	−0.044 (−0.06)	0.702 $(2.24)^1$	−	0.60 (0.98)	0.80	1.66	21
4.7	−4.57	1.18 $(3.54)^2$	0.056 (0.09)	0.319 (0.39)	0.60 (2.00)	−	0.79	1.50	20
4.8	−4.55	−	0.072 (0.10)	0.39 (0.37)	1.16 $(3.64)^2$	1.62 $(2.18)^1$	0.72	1.61	20
4.9	−4.63	1.01 $(2.69)^1$	0.119 (0.19)	−0.162 (−0.17)	0.7 $(2.19)^1$	0.712 (0.97)	0.80	1.72	19

strategy, (3) their highly skewed economic structure toward manufacturing and service industries, (4) their almost complete urbanization, (5) their full participation in the international division of labour, (6) the high proportion of their younger people engaged in secondary or tertiary education, (7) a consistent policy of export led growth and (8) a generally sympathetic ethos towards both inward and outward direct investment. These economies moved fairly quickly from stage one to three of the investment development cycle within a period of about 20 years, and in 1985, are both the wealthiest of the newly industrializing countries (NICs) and those which have the highest *per capita* outward capital stock.

Group 2 economies comprise those which, in the 1960s, were moving from the first to the second stage of their economic development via a policy of indigenization. During this period, inward investment was confined to manufacturing and service activities which assisted this objective; and, in general, joint ventures were preferred to 100 per cent foreign ownership. The affiliates were closely monitored and expected to adhere to fairly rigidly defined performance requirements, e.g. with respect to technology transfer, employment of local personnel, capital financing, procurement policies, reinvestment of earnings, etc. As the economies moved from this phase to one in which development was more closely linked with establishing a particular stance in the world economy, their attitudes towards inward investment shifted; while the *O* advantages of domestic firms

Table 8 Outward direct investment per capita for selected developing countries and selected economic variables 1960–82

| | No. in secondary and higher education as a %ᵃ of age group[1] | | | | | | | | Percentage of labour force in industry and services | | | | GNP per head ($US) | | | | Trade as % of GNP[2] | | | | R & D % of GNP | | | | Outward direct investment per capita | | | |
| | Secondary | | | | Higher | | | | | | | | | | | | | | | | | | | | | | | |
	B	C	K	P	B	C	K	P	B	C	K	P	B	C	K	P	B	C	K	P	B	C	K	P	B	C	K	P
1960	11	12	27	26	2	2	5	13	48	49	38	39	270	258	153	250	5.8	11.5	4.9	9.8	–	–	–	–	neg	neg	neg	neg
1965	16	17	35	41	2	3	6	19	51	55	42	43	286	317	107	188	4.7	8.1	10.5	13.3	–	–	–	0.17	neg	neg	neg	neg
1970	–	–	–	–	–	–	–	–	54	62	49	47	540	340	270	230	6.1	11.5	16.9	16.9	–	–	0.39	–	0.1	0.2	1.0	1.0
1975	18	36	59	56	10	7	10	20	70	74	51	–	1,029	578	563	377	8.9	11.6	33.0	18.8	–	–	–	0.15	0.8	1.7	0.8	0.2
1980	–	–	–	64	–	–	–	–	–	–	–	54	2,050	1,180	1,520	690	9.5	14.2	19.3	19.3	–	–	–	–	2.4	3.1	0.3	3.5
1982	32	46	89	64	12	12	24	27	–	–	–	–	2,240	1,460	1,910	820	7.8	12.3	38.7	16.6	–	–	–	–	2.6	1.0	3.4	3.2

Notes:
[1] 20–24 age group in case of higher education.
[2] GDP in 1960.

B = Brazil, C = Colombia, K = South Korea, P = Philippines.

Source: *World Development Report* (various issues); *IMF Balance of Payments Yearbook* (various issues). *OECD Geographical Distribution of Financial Flows to Developing Countries* (various issues).

started to be exploited in overseas markets. In this stage, the emphasis of government policy switched towards export-promoting activities, including the encouragement of rationalized export processing activities by subsidiaries of foreign MNEs. At the same time, the required upgrading of the foreign technological, managerial and organizational expertise made the supplying firms less willing to risk dissipation or infringement of property rights through joint ventures or contractual relationships.

Countries in Group 2 include Korea and Taiwan, which have moved fastest towards an economic system practised by Group 1 countries; and Brazil, Malaysia, the Philippines and Thailand, which are both (1) more diversified in their economic structure and (2) whose political preferences remains the indigenization (or nationalization) of their industries. Each of these countries has a reasonably large domestic market; and foreign affiliates perform a dual role, in supplying both this and the export market. Outside the developing countries, Portugal is also moving swiftly from stage two to stage three of its development cycle (Simoes, 1985). In all these economies, the structure of inward investment has changed from being directed towards basic and/or resource-based manufacturing activities (e.g. cement, iron and steel, textiles, lumber, heavy chemicals) to favouring the more technologically and labour-intensive sectors (e.g. electronics, consumer chemicals, plastics, motor vehicles, and services e.g. construction, insurance, banking and so on).[40]

Group 3 countries continue to pursue import substitution policies with the government playing a key role in influencing the level and pattern of economic activity. India and Kenya are cases in point, although until recently Mexico and Argentina were also members of this group. Usually the political emphasis is strongly oriented towards promoting economic self-reliance, with foreign direct investment tolerated only so far as it provides new resources or helps to upgrade existing resources, and plays a tutorial role to accomplish this objective. Rationalized investment is not generally welcomed as this usually involves some surrendering of decision taking over resource allocation to the parent company. Neither is 100 per cent ownership normally permitted; to this extent then these countries remain in stage two of the development process – with their stage three being a gradual indigenization of economic activity. Yet, rather paradoxically, if these constraints are coupled with an uncongenial local investment climate, outward investment may exceed inward investment and these countries take on the guise of their stage four equivalents.

The great majority of developing countries remain in stage one or at the beginning of stage two of their investment development cycles. As far as one can tell, most seem likely to develop on the lines of the Group 2 countries, though some (e.g. Nigeria) may veer towards Group 3, and others (e.g. Thailand and Indonesia) veer towards Group 1. Some, like Chile and some African and Middle Eastern countries may fluctuate violently according to the economic strategies and policies of the government in office.[41]

Though none of the developing countries has reached the stage of being a net exporter of direct investment capital, both Hong Kong and Singapore are already demonstrating some of the characteristics of economies which both embrace and emanate a strategy of international corporate integration. But, as with MNEs from other groups, their own MNEs rarely possess ownership advantages arising from their ability to co-ordinate home and foreign activities and minimize the volatility of international environmental risk. Instead their competitive strengths derive from the possession of intangible assets or a set of assets, the origin of which reflects the structure of their resource endowments (and sometimes that which they are able to acquire from foreign affiliates in their midst). Of Group 2 economies, Korea and Taiwan are moving along this route, but, for the rest, it is premature to forecast the likely structure of their eventual international economic involvement.

In Table 9 a summary is set out of the relationship between the development stages of the countries considered in this paper, and the likely changes in configuration of the *OLI* advantages facing their own firms as they seek to engage in outward direct investment.

Conclusions

Let us summarize now the main findings of this chapter. All developing countries now emerging as outward investors are able to do so firstly because their firms – private or state-owned – are now generating *O* advantages which are, in part or in whole, country specific in origin. Second, for one reason or another, it is in the best interests of these firms to employ these assets together with other (and usually immobile) resources in another rather than in their home country. Third, to appropriate the maximum economic rent from these assets (discounted for risk) it pays such firms to internalize their use rather than license the right to do so by foreign firms.

The nature of the *OLI* configuration will vary both over time and between developing countries at a given moment of time. We have suggested that all countries – irrespective of their economic structure, and of the strategy and policies of governments towards development – tend to pass through various stages of development. The speed and direction of the development process will depend *inter alia* on the political objectives of governments, and in particular on how they see their role in the international economy, and the risks – as perceived by domestic and foreign firms – attendant on these objectives. But, except in countries pursuing a policy of self-reliance, one would expect the significance of international

Table 9 Relationship between OLI advantages of investing country firms and development stages

	Least developed →	→	→ Most developed
O	Transferable asset advantages, based on country-specific factor endowments: mainly capital, labour, natural resources, and individual entrepreneurship; ability to adapt (recycle) imported skills and technology.	Upgrading of factor country-specific endowments via education and training, capital accumulation, technology; asset advantages switch from labour/resource intensive industries to more human capital and technology or resource intensive industries. Less emphasis on import-substitution development strategy.	Sophisticated innovations, advanced technology; factor endowments advantage in technology intensive sectors.
	Transaction cost advantages	Firms become larger and multi-activity: economies of common governance, e.g. joint overheads, economies of scope begin to show themselves.	Associated with diversification, spreading of risks and oligopolistic behaviour; MNE galaxies/conglomerates. Gains through vertical/horizontal integration; scale economies.
L	Obstacles to exports: transport costs, import controls, tariffs. Adaptation of product to local customer needs. Uncertain or unfavourable domestic political climate, economic environment inhibiting to entrepreneurship and growth.	Increasing importance of difference in production *et al.* Costs as foreign markets expand.	To escape from locational disadvantages of home country, e.g. real costs of immobile resources.
	Better infrastructure and productivity of labour force of host countries; incentives to local production.	To maintain or advance international competitive position to forestall market entry.	As part of regional or global strategy. To reduce global tax burden: foreign exchange risk: to exploit country-specific differences in market failure and/or factor cost differences.
I	Imperfect markets: (i) to acquire needed resources e.g. technology (ii) for sale and protection of property internalization of markets necessary to appropriate economic rent fully.	Need to safeguard supplies of essential inputs; protect quality control of intermediate products.	Market for advanced/idiosyncratic technology likely to become more imperfect.
		To exploit transaction cost advantages identified above; economies of scale and scope.	Internalization of external economies to single activities; risk aversion becoming more important.
	Stage 1 and 2	Y per capita →	4 and 5

trade and investment to be positively related to growth, and for there to be some acknowledgement of the benefits of international specialization. Such specialization immediately enlarges the opportunity for trade and international production based upon the creation and exploitation of O-specific advantages.

At any given moment of time, countries are at different stages of the development cycle. What state they are in, relative to their income levels, will depend on the relationship between the OLI configuration perceived by MNEs (or potential MNEs) and the economic, social and political (ESP) configuration of the country in question. Again we have suggested, here and elsewhere, the factors influencing the international investment position of countries as they pass through different stages in their development.

The main difference between the operations of Third World MNEs and those from the developed countries lies in the nature and extent of their O and I advantages and in the role played by governments in affecting the strategy of development. In the developed world, the theory of market failure (based on transaction-cost minimization) is becoming increasingly relevant in explaining the level and structure of O advantages of MNEs, and also the location of their use. But for the vast majority of Third World MNEs, these advantages stem from the possession of specific (and usually intangible) assets; and, here, we believe that the theory of factor endowments offers a cogent explanation of both the origin and the geography of their use. The theory of market failure is relevant in suggesting the appropriate form of organization for exploiting these advantages at home or abroad. If there is, then, to be a distinctive appreciation of and understanding of Third World MNEs, it must surely be based on the difference in emphasis accorded to the role of factor endowments and that of market failure in explaining their activities.

Notes

1. As set out in Chapters 1 and 2 of this volume [*EIP*].
2. The proceedings of this Conference were published in Kumar and McLeod (1981). Later monographs on Third World multinationals include those of Lall (1983) and Wells (1983).
3. Note that the former theory addresses itself to the question of why part of the production of all firms of a particular nationality should be produced outside their national boundaries, and draws heavily on the tradition of trade and industrial organization theory. The emphasis of the latter is more micro-oriented and is a natural extension of the theory of the uninational firm. Put in a slightly different way, while the theory of international production is interested in the determinants of which activities are undertaken in different countries under the common governance of MNEs, that of the MNE is mainly concerned with the ownership and location of a particular activity or set of activities. See also Chapter 1 of this volume [*EIP*].

4. As it also was used *inter alia* by Ranis (1976), Chenery (1979), Balassa, (1979) and Stoever (1984).

5. Notably of the Hecksher/Samuelson/Ohlin (HSO) kind; but modified to take account of the role of government (see Chapter 1 [*EIP*]).

6. Again, it is important to identify the exact question one is trying to answer and from which perspective. For example, as far as we are aware, no one has suggested a modification of the theory of the firm to take account of its exporting activities, yet a separate theory of international trade has emerged in the literature mainly because of the assumption that factor endowments are immobile across national boundaries. Similarly it may be argued that the need for a separate explanation of international (cf. domestic production) must rest primarily on the assumption that at least *some* factor endowments are both immobile and unevenly distributed between countries.

7. Exceptions include Gray (1982), Ethier (1986), Helpman (1984) and Markusen (1984).

8. Or that the two forms of foreign involvement are indistinguishable from each other.

9. Without such a difference, then market failure may play a minor role in explaining *foreign* direct investment; indeed the choice between domestic and foreign investment might be determined entirely by locational advantages.

10. As analysed in Chapter 6 [*EIP*].

11. In this case arising partly, at least, from government fiat or intervention.

12. Except in so far as co-ordination and entrepreneurship related to co-ordination can be thought of as a resource.

13. In Michael Porter's language, co-ordinating advantages are high, but the configuration of locational needs suggests a decentralization rather than a centralization of economic activity (Porter, 1986).

14. Again we make reference to the ESP (environment, system and policy) paradigm, to identify ways in which country-specific endogenous variables might influence production decisions of firms (Koopman and Montias, 1971). Here we are primarily concerned with the way in which ESP might affect international market failure.

15. One exception may be trade between neighbouring territories.

16. There are exceptions, e.g. where less well developed countries invest in more developed countries to acquire technology, marketing and other kinds of knowledge.

17. In 1983, the leading five countries accounted for 75.3 per cent of the stock of outward directed investment and 53.1 per cent of inward investment. In that same year, developing countries accounted for about 3 per cent of outward and 25 per cent of inward investment. In 1982 only 24 of the world's largest industrial enterprises were from the developing countries (nine from Korea); this compares with only three (of the same number) in 1962.

18. For example, see those of Schive and Hsueh (1985, Taiwan), Jo (1984), and Kumar and Kim (1984, Korea), Chen (1983, Hong Kong), Tolentino (1987, Philippines), Katz and Kosacoff (1983, Argentina), Agarwal (1985, India), Villela (1983, Brazil). For a general analysis of TNCs from Asian developing economies see ESCAP/UNCTC Joint Unit (1985) and Escho (1985) and from Latin America, UNCTC (1983b).

19. E.g. investment by Liberian-registered companies in Europe and Latin America, and 'entrepôt' financial operations of American and European subsidiaries in Hong Kong and Singapore.

20. The importance of international ethnic minorities as a factor explaining the

greater intensity of Asian compared to Latin American investment is highlighted by Wells (1983).

21. For a general analysis of these investments see Wells (1983).

22. Unskilled or semi-skilled labour is usually regarded as among the least mobile of factor endowments; with improvements in international transport this is no longer the case. There is a substantial flow of temporary workers from Asia to the Middle East.

23. One example is Korean investment (approved) in mining and lumber projects in Central and South America which by 1984 had totalled $109 million (Kumar and Kim, 1984). At the same time Korean firms have set up timber processing plants in Indonesia to overcome the threat of the Indonesian authorities to forbid the export of unprocessed raw materials.

24. This is an important form of direct investment by some countries, notably Argentina, Zimbabwe, Libya and the Philippines in recent years.

25. Examples include a Korean cement plant in Singapore and a tyre plant in Sudan.

26. Schive and Hsueh give an example of an adaptation of a technology originally imported from a developed country by a Taiwanese firm to manufacture polyester fibre to suit the needs of a joint venture with an Indonesian company.

27. Such entrepôt trade does not only apply to developing countries. Parry (1983) has shown this to be an important form of technology transfer from Australia to neighbouring developing countries.

28. Examples quoted by Kumar and Kim (1984) include Korean firms producing garments, shoes, jewellery and fountain pens. The authors argue that both quota restrictions and a relatively inexpensive labour force in other developing countries, e.g. Sri Lanka, El Salvador and the Philippines, cause Korean firms to relocate activities, the initial advantage of which was partly the low cost of Korean labour. According to Kumar and Kim about one-third of all Korean foreign manufacturing projects are solely designed to export to Third World locations and are located in export processing zones.

29. For example, 90.5 per cent of Taiwanese direct investment in Asian countries takes the form of joint ventures (Schive and Hsueh, 1985).

30. These and other influences on Third World investments are examined in more detail in Wells (1983).

31. As set out in more detail in Chapter 5 of Dunning (1981).

32. For more detailed analysis see: Cantwell (1985) and Wyatt, Bertin and Pavitt (1987).

33. These may be both short and long term. For a discussion of a model which traces movements in the competitive strength of European and American firms since the Second World War, see Pavitt (1987) and Cantwell (1985).

34. The two are not necessarily unconnected. Innovations may initially strengthen the international competitive position of the innovative country, but over time this position could be eroded if the share of the additional output created going to the non-innovating sector of the economy exceeded its increase in productivity. In practice, this tends to reflect an increase in the real cost of labour which may cause firms to reappraise their locational strategies.

35. Canada is one exception. With an R&D as a percentage of GNP of 1 per cent in 1971, she had the fifth largest outward investment per capita over the 1967–75 period.

36. Also some variables may 'push' and 'pull' at the same time. For example, high earnings per head may reflect high costs (a 'push' factor), but also high spending power (a 'pull' factor).

37. The economics behind this suggests that as GNP per head increases, owner-ship, internalization and locational advantages combine to encourage a greater proportional increase in outward direct investment. The association between the other independent variables (notably industrial structure and trade intensity) and outward direct investment appears to be a more linear one.

38. The dramatic shift from an import substitution to an export bid growth strategy of the Korean Government in the 1970s led directly to an increase in outward/inward investment, ratio from 0.11 in 1970–6 to 0.44 in 1977/1982 (Koo, 1985).

39. Taiwan also exhibits certain of the characteristics of a city-state (i.e. a limited home market) but because of its more diversified economic structure we have classi-fied this country in Group 2.

40. For further details: see the sources identified in Note 1 and especially Schive and Hsuech (1985) [not listed] and Kumar and Kim (1984).

41. For an extended analysis of the evolvement of government policy towards (inward) foreign direct investment as development proceeds see Stoever (1984). In his book, Wells (1983) argues that a major reason for the difference in the scope and pattern of Latin American and Asian outward investment is that in most of the former countries the emphasis has largely been on import substitution while in the latter it has been on export promotion.

References

Agarwal, J. P. (1985) *Pros and Cons of Indian Multinationals Abroad* (Tubingen: Mohr).

Aliber, R. Z. (1971) 'The multinational enterprise in a multiple currency world', in Dunning, J. H. (ed.) *The Multinational Enterprise* (London: Allen & Unwin).

Balassa, B. A. (1979) 'A stages approach to comparative advantage', in Adelman, I. (ed.), *Economic Growth and Resources: National and International Issues* (London: Macmillan).

Cantwell, J. A. (1985) *Technological Competition between Europe and US Companies in the Post War Period.* A report submitted to the Commission of the European Communities, October.

Casson, M. C. (1979) *Alternatives to the Multinational Enterprise* (London: Macmillan).

Casson, M. C. (1985) 'The theory of foreign direct investment', in Buckley, P. J. and Casson, M. C., *The Economic Theory of the Multinational Enterprise* (London: Macmillan).

Casson, M. C. (1987) *The Firm and the Market* (Oxford: Basil Blackwell).

Casson, M. C. *et al.* (1985) *Multinationals and World Trade* (London: Allen & Unwin).

Chen, E. (1983) 'Multinationals from Hong Kong', in Lall, S. *et al.*, *The New Multi-nationals: The Spread of Third World Enterprises* (Chichester: John Wiley).

Chenery, H. (1979) *Structural Change and Development Policy* (Oxford: Oxford University Press).

Davidson, W. H. (1976) 'Patterns of factor saving innovation in the industrialized world', *European Economic Review, 8*, pp. 207–17.

Dunning, J. H. (1981a) 'A note on intra-industry foreign direct investment', *Banca Nazionale del Lavoro Quarterly Review*, no. 139, pp. 427–37.

Dunning, J. H. (1981b) *International Production and the Multinational Enterprise* (London: Allen & Unwin).

Dunning, J. H. and Pearce, R. D. (1985) *The World's Largest Industrial Enterprises 1962–83* (Aldershot: Gower).

Dunning, J. H. and Rugman, A. (1985) 'The influence of Hymer's dissertation on theory of foreign direct investment', *American Economic Review*, 75, May, pp. 228–32.

Ergas, H. (1984) *Why Do Some Countries Innovate more than Others?* (Brussels: Centre for European Policy Studies).

Ergas, H. (1985) 'Corporate strategies in transition' in Jacquemin, A. (ed.), *Industrial Policy and International Trade* (London: Cambridge University Press).

ESCAP/UNCTC (1985) *Transnational Corporations from Developing Asian Economies* (Bangkok: ESCAP/UNCTC joint units).

Escho, H. (1985) 'A comparison of direct investment from India, S. Korea and Taiwan by size, region and industry', *Journal of International Economic Studies*, 1, pp. 1–37.

Ethier, W. J. (1986) 'The Multinational Firm', *Quarterly Journal of Economics*, 101, pp. 806–33.

Giddy, I. H. and Young, S. (1983) 'Conventional theory and unconventional multinationals: do new forms of multinational enterprises require new theories?', in Rugman, A. (ed.), *New Theories of the Multinational Enterprise* (London: Croom Helm), pp. 55–78.

Gray, H. P. (1982) 'Towards a unified theory of international trade, international production and direct foreign investment', in Black, J. and Dunning, J. H. (eds.), *International Capital Movements* (London: Macmillan).

Helpman, E. (1984) 'A simple theory of international trade with multinational corporations', *Journal of Political Economy*, 92, pp. 451–67.

Jo, Sung Hwan (1984) *International Production in Different Phases of LDC Industrial Growth: the Case of South Korean Experience*, mimeo.

Katz, J. and Kosacoff, B. (1983) 'Multinationals from Argentina', in Lall, S., *The New Multinationals* (Chichester and New York: John Wiley).

Kogut, B. (1983) 'Foreign direct investment as a sequential process', in Kindleberger, C. P. and Audretsch, D. (eds.), *The Multinational Corporation in the 1980s*, (Cambridge: MIT Press).

Kojima, K. (1978) *Direct Foreign Investment: A Japanese Model of Multinational Business Operations*, London: Croom Helm.

Kojima, K. (1982) 'Macroeconomic versus international business approach to foreign direct investment', *Hitotsubashi Journal of Economics*, 23, pp. 1–19.

Koo, Bohn-Young (1985) 'Korea' in Dunning, J. H. (ed.), *Multinational Enterprises, Economic Structure and International Competitiveness* (Chichester and New York: John Wiley).

Koopman, K. and Montias, J. M. (1971) 'On the description and comparison of economic systems' in Eckstein, A. *Comparison of Economic Systems* (California: University of California Press).

Kumar, K. and McLeod, M. G. (eds.) (1981), *Multinationals from Developing Countries* (Lexington, Mass: Lexington Books).

Kumar, K. and Kim, K. Y. (1984), 'The Korean manufacturing multinationals', *Journal of International Business Studies*, 15, spring/summer, pp. 45–62.

Lall, S. (1983) *The New Multinationals* (Chichester and New York: John Wiley).

Markusen, J. R. (1984) 'Multinationals, multi-plant economies and the gain from trade', *Journal of International Economies*, 16, pp. 205–16.

Oman, C. (1984) *New Forms of International Investment in Developing Countries* (Paris, OECD).

Pavitt, K. (1987) 'International patterns of technological accumulation', in Hood, N.

and Vahine, J. E. (eds.), *Strategies in Global Competition* (Chichester and New York: John Wiley).

Porter, M. E. (ed.) (1986) *Competition in Global Industries* (Boston: Harvard Business School Press).

Ranis, G. (1976) 'The multinational corporations as an instrument of development', in Apter, D. E. and Goodman, L. W. (eds.), *The Multinational Corporation and Social Change* (New York: Praeger).

Rugman, A. M. (1979) *International Diversification and the Multinational Enterprise* (Lexington, Mass.: Lexington Books).

Simoes, V., 'Portugal', in Dunning, J. H. (ed.) (1985) *Multinational Enterprises, Economic Structure and International Competitiveness* (Chichester and New York: John Wiley).

Schive, C. and Hsueh, Kuangtao (1985), *Taiwan's Investment in Asean Countries and its Competitiveness* (mimeo).

Schneider, F. and Frey, B. S. (1985) 'The economic and political determinants of foreign direct investment', *World Development, 13*, February, pp. 161–76.

Stoever, W. A. (1984) *The Stages of Developing Country Policy towards Foreign Investment*, mimeo.

Tolentino, P. (1987) *The Global Shift in International Production. The Growth of Multinational Enterprises from the Developing Countries: The Philippines.* Ph.D. Thesis, University of Reading.

UNCTC (1981) *Transnational Corporation Linkages in Developing Countries* (New York: UNCTC) ST/CTC/17.

UNCTC (1982) *Regional Integration Cum/Versus Corporation Integration* (New York: UNCTC) E.82 II A.6.

UNCTC (1983a) *Transnational Corporations in the International Auto Industry* (New York: UNCTC) E.83 II A.6.

UNCTC (1983b) *Transnational Corporations and World Development Third Survey* (New York: UNCTC) E.83 II A.14.

UNCTC (1983c) *Joint Ventures among Firms in Latin America: A Technical Paper* (New York: UNCTC) E.83 II A.19.

Vernon, R. (1983) 'Organizational and institutional responses to international risk', in Herring, R. J. (ed.), *Managing International Risk* (Cambridge, Mass.: Cambridge University Press).

Villela, A. (1983) 'Multinationals from Brazil', in Lall, S. (ed.), *The New Multinationals* (Chichester and New York: John Wiley).

Wells, L. T. (1983) *Third World Multinationals* (Cambridge, Mass. MIT Press).

World Bank (various dates), *World Development Report*, annual publication (Oxford: Oxford University Press).

Wyatt, S., Bertin, G. and Pavitt, K. (1987) 'Patents and multinational corporations: results from questionnaires', *World Patent Information, 7*, 196–212.

6

New Forms of Investment in Developing Countries*

Charles P. Oman[†]

*Source: T. Moran, ed., *Investing in Development: New Roles for Foreign Capital?* (New Brunswick, Transaction Books, 1986), pp. 131–155.

During the postwar period and into the 1960s, international investment primarily involved transactions whereby corporations based in one country acquired or created firms in other host countries. Today statistics on foreign direct investment reflect mainly this 'traditional' kind of foreign direct investment. What they fail to show, however, is a variety of 'new' forms of investment that have been gathering impetus since the late 1960s and that are now playing a more important role in North–South activities. This chapter looks at the patterns of these new forms of investment and illustrates them with specific examples from the extractive and manufacturing sectors. It examines some of the principal causes of new forms of investment and tries to weigh some of their consequences.[1]

The term "new forms of investment" (NFI) covers a broad, heterogenous range of international business operations that all have a common denominator: For an investment project in a host country, a foreign company supplies goods, either tangible or intangible, which constitute assets, but it does not own the project itself. In other words, the foreign partner's equity share, if any, does not constitute ownership control, as it did in traditional investments. But this does not mean that the foreign company cannot exercise partial or total control over the project by other means.

Among the new forms of foreign investment are joint ventures in which foreign equity does not exceed 50 per cent, licensing agreements, management contracts, franchising, turnkey and "product-in-hand" contracts, production sharing and risk-service contracts, and international subcontracting (when the subcontracting firm is at least 50 per cent locally owned). Many of these business forms of course are not particularly new; examples of many of them predate the 1960s. Use of the adjective 'new'—it could be replaced with 'non-traditional'—is meant to focus attention on the new *importance* of these business forms as a whole, given their significant growth in recent years.

An important question here is whether all these business forms can legitimately be considered investments. From the point of view of the host-country participants, they almost invariably do represent investments. But from the perspective of the foreign firms supplying technology, equipment, or access to export markets, the answer can vary from one project to the next. Nor does the answer depend on the type of resources the firm supplies; rather, it rests on the nature of the firm's involvement in the project.

This distinction between what a given international business operation represents for the host country and for the foreign supplier of assets—an investment or a sales operation[2]—may seem academic; but it is in fact crucial: It sheds light on the underlying logic of conflicts and convergences of interest between the two parties. When a foreign company participates as an investor, it shares with its host-country partner an interest in maximizing the difference between the costs of producing the project's output on the one hand and the value of that output on the other. Often the two parties also share an interest in generating or defending the market share of the project's output and, if possible, in generating monopoly rents in that market. In short, they share an interest in the project's success as an investment, in its future ability to generate a surplus. Conflicts of interest between the two partners arise primarily over how profits or losses are shared. In some cases, conflict may also arise over the definition of the geographic boundaries of the market (for example, over whether or not the product is to be exported from the host country, as this could conflict with the company's international marketing strategy).

Whenever, however, an investment project in a developing country basically represents a sales operation for the foreign company supplying the assets, the foreign company's interest lies primarily in *maximizing* the difference between the pre-negotiated price to be paid by the host-country partner for the assets (technology, equipment, and so on) and the cost to the foreign company of supplying those resources. The company's concern about the future surplus-generating capacity of the project is secondary at best.[3] The interest of the host-country participant is usually just the opposite: It wants to *minimize* the price-cost difference for resources supplied by the company and is concerned above all with the success of the project as an investment.

Returning to our definition, then, it is possible to distinguish between a broad and a narrow, more rigorous definition of the "new forms of investment" concept. The broad definition was sketched out above: NFI investment projects are ones that are at least 50 per cent locally owned, with some assets supplied by one or more foreign companies. For such a project to qualify as NFI in the narrower definition, the project should represent an investment not only for the host-country participant(s), but also for at least one of the participating foreign companies. The foreign company should regard the surplus-generating capacity of the project in the host country as a, if not the, source of income and profit. This implies both that the company has a direct interest in the project's economic viability as an investment and that it has some way to appropriate or control at least part of the surplus generated. The project then represents an investment for the foreign company irrespective of its equity participation. In this definition, the foreign company must perceive its contribution to the project as an asset not only for the project, but for itself.[4]

New versus Traditional Foreign Direct Investment: The Trends

Are the new forms of investment superseding traditional foreign direct investment (FDI) in the developing countries? In the 1970s, NFI grew more quickly than traditional FDI, but will this trend be reversed in the 1980s? To what extent is NFI a substitute for, and to what extent does it complement, traditional FDI?

Overall, the evidence points to two broad tendencies. During the last decade, some developing countries promoted NFI over traditional FDI so as to enhance local control over industry and to circumvent the rent-extracting powers of multinational firms, seen as being embodied in FDI. Today they may feel as if they had jumped from the frying pan into the fire. When real interest rates were low in the first half of the 1970s, many developing countries no doubt found it easier and cheaper to pursue strategies of debt-financed growth, with greater reliance on NFI for access to non-financial assets when necessary. It was then frequently easier to negotiate with multinational firms over the terms of NFI. But by the 1980s, higher interest rates and a feeling that the international banking community and the International Monetary Fund have quasi-monopoly powers in the financial markets—as well as awareness of their continuing, heavy reliance on multinational firms for access to technology and export markets—made many developing countries change their minds. That is why many of these countries, including some of the more ardent promoters of NFI during the 1970s, are liberalizing their investment policies and trying to attract traditional FDI.

Even so, there is considerable evidence of a changing division of risks and responsibilities among the three principal groups of participants in North–South investment: multinational firms, international lenders, and host-country elites. It suggests that NFI will continue to gain importance—superseding traditional FDI in some cases and complementing it in others. In part, this reflects continued interest by some developing countries in acquiring only those components of the traditional FDI package (technology, management, marketing, and finance) that cannot be obtained locally. Such "unpackaging" and selective overseas acquisition of assets via

NFI may be seen by some countries, including some of the more industrialized or heavily indebted developing countries, as a way to minimize the foreign-exchange costs of obtaining only those particular assets required for industrial restructuring or for sustaining local industrial capital formation. But more importantly, the changing international division of risks and responsibilities also reflects a tendency for some multinational companies to modify their views on the advantages and disadvantages of NFI over traditional FDI in developing countries.

Some companies, for example, are finding that they can earn attractive returns from certain tangible or intangible assets that they can supply without necessarily having to own or finance projects. By supplying assets via NFI, they can also, in some cases, benefit from increased leverage on those assets because, for example, local partners or international lenders absorb start-up costs and provide working capital. And, especially important, NFI often means reduced exposure to commercial and political risks that accompany traditional FDI.

There is also evidence that 'newcomer' multinationals and market-share 'followers' frequently use NFI to compete with the more established multinational firms. In some cases, they use it *offensively*—to penetrate or increase market shares in industries or countries where the 'majors' are reluctant either to share equity (and rents) or to relinquish the decision-making power and information that might dilute their particular competitive advantages (e.g., state-of-the-art technology, brand names, etc.). Newcomers and followers may offer host countries shared ownership or greater access to technology in return for preferred (or exclusive) access to local markets.

In other cases, newcomers and followers are using NFI more *defensively*—in a context of globalized oligopolistic rivalry in which their managerial and especially financial resources are stretched thin because of increased competitive pressures to take investment positions in numerous markets. By sharing technology, control, and profits with local partners, they can benefit from the latter's knowledge of local markets, access to local finance, and willingness to share or assume important risks. This phenomenon may have received added impetus during the 1970s because of rising capital costs and cash-flow problems that some firms experienced due to depressed demand conditions in their home markets. And whether they have resorted to NFI as a competitive tool in developing countries offensively or defensively, newcomers and followers have sometimes brought considerable pressure to bear on the majors to follow suit.

Moreover, as technologies diffuse and products mature and become increasingly price-competitive, even the majors and market-share leaders sometimes initiate the use of NFI as part of a strategy of divestment. For example, if a company perceives that its control over a particular technology is waning, it may decide to obtain additional, marginal returns from that technology by licensing it and using those returns to help finance movement into newer, higher-growth activities—often in its home market or in other industrial countries. Another example is the phenomenon of 'industrial restructuring' in Japan, where the government (MITI)—either because of changing comparative advantage or for environmental reasons—has joined forces with firms and large trading companies to transfer entire industries or industry segments to developing countries by using the new forms of investment.[5]

Still, industry leaders often resort to NFI only in fairly protected and isolated markets; the new forms generally are considered marketing tools in countries where local production by the joint venture, licensee, or purchaser of a turnkey plant stands little chance of competing internationally with the company's 'core' activities. This may be because the company will not supply its most advanced technology or because of relatively high production costs in the host economy, for example, due to inefficiencies of small-scale production behind tariff barriers. Industry 'majors' that do incorporate production from developing-country affiliates into their global networks, on the other hand, still tend to rely heavily on traditional FDI for such affiliates.

Thus the ultimate importance of NFI relative to FDI in coming years is likely to be determined less by unilateral developing-country government decisions on whether to increase their efforts to attract traditional FDI or to emphasize selective acquisition of assets through NFI, than it is by the dynamics of inter-firm competition—and by the interaction between those dynamics and host-government policies. And even though those dynamics reflect patterns of technological innovation and of supply and demand that are global in scale, they tend to be industry-specific. Hence, it is important to look at investment trends at the level of sectors and industries.

Overall, the evidence points to an emerging international, inter-actor division of risks and responsibilities, the principal characteristics of which can be summarized as follows:

(1) *Multinational firms* will tend to concentrate their efforts in industry segments where barriers to entry and hence value-added and profitability ratios are highest, while at the same time seeking to maintain or increase flexibility. They will thus generally focus on such strategic activities as technological innovation, marketing, and certain key aspects of management. These activities could increasingly become their primary bases of control and profits in a world economy characterized by the growing internationalization of production and inter-firm competition, coupled with rapid technological change and considerable instability in world product and financial markets. In other words, multinational companies may increasingly become intermediaries for both the input (technology and management) and output

(world market) sides of industry in developing countries, while shifting a greater share of the investment risk associated with the investment process onto international lenders and, perhaps even more so, onto their host-country partners.

(2) *International lenders*—notably multinational banks, but also public national and multilateral financial institutions—may continue to play a leading role in channeling financial capital to developing countries in need of liquidity, particularly those with the industrial or primary-products export potential needed to service their debt. Financial institutions will thus continue to assume or will be delegated control over the financial dimension of the international investment process in developing countries. Within the financial community, however, the division of risks and responsibilities will vary from project to project and period to period, with private banks playing a clearly predominant role in some cases, and national or multilateral financial agencies playing an increasingly important role (via co-financing, export credits, or mixed credits, for example) in others.

(3) *Host-country elites* in the private and public sectors may increasingly retain legal ownership of the investment projects in their countries and assume, or be delegated, certain managerial responsibilities. In addition, they may take on important risks and increase their share of returns.

Risk and Responsibility Sharing in the Primary Sector

It is in the primary products sector that one finds the strongest empirical evidence to support the argument that traditional FDI is being superseded by NFI. In *petroleum extraction*, the shift to NFI began to gain momentum in the 1950s and was virtually complete in Third World petroleum-producing countries by the late 1970s. In the major capital-surplus petroleum-exporting countries, service contracts are commonly used, often in conjunction with joint ventures. In contrast, petroleum-producing countries that do not have large financial surpluses (many of which are major borrowers) often use the production-sharing formula. In the first group of countries, the inter-actor division of risks and responsibilities is often bilateral, between the host country and the multinational petroleum company. But in the second group, the financial dimension often involves international lending institutions. Mexico's PEMEX and Brazil's PETROBRAS, for example, received huge loans to finance exploration, production, and refining during the 1970s. Less spectacular but also important were loans to state oil companies in Algeria, Indonesia, Nigeria, and Peru. In both groups of countries, however, there is ample evidence that multinational petroleum companies are concentrating on supplying technology, certain key managerial functions, and international marketing, while the host countries assume ownership of the investment projects along with some important managerial responsibilities.

In *metals mining*, the shift toward NFI became clear in the late 1960s, and the desire for national sovereignty over mineral resources led many developing countries to put ownership of mining operations in the hands of state or private local enterprises. Management contracts in which the managing company's remuneration is based at least in part on profits or production levels are not uncommon in new projects, and they are sometimes combined with minority equity participation by the managing company. Turnkey contracts, which typically call for the contractor to conduct a feasibility study, to provide technology and know-how, and to carry out or supervise the design, engineering, and construction as well as supply capital equipment, have been widely used in minerals-processing projects. They are less frequent in minerals extraction itself, although they have been used in some mining projects that required major infrastructure investments. The most typical contracts since the late 1960s, however, have been between major developing-country state mining companies and international contractors (for example, a specialized engineering or construction company), in which the latter receives a fixed fee or percentage of total costs and assumes little risk associated with or control over the mining project.

In sharp contrast to petroleum, the rapidly rising investment costs in metals mining have been accompanied since the early 1970s by fluctuating and, on average, depressed output prices on the world market. One result is that relatively few new mining projects are being brought to fruition. Another is that, following a period of increased restrictions on FDI in the late 1960s and early 1970s, a number of mineral-producing countries have switched back to active promotion of traditional FDI. But the multinational mining companies have shown considerable reluctance to undertake major equity investments in developing countries. Those which are still active increasingly operate as mobilizers of international loan capital from public and private sources, as innovators and suppliers of production and processing technology, as project managers, and, above all, as providers of access to world-market outlets.[6] Engineering companies that often worked as contractors to these multinationals are now contracted directly by state mining companies in developing countries.

Although traditional FDI has not been as completely displaced by NFI in mining as it has been in petroleum extraction, the evidence nevertheless points to major changes in the international inter-actor division of risks and responsibilities, with the host countries assuming major risks and costs. And the requirements of finance capital are such that "the attitudes of lenders, be they international agencies, banks, or export credit insurers, are likely to be of critical importance and may well seriously limit the freedom of maneuver of the host countries and mining enterprises as they reach for new models of mining agreements for the remainder of this century."[7]

As for international investment in *agriculture* (see Chapter 4 in this volume [Moran, 1986]), there has been considerable movement away from traditional FDI in the plantation system to NFI, particularly contract growing, both in traditional export products (sugar, bananas, and meat) and in primary products supplied to foreign-owned food processing firms whose output is largely sold locally (a trend discussed later in this chapter).

The Manufacturing Sector

The evidence on NFI in manufacturing as a whole is less clear-cut than in the primary sector, both as regards the extent to which it is superseding traditional FDI and the extent to which a new inter-actor division of risks and responsibilities is emerging. These new forms of investment obviously have gained considerable importance over the last ten to fifteen years, but what stands out most in the manufacturing sector is the great diversity among host countries both in the importance of NFI as a group relative to traditional FDI and in their importance in gross domestic capital formation in industry.[8]

This wide diversity among host countries clearly reflects differences in host governments' policies on foreign ownership of investment. But it also indicates a complex interaction of other factors whose combined import- ance, especially in recent years, may well outweigh that of host govern- ments' FDI policies. These factors include foreign firms' perceptions of: the size and growth potential of a country's market, its political stability, its bureaucracy and the nature of relations between government and the private sector, its long-run development strategy, its macro-economic and industrial policies, and the availability of local managerial talent and skilled labor.

If one controls for such country-specific factors (and company-specific views of them), a few sector-wide patterns nevertheless seem to emerge. First, other things being equal, the NFI are more likely to be found in investment projects whose output is destined for the host-country's local or regional market than in export-oriented projects. Second, NFI are more frequent in projects using relatively stable or mature technologies than in those using 'high' or rapidly changing technologies. Third, like traditional FDI, NFI tend to concentrate in host countries' principal growth industries or in high value-added segments within industries.

This last observation of course reflects the rent-seeking nature of foreign investment. But it also points to an important corollary: NFI in projects with promising growth and surplus-generating potential more often repre- sent *investments* for the foreign participants (that is, they correspond to our narrower definition of the term), whereas projects whose growth potential appears limited or doubtful more than often correspond to *sales* operations for foreign participants.

Because NFI patterns differ greatly among host countries and because many projects use NFI in conjunction with traditional FDI, it is important to analyze North–South NFI trends on an industry-by-industry basis.

Petrochemicals

Until recently, petrochemicals were produced almost exclusively by the industrial (OECD) countries; but today a spectacular change is taking place, to a large extent via NFI in developing countries. Whereas in 1970 only 2–3 per cent of world capacity in ethylene was found in developing countries, by 1982 that share had surpassed 8 per cent, and by 1990 it is expected to reach 20–22 per cent. Similar patterns can be seen in the cases of the five major thermoplastics.

Since the mid-1970s, a large proportion of this expansion in developing countries' production capacity has been on the basis of fifty-fifty or minority foreign-owned joint ventures, technology licensing agreements, and turnkey contracts. The foreign companies involved in these new forms of investment are some of the world's leading petrochemical producers, including the largest chemical companies as well as the chemical divisions of major petroleum firms.

In Latin America, the transition from a rather limited development of petrochemicals production in the 1950s and 1960s, when foreign investment was primarily via traditional FDI, to the emergence of large-scale, state-led petrochemical programs during the last fifteen years has been accompanied by a marked shift to NFI—primarily joint ventures, but also licensing and turnkey contracts. In Argentina and Brazil, this shift was triggered by the general lack of interest on the part of the petrochemical multinationals in further developing local capacity through traditional FDI. In Mexico, U.S. companies might have been interested, but the Mexican government's extension of PEMEX's monopoly to basic and secondary petrochemicals in 1960 hindered such a move.

A notable feature of the big petrochemical joint ventures established during the 1970s in Brazil and Mexico (now the major producers in Latin America) and in Asia is the foreign firms' contribution of technology in return for equity shares. In Mexico, despite legislation in 1970 that restricted foreign ownership to 40 per cent and despite a sluggish economy since 1982, the local market remains a major attraction to foreign investors—especially to U.S. firms and some large European companies (BASF, Bayer, ICI)—in downstream production. In Brazil, most production is also for the local market, although foreign partners are now being asked to promote exports and to help develop high value-added products as well.

Another important feature is the extent to which the NFI in Brazil and Mexico have led to major advances not only in substituting local for foreign hardware and detail engineering services, but also in local appropriation of skills and know-how in state-of-the-art process design engineering and in research and development. This trend is reflected, for example, in Brazil's third and most recent major NFI agreement signed in 1977 with Technip (France) and KTI (the Netherlands). These firms agreed to supply all the technical engineering data, including the technology to obtain and update those data, along with technical assistance and training of local technicians. In fact, Brazil now supplies some other developing countries with petro-chemical technology and production know-how.

In Asia, several developing countries—India, the Republic of Korea, Taiwan, and the member countries of the Association of Southeast Asian Nations (ASEAN)—have significant petrochemical capacities, and the People's Republic of China is expected to have substantial capacity by the end of the decade. India's production dates back to the 1950s. Its 1963 petrochemical development plan, prepared with the help of the French Petroleum Institute, aimed for a pattern where basic production would be in local hands and downstream production would be in those of joint ventures. But India's experience has been less successful than Mexico's, and there is no clear division of responsibilities between sectors. Some traditional FDI still exists; some NFI came in, largely during the 1960s (mostly joint ventures with U.S. and European firms); and production is almost exclusively for a not very dynamic domestic market.

In the Republic of Korea, state-led development of the industry by private firms has resulted in considerable use of joint ventures and licensing, mostly involving U.S. and Japanese partners in downstream products, with ethylene now totally in Korean hands. Korea's first complex was completed in 1973, and a world-scale complex came onstream in 1979; the former relied heavily on fifty-fifty joint ventures, whereas the latter involved fewer joint ventures and more domestic firms with licensing agreements. Downstream production appears to be moving into Korean hands as well: Some foreign partners, such as Dow, have been bought out; and technology has been acquired through arm's-length licensing, as happened in 1984 with Union Carbide.

In Taiwan, the pattern is not unlike that of Korea, with the notable difference that all the foreign partners in Taiwan are U.S. 'majors'—perhaps reflecting U.S. political motivations to help develop the Taiwanese industry. Korea's Lucky Group and Taiwan's Formosa Plastics Corporations have become important suppliers of technology to other developing countries. In 1983, Saudi Arabia's SABIC chose Lucky to be its joint-venture partner in its largest polyvinyl chloride plant, and the Taiwan company as its partner in the urea plant.

In the ASEAN region, Japanese firms are involved in petrochemical joint ventures in most countries but, apart from Singapore, this is largely through turnkey and licensing contracts, with little capital contribution. In Singapore, by contrast, the Japanese have played a leading role since the late 1970s in setting up a world-scale complex in which the Singapore government is a 50-per cent shareholder. (Philips and Shell are participants in two downstream facilities.) The project was designed to produce for export to the ASEAN region as well as for the Japanese home market as part of Japan's vertical integration/relocation strategy. Now, however, Japanese commitments to import from Saudi Arabia are highlighting problems of excess supply.

The creation of major petrochemical capacities in the Middle East is undoubtedly the most striking recent development for the industry worldwide and for the OECD countries in particular. Saudi Arabia alone has eleven major production facilities, all of which are fifty-fifty 'first-generation' joint ventures between Saudi Basic Industries Corporation (SABIC) and one or more multinational firms (primarily Japanese and U.S. ones, with the latter being mostly petroleum companies). In every instance, SABIC and the foreign partner each put up 15 per cent of the project's capital needs as equity, 60 per cent is provided by the Saudi Public Investment Fund in the form of long-term low-interest loans, and the remaining 10 per cent is raised from commercial banks; a ten-year tax holiday is also provided. Technology has not been capitalized as part of the foreign partner's equity share, but is the object of separate contracts, and usually third-party technology has been chosen. Thus it is obviously the foreign firms' ability to penetrate OECD petrochemical markets that constitutes their key 'immaterial asset'; it also explains both the highly favorable financial and fiscal arrangements provided by the host country and the difference between the foreign firms' 15-per cent contribution to financial needs and their 50-per cent equity shares.

By and large, the major petroleum and chemical companies' decisions to meet the demands of various Third World countries to help develop their local petrochemical capacities and to use NFI to do so reflect strategies these companies came up with in response to important changes in the industry starting in the early 1970s. One such change was the shift from rapid growth and high profitability during the 1950–1970 period to a maturation of the industry in the OECD area, with a slackening of growth potential and profits. Another major change came with the two successive oil-price hikes, which greatly increased the share of naphtha feedstocks in total output costs. The latter has had a crucial impact on profitability as well as on cost structures. In virtually every OECD country except the United States, which has oil and natural gas resources, the petrochemical industry that developed prior to 1973 has been caught between the need to pass on cost increases to safeguard financial viability and the difficulty of doing so because of depressed demand conditions.

The pattern of petrochemical investments in the developing countries points up the fact that 'newcomers'—which in this industry include the Japanese petrochemical firms and U.S. petroleum companies—often use the new forms of investment to gain favored access to new markets and to force some of the 'majors' to follow suit. The substitution of NFI for traditional FDI now appears irreversible. Some of the major developing-country producers are apparently trying to do without foreign investments altogether, except when foreign partners can help penetrate OECD markets. It is also worth noting that South–South collaboration has been growing primarily through NFI. This movement may well be accentuated by China's large demands for technological and industrial NFI in this industry.

The Auto Industry

Traditional foreign direct investment clearly dominates investment in vehicle production in developing countries. (*Production* implies over 50-per cent local content, whereas *assembly* implies over 50-per cent of imported parts and components.) But such investment is heavily concentrated in only a few countries: Brazil, Mexico, and Argentina. There were a fair number of joint ventures and licensing agreements during the early years of auto production, notably in the 1960s, but even then traditional FDI accounted for a larger share of production. Since then, most majority locally owned producers based on NFI have folded or have been absorbed by majority or wholly foreign-owned subsidiaries.

The other major auto-producing developing countries today are India and Korea. Foreign investment in India has been limited mostly to licensing, and production has been largely confined to models quite outdated by international standards. Now, however, Japanese investments in minority joint ventures are growing rapidly. In Korea, two firms dominate production. Hyundai was a wholly Korean-owned producer, and is now 85-per cent Korean-owned. (Mitsubishi has taken a 15-per cent equity share in return for its contribution to finance and international marketing.) Hyundai's "Pony" automobile, developed with the collaboration of various foreign suppliers of design, technology, finance, etc., is now a competitor in world markets. Daewoo is in a fifty-fifty joint venture with General Motors (GM); the venture is not active in exports, and Daewoo took over management from GM in 1983.

Car assembly presents a very different picture. Minority joint ventures and licensing play an important role in numerous developing countries (including ASEAN members, the Andean countries, Iran, Nigeria, and several North African nations). The investment pattern in assembly operations suggests that: a) host-government restrictions on foreign ownership are a major factor behind NFI; b) auto companies that are market-share followers often use NFI offensively to gain favored access to local markets (pressuring the leaders to follow suit in some cases); and/or defensively—to benefit from local partners' sharing risks and contributing to finance and marketing efforts; and c) the industry leaders tend to use NFI only when local production cannot compete internationally with the core activities of their international integrated production and marketing systems. NFI, notably joint ventures and licensing, are also somewhat more prevalent in the commercial-vehicle and component segments of the industry than in auto production per se.

The pattern of North–South investment in the auto industry reflects above all the high level of worldwide concentration in this industry; the very significant economies of scale in production (which are greater in passenger cars than in commercial vehicles); and the financial and techno-logical advantages of subsidiaries of the major auto multinationals *vis-à-vis* majority locally owned firms that rely on NFI. It also reflects the import-ance that such industry leaders as GM and Ford attach to retaining full control and ownership of their affiliates, which operate within increasingly integrated worldwide production and marketing networks. Meanwhile, the Japanese majors continue to prefer to keep production at home. Korea's experience is thus unique among developing countries; and its success is far from assured, particularly given the relatively limited size of the country's domestic market.

Electronics

The electronics complex may be defined as covering three distinct segments: microelectronic components (semiconductors and integrated circuits), consumer electronics (radios, television, hi-fi equipment, elec-tronic watches, hand calculators, and toys), and computers.

In *microelectronics*, increasing price competition, the relatively labor-intensive nature of the assembly and testing of semiconductors, and the relatively modest fixed-capital requirements led a number of major firms to set up assembly and testing operations in some Asian and Latin American countries in the early 1960s. But those operations, which produce virtually exclusively for OECD markets, involved mostly traditional FDI. In the late 1960s and especially in the 1970s, however, locally owned subcontracting companies were set up in a number of countries, including Hong Kong, the Philippines, and Taiwan. They were often established on the basis of contracts with smaller OECD-based firms that supplied equipment and technical and marketing assistance. Furthermore, in countries like Brazil, Korea, and Taiwan, recent efforts to increase semiconductor production capacities have given rise to a number of NFI arrangements. A few examples are the licensing agreements between the Brazilian firms, Itan and Docas, and several European firms; licensing between Korea's San Sung and the U.S. firm, Micron Technology; a joint venture between Gold Star (Korea) and AMI (United States); and licensing between Taiwan's state enterprise, ERSO, and RCA (United States).

In *consumer electronics*, licensing and joint ventures provided the basis for some developing-country producers, especially in East and Southeast Asia, to develop their production capacities. In the early years, assembly of radios and black-and-white television sets was the principal activity; but this led to greater local production of components, to the production of more sophisticated products, and finally, in countries like Korea and Taiwan, to the mastery of production techniques and technology by local firms. In the past few years, some of these firms have actually set up production subsidiaries in OECD countries: There are Korean subsidiaries in the United States and Portugal, and a Taiwanese color TV producer in the United Kingdom.

In *computers*, foreign investment in developing countries remains limited. This is particularly so in the case of large computers, in which what investment there is tends to be dominated by the traditional FDI of a few major companies. Efforts to promote the development of national production capacities, notably in Brazil, have given rise to licensing in mini- and micro-computers and in such peripherals as printers, screens, and disks. And it is principally market-share followers—like Sycor (United States), Logabax (France), Nixdorf (the Federal Republic of Germany), Fujitsu (Japan), and Ferranti (United Kingdom)—that have supplied production technology through NFI. On a much smaller scale, China, Korea, and Mexico have also begun to develop national computer industries, mainly through licensing and joint ventures.

In short, the pattern of NFI in the electronics complex points up the importance of rapid technological change, which explains why the majors are reluctant to share ownership or to license their most up-to-date technologies with developing-country producers. It also highlights the use of NFI by some 'followers,' primarily as an offensive tactic to gain access to potentially important markets in some newly industrializing countries. Such companies may also seek to amortize research and development expenditures through licensing activities in developing countries.

Future negotiations in this industry undoubtedly will focus on the issue of access to developing-country markets in exchange for access to rapidly changing production technology, particularly in microelectronics and computers.

Textiles

In the textile industry, international investment has played a less important role in the development of production capacity in developing countries than it has in other manufacturing industries of comparable importance. This is consistent with the observation that both traditional FDI and NFI tend to concentrate in host countries' major growth industries. The textile industry has not been a major growth industry for the Third World as a whole during the past two decades.

But in those developing countries where the industry has been a growth leader, foreign investment—and especially NFI—usually has been important. Such is clearly the case of the three leading exporters: Korea,

Taiwan, and Hong Kong. It is also true in a number of emergent textile-producing countries, with the notable exception of India.

To understand the patterns of international investment in this industry, it is important to recall that the industry comprises three main segments: fibers (synthetic and natural), textile-mill products (fabrics), and end-use products (notably apparel). Also key is the role played by the international quota system in apparel trade under the Multi-Fibre Arrangement (MFA), which strongly influences the flow of textile production and technology from developed to developing countries, and within the Third World.

World production of synthetic fibers is dominated by a handful of OECD-based multinational chemical companies; the top twelve alone accounted for some 60 per cent of world output in 1980, for example. One result is that traditional FDI plays a bigger role than NFI in this segment, especially compared with the other two segments. Large capital costs, economies of scale, and patent protection constitute major barriers to entry; and relatively few developing countries have embarked upon synthetic fiber production. New forms of investment—especially by a few U.S. and European fiber producers (the latter are an integral part of their countries' larger, oligopolistic chemical industries)—have been important in some of the larger Latin American countries. Nevertheless, new forms of investment have helped develop fiber-production capacity in some Third World countries. The most active investors have been the Japanese fiber companies, which are part of vertically integrated textile groups; and they have done so primarily through joint ventures, licensing of know-how, and plant exports with technical assistance—particularly in Asia and to some extent in Latin America.

Compared with the fiber industry, the role of international investment in textile-mill products has been limited. This segment has been developed in many Third World countries on the basis of imported, often second-hand machinery. Only Japanese firms have been really active in this segment, and, again, their involvement has been largely through minority joint ventures, licensing, and plant exports with technical assistance. Many of the smaller Japanese firms have used NFI (and especially joint ventures) to relocate production capacity, often under the umbrella of the large *sogo shosha* (general trading companies) in conjunction with Japan's restructuring of its textile complex during the 1960s and early 1970s. It is worth noting that about two-thirds of the sales of Japanese textile affiliates in developing countries go to local markets, about a quarter to third-country markets, and less than a tenth to Japan.

But it is in the apparel industry, more than any other segment of the textile complex, that NFI has been of crucial importance—and traditional FDI, insignificant—in recent decades. Textile and clothing manufacturers as well as apparel retailers and buying groups in the OECD countries have played a major role in the development of apparel production for export from developing countries. These 'principals' supply designs and raw materials, organize shipping, provide advertising and brand names, and control distribution channels. Most of this is done through international subcontracting with locally owned firms. The contracts are normally short-term (about one year), which allows the principals to shift important risks and costs associated with demand fluctuations onto the subcontractors while retaining virtual control over operations.

Among the first to make extensive use of international subcontracting were Japan's trading companies, which set up agreements with local producers in Hong Kong, Taiwan, and Singapore. Starting in the late 1960s, they worked mostly for export to the U.S. market. Some of this activity has been taken over by U.S. buying groups, and it has been expanded considerably both by these groups and by U.S. textile and apparel manufacturers. Among the European firms, German manufacturers have been the most active in using Asian subcontractors. The main motivations have been labor-cost reductions in a context of slow demand growth and intense price competition (and, in Japan, rapid wage increases).

Whether or not this type of offshore apparel processing continues to grow will depend largely on the nature and speed of technological change in the clothing industry. One of the major transformation that industrial countries may be able to carry off is to reduce labor costs markedly while increasing production flexibility through robotization; apart from high-fashion apparel, they have no comparative advantage today. (If import pressures on textile and clothing manufactures are creating serious difficulties in some OECD countries, these problems should be attributed less to NFI in developing countries than to domestic restructuring difficulties—for example, in moving up-market or, as in the United States, in modernizing production.) Obviously, continued expansion will also depend on protectionist trends in the OECD region and the distribution of Multi-Fibre Arrangement quotas among developing countries.

It should also be noted that the MFA quotas, along with the high costs of new production technology and other barriers to international marketing, create major obstacles to developing countries aspiring to join the ranks of major textile and apparel exporters. The quota system has had a major influence on the spread of production to second-tier producing countries, a movement in which NFI have played a central role. But the consensus seems to be that most of the emergent producers, with the exception of China, are not likely to join the ranks of the major exporters in the foreseeable future.

Food Processing

Although traditional FDI predominates foreign investment in food-processing plants, the trend is clearly one of increasing use of NFI. Particularly important are joint ventures in which the foreign partner supplies more sophisticated product technology and, often, a brand name and advertising experience, and the local partner provides assured access to raw materials. Other NFI of growing importance in the industry include licensing and franchising, the latter especially in "fast foods."

The fact that the majors and market-share leaders in food processing still rely heavily on whole or majority ownership of their processing plants suggests that such firms are reluctant to share equity (and rents) or to relinquish decision-making power that might dilute their competitive advantages, notably in marketing and brand differentiation. But there is also considerable evidence that some newcomers and followers are using NFI offensively, to penetrate markets in competition with some of the majors. Sharing production technology and control with local partners, such firms benefit from the latter's knowledge of local markets and ability to share risks (as well as to ensure supplies of raw materials). They have thus sometimes exerted considerable pressure on competitors, including the majors, to follow suit.

These patterns in turn suggest that the future of NFI will depend largely on the dynamics of inter-firm rivalry, and especially on whether more newcomers and followers will want to expand through NFI. Although a relatively low level of concentration in the industry works in favor of such a trend, it is important to remember that most international investment is still in the OECD region, where the emphasis is on acquisitions and mergers.

Several observations confirm that the new forms of investment, like traditional FDI, tend to be concentrated in the high value-added segments of this industry. The branches in which both the majors and the newcomers have become the most involved are brand-name and differentiated processed foods as well as milk products, fruits, and vegetables. They are not usually in mass-consumption food products, as they tend to concentrate their activities in the higher-income markets. An important exception is, of course, beverages. Some foreign companies have used mass-marketing techniques to create mass-consumption markets for their drinks.

Another phenomenon is the use of new forms of investment, and notably contract growing—as discussed in Chapter 4 [Moran, 1986]—to shift the risks of primary production onto local growers, while keeping control over the high value-added segments of the food chain, processing and marketing.

Structural changes in developing countries also account for some increased use of NFI. In many countries, especially in Latin America, the process whereby modern elites have consolidated their power has been accompanied by, and indeed has sometimes depended on, import-substitution industrialization. This has usually created internal terms of trade that are unfavorable to agriculture. Consequently, there has been a massive migration to urban centers with an accompanying rise in urban food demand. It was in this context that the change in foreign-investment patterns in Latin American food production took place: From heavy reliance on traditional FDI in the production of mostly unprocessed export produce, there was a shift to contract-growing by food processors producing primarily for local urban markets.

Implications of New Forms of Investment

There can be little doubt that many developing countries adopted policies in the late 1960s and early 1970s that were designed to increase national control over investment and returns on investment through NFI. But, as noted earlier, many of these countries now feel that they achieved only limited success at best. One reason, in their view, is that even with new forms of investment, they continue to depend on foreign firms for access to competitive technology and world markets. Another is a feeling of greater vulnerability to conditions in the international financial markets. A third may be that firms supplying assets through new forms of investment frequently approach these projects as sales rather than investment operations, which gives rise to the types of conflicts of interest cited in the discussion of the NFI concept.

Clearly, in a global investment scene characterized by changing economic conditions and investment strategies, the NFI offer important potential advantages to developing countries compared with traditional FDI, but greater risks as well. Among the advantages, the most important is undoubtedly the potential for increased host-country control over the process of capital formation, and for a larger share of returns from investment. There can be little question that NFI has favored such control in some cases: Witness the Japanese postwar experience, for example, as well as that of the Republic of Korea during the 1960s and 1970s.[9] In other cases, NFI have at least favored a higher host-country share of profits: Petroleum extraction is a case in point. Moreover, by combining the strengths and interests of host-country elites and the international business and finance communities, certain new forms of investment have broken ground in the development and capitalization of activities in the developing countries that were either new, like petrochemicals, or backward, like peasant agriculture.

Indeed, these new patterns could have significant implications: Given the vast development needs and growth potential of the Third World at a time when growth in the OECD region has slowed considerably by postwar standards, it would be reasonable to infer that by opening important new avenues of growth and longer-term business opportunities, NFI may hold important positive-sum-game implications for contributing to growth not only in host countries but in the global economy. In the extreme, it is conceivable that NFI may in the long run do for accumulation and growth internationally what the advent of the limited-liability joint stock corporation did a century ago in the national context of today's industrial economies. Like the corporation, NFI provide a legal and institutional framework in which entrepreneurs, owners of physical assets, and financiers can join forces, separate effective control from equity ownership, and divide risks and responsibilities.

The question, then, is to determine how a host country can take advantage of what NFI can potentially offer—and whether it might or might not do better with traditional FDI (perhaps in conjunction with improved fiscal policies). The evidence suggests that the answer generally depends less on the host country's foreign-investment policies per se (although these should be reasonably stable and transparent) than on the coherence and effectiveness of the country's overall industrial and macro-economic policies. Much also depends, of course, on the relative bargaining strength of local elites vis-à-vis their international counterparts. This bargaining strength in turn depends on such factors as the size and dynamism of the local market and the level of development of local technological, managerial, and entrepreneurial capacity, and hence also on the ability of local elites to take advantage of rivalry among foreign firms.

But in assessing the potential advantages of new forms of investment to developing countries, and, indeed, in explaining why some countries favor such forms, it is important not to confuse often nationalistic declarations with local reality. In some developing countries, an important reason why local elites may favor NFI over traditional FDI may be that they find it useful in competing with or consolidating their economic and political power vis-à-vis other groups at home. That is, new forms of investment may reflect and reinforce two simultaneous movements: one of increased horizontal integration by some local elites internationally (where NFI serve to strengthen ties between them and the international business and financial communities), and another of vertical hierarchization and concentration of power within host countries. Viewed from the broader national perspective, however, and particularly from that of local groups excluded from direct participation in NFI, the new forms may not hold any intrinsic advantages over traditional FDI. Indeed, the rising pressure in some developing countries in favor of NFI during the 1970s—a period of relatively rapid growth—may have been as much or more a reflection of struggles among groups to consolidate power as it was an expression of national interests vis-à-vis foreign capital.

For some countries, those pressures may diminish during the 1980s—either because of the relative success of certain groups in consolidating their positions of local power (some may even become international investors in their own right[10]) or because today's lower economic growth rates and debt problems leave them less room to maneuver vis-à-vis the international business and financial communities. But in other developing countries, pressures for NFI may remain strong for domestic political reasons if not for clearly justifiable reasons of national economic interest. Both possibilities reflect the continuing, complex interaction among local power structures, competition for control of the state and local economic conditions, and the forms of foreign investment in developing countries.

Among the potential risks of NFI for host countries, perhaps the most important are those associated with the decision of whether to invest and with the choice of the size of the capacity to be installed. Under NFI, these decisions are frequently assumed by host-country firms or governments and are thus more likely to be de-linked from world market conditions and the supply of technology. Under traditional FDI, the risks and responsibilities associated with long-term investment decisions, supply of technology, financing, and marketing output are normally assumed by the multinational firm; its decisions are likely to be based on a careful and knowledgeable assessment of worldwide conditions of supply and demand. The local participant in an NFI venture rarely has an information and planning horizon as international in scope as a multinational, and its ability to keep abreast of technological innovation and changing world-market conditions is likely to be more limited. Decisions may be influenced more by local production potential, investment costs, the country's need for foreign exchange, or even local political considerations than by projected global supply and demand.

One result may be continued host-country dependence on foreign firms for access to new technology and world-market outlets, even though those firms may be less committed to the success of the investment project than they would be under traditional FDI. (They may even take measures to ensure that the NFI project cannot compete with their global system.) The danger is that the gains in local control or share of returns obtained by the host country may not be commensurate with the increase in risks assumed and the costs incurred. There have been cases of large NFI projects whose viability depended on exports (as, for example, in mining, steel, petrochemicals, or autos), but whose output could not be sold profitably on world markets. There also have been cases of NFI in highly cost-inefficient, local-market projects to which local elites were more economically and politically committed than they would be to a traditional FDI project. But their survival called for high output prices behind even higher import barriers and large public subsidies. Traditional FDI projects are not immune to such problems, of course, but the potential risks and costs to the host country may be considerably greater under NFI.

Exacerbated long-run disequilibria in global supply and demand trends, with a tendency toward over-production and over-capacity worldwide in some important industries, is also a danger for host countries—and for the global economy. This danger undoubtedly explains why some industrial firms approach certain investment projects in developing countries as sales operations rather than as investments.

It is of course conceivable that the long-term planning perspective relinquished by multinational firms in such projects may be assumed by international lenders, provided foreign loans are necessary. Such a possibility is consistent with studies of trends in offshore financial markets and multinational banking, which found that banks were making more credit-allocation decisions on a global scale, focusing on outcomes—"choosing winners and losers"—by firm and industry.[11] Indeed, the potential for global rationalization might even be enhanced by the lenders' participation under NFI, because in traditional FDI, oligopolistic inter-firm rivalry in some industries can have a destabilizing effect.

But the international financial community's potential power to contribute to a rationalization of productive investment on a global scale tends to be undermined by a number of factors. One is the limits that banks now place on lending to specific debtor countries, sometimes irrespective of the soundness of a particular project, because of the debtor country's overall debt level. Other factors include the pressure on banks to create relatively short-term assets and the relative instability of international financial markets (not to mention their capacity to devote large sums to short-term speculative-type activities). Nor do industrialized countries' national credit agencies, whose export credits and guarantees are often used in conjunction with large NFI projects, appear likely to resolve the problem of international investment rationalization. Indeed, their decisions are often heavily influenced by pressure to favor the competitive positions of firms from their own countries.

Thus, by opening up new avenues of lucrative investment and sales opportunities for foreign firms in developing countries, certain new forms of investment may be a response to short-term problems of host countries and foreign firms alike. But they risk creating or aggravating both financial and "real" disequilibria in host economies and internationally. And, insofar as new forms of investment not only reflect but also reinforce the tendency of firms to shorten their investment-planning horizons, these disequilibria may be accentuated. Such disequilibria can and in some cases already do pose serious problems for host and industrial countries, individually and collectively.

Such imbalances could in turn aggravate international trade and investment relations, notably but not exclusively, in the North–South context. This aggravation could lead—and, in some cases, has led—to increasing state intervention in world trade relations, financial markets, and even investment activities.[12] Intervention can take the form of inter-governmental investment treaties,[13] but it can also intensify protectionism, through actions including "anti-dumping" measures and "voluntary export restriction" agreements, not only between countries in the North and the South but also among industrial countries.

To put these global disequilibria and negative-sum-game scenarios into proper perspective, it is important to recall that the bulk of international investment by firms takes place, and increasingly so, in the industrial OECD countries. Although new forms of investment in developing countries offer potential advantages as well as risks to the host countries, their impact on the global economy could, at worst, be one of exacerbating difficulties in some industries. The origins of these difficulties clearly lie in the industrial countries. And that is where the solutions must be found.

Notes

†Note: The views expressed are those of the author and do not necessarily represent those of the Organisation for Economic Co-operation and Development.

1. Many of the points discussed in this chapter are developed more fully in the author's forthcoming book, *New Forms of Investment in Developing Countries, Industry Studies* (Paris: OECD Development Centre, forthcoming). See also Charles Oman, "New Forms of International Investment in Developing Countries," OECD Centre Studies, No. 1 (Paris: OECD, 1984); and Charles Oman, ed., "New Forms of Investment in Developing Countries: The National Perspective," OECD Development Centre Papers, no. 1 (Paris: OECD, 1984).

2. A trade (sales) operation is an exchange transaction in which the seller (exporter) supplies a certain value of goods and/or services to the buyer (importer) in exchange for an *equivalent value,* but in a different form. Payment by the buyer is usually in money, but it may also be in other goods or services. Investment, on the other hand, implies the use of money and/or other goods (tangible or intangible) as assets, as capital, by one or more parties for the purpose of generating and appropriating *new value* ("value added") or a surplus of value over that embodied in the money/goods invested. For a fuller discussion of the conceptual distinction between "sales" and "investment," see Oman, "New Forms of International Investment." OECD Development Centre Studies, No. 1, op. cit.

3. Companies whose principal activity is the supply of turnkey plants, for example, may, of course, take an interest in the project's success insofar as their reputation benefits from successful projects and suffers from unsuccessful ones. But their own balance sheet is not normally affected. Furthermore, firms whose core business is the same as that of the investment project may actually have an interest in making sure that the project does not compete with their business outside the host country, they thus have rather ambivalent interests, at least, regarding the commercial success of the investment project.

4. For example, although the term "technology sale" is often used to describe licensing agreements, the term "sale" is generally inappropriate since strictly speaking a sale implies the transfer of property rights from the seller to the buyer. Rather, the licensee is usually given carefully defined rights of access to and use of proprietary knowledge possessed, and retained by the licensor. This is reflected in the fact that payments to the licensor frequently take the form of a percentage of sales or, occasionally, of profits. But even when the payment or "price" paid by the licensee is a lump sum, what the licensor is selling is in fact not the technology as such, but the firm's rights to future income—as the supplier of technological capital—from the licensee's operation. The licensor is "capitalizing" those rights. In either case (percentage on sales or lump sum), the technology plays the role of an

asset, of capital, for the licensor, as well as for the licensee's operation. See also Oman, "New Forms of International Investment," op. cit.

5. K. Kojima and T. Ozawa, *Japan's General Trading Companies: Merchants of Economic Development* (Paris: OECD Development Centre, 1985); T. Ozawa, "Japan's 'Revealed Preference' for the New Forms of Investment. A Stock-Taking Assessment," in Oman, "New Forms: The National Perspective," OECD Development Centre Papers, No. 1, op. cit.

6. Some important copper companies, for example, have either disappeared completely (Anaconda was purchased by the oil company Arco and then taken out of the copper business) or have been absorbed into larger firms, where copper mining is only a minor activity (e.g. Kennecott, acquired by BP's subsidiary, Standard Oil Company of Ohio, and St. Joe Minerals, acquired by the construction-engineering firm Fluor).

7. D. Suratgar, "International Project Finance and Security for Lenders," Paper presented to German Foundation for International Development Conference on International Mineral Resources Development—Emerging Legal and Institutional Arrangements, Berlin, August 1980, p. 1.

8. Algeria, for example, has relied very heavily on NFI, and in particular on turnkey and "product in hand" contracts as a basis for industrial capital formation since independence. At the other end of the spectrum, Singapore shows little use of NFI. But compared with Korea, for example, both Algeria and Singapore rely heavily on foreign investment (NFI and/or traditional FDI) as a proportion of domestic capital formation. When Korea is compared with Brazil, it clearly has less foreign investment, but what it has is predominantly NFI. In both Brazil and Korea, joint ventures and technology licensing are the principal NFI. See Oman, "New Forms. The National Perspective," op. cit.

9. See Bohn-Young Koo, "New Forms of Foreign Investment in Korea," in Oman, "New Forms: The National Perspective," op. cit.

10. See Charles Oman, *New Forms of Investment by Developing Countries* (Paris: OECD Development Centre, forthcoming).

11. See, for example, R.B. Cohen, "Structured Change in International Banking and Its Implications for the U.S. Economy," prepared for the Joint Economic Community, U.S. Congress, Washington, D.C., December 1980.

12. See, for example, Richard E. Feinberg, "LDC Debt and the Public-Sector Rescue," *Challenge*, Vol. 28, No. 3 (July/August 1985), pp. 27–34. The author argues that "despite the Reagan Administration's free-market rhetoric, its response to the debt crisis relied on government action. Ideologies aside, governments and international agencies acted quickly, pragmatically and effectively" (p. 27). He analyzes U.S. government involvement in debt rescheduling, in regulation of banking, and in direct foreign investment in developing countries. He also argues that "the same forces that drove the Reagan Administration to intervene in financial markets forced governments in the Third World to intrude more deeply into their own domestic economies" (p. 32).

13. See Alexandra Gourdain Mitsotaki, "Les Accords Intergouvernmentaux Relatifs aux Investissements," (Paris: OECD Development Centre, 1982).

7

Debt-equity Swaps and Foreign Direct Investment in Latin America*

Joel Bergsman and Wayne Edisis

*Source: *International Finance Corporation, Washington D.C., 1988, Discussion Paper No. 2*, mimeo.

Introduction

Objectives of the Research

This paper is about how debt-equity swaps affect flows of foreign direct investment (called here "FDI"). It is based on research that concentrated on four major Latin American debtors, Argentina, Brazil, Chile and Mexico. The paper examines how investment decisions of multinational corporations and commercial banks have been influenced both by the opportunity to use swaps, and by the different features of swap programs. The primary question is to what extent the availability of swaps has motivated investors to undertake projects that they otherwise would not have attempted. The paper also analyzes the many different ways that investors have used swaps (e.g., buy-outs, financial restructuring, technological improvements, or new capacity creation; export markets or domestic sales; privatization). From the analysis of the effects of swap programs on investors' behavior, the paper also draws some lessons about the usefulness of swap programs and about their designs.

It is important to state these purposes at the beginning, because there are many things this paper does not try to do so. First, the paper does not cover many other kinds of swaps. The debt-equity swaps considered in this paper involve the exchange of *public* external debt for local currency which is then used to invest in *equity* (or quasi-equity) in companies in the debtor country. Not considered are many other kinds of swaps, such as debt-for-debt, debt-for-commodities, and *private* debt for equity swaps in which a foreign parent company exchanges private debt issues by a subsidiary in the debtor country for equity in that subsidiary. Some of these other kinds of swap programs have generated a large volume of transactions, and are having important effects in the debtor countries.

Second, this paper does not cover all the material that would be required for an overall evaluation of swaps. A final verdict on the value of swaps depends not only on how they function as investment incentives (the subject of this paper), but also how they affect debt burdens, impose potential fiscal costs or add to inflationary pressure. As well, a final evaluation of swaps must take into account concerns that are more issues of judgment or personal values than of verifiable facts, such as whether the debtor countries will or should fully service their debts, and whether higher levels of foreign investment are good or bad for national development. The paper touches on some of these points but does not evaluate them fully.

Methodology

To summarize briefly, we relied mainly on interviews of executives of the companies that were involved in making the investment decision. We also talked with many government officials, intermediaries and others familiar with the programs. Some published information was also taken into account. Most of the foreign investors covered were based in either the United States or Japan. In over 125 interviews, we were able to obtain useful information on 104 of the approximately 450 public-debt-for-equity swaps that took place in the four countries studied.[1] There are serious difficulties in identifying all swap transactions, and others in accessing some of the investor companies' decision makers involved. For these reasons it is not possible to construct any kind of scientific sample of all transactions made. Our data are relevant to the larger, more established companies that did swaps, and we are confident that we have come to understand the effects of swaps on their behavior.

The Context of Debt-Equity Swap Programs

The debt "crisis" has entered its seventh year. It has not been brought to a head by wholesale refusal to service debts, nor has it been resolved by any sweeping bail-out. Rather, we are witnessing a protracted period of muddling-through, where both creditor banks and debtor countries share an interest in dealing more or less with small changes in the *status quo* or, in other words, not rocking the boat. Banks want to avoid the necessity of declaring default, and are fending off proposals for debt relief, all the while adding to their loss reserves. Many debtor governments are similarly acquiescing to muddling through, paying the least amount of debt service sufficient to ensure that they are spared the possibly severe repercussions of formal or extended non-performance.

Six years of this muddling through the debt problem have created a long-term environment discouraging to foreign direct investment in Latin America. A debt problem of shorter duration would not have had such a devastating impact on foreign investment. The problem's scope is reflected not merely in the cumulative loss of six years of investment flows; it is additionally the chilling effect on planning for future investment that comes

Table 1

A: *Foreign direct investment in four Latin American countries (US$ millions)*

	1983	1984	1985	1986	1979–82 average	1983–86 average	Percent change
Argentina	104.7	134.6	171.5	283.4	641.1	173.5	−72.93
Brazil	674.0	1,478.5	549.2	195.5	1,296.4	724.3	−44.13
Chile	25.3	22.8	106.4	103.7	138.7	64.6	−53.45
Mexico	−325.5	580.2	359.4	−49.5	790.9	141.2	−82.15
				Total	2,867.0	1,103.6	−61.51

B: *Swaps compared to other flows (US$ millions; annual averages)*

	FDI through swaps	'Normal' FDI (1979–82)	'Depressed' FDI (1983–86)	Service on official debt 1986
Chile	400	139	65	281
Mexico	1,133	791	141	2,087

Sources: FDI flows: OECD; flows from DAC members
Swaps: Host government data
Debt service: World Bank, *Debt Tables*

as the special burden of a protracted debt situation. Many companies spend two or more years planning and evaluating investments; in this context, a short-term doubt problem may cause planning to be temporarily suspended, but a long-term debt situation that shows no sign of ending, and the stagnation and uncertainties that go with it, may well convince companies to quit planning investments entirely – not only for the moment but for the indefinite future.

Table 1, part A, shows the decline in foreign direct investment to major Latin countries. At the beginning of the decade, Latin America attracted over half of all direct investment flowing to the Third World; by mid-decade, however, it was attracting less than a quarter – and of a significantly smaller total. In nominal terms, the flow of direct investment to the four major Latin American debtors fell by 62% between 1979–1982 and 1983–1986.

Muddling through the debt problem and the decline in foreign investment make debt-equity swaps a potentially interesting instrument, because swaps both help to lower indebtedness and to increase investment. But it is necessary in the same breath to say that swaps *alone* neither will unstick the morass of debt nor bring record levels of investment. The international financial community looks to swaps mainly for their potential to reduce debt and to increase its price in the secondary market, while debtor governments see swaps primarily as a way to attract investment, and secondarily as a way to reduce debt. But neither group expects swaps to produce a breakthrough in these areas. Although for a brief period a few years ago swaps were being touted by some promoters as the hot entree on the debt problem "menu," swaps are now seen more correctly only as an appetizer.[2]

Nevertheless, if the effects of swaps are examined on an incremental basis (rather than judged against the entire magnitude of Latin America's debt outstanding), than their impact appears more impressive. As shown in Table 1, part B, the amounts of FDI that came through swap programs in Mexico and Chile have been quite significant in comparison to earlier flows of FDI to those countries, as well as to other relevant balance of payments items such as their debt service obligations.[3]

Although the magnitude of swaps has been important in some ways, their contribution must be kept in perspective. First, as mentioned earlier, the role of swaps is only incremental; swaps can never substitute for fundamental changes in the overall investment climate that would be necessary for Latin America to reach its potential for attracting foreign investment. Second, the volume of swaps reported in the table are not proof that swap programs were the reason motivating these investments, nor are the data evidence that the swap investments were put to good use in the recipient countries. One point however is evident just from the numbers: swaps do offer an attractive incentive to foreign investors. The swap incentive is in essence an *up-front discount* on the cost of an investment. Even after deducting fees plus the portion of the discount captured by the government, the incentive accruing to the investor typically equals a quarter or a third of the total cost of the investment. (See Table 3.)

The incentive offered by the swap may be partially offset by restrictions on how the investor may use the local currency. Regulations vary from country to country, but the debtor governments in general impose longer delays on both dividend and capital repatriation for investments made by swaps, than for foreign investment through normal channels. Taxation and additional restrictions may undermine even more of the value of the swap. But the fact remains that swaps are a potentially powerful form of investment incentive, because (a) the incentive can be large, and (b) the incentive comes at the time of the investment, so that unlike most fiscal incentives it is neither delayed nor dependent on uncertain future events such as profits. That the amounts of foreign investment shown in Table 1 B have been done through swaps rather than the normal channels shows that the former, more difficult route must be of some value to investors.

The Costs of Swap Programs

Swaps, as has been noted, are instruments with two functions: they help to reduce foreign debt and they help to attract foreign (and sometimes domestic) investment. They also have some costs, and some observers argue that swap programs are on balance not worthwhile. Many of these arguments are really arguments about the desirability of the *products* of the programs. They are arguments that foreign investment is not such a good thing, or that prepaying the foreign debt is not a good idea. There may be valid questions about these points, but we do not analyze them here.

Although this paper is focused on questions about how swaps work in attracting investment, there are two points about the costs of swaps that we wish to note. First, one possible cost of swaps to a host country, perhaps psychological or perhaps real, is what might be called "overpayment" in redeeming the debt. To the extent that the country is not fully servicing, and intends not to service fully its foreign debt, the net present value of the payments it expects to make may be less than the amount at which it redeems the debt in the swap transaction. This viewpoint, is naturally, more common in the debtor countries than among the creditor institutions; the latter point out that the debtors received the resources they borrowed and are now obligated to service the loans fully. Leaving aside moral hazard, legal and other related considerations, the question does arise as to whether the debtor country is paying more to redeem its debt than the present value of the payments it expects to make to service the debt. The factual basis for concluding that swap programs do involve such "overpayment" is strengthened by international discussions of debt relief that seek methods for refinancing sovereign debt at its secondary-market price, and by actual buy backs, such as the one recently arranged for Bolivia.

Second, we have encountered considerable confusion about what is perhaps the most important cost of swaps, i.e., their impact on a country's monetary situation. In redeeming foreign debt with local currency, a government must choose some combination of allowing the payments to increase the money supply or else sterilizing this expansionary impact by restricting credit (or expenditure) elsewhere. Since most of the countries involved are experiencing high rates of inflation (Chile is a notable exception), these effects are a grave concern to most debtor governments.

In an attempt to clarify this negative effect of swaps, we present in Note[1] a brief analysis. The conclusion is that "... allowing a transaction through a swap always results in reducing foreign debt; it can cost the government *either* foreign exchange [if the investment was not additional] *or* the need to come up with domestic currency [if the investment was additional], *but not both*. Also, *if the swap investment is not additional then the swap program does not add to inflationary pressures*. These two criticisms that are often leveled at swap programs – lack of additionality, and inflationary impact — logically cannot apply simultaneously. A swap program leads to inflationary impacts only to the extent that investments made through it would not have happened if there were no swap program."[4]

Results

Additionality

The concept of additionality, and its measurement, are complex. Conceptually, additionality depends on how wide a range of other possibilities the analyst considers. At the broadest level, the inflationary or interest-rate effect of swaps will partly reduce domestic investment elsewhere in the economy. Thus, the total level of investment in a country will not increase by the full amount of foreign investment attracted by swaps. At a somewhat narrower level, an investment for which a swap was crucial to a particular investor might have been done by a different investor without a swap program. Investments in hotels in Cancun (Mexico) are sometimes cited to illustrate this point. Even if the actual investors were in fact swayed by swaps, it is alleged that the occupancy rate in the area was so high that other investors would have made the same investments without swaps.

Our research is limited to a narrower concept. We analyzed additionality only at the level of the individual transaction. We defined additionality as meaning that the particular investor would not have made the investment if a swap deal were not available.

Even with this simpler definition of additionality, measuring this phenomenon was not always clear cut. The information gathered in our interviews enabled us to classify the great majority of transactions as either additional or not additional. Nevertheless, for a few transactions, the question of additionality was not as straightforward. In these cases, the swap program affected the timing and/or the amount of the investment. It seemed likely that, in the absence of a program, something like the actual investment would probably have been made at some time. For these cases we established a category of "partial" additionality. Only a small percentage (7%) of transactions fell into this category, but some of these were large investments.[5]

We were able to come to conclusions about additionality for 99 of the transactions we studied.[6] Of these, 30 were made by banks and every single one was additional. Of the 69 made by MNCs, 23 (33%) were clearly additional and another 7 (10%) were partly additional. Thus for 61% of the transactions (43% for the MNCs and 100% for banks), swaps made a difference.

The larger degree of additionality for banks than for MNCs reflected an important underlying difference. These two kinds of investors responded in fundamentally dissimilar ways to the existence of swap programs. In recognition of these differences, it is appropriate to divide the discussion of additionality into two parts – one for banks and another for MNCs.

Additionality and banks: The attitude of most bankers toward equity investments helps to explain why additionality was 100% for the transactions studied. Most banks and bankers are by profession lenders and not equity holders. They normally would not, and do not, invest in non-financial businesses in Latin America. When most banks invest through swaps, they do so because they are dissatisfied with the performance of the debt they hold. Their main objectives are to diversify, and ultimately to liquidate a part of their portfolio sooner than would otherwise occur. The upside potential of equity investing is studied, but for most bank investors it is not the primary motivating force. A corporate investor, by comparison, does a swap transaction in order to reduce the cost of an investment which is expected to yield profits. For the corporate investor, the upside is a driving force and the swap increases it. Thus, it can be generalized that in most swap transactions "corporate investors want to get rich, while banks want to get out."

The media sometimes portray swaps as if they were a technique expressly designed and used by banks to transform their own loans into equity. The banks have been, in fact, among the main proponents of swap programs. However, the number to date of swap investments by banks has been considerably smaller than might be expected. There are a few well-known exceptions, but as of the beginning of 1988, many of the large US creditor banks had yet to make a single investment for their own account through a debt-equity swap, and others had made only a few. (We do not count here transactions to recapitalize their own wholly owned sub-sidiaries.) Japanese banks have been similarly reluctant, and in addition have been strongly discouraged by their regulatory authorities. No Japanese bank had made an equity investment through debt-equity swaps as of February 1988.[7]

While it may seem ironic or perhaps even erroneous, bankers shy away from what they perceive as the higher risks of equity. In every bank, we met some individual officers who believed that the upside potential of equity outweighed the risk of swapping some of the banks' poorly performing public debt for private equity. In most banks, however, top management was less ready to adopt this "entrepreneurial" view of risk. Instead, the closer a swap could be made to resemble debt, the more top management would be willing to consider the deal as worthwhile. For example, one banker told us that his bank would look more favorably on debt-equity swaps if it could be guaranteed that the resulting equity invest-ment would return LIBOR plus two basis points over five years.

A few banks, however, do not fit this general case. They include, among others, American Express Bank (which does not do commercial banking in the US and therefore is not subject to the same restrictions as other banks, and which of course is part of a larger group that is active, *inter alia*, in tourism), Bankers Trust and Security Pacific. These and a few other banks have a history of merchant banking operations, and consequently they have less institutional resistance to equity investments. Predictably, these are the banks that have made the most swaps for their own books. In some countries, especially in Chile, these merchant banks were among the first of all foreign investors to apply for swaps.

Tax considerations are a second significant factor restraining the number of swaps by U.S. banks. When a bank completes a swap, it may be able to take a loss equal to the difference between the face value of the debt and the (discounted) amount in local currency received from the debtor government. Moreover, in spite of a contrary opinion by a committee of the American Institute of Certified Public Accountants, some US auditing firms still take the position that all similar loans still held by the bank would have to be written down. Since many banks have been generating at best small profits in Latin countries, or indeed overall, a decision to make any particular swap must compete against all other types of losses that a bank may wish to take for tax reasons. A bank faces a fixed ceiling of usable tax losses, set by its own profitability. In recent years, this ceiling has been low, allowing little room for the possibility of large write-downs that doing swaps might imply.

A related reason has to do with the banks' wish to present healthy income and balance sheets. Even if the losses could be used to reduce taxes, some banks do not want to reduce their reported earnings by the amounts that might be involved if they were to do swap transactions. However, there have been reports in mid-1988 that some banks, having made investments for their own accounts through swaps, are putting such investments on their books at values not only higher than the secondary market prices of the debt, but even higher than the prices at which the debt was redeemed by the governments.

A final factor discouraging banks from making swaps is their own reluctance to commit fresh dollars, or even fresh local currency, in the debtor countries. Most investments require a foreign exchange component to pay for imported machinery, etc., which cannot be financed with swaps. Even straight buy-outs, such as have occurred in Chile, are often part of a corporate plan which includes some improvements in physical assets. For multinational corporations, these *de facto* fresh money requirements are not usually major obstacles to a swap. Banks, however, see an important difference between swapping their own paper, which involves no added exposure, and the need to inject fresh resources into countries where they feel already seriously overexposed. In interviews, American bankers expressed virtually unanimous and complete unwillingness to make any sort of swap investment that would require investing anything beyond the paper they already hold. This attitude clearly places tight constraints on the kind and the number of swaps that banks are willing to make.

Among the factors that restrain banks from becoming more involved in debt-equity swaps, one is conspicuous by its lack of importance. Federal regulations restricting the amount of equity a bank may hold in a non-financial institution have, in general, not greatly hampered U.S. banks from making swaps. Up to mid-1987 Regulation K required American banks to keep the level of their investments below $15 million, and below 20% of voting shares, in any one non-financial company. Moreover, ownership was circumscribed by a five year limit. These restrictions were liberalized in August 1987 and again in February 1988, for certain investments in heavily indebted developing countries. Moreover, Regulation K was flexibly administered in regard to swaps, with exceptions allowed, and both Federal Reserve officials and commercial bankers report that it was not a serious obstacle to the banks' investment desires.

As of the first quarter of 1988, however, many US banks said they were about to begin to make swap investments. The large write-downs of debt taken by many of them in early 1987 led to more active searching for good investments, and as of early 1988 a number of these banks had a significant pipeline of possible swap transactions for their own account under active consideration. Another factor that will lead banks to somewhat more swapping for their own accounts is the advent of mutual fund type institutions in some of the debtor countries (e.g. Brazil and Chile), to be capitalized by swapped debt. These funds are small in size – a few hundred million dollars cach, or sometimes even less — but are likely to attract smaller banks who want to convert some of their LDC debt to equity but lack the resources to select the investments or to manage the equity.

If more banks do make more investments for their own account through swaps, whether directly or through mutual funds, then recipient countries can expect the level of additionality in their swap programs to increase. Indeed, greater involvement by banks may be the most significant single development that could lead to a rise in overall additionality.

Additionality and corporate investors: For the investments we studied made by MNCs, swaps were a determining factor in 33% of them and were influential in another 10%. Why did swaps motivate these investment decisions, and not others?

The nature of swaps as investment incentives suggests some possible answers. Swaps create an incentive equivalent to an up-front cash grant. The incentive is certain, and it comes at the time of the investment. This differs strongly from many other kinds of incentives, which may offer benefits to investors only in the future, and only if projects become profitable. By reducing the initial cost of an investment, a swap not only increases the expected rate of return, but also reduces the absolute amount that the investor has at risk. As one swap investor said in an interview, "I wouldn't have made this investment if it cost me $40 million, because I wouldn't put that much money in this country. But for $25 million I was willing to take the risk."

Another feature of up-front incentives also helps to differentiate between additional and non-additional swaps. Experience has shown that up-front incentives have more effect on export-oriented projects than on projects aimed at the domestic market.[8] This is because costs are more important to export projects. They must compete in world markets and usually cannot pass higher costs on to their customers. Domestic projects, by comparison, are competing with others in the same market and are more able to pass costs on to customers, as long as their costs are not higher than their competitors. Producers for the domestic market are most concerned about the size and expected growth of that market, and consider costs as a secondary factor. The data from our interviews confirmed this greater importance of swaps for export-oriented projects. Among MNC investments aimed wholly or in large measure at export markets, 54% of those we studied were a directly additional result of the incentive created by swaps. By comparison, 40% of domestic-oriented projects were additional.

The difference between the results for export and domestic projects would be even larger if maquiladoras in Mexico were deleted from the sample. Maquiladoras are assemblers of parts mainly imported from the USA, for re-export to the USA. They are typically light manufacturing of garments, electronics and electrical products, not very capital-intensive, where labor is by far the greatest part of value added. We found a number of investments where swaps were used to buy or construct buildings for these operations. The swaps were, for the most part, not additional because capital costs are not a very important part of the cost of these operations.

This greater additionality in the case of export-oriented investment in general applies only to *manufacturing* investments. It does not apply to most mining or other natural resource projects for which the quality of the resource is the main factor determining location.

Additionality also depends on how long a swap program has been operating. Most of the programs in Latin America have existed only for a short time; even the longest (in Chile) had been in place for less than three years at the time of our interviews. Yet, many of the investments made in Latin America over the past few years were in the planning stage for a considerable time. Indeed, most foreign projects often spend at least a year or two in gestation before getting off the ground. This fact of corporate life means that most of the investments during the first six months to a year of a swap program had to be planned well in advance of the start of that program. Consequently, few such investments can possibly be additional. The existence of a swap program may cause a few such investments to be made sooner, or perhaps to be expanded. But for most of the early investments, there simply had not been sufficient time for an incentive to take effect.

This point may be extended in a further step; if in its early days a swap program cannot attract many additional investments, then the later years should see a rise in additionality (assuming all else is held constant). The interviews confirmed this. In Chile, for example, investors from many parts of the world, including from countries which did not have close business ties with Chile, have started to look for investment possibilities. This is, of course, attributable not only to the relatively long standing swap program available, but also to other important positive aspects of the investment climate there. However, it was clear from our interviews that the swap program was a significant part of the whole picture.[9]

Quantitative results also show the effect of the duration of the program. Countries with the longest lasting swap programs achieved the highest degree of additionality, if the Mexican data is interpreted in light of the effect of maquiladoras. Chile registered 64% additionality, Mexico 44%, Argentina 45% and Brazil 0% in the MNC transactions studied. (Our sample for Brazil was quite small and did not include transactions under the scheme that began in early 1988.)

Uses of Swaps

This section reports qualitative results on the kinds of investments being made through swaps. Generally speaking, two separate forces play a part in determining how swaps are used. One force is the regulations issued by the debtor governments, defining the permissible types of expenditures that a swap can finance. The other force is corporate strategy, defining the kinds of investment a foreign company wants to make. Frequently, these forces collide, and their conjunction results in a compromise and/or a partial use of swaps. Investors are often told they can use a swap to finance only the "qualified" part of their projects, and they are forced to provide the remainder in fresh money. Sometimes, though, an investor refuses to bend and the country yields, permitting the investor to use a swap for purposes outside the normal limits.

The uses of swaps encompass a wide spectrum of activities. Figure 1 presents a continuum that stretches from the least change in the recipient company to the maximum.

(Least)			(Most)
Buy-Out	Financial Restructuring	New Capacity	New Company

Figure 1 The spectrum of uses

In a buy-out only ownership changes, leaving the physical plant largely unaffected. Next is a financial restructuring, which improves a company's balance sheet but again does not alter production facilities. This is followed by a modernization and/or the addition of new productive capacity. At the far end of the spectrum is the creation of a new firm, which is the maximum change possible.

Buy-outs: Argentina does not permit swaps to be used for pure buy-outs, and in Brazil and in Mexico there are significant restrictions on such use. Chile permitted it, although now limits pure buy-outs to privatization transactions. These restrictions reflect an implicit viewpoint that foreign investors should be entitled to the incentive of a swap only if they use the local currency to increase a firm's productive capacity.

Buy-outs, however, can serve a potentially good purpose. When a foreign investor uses a swap to buy an existing local company, the enterprise may benefit from an immediate injection of managerial know-how. Even if new capacity is not immediately added, the buyer may be in a better financial position than previous owners to pay for future investments, and to put the recipient company's balance sheet in better shape. In fact, our interviews found a few cases where swap transactions that were originally limited to buy-outs led quite soon to increases in capacity and, often, to start-ups of entirely new lines of production.

An example from the interviews illustrates the advantages of swaps at the buy-out end of the spectrum. A foreign investor was prepared to close down a heavily indebted manufacturing subsidiary. Instead, when a conversion program becomes available, the parent company elected to use a debt-equity swap to repay the subsidiary's loans. The parent was then able to find a buyer for the recapitalized company, selling it to a new foreign investor who had a more specialized knowledge of the industry and who was committed to making the plant succeed. Although the swap transaction itself did not create new productive capacity, it nevertheless made the difference between the life and death of the enterprise.

Many buy-outs tend to involve banks as purchasers. In general the banks recognize that they do not have the expertise – or the desire – to run non-financial businesses. So these transactions are generally either (a) banks buying out, and running, financial businesses such as banking or insurance, or (b) banks using swaps to buy minority shares in existing firms, acting as silent partners and leaving the managements intact (this is common in Argentina), or (c) banks coming in jointly with a foreign company to buy or establish a local company, with the banks providing most of the finance and the foreign company providing management. In the latter two variants, the bank seldom takes true straight equity. Rather, it usually has some sort of agreement that gives it a semi-preferred access to earnings and thus limits its risk on the downside, correspondingly limits its potential gain on the upside, and provides for an exit after a specified period of time.

Financial restructuring: Only Mexico and Chile permitted swaps to be used for financial restructuring. A large number of investors used this option to retire debts (owed to others) by their local subsidiaries. Mexico reports that almost 25% of the total value of swaps in 1986 and 1987 was used for financial restructuring.

Traditionally, many foreign investors have preferred to finance a large portion of their Latin American operations with local borrowing; this minimized the parents' capital requirements and business risk. The higher real interest rates seen during the last decade have made these heavily leveraged capital structures too expensive, and swaps for financial restructuring have provided an inexpensive way to repay this debt, transforming it into equity at a lower cost. In most of the cases we studied, the transaction was entirely additional; the parent companies would not have restructured to increase their equity in their subsidiaries without access to a swap program. Moreover, in countries such as Argentina and Chile, where private debts have been assumed by the Central Bank, swaps for restructuring are non-inflationary, since they do not increase the amount of money in circulation.

Our earlier observations on the advantages of buy-outs also apply to financial restructuring. Since a restructuring will ease the financial constraints on a local company, it can subsequently lead to plant moderniz-ation and expansion of capacity. Countries such as Brazil and Argentina that do not permit swaps to be used for financial restructuring may be denying themselves these follow-on benefits. Moreover, these countries would not have to bear much added cost for these benefits, since most restructuring swaps are additional and some are non-inflationary.

New capacity: In the most general terms, companies add new capacity when they perceive a market opportunity for higher sales. The decision to add capacity is therefore tightly linked to market conditions. The charac-teristics of export markets and domestic markets are quite different. Accordingly, one would suspect that companies serving these dissimilar markets from the same home country base would not be influenced by the same factors when evaluating whether to add new capacity. They would not, therefore, be similarly influenced by the existence of swaps. For this reason, the following discussion treats export companies and domestic companies separately.

As noted earlier in the section on additionality, export companies are more sensitive to costs and therefore (in the manufacturing sector) are more likely to be swayed by the existence of swaps to make investments that they otherwise would not. This was true in our sample, especially of export companies that decided to add new capacity. Many of these would not have proceeded with their plans without the swaps. (Maquiladoras remained an exception, as explained above.) For example, one export company, which was unsure whether its plans for expansion would qualify under the new Brazilian rules, said it would not move ahead with its plans if a swap were denied.

By comparison, companies oriented toward sales in the domestic market would have proceeded with most of their investments to add new capacity, even without swap programs. They based their investment decisions on strategic considerations, such as an opportunity for greater sales of an existing product, a chance to introduce a new item into a prior distribution network, or a need to fend off a competitor to protect market share. These investors faced a difficult domestic situation; they were typically willing to expand capacity only when they perceived that a *sound business reason* justified risking additional capital. They did not believe that the strictly financial benefit provided by a swap could substitute for strategic consider- ations in determining whether to invest. Some firms even went so far as to evaluate a proposed expansion solely on its merits as a business decision and to explore the possibility of a swap only after the investment was approved. This behavior was especially common among Japanese MNCs, for which swaps were a determining factor in only two of 15 cases studied.

New company: Once again, in the decision to use a swap to create a new company, export companies and domestic companies are generally influ- enced by different factors.

Export companies are highly conscious of costs when evaluating whether to create a new manufacturing subsidiary in Latin America. They are thus influenced by the existence of swaps, which could make the differ- ence in the investment decision (maquiladoras again being an exception). Our research even found a few instances in which swaps were responsible for decisions to create new export-oriented capacity in Latin America rather than in Southeast Asia. We found examples of companies that were set up both to produce components and to assemble final products. In each case, corporate strategy dictated a need for a plant that could produce competitively at world market prices, and the cost savings created by the swap made a difference in the location decision. Other factors, including labor costs and competitive exchange rates, were also important; indeed, it is fair to say that the investments would not have occurred without this supportive environment. But the other elements of the environment alone did not attract the investments away from Southeast Asia, where general conditions were also suitable to exports. Swaps were the decisive factor. The number of these cases we encountered was small but, we think, interesting. Seen in conjunction with increased use of robotics and other automation techniques that are reducing the competitive importance of Asian labor, these location decisions may mark the start of what could be an important change in how exporting MNCs view at least some Latin American countries.

Companies aiming at domestic sales tended to follow the same pattern as when they decided to expand capacity; new companies were typically established only for "sound business reasons," in which swaps did not play a decisive role. There were a few exceptions, where swaps were decisive in the creation of companies oriented to domestic sales. Interestingly, these investments had been made, or were being planned, by multinationals that had previous experience in Latin America, but which had withdrawn or were about to withdraw for lack of profitability. These companies saw swaps as a way to gain enough leverage to justify re-entering or retooling for their traditional markets. This phenomenon, though, was limited to "old hands". Our interviews did not find a single company without previous experience in Latin America that was motivated by swaps to create a company to produce for the local market. The incentive provided by swaps did not seem to be powerful enough to persuade *new* investors to go to Latin America to produce for the generally depressed internal markets there.

Privatization: Privatization represents a special use of swaps for a buy-out. In such a transaction, a state-owned company is sold to a foreign investor, who pays for it with local currency generated through a swap. Since the seller is the government, such transactions are not inflationary. In these cases swaps can be useful not only in their two main functions of increasing the incentive for the investment and at the same time permitting the government to retire external debt at a discount. Using swaps may in some cases also ease the political problems of privatization. The sale price of a national company is often a controversial issue in privatization efforts. The market values of most of the enterprises are below cost. Opponents of the move (or simply political opponents of the government) often accuse governments of selling public firms too inexpensively. Swaps can help with these problems by making foreign investors willing to pay a higher local currency price. Governments may enhance the attractiveness of swaps for privatization by reducing the amount of the secondary-market discount that they retain for themselves; Mexico, for example, redeemed debt at full face value for investors who have applied to use the proceeds to privatize state-owned companies. Swaps have been made in Mexico, and even more in Chile, for privatization. Argentina, however, expressly forbids the use of swaps for privatization, and in Brazil swaps may not be used by foreigners to gain control of a Brazilian-owned company.

Environmental influences on the use of swaps: The discussion so far has focused on how different characteristics of companies, and of government regulations, affect the uses of swaps. The economic environment also makes a difference. Two factors of importance that the research found are (a) the state of financial markets and (b) the investment climate.

In Argentina, and to a lesser extent in Mexico, long-term financing for industrial expansion is not easily available on reasonable terms. Moreover, in Argentina relatively few foreign investors are interested in new invest-ments. In these circumstances, a principal use of swaps in Argentina (and to a lesser extent in Mexico) is by good local companies to obtain long-term financing for expansion programs. In some cases the company approaches creditor banks and offers them the opportunity to become a silent partner, using swaps to help finance their investment program. The bank takes not straight equity, but some sort of paper with a somewhat more fixed and limited return, and a date for sale back to the company. The bank adds some company risk to its portfolio, but in return gains a good chance of full service on its paper and a clear exit in something like 10 or 12 years (or perhaps less). Such a use of swaps may not resemble traditional FDI very closely, but is useful in the constrained situations existing in many of the debtor countries, permitting sound firms to grow more rapidly than they otherwise could. In other cases the Argentine company may itself be the investor using swaps, employing foreign exchange it owns to buy the debt. Here the swap scheme is acting as an incentive to capital repatriation, as well as a source of industrial financing.

This kind of transaction seems much less common in Chile, where financial and capital markets are working better. There, with a better investment climate, a different kind of additionality occurs. The creditor bank again becomes a silent partner, but in this case the managing partner is a foreign company that the bank brings into Chile. The bank will take a company from its own home country, usually a company with which it already has important relations, and offer to finance a large share of an investment in the debtor country if the company finds one it wants to run. The bank again takes on some company risk but gains a good chance of full service and exit; the company gets an investment with very little of its own capital at risk, and the debtor country gets a new company and/or an injection of management talent, and often additional exports.

Final thoughts on uses of swaps: These varied uses of swap facilities, as well as the continued demand for them in all four Latin American countries, show that one early idea about a very limited absorptive capacity for swaps was not correct. Some observers, seeing the early use of swaps in Chile concentrated on buying up existing companies, concluded that once the "interesting" candidates were sold there would be little or no demand to use swap facilities for investment. The total ability of a country to attract investment and to reduce its debt through swaps was thus thought to be limited to this relatively small *stock* of potentially decent enterprises that were for sale. Experience shows, however, that a reasonable swap facility can be used not only to transfer ownership of existing companies but also to create new productive capacity. The absorptive limit for swap transactions is thus set more by *flow* concepts: a share in the total investment that may take place in the country each year; the amount of foreign investment that the government is willing to accept in that flow; or the amount of inflationary impact that the monetary and fiscal authorities feel able to deal with. A reasonable swap program in a reasonable environment will, it appears, attract more potential investors than the host country government may want, as long as the price of debt in the secondary market remains low enough to make the incentive significant.

Swaps are thus used for at least as many different purposes as regular FDI. Excluding the special case of maquiladoras, export-oriented swaps tend to be additional and to fall at the end of the spectrum toward starting new companies or adding extra capacity. Domestically-oriented investments tend to be made by companies that already had experienced in Latin America. Many of the projects that were intended to expand existing capacity to serve the local market were justified by strategic factors and were not decisively affected by the existence of a swap program. Swaps that were used for financial restructuring were usually additional investments which often led to further investments in new physical capacity. Banks were the main players at the end of the spectrum where swaps were transacted only to transfer ownership, and in most cases, especially for investment in non-financial companies, this investment is intended to be only temporary and is often in the form of quasi rather than straight equity.

Features of Swap Programs and their Effects

Table 2 summarizes what we have learned about the effects in practice of different features of swap programs on investors' behavior. Nine different kinds of features are listed, along with their effects on three kinds of results: additionality, channeling investments into priority uses, and financial benefits to the debtor government.

Auction vs. negotiation:[10] Around the end of 1987, Argentina and Brazil began using auctions to let the market set the price at which they will redeem debt in swap transactions. Chile (in Chapter 19, its public-debt-for-equity program), and Mexico when it had a program, used mechanisms that more or less set the price administratively. (Both Argentina and Brazil also, however, allow for transactions negotiated separately and independently of the auctions; these are large or otherwise special investments.)

Table 3 presents data on the secondary market price of debt, the government's share of the secondary market discount, and the incentive to the investor. While there are by no means enough data points to be sure of any inferences, these numbers are consistent with two common-sense conclusions: First, a lower secondary market price is associated with both a higher incentive for the investor and a higher share of the discount going to the government. When the pie is bigger, both the investor's and the government's slices are larger. Second, using auctions to set the redemption value may give the government a larger share of the discount than using administratively set rules or negotiation. Comparing Brazil and Chile, the secondary market prices were similar but Brazil, which used auctions, captured a higher share of the discount than did Chile. A different explanation, not necessarily mutually exclusive, is that the data for Argentina and Brazil (the countries using auctions) are for the first few months of their programs. Additionality was likely to have been low in these transactions. Investors therefore may have been willing to cede a higher share of the discount, since they were prepared to proceed even without a swap.

Some observers say that using negotiation rather than auctions helps the government to increase additionality. We find no evidence or reason to believe this. Using auctions need not preclude screening for additionality; the government can screen before allowing participation in the auction. Moreover, negotiating fine gradations of incentive depending on the government's perception of additionality is likely to be ineffective, for two reasons: First, it is not easy for the government officials to be sure about additionality, and the best that a government can hope for is to screen out a decent percentage of the obviously non-additional cases. Second, even if the screening were perfect, giving a low incentive to non-additional investors is silly; if they can be identified, why give them any incentive at all?

Negotiation or administrative rules giving different redemption prices for investments of different priority may also seem to be useful in channeling investments into higher priority sectors, places, etc. But if the number of priority categories is high, the differences in incentive will be small. We doubt that small differences in incentives have any important predictable effects on investment decisions. For a very small number of different priority categories (say, two), and if the high-priority category for the government is unattractive to investors, than a segmented program that gives a moderately high incentive in the low-priority category and a very high incentive in the high priority category may be effective. Such segmentation could be achieved either administratively or by (separate) auctions.

Another effect of using auctions rather than negotiations may stem from the greater transparency of the auction process. Auctions may in fact reduce the possibilities for bribery and corruption, and also may give the appearance of a more honest and fair process. Nevertheless, no government grants admission to the auction without a case-by-case review of proposed transactions. So while detailed negotiation probably does provide a somewhat more flexible field for corruption, using auctions does not completely guarantee an honest or fair process.

Fresh money requirements: Argentina is the only one of the countries studied to impose a general requirement for fresh money. (Chile sometimes requires it, on a case-by-case basis, when the government thinks that a particular investment is highly likely to occur even without access to swaps.) Under the Argentine scheme in effect from mid to late 1987, an amount of foreign exchange equal to the amount of debt swapped was required. This absolutely killed the interest of commercial banks and did pretty much the same for other potential investors. Thus, greater additionality (which was the stated goal of the requirement) was not achieved because there were no transactions.[11] (We did encounter one investor who was going to use this program for an investment that would have gone ahead even without any swap incentive. But the rules were changed before he applied.)

Starting in late 1987, however, the requirement was changed to only a ratio of 30 cents fresh money per 70 cents swapped debt. More important than the change in the ratio, the fresh money could be in local currency, and it could be in the form of loans or equity, at the choice of the investor. The exchange rate used was also changed from the official to the free rate.

Table 2 Effects of different features of swap programs

	Additionality	Prioritizing investments	Impacts on debtor government*	Other comments
I. Features whose main effect is on price				
1. Auction vs. negotiation	No direct effect	Negotiation can channel investments to desired uses	Auction probably increases government's share of discount	To a limited extent, segmented auctions can substitute for negotiations in regulating the discount and channeling the investments
2. Fresh money requirements in foreign exchange	Very few deals; most not additional	No direct effect	Drastically reduced demand for swap and hence amount of investment and debt reduction	Banks won't participate
3. Fresh money requirements: local currency OK	May reduce additionality	No direct effect	May reduce government share of discount	Reduces both the incentive to investors and the government's share of discount
4. Incentive taxed as gain at time of swap	No direct effect	No direct effect	One way to increase government share of discount	May decrease foreign investors' tax liability in USA. *Increases* tax liability in Japan
5. Convert at official rate which differs greatly from free market	Decreases additionality	No direct effect	Will reduce demand for swaps but increases government share of discount	Investors hate it

6. Allow domestic participants	May increase round tripping, and additional investments as well	No direct effect	Increased demand should allow government to capture more discount	They do it anyway. Allowing it reduces evasion and perception of unfairness
7. Screen investments: (a) for additionality and to reduce round tripping	Can be somewhat effective	No direct effect	May reduce government's ability to capture discount	Probably worth doing if expectations are modest and it's done quickly
(b) for sector, exports, technology transfer, etc.	Favoring exports will increase additionality	Can be very effective	No direct effect unless overall demand is greatly reduced	
(c) only new capacity allowed; no financial restructuring	Decreases additionality	Could be slightly positive	Ditto above	Counter-productive because financial restructuring often precedes new capacity, and is not inflationary
(d) for financial or economic soundness	No direct effect	Could be positive but this is doubtful	No direct effect	Probably not very useful
III. *Primarily regulatory, administrative or other features*				
8. Timing restrictions on dividends or capital repatriation	May channel some non-additional investments out of swap program	No direct effect	May improve near-term future balance of payments	Not a major disincentive for most investors — but there are some exceptions
9. Continuity of swap program	Significant positive effect	No direct effect	Probably no direct effect	Very important to increase additionality

* In addition to the effects noted, more additionality implies inflationary impacts (as explained in Note[1]), except in cases of financial restructuring.

These changes have greatly increased the attractiveness of the Argentine program; even banks can often arrange for some other investor to provide the fresh money. Demand at Argentina's first three auctions was strong.

Under the present Argentine system, many investors satisfy the fresh money requirement with loans from third parties, or in some cases a mixture of equity and loans from third parties. The fresh money requirement may have little or no effect in reducing the incentive in these cases. In other instances, however, no acceptable third parties may be available, and the investor may have to contribute the fresh money himself. In this case a fresh money requirement reduces the incentive for the investor. Even when a suitable third party may be available, the investor might have preferred the simpler alternative of going without him if fresh money were not required. Now, the fresh money requirement might bring in more cash to the country, but it brings no fiscal benefit to the government. Dropping the fresh money requirement altogether would probably increase the price that investors would bid in the auction, thus increasing the share of the secondary market discount that the government could capture. Moreover, in the present Argentine environment, the fresh money requirement, even in local currency, may turn away some investors and thus reduce additionality. So it might be better for a government not to impose a general fresh money requirement, and to profit from the higher demand which will result in a lower redemption price as set in the auctions.

Taxing the gain: The incentive actually appropriated by the MNC investor presumably represents a gain for him, which may be subject to tax in the host country. If so, there is a question whether the host country should tax that gain at the time of the swap, or rather just reduce the investor's cost basis, wait for the investor to sell the equity and tax the realized gain, whatever it turns out to be, at the later time. In Argentina the amount of the incentive is subject to the regular corporate income tax. Mexico is considering taxing the gain at a rate of 30% at the time of the swap. For a US-based MNC investor, such a tax might reduce its tax liability in the US and therefore the Mexican tax might be a way of transferring resources from the US Treasury to the Mexican. In Japan, however, the Ministry of Finance has apparently decided that if Mexico taxes the gain at the time of the swap, it will do the same – thus for a Japanese-based MNC such an action would greatly reduce the attractiveness of swaps.

Exchange rate used: More than any of the four countries studied, Venezuela has a market exchange rate which differs greatly and steadily from the official rate. Venezuela opened its swap program in early 1987 offering to redeem debt at full face value but at the official exchange rate. Even though the Government guaranteed to convert at the official exchange rate for future dividends and capital repatriation, most potential investors were skeptical – they feared large real devaluations. They would strongly prefer conversion at the free rate, and accept converting sub-

Table 3 Discounts and market prices

Country and date	Redemption value	Market price	Incentive to investor	Government's share of discount
Argentina				
January 20	0.620	0.320	48.4%	55.9%
March 29	0.641	0.270	41.4%	73.8%
June 10	0.423	0.250	40.9%	76.9%
Average			43.6%	68.9%
*Brazil**				
March	0.730	0.460	37.0%	50.0%
April	0.680	0.500	26.5%	64.0%
May	0.780	0.510	34.6%	44.9%
June	0.865	0.530	38.7%	28.7%
July	0.730	0.540	26.0%	58.7%
Average			32.6%	49.3%
Chile				
Average	0.890**	0.670	24.7%	33.3%
Mexico				
Average	0.850	0.550	35.3%	33.3%

* Free area auctions
** Net market value to investor

sequent repatriation flows at the future free rate; for them the Venezuelan scheme effectively reduced the incentive to use swaps to zero benefit in the present and an uncertain gain in the future. A government in this kind of situation can probably attract more swaps – especially more *additional* investment – and still capture a good share of the secondary market discount by redeeming at the free rate but using an auction or a preset discount to regulate the amount of the incentive.

Allowing domestic participants: The Argentine program allows domestic companies or persons to use it. In Chile, Chapter 19 can be used only by nonresidents.[12] Mexico's agreement with the creditor banks allowed local residents to participate from March 1987, but the government never included that right in its regulations governing swaps (although it was legal for a Mexican-owned foreign firm to use it). A few domestic firms were nevertheless allowed to use swaps in late 1987, before the receipt of new applications was suspended in November. The Brazilian program allows domestic participants but there is little incentive for them to use it, given the difference between the official and secondary market exchange rates. (Brazilian investors did make considerable use of swaps in earlier periods, under the old rules and at times when the difference between the official and parallel rates was smaller.)

Our interviews showed conclusively that domestic investors had no difficulty in circumventing restrictions on their participation, by establishing offshore dummy corporations or otherwise.[13] The restrictions, apparently meant to reduce round-tripping, do not appear to be effective, and they create resentment and political opposition at home because they say that foreigners are given access to an incentive which locals are denied. Moreover, in a situation such as that in Argentina and Mexico, with domestic interest rates high and only very short-term financing available at all, swaps may perform a very useful legitimate function for local companies in giving them access to long-term financing at reasonable rates.

Screening proposed investments: Every government screens every applicant for a swap on a case-by-case basis. Perhaps surprisingly, few investors had serious complaints about this process in any of the countries studied. The purpose and criteria of the screening differ widely, however, from country to country.

Screening for additionality and to prevent round-tripping has been recently increased in Chile and in Brazil. It seems to be effective enough to be worth doing, even though it is bound to give less than perfect results, and should be done on an expeditious basis with these limitations in mind.

Screening for priority sectors, priority regions, export orientation, etc. can be quite effective. It of course replaces market signals by administratively determined priorities, with the well-known dangers this entails. Given the strong positive association of export orientation with additionality, it is tempting to recommend a screening, auction or negotiation process that either restricts swap programs completely to export projects, or else screens non-export projects much more rigorously than export projects for additionality.

Restricting swaps to creation of new capacity may be counter-productive on balance because of the strong linkage between initial swap-financed buy-outs and later additional investments. Moreover, some of the swaps for financial restructuring are used to retire debt that has been taken over by central banks. These swaps are not inflationary and hence have less real resource cost to the host economy.

Screening swaps for financial and/or economic soundness of the investment may not be very productive. Some kind of quick, qualitative look to weed out investments that are not legitimate or in some other way clearly counter to national priorities may be useful, but detailed quantitative evaluation may not be effective without access to information and a commitment of time and resources to each evaluation that are probably not possible.

Screening of any sort of course increases the possibilities for corruption. We have gotten strong hints of systematic corruption in the screening process of one country.

Timing restrictions on dividends and repatriation: Every program forbids the payment of dividends, and/or the repatriation of capital, for several years – typically four years for dividends and ten or twelve years for capital. Perhaps surprisingly, we found only a few investors (including some who did *not* use swaps) who regarded these restrictions as serious deterrents. This seems to be because most non-bank users of swap programs are committed to staying in the countries for the long term. Most banks, on the other hand, want to get out as soon as possible. But those few that make investments for their own account through swaps do so because they find their alternatives to be no better in regard to timing of exit – and often they have mechanisms that will circumvent the limitations. On balance, such restrictions may be of some use in improving the country's near-term balance of payments, and also in diverting a few non-additional investments out of the swap program and into normal channels.

Continuity: We repeat here our conclusion that a stable and continuous program after a year or two starts to generate significantly more additional investments. A stop-go program is a good way to assure a lot of free riders, while not changing the behavior of very many investors (other than banks).

Main Conclusions on Program Design

The results described above can be summarized according to the three criteria used to evaluate swap programs as investment incentives:

(i) *To Increase Additionality*, these results suggest five practical steps to take:
- Keep the level of the incentive to the investor reasonably high, but screen proposed swaps to eliminate the most obviously non-additional investments. Keeping the incentive low is self-defeating and results only in a large percentage of free riders.
- Maintain continuity in the program over time – i.e. several years at least. The basic thrust of the rules and regulations, and the incentive levels, are important things in which to avoid too much variation if additionality is to be enhanced.
- Since additionality is greater in investments aimed at producing manu-factures for exports, screen non-export proposals and mining proposals much more rigorously for additionality than manufacturing export proposals. In the extreme, if a very limited swap program is desired, it could even be limited to export-oriented manufacturing investments.
- Similarly, since virtually all investments made by banks are additional, adopt measures that encourage banks to use swap programs. Investment funds financed by swapped debt can be one important mechanism. Also, bank proposals could be subject to less intensive screening for addition-ality.
- Maintain reasonable timing restrictions on the repatriation of dividends and capital.

(ii) *To channel investments into priority sectors or areas*, the most effective procedure is simply to screen proposed swap deals and permit only high-priority investments to use the program. Alternatively, for high-priority areas that are relatively unattractive to investors, two different levels of incentives (set either in auctions or administratively) can work if the incentive level for the high-priority area is allowed to be very high. Allowing low-priority investments to use the program, at low incentive levels, will just waste the incentive on a high percentage of free riders. Similarly, a finely-graduated scale of priorities, with smaller differences among categories, will not have much channeling effect and will result in many free riders in categories, if any, where the incentive is small.

(iii) *To capture a larger share of the secondary market discount for the government,* our results again suggest four ideas:

– Use auctions to set the redemption price of the debt.
– Allow domestic participants.
– Don't screen out too many applicants.
– Don't require fresh money.

There are some unavoidable tradeoffs among the objectives or criteria that have been discussed here. Channeling investments into priority sectors or areas will decrease both additionality and the government's share of the secondary market discount, unless the priority happens to coincide with the effect of swaps on investors. (The only such coincidence we found is export-oriented investment, and this is an important one.) Using auctions to determine the redemption price of swapped debt will probably increase the government's share of the discount, but if it leads to large variations in the redemption price it may decrease additionality. Keeping the incentives high will increase additionality but will also increase the amount of subsidy given to free riders – this being a conflict not peculiar to swaps but rather common to all investment incentives. Allowing domestic participants will increase additionality and also the government's share of the discount, but may also increase pressures on a parallel foreign exchange market. For a particular government designing a swap program, the right balance among these tradeoffs will depend on the particular objectives and constraints that the country has, as well as on knowledge of just how these details are likely to affect the behavior of potential investors in that country.

A Final Word

We hope the information in this paper will be of use to debtor country governments in deciding whether to allow debt-equity swaps, and in designing a program if the decision is positive. Each government must decide for itself whether it wants to use swaps to prepay foreign debt, even at a discount, and how much inflationary impact it can handle (from the part of that prepayment that will be financed from local currency). It must also decide whether it wants to attract more foreign investment than it is currently getting.

We found swaps interesting, even before studying their effects in practice, because of their double function. After learning more about how they do work, our own evaluation is that:

(i) A well designed swap program can lead to a small but significant reduction in foreign debt. Having a debt-reduction program in place may, in and of itself, also help towards the restoration of creditworthiness. These effects are benefits to a country that is making serious efforts to service its debt insofar as is feasible; they are of little use to a country that expects to receive debt relief or to default soon.

(ii) The more important benefit of a swap program can be in helping to reactivate both foreign and domestic investment. This effect will be greater to the extent that other aspects of a country's investment climate are reasonably positive, although swaps can also be valuable in providing a source of long term financing for domestic companies when the domestic financial market is not functioning well. The tendency of swaps to attract export investment more than domestic market-oriented investment is an added bonus. In spite of inevitable losses through free riders and outright abuses of the program, swaps do attract a fair amount of additional private investment – which in most if not all of the debtor countries could be useful.

Notes

1. Three of the 104 transactions studied were in other highly indebted countries. Also, we were able to analyze a number of other investments in the four countries for which the investors decided not to use the swap programs that were available.

2. Although in Chile, where the program has been in place since May 1985, debt-equity conversions under Chapter 19 through December 1987 amounted to US$1.0 billion, equivalent to 5.7% of its stock of long-term debt at the end of 1985. (Conversions through other schemes amounted to even more.)

3. In constructing tables such as Table 1, there are serious data and conceptual problems. Three major ones are: First, data on FDI are poor in quality and not comparable across countries. The two generally used sets of data are the IMF numbers, which reflect actual balance of payments flows as reported by the host countries, and OECD estimates which reflect something closer to commitments than to actual cash flows and are as reported by source countries, the latter limited to members of the OECD. These two sources typically differ greatly for a specific country in a specific year, but are usually not too far from each other for a specific country over a period of several years. We used the OECD numbers for two reasons: (a) they are comparable across host countries, while the IMF numbers are not; (b) they are conceptually closer to the estimates of swap transactions, which also reflect something closer to commitments than to cash flows. Second, of the four

countries studies, only two – Chile and Mexico – had generally available and relatively stable swap programs in place for significant periods of time. Third, the advent of the swap programs more or less coincided with other positive changes in the investment climate in both Mexico and Chile (notably more attractive exchange rates in both countries, and other elements as well in Chile), so that the high levels of swap transactions cannot be fully attributed to the availability of the swap programs.

4. From Annex 1, para 6.

5. The swap investments of two auto companies in Mexico illustrate this gray area. As early as 1982, Volkswagen and Chrysler had decided to invest to expand their facilities, but they did not move ahead with these projects until 1986, when they used swaps to finance their investments. Chrysler, moreover, decided to create significantly more additional capacity than it otherwise would have done, because oi the cost-reduction effect of using swaps. We scored both these cases as "partly additional." See Debs, Richard A., David L. Roberts and Eli M. Remolona, *Finance for Developing Countries*, Group of Thirty, 1987, p. 29.

6. The sample contained five transactions from which we learned other useful information, but were unable to determine anything about additionality.

7. The research did not cover European banks, but they appear to have been more willing to make swaps than either the U.S. or Japanese banks.

8. See, e.g., Guisinger, Steven and Associates, *Investment Incentives and Performance Requirements*, Praeger, 1985.

9. It should be mentioned that in recent months the Chilean authorities have been somewhat more rigorous than previously in screening investments that are allowed to use the swap program. One of the criteria in this screening has been additionality. Most of the transactions analyzed here were approved before this more rigorous screening took place, but there might have been some effect from it on them.

10. Some clarification of our terminology about different prices and discounts may help here. As shown in the schematic diagram, we refer to three different *prices*: the face value of the debt being swapped, the secondary market price of that debt, and (somewhere in the middle) the price at which the debtor country redeems the debt to the investor. The "discount in the secondary market" is the difference between the face value and the secondary market price, expressed as a percentage of the face value. This difference is divided between the "incentive to the investor," which is the difference between the secondary market price and the redemption price, expressed as a percentage of the latter, and the "government's share of the discount," which is the difference between the face value and the redemption price.

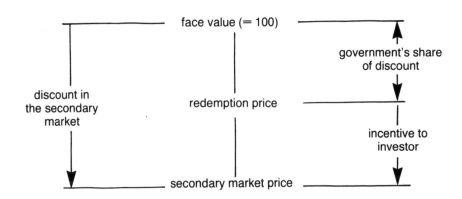

11. It is true of incentive schemes generally that very low incentives do not change the decisions of many investors. Thus, a low incentive will usually result in a high percentage of free riders – low additionality in percentage of decisions affected – but only a small subsidy per transaction. A high incentive will produce more additionality, but will of course give a higher unnecessary subsidy to the (smaller percentage of) free riders. Designing any incentive program involves a trade off in that to attract more investment, more must be given away to those who would have invested anyway.

12. Annex 4 of Chapter 18, usually referred to as "Chapter eighteen and a half," permits Chilean residents to make investments in existing firms under the higher incentives available under Chapter 19. This facility is limited to the investee company buying and swapping its own publicly guaranteed foreign debt, and has been used mainly for financial restructuring by a few local banks and other companies.

13. Chile has increased its efforts to screen out applicants from dummy offshore corporations owned by Chileans, and participants in the process say these efforts have been reasonably successful.

8

New and Old Multinationals: Competitors or Partners*

Louis T. Wells, Jr.

*Source: K. Khan, ed., *Multinationals of the South* (New York, St Martin's Press, 1986), pp. 196–210.

The spread of 'Third World' multinational enterprises is a relatively new phenomenon.[1] These firms, with home bases in developing countries, have multiplied rapidly in Southeast Asia in particular, but also in Latin America, South Asia and, to a considerably lesser extent, in Africa. An important question for the managers of the traditional multinationals from the industrialized countries is whether these new multinationals are competitors or potential partners in the battle for world markets. The answer, it will be argued in this chapter, is a mixed one: in some cases the new multinationals are a threat to the profitability of the traditional firms; in other cases, there are opportunities for beneficial collaboration between the old and the new multinationals.

Like the multinationals from the industrialized countries, the new multinationals from the developing countries are of several types. In discussing the competition that they pose for traditional multinationals as well as the opportunities that they offer, it is useful to consider in one category those firms that have subsidiaries which manufacture for the market in which they are located. As another, separate category, one can consider the several types of firms that produce for export. This chapter will not deal in depth with a third category, the service firms: banks, contracting companies and so on.

Firms that Manufacture for the Host Country Market

By far the largest number of subsidiaries of multinational enterprises manufacture almost entirely for the market in which they are located.[2] Third World multinationals of this type often do not compete head-on with the traditional multinationals for local markets. But the exceptions are numerous and important. Moreover, where resources are complementary, there are opportunities for collaboration.

Different Geographical Focus

In many markets of the world investors from the industrialized countries simply do not meet the multinationals from developing countries. While a large part of foreign investment from the industrialized countries goes to other developed country markets, an overwhelming majority of investment from developing countries is placed within the Third World. About 54 per cent of the subsidiaries of multi-nationals of Europe and Japan were located in developed areas in 1971; for American-based multinationals the equivalent figure, for 1968, was close to 60 per cent.[3] In contrast, 428 out of 494 manufacturing subsidiaries of Southeast Asian parent firms were located within the developing countries of the parent's own region. Similarly, 118 of 157 subsidiaries from Latin America were located within Latin America. Many of the remainder were also located in other developing areas, rather than in North America, Japan or Europe. Consequently, it is principally in developing countries that the two kinds of investors are likely to meet.

To be sure, developing country firms do occasionally establish manufacturing subsidiaries in the advanced countries. But most such subsidiaries are established as export supporting entities. Most are simply assembly operations that put together components manufactured in the home country. The rationale for these relatively scarce types of subsidiaries is to lower transportation costs or to escape import restrictions in the host market.

Different Industry Focus

Even when investors from the advanced countries and the Third World find themselves in the same country, they may well not be in head-on competition. A major reason for the lack of direct competition is that manufacturing multinationals from the industrialized countries and those from the developing countries do not typically focus on the same industries.

Data on industry distribution of different investors demonstrate that the new multinationals tend to concentrate in industries that are not at the forefront of technology in the advanced countries and in industries in which advertising is not a principal competitive weapon. The patterns of concentration are consistent with the view that the major strengths of the multinational manufacturing firms from the advanced countries are in technology and in product differentiation through marketing techniques. The strengths of the multinationals from developing countries, on the other hand, tend to be in low-cost manufacture of more standardized products or those in which trade name plays a lesser role.

Many of the multinationals from the advanced countries have depended on a technological edge to survive abroad. That edge has often been at the forefront of research and development. Such firms rarely encounter intense competition from Third World multinationals. Although the multinationals from the developing countries have often had technological advantages, these have been of a different sort.

The differences in mix are quite apparent when one examines the industries in which the two types of firms invest. One approach is to classify industries by their R & D intensity. About 58 per cent of the subsidiaries of firms from the developing countries are in industries characterized by low R & D expenditures (calculated in the United States as less than 1 per cent of sales). Such industries account for only 30 per cent of subsidiaries of American multinationals and about 36 per cent of subsidiaries from other industrialized countries. The figures are almost exactly reversed for high R & D industries (2.5 per cent or more of sales spent on R & D). Only 26 per cent of the subsidiaries of Third World multinationals are in high R & D industries, whereas almost 55 per cent of the subsidiaries of American multinationals and 52 per cent of the subsidiaries of multinationals from other industrialized countries are in such industries. Detailed data from Indonesia, Brazil, Taiwan and the Philippines cover a larger sample of multinationals and confirm this pattern.[4]

Although the comparisons are less striking, the industries in which the new and the old multinationals focus also differ in their advertising intensity. Multinationals from developing countries have 84 per cent of their subsidiaries in industries characterized in the United States by advertising expenditures of under 1 per cent of sales. American-based multinationals have only 74 per cent of their subsidiaries in such industries. The contrast is sharper at the upper end (2 per cent or more spent on advertising). There, Third World multinationals have 2.7 per cent of their subsidiaries; American multinationals have more than four times the proportion. Again, the same pattern appears when one examines the more comprehensive data from individual countries.[5] Consequently, the Unilevers and the Colgates of the advanced countries are somewhat protected from the multinationals of the developing world.

Even though the focus of the investments of the new and the old multinationals is different, there is sufficient overlap in the industries in which they invest for there to be real potential for competition. Moreover, the overlap may well be increasing as developing country firms master the marketing techniques that are so common in the industrialized countries.

Price versus Differentiation

In some cases, the new multinationals have found ways of competing on price in industries in which product differentiation is the principal means of competition in the industrialized countries. In industries such as detergents, soft drinks and much of the pharmaceutical market, price competition seems to play a minor role in the advanced nations. The market is dominated by firms that have created powerful brand names. Although little-known brands compete at the periphery by lowering prices, they capture only a small share of the market. On the other hand, in some developing countries, price plays a significant role even in such industries. Although multinationals from the advanced countries have usually entered these markets by following the strategies that have worked well at home, branding and advertising, some firms from developing countries have entered the same markets with a strategy based on price competition.

These latter firms are, on occasion, powerful competitors to the multinationals from the advanced countries. Although they may initially appeal to different segments of the market, the price competitive sector of the market may well be much larger than that to which the traditional multinational is accustomed. Further, the presence of popular products at lower prices puts competitive pressure on the traditional multinationals even in their higher-income segment.[6]

Learning to Differentiate

In a few cases, firms from the developing countries have learned the skills of brand creation and have exported the expertise. Well-known examples include Inca-Kola of Peru (soft drinks) and San Miguel of the Philippines (beer). They are companies that have learned to create brand images and to transfer the skill to other countries, often in direct competition with the traditional multinationals.

A few years ago, firms that had created well-known brand names were exceedingly rare in the developing countries. Today the traveller in developing countries encounters increasing numbers of local firms that have mastered such such marketing skills and are competing successfully with the traditional multinationals. In Indonesia, for example, a local firm has created a strong brand name for dry-cell batteries (ABC) and has captured such a large share of the local market that Union Carbide has recently suspended production of its Everready batteries. Like Inca-Kola and San Miguel, many more of these successful firms will, no doubt, be tempted to venture abroad with their skills.

Technological Development

The figures presented earlier suggested that Third World multinationals tend to be strong in low-technology industries. That fact should, however, not lead to the conclusion that these companies are not innovative. It is well known that a number of Third World firms have adapted imported technology to the requirements of small-scale manufacture, for example. Thus, to picture firms in these countries as being solely copiers of technology from elsewhere would be quite incorrect.

Many of the new technologies are developed to enable the firm to utilize local inputs. Firms in developing countries have learned to use tropical hardwoods, rice or wheat stalks and other local raw materials for the manufacture of paper. Less dramatically, they have learned to use standard steels in place of speciality steels not available locally, standard screws and knobs that do not have to be imported and so on. Such innovations or adaptations can give the firm a significant advantage over other firms that must import their inputs. The multinationals from the industrialized countries are particularly likely to be at a disadvantage. Often they manufacture global products that require specialized inputs. Those inputs can be exceedingly expensive in the developing countries because of protective tariffs and long lead times in ordering from abroad.

In other cases, the innovations of firms from developing countries are addressed to special needs of the developing country customer. For example, Brazilian appliance makers claim to build models that are particularly resistant to high humidity and to fluctuations in voltage, while an Indian firm claims that its dyes are especially sun-fast. These products are occasionally effective competitors against the global products of the advanced country multinational, even outside the Third World firm's home market.

Tail of the Product Cycle

Probably the most severe competition between multinationals of the advanced countries and those from the developing world occurs at the tail of the product cycle.

The pattern is similar to the competition that has for decades faced America-based multinationals as their product lines mature. But the source is different, and the severity greater. According to the well-known product cycle model, since the late 19th century, firms from the United States have innovated labour-saving products or processes and products that appealed to high-income consumers.[7] In so doing, they were simply responding to the needs of their home markets. Eventually markets developed abroad for their innovations. Although those markets might well be served initially by exports, eventually transportation costs, import restrictions and potential local competition led the firms to invest in foreign plants. With the passage of time, the technologies became more widely available and foreign producers grew to be effective competitors to the American innovators. First, it was the Europeans in most cases; then the Japanese entered the markets and provided competition for American multinationals, even in third countries.

In recent years, the power of the product cycle model for explaining trade and investment patterns among the industrialized countries has weakened considerably.[8] Income levels, market sizes and wage costs are now sufficiently similar among the principal industrialized areas that it is increasingly difficult to predict where innovations will occur. Japanese, European and American firms face similar markets and are thus likely to innovate for high-income consumers or to save on high-cost labour.

Although there has been a dramatic decline in the power of the product cycle model to explain trade and investment among the advanced countries, it is still a rather powerful tool for understanding the differing patterns of the advanced and the developing countries. The markets in the Third World are sufficiently different in income levels, size and labour costs that local firms are unlikely to undertake the same kind of innovative activities that are typical of firms in the richer countries. For high-income and high-technology products, customers in the developing countries must generally turn to the multinationals from the industrialized world. It is the special nature of their products and production processes that grant most multinationals from the advanced countries the ability to compete in the Third World. Most firms depend on their technology to compensate for their higher overheads and the penalties bestowed on them by developing country governments because of their nationalities.

As incomes grow in the developing countries, markets for the higher-income and labour-saving products and processes grow. Eventually, local firms learn the technologies, and, in some cases, contribute to the know-how. Often with lower costs, and with preferential treatment from local government in many cases, local firms become serious competitors for the traditional multinationals in the richer developing countries. But recently, some of these new competitors have also ventured abroad, almost always to countries at similar or lower levels of development. As a result, the firms from the newly industrializing countries (NICs) are providing competition for the traditional multinationals much like that posed by the Europeans to the Americans especially in the late-1950s, and by the Japanese to both the Europeans and the Americans from, say, the mid-1960s.

The most common competitive tool of the developing country multi-nationals in the battle with multinationals from industrialized countries is price. Many of the Third World multinationals have advantages over other multinationals that enable them to manufacture at lower costs. First, their salaries for expatriate managers and engineers are only a fraction of the salaries for expatriates that accompany the traditional multinationals.[9] Second, as was pointed out, their manufacturing processes have, in many cases, been adapted to the requirements of small-scale manufacture.[10] Small markets, after all, were what they faced in their home countries only recently. Third, they have, in some cases, learned to lower costs by using locally available inputs to the manufacturing process. Finally, they have experience in operating in developing countries. An examination of foreign investors' proposals in one developing country showed clearly that firms from India, for example, understood the concerns of government much better than the multinationals from the industrialized countries.[11] Their proposals addressed directly issues such as effects on their host's balance of payments, concerns with the use of scarce resources, economic as opposed to private returns, and so on. In addition, American-based multinationals occasionally claim a further advantage for Third World multinationals:

they have no constraints from their home country in paying the bribes that are often necessary to accelerate approval processes.

Ironically perhaps, it is the Japanese multinationals that are most likely to be head-to-head in competition with Third World multinationals. First, Japanese firms are particularly strong in the geographical areas where Third World multinationals are most developed, in Southeast Asia. Maybe even more important, the Japanese are particularly likely to have investments in developing countries for products that are at the tail end of the product cycle. In the poorer countries, they have invested in industries such as textiles, kitchen utensils and simple metal fabricating. These are exactly the kinds of industries in which Third World multinationals have gained increased strength.

The Pattern of Competition

In sum, the principal form of competition between Third World multinationals and the traditional multinationals occurs when the advantages of technology have been eroded and the new multinationals can use their low costs to advantage. This is late in the product cycle. There are exceptions, to be sure. On occasion one encounters Third World multinationals that have mastered marketing techniques and can exploit the advantages of branding. Indeed, casual observation in the developing countries leads one to speculate that the numbers of such firms are on the rise. Furthermore, innovations of a special character, suited to Third World markets, can create small numbers of competitors. But bitter competition is most likely at the tail end of the product cycle, and for products where lower prices are likely to attract a significant customer base.

Opportunities for Collaboration

Perhaps surprisingly, it is late in the product cycle that the opportunities for collaboration between the traditional and Third World multinationals are most apparent. There, opportunities exist to combine the marketing skills of the advanced country firms with the low costs of firms from the NICs.

Collaboration can, in some instances, take the form of conventional joint ventures. Thus, I encountered a paint factory in one Asian country that was jointly owned by an American-based multinational and a firm from another Asian country. The American company provided brand name and formulations; the Asian company, management and knowledge of operating in a developing country environment. In another joint venture, a Japanese manufacturer had joined with an East Asian firm in joint ventures for significant Asian markets to manufacture consumer electronic products. These joint ventures drew together complementary skills much like those in the paint venture.

Theoretically, at least, one could imagine that Third World partners might bring political benefits to a partnership as well.[12] Their presence might soften the political reaction to a foreign investment. Thus, an American multinational might join with a developing country firm in a third market and find its proposals more acceptable because of the partnership. The facts may, however, be different. In much of the world the obvious Third World partners are little more acceptable than the traditional foreign investors. Chinese partners from Hong Kong, Taiwan or Singapore grate on ethnic sensitivities in much of Southeast Asia. Indian or Pakistani partners can create adverse reactions in East Africa. And it is not clear that Mexican investors are more loved in Central America than are the Yanquis—or Chileans in Peru or Argentinians in Brazil, for that matter.

The experiences of the few formal joint ventures that I have seen suggest that they may not be very stable. Disputes appear to be frequent. The joint venture for paint, for example, apparently broke up eventually. One of the important causes of the break-up appears to have been disputes over the effect of local inputs on the quality of the paint. The Asian partner wanted to use raw materials that were available in the host country; reasons ranged from lower costs to improved government relations. The American firm insisted on imported ingredients to maintain the same standards for the product that were to be met at home. Although I do not know the current status of the electronics venture, I can imagine increasing dissatisfaction on the part of the Japanese partner as its strategy becomes more global. Growing interest on the part of the Japanese parent in integrating overseas manufacturing facilities is likely to lead to conflict, especially since the joint ventures were in potentially important markets. With increasing integration, partner conflicts are likely to occur over allocation of production, transfer prices and quality standards.

In other cases, collaboration may be less formal than that of joint ownership of projects in third countries. One South Asian firm, for example, had originally obtained its expertise from a European enterprise. Relations between the two enterprises remained good. New technology was supplied from time to time, and machinery was occasionally purchased from the European company. Moreover, the two firms had cooperated when opportunities were identified in other countries. Cooperation was usually in small, less-developed countries. The European firm realized that its overhead costs would be high in such countries. Further, its skills generally lay in larger-scale production than would be appropriate for the local market. The South Asian collaborator, on the other hand, had adapted European techniques to the needs of small markets. Collaboration took the form of the European firm passing on to the Asian firm information about opportunities that it encountered in other areas of the world. If the Asian partner proceeded with the project, the European firm would supply some machinery and, perhaps, special technical knowledge.

This looser form of collaboration is likely to generate fewer conflicts between partners than the type described earlier. First, the collaboration was in markets that were very peripheral to the interests of the European firm. And the odds were good that they would remain peripheral. The European firm would be unlikely to consider integrating production in these countries into a global system. Further, the lack of an intimate relation meant that issues of transfer pricing, allocation of production, and so on would not arise regularly. Finally, the collaboration did not involve the use of a brand name that might suffer if the new operation produced a non-standard version of the product.

A third kind of collaboration was also encountered. In these ventures, firms from advanced countries combined with developing country enterprises to build vertically integrated systems. One of these ventures was born out of an earlier relationship. Toray, of Japan, had supplied inputs to the textile and garment operations of TAL, a Hong Kong enterprise. When TAL encountered financial difficulties, Toray acquired almost half its shares, largely to maintain the outlet for its Japanese production. The two firms then jointly expanded into South-east Asian countries, building a vertically integrated network, from synthetic materials to garment manufacture. Toray provided skills for the upstream industry, TAL for garment making.

Over time, Toray acquired more and more of the equity of TAL. This was, perhaps, inevitable. Garment-making skills are probably easily mastered, compared to the skills involved upstream in the industry. The importance of inputs from TAL would decline with time. Increasingly it would be viewed primarily as a customer with little to offer aside from markets. Integration into the Japanese enterprise was the response to continued financial difficulties.

Still another kind of collaboration was encountered in my field work, a type that usually involved no equity participation on the part of the multinational from the industrialized country. In some cases, a traditional multinational had established a network of local suppliers in one developing country. It had, perhaps, provided the original technology for the start-up of these suppliers and had trained management to meet quality and delivery standards. When the multinational set up facilities in another developing country, it would occasionally invite these earlier suppliers to follow and establish parts or component plants in the new site. Thus, the close links between the multinational from the advanced country and local suppliers would be maintained as the suppliers themselves became multinational. Indeed, on occasion the new projects might be jointly owned. Exchange controls and weak capital markets in the new multinational's home country could mean that it has to turn to the traditional multinational to provide capital. The result might be an equity joint venture between the advanced country multinational and the newly multinational Third World enterprise.

The Exporters

Raw Material Producers

Third World multinational producers of raw materials are, at least today, so few in number that they can hardly be considered as serious competition for firms from the industrialized countries. Although they account for a very small percentage of the total overseas projects undertaken by firms from developing countries, investments that provide sources of raw materials are important because of their political sensitivity and because they quite frequently involve collaborations with firms from the industrialized countries.

Some such projects are undertaken with strong home government support, often by state-owned enterprises. In these cases, the goal is to secure for the nation a reliable, and perhaps low cost, source of raw materials. Most such ventures have been undertaken in the search for oil and involve partnerships with the older international oil companies. YPF, of Argentina, for example, has worked with major international oil companies in some of its overseas concessions, which have been located in Bolivia, Ecuador and Uruguay.

Other raw material projects are undertaken by private firms on their own because of the need to secure raw materials for themselves, even though they may be of little strategic importance for the nation. Thus, Hong Kong furniture makers and Korean plywood manufacturers have, on occasion, integrated backwards into timber extraction when faced with unreliable sources. These ventures have generally not involved collaboration with multinationals from the industrialized countries. An exception is Formosa Plastics' joint venture with ARCO in the United States to obtain low-cost gas to be turned into polyvinylchloride, vinylchloride monomer and ethyl dichloride.

In the case of YPF, the Argentine national oil company, the goal in its overseas joint ventures was to obtain technology and experience in exploration and development that it could apply in Argentina. This technology could, management believed, be obtained most quickly by working together with the major international oil companies. At times, they were not encouraged to invest in Argentina, but the state company would work with them abroad. In turn, the presence of the Argentine company in a concession in Latin America would, perhaps, lower the political costs of turning potential oilfields over to foreign enterprises.

Whether the state enterprises of the developing countries are likely to become significant producers of oil, or other raw materials, outside their own borders is an open question. To date there are few indications of such firms posing a major threat to other multinationals.

Marketing of Raw Materials

Some of the most interesting foreign investment plans of firms from the developing countries have not been in raw materials themselves, but rather in the processing of their raw materials. In many cases producing countries have felt that they were at the mercy of foreign processors and that they could obtain higher prices for their materials if they could break the control of foreigners over downstream processing and distribution. Consequently a number of projects were proposed to weaken the hold of foreign enterprises over downstream stages of industries that were important to the developing countries. Examples abound. A Brazilian sugar cooperative bought an American coffee firm in the hope of using its distribution system for sugar. Algerians tried to buy into the French packing industry to market their dates. And so on.

With the principal goal that of breaking the power of the traditional firms over the downstream stages, such ventures have tended to stay clear of collaboration with multinationals from the advanced countries. But not always. The Iranian National Oil Company, for example, had, before the revolution, cooperated with ENI, the Italian state company, in developing refineries and distribution systems abroad. When such cooperation occurs, it may be most likely with a maverick firms, such as ENI, which is somewhat outside the traditional group of oil companies. Thus Caribbean efforts to establish aluminium smelters to break their dependence on the major aluminium multinationals falter due to their lack of technology and capital. Although both are in the hands of the traditional aluminium firms, collaborations appear to be in the interests of neither party. Proposals that have been floated for collaboration are with Eastern European firms, who are not viewed as a part of the 'enemy'.

Although efforts to break the hold of traditional multinationals are behind many of the interesting foreign investment proposals that involve vertical integration, some are of a more conventional kind. They are attempts to tie user and supplier in ways that assure stability to both. Thus the Korea Electric Company has explored for uranium with a French group in Gabon. Presumably the Koreans were interested in secure sources of uranium, the French in secure outlets for uranium.[13] The French influence over a former colony may give the French partner preferred access to raw materials. Moreover, the Korean Electric Company is unlikely to have the required mining skills, but can provide an outlet for uranium. With few importing customers and few export sources within the industry, a joint venture between supplier and user might well be useful to both parties.

The Quota Hoppers

Of all the Third World multinationals, perhaps the most significant from the point of view of politics in the advanced countries are the so-called quota hoppers, the firms that establish subsidiaries abroad to provide platforms to continue exports to the industrialized countries. These investments are usually primarily in response to restrictions on exports from their home country that have been imposed as a result of negotiations between their home country governments and the advanced countries. To avoid these restrictions, local companies establish plants in other low-wage countries not yet subject to quotas.

The earliest illustrations of such investments were the textile companies of Hong Kong, which, when faced with restrictions on exports from Hong Kong to Britain and the United States, established subsidiaries in Macao, Singapore, Malaysia and other sites. They have been followed by electronics firms, shoe manufacturers and other producers who draw heavily on low-wage labour. Their projects have extended from East Asian home bases as far as Sri Lanka and Mauritius.

Perhaps not surprisingly, these investments have not typically involved collaborations with firms from the advanced countries. Most such companies have the technical skills and access to foreign markets before the quota issue arises.

Service Firms

Although we shall not devote much attention to service firms, note that collaborative efforts are quite common for such activities.

Perhaps the most common are in the banking sector. Collaboration ranges from very loose forms such as correspondence arrangements to the creation of jointly owned institutions. In many cases, joint activities result simply from the gains that arise from pooling complementary geographical expertise.

Joint activities are also not unusual for construction and engineering firms. Thus American enterprises have joined with Korean or Indian firms in the Middle East for construction projects.[14] In these cases, the American partner is likely to bring a well-known name and, perhaps, technology, while the Third World partner brings low-cost labour and, on occasion, special expertise in simple construction techniques in difficult environments.

There are numerous other collaborative efforts in the service sector. For example, First Pacific, a Hong Kong based firm owned by ethnic Chinese from Indonesia, has joined with Sears World Trade for international trading. Little information about the arrangements is public, but there appears to be joint equity involved.[15] The collaboration apparently grew out of complementary geographical coverage and skills. First Pacific had earlier acquired a faltering Dutch trading company. Sears World Trade was having considerable difficulty. The two trading enterprises had, it seems, strengths in different parts of the world. Moreover, Sears seemed better at obtaining product; the old Dutch firm, at selling. The hope appears to be that the combination will strengthen the firms so that they can survive. In this case, however, the Third World nationality of one of the partners appears to be accidental and of no particular relevance to the future.

Conclusions

Competition

By far the most common subsidiaries of Third World multinationals are those that manufacture in developing countries for the local market. Many of these produce in industries that are not the focus of the multinationals from the industrialized countries. Consequently the two types of multi-nationals are, often, not in direct competition. Nevertheless, as the product lines of the advanced country multinational mature, the firm is likely to face increasingly severe competition from Third World multinationals. What is more, that competition is likely to be of a particularly difficult kind. The Third World multinationals are effective low-cost producers, especially at the relatively small volumes that are required in many developing countries. And their principal strategy involves the use of that cost advantage to cut prices.

Third World multinationals are, in fact, a varied lot. Although the previous paragraph describes a large fraction of them, many are quite different. Increasingly, firms from the developing countries create trade names that can compete with the traditional multinationals. Some firms are also particularly innovative when it comes to the special demands of the Third World markets.

Further, there are strong developing country multinationals in a wide range of extractive and service industries. Although they account for only a small fraction of their markets, they are in some ways new competitors for the old multinationals. But the efforts on the part of developing countries to develop vertically integrated multinational chains to weaken the control of traditional firms over markets have had only very limited success. And where such chains have been built, the industry has usually been one with rapidly declining barriers to entry. As the oligopoly weakens, the traditional multinationals have been facing new competition from entrants from the advanced countries as well as from the developing countries.

Collaboration

A number of firms from the industrialized countries have found opportunities for collaboration with the new Third World multinationals based on their complementary skills.

Perhaps the most common have been ventures that combine the

marketing skills of firms from an industrialized country with the small-scale technology or the knowledge of business practices in developing countries of Third World multinationals. Problems have often arisen in these ventures, however, as one partner has mastered the skills of the other, when the developing country partner wants to modify the product of the industrialized partner or when the traditional multinational begins to follow a more global strategy that incorporates the joint operation into its world-wide system. For the firm from an advanced country with limited interests in Third World markets, for which eventual integration is unlikely, collaboration with firms from developing countries is, however, promising.

Notes

1. For recent books and bibliographies on the subject, see: Sanjaya Lall, *The New Multinationals: The Spread of Third World Enterprises*, Chichester, John Wiley and Sons, 1983; and Louis T. Wells Jr., *Third World Multinationals: The Rise of Foreign Investment from Developing Countries*, Cambridge, Mass., The MIT Press, 1983.
2. Only about 4 per cent of the manufacturing subsidiaries identified in my study of Third World multinationals were export platforms. And very few of the other manufacturing subsidiaries exported at all.
3. Data calculated from tables on p. 38 and p. 112 of James W. Vaupel and Joan P. Curhan, *The World's Multinational Enterprises* Boston, Division of Research, Harvard Business School, 1973.
4. These and other data are presented and explained in detail in Wells, op. cit., pp. 44–7.
5. Ibid., pp. 60–2.
6. See Sushil Vachani, *Strategic Product Market Choices by Multinationals and Local Firms in a Newly Industrializing Country*, unpublished D.B.A. thesis, Harvard Business School, 1985, for some corporate responses.
7. See Raymond Vernon, 'International Investment and International Trade in the Product Cycle', *Quarterly Journal of Economics*, May 1966.
8. Raymond Vernon, 'The Product Cycle Hypothesis in a New International Environment', *Oxford Bulletin of Economics and Statistics*, November 1979.
9. See Louis T. Wells Jr. and V'Ella Warren, 'Developing Country Investors in Indonesia', *Bulletin of Indonesian Economic Studies*, March 1979, pp. 69–84.
10. See Wells, op. cit., Chapter 3.
11. From my field work with Dennis Encarnation for Encarnation and Wells, 'Evaluating Foreign Investment' in Theodore H. Moran (ed.), *Investing in Development: New Roles in Private Capital?*, New Brunswick, N.J., Transaction Books for the Overseas Development Council, 1986.
12. See, for example, Seamus G. Connolly, 'Joint Ventures with Third World Multinationals: A New Form of Entry to International Markets', *Columbia Journal of World Business*, Summer 1984, p. 19.
13. Ron Richardson, 'South Korea Tries to Buy a Guarantee', *Far Eastern Economic Review*, 31 August 1979, p. 77.
14. Raj Aggarwal and Inder P. Khera, 'Strategic Planning for Western Direct Investment in Developing Countries: A Response to the New Realities in Growth Markets', *The Mid-Atlantic Journal of Business*, Summer 1983, p. 1.

15. 'First Pacific: On the Move Again', *The Economist*, 24 August 1985, pp. 64–5, and 'Sears' Trade Unit Shifts Focus', *New York Times*, 2 December 1985, pp. D-1 and D-5.

PART THREE: Impact on Developing Countries

This part combines chapters on selected issues, as well as on important host countries in the developing world. Of the enormous range of possible publications available, this part includes three which deal primarily with issues, and two that describe the role of TNCs in the most dynamic of developing economies, the Republic of Korea and Taiwan, Province of China.

The chapter by Lall deals with the impact of TNCs on technology development in host countries, with empirical evidence drawn from India. It distinguishes between different levels of technological development in developing countries and traces, in particular, the impact of TNCs on "know-how" (production skills) and "know-why" (innovative capabilities). The evidence suggests that TNCs are efficient transmitters of know-how and have beneficial effects on local competitors' know-how. As far as know-why is concerned, the effect of TNCs is more ambiguous. There remains a grey area where genuine concern can be voiced about the effects of TNCs on firms in lesser industrialized countries. The pace at which these firms are prepared to launch innovative efforts in developing host countries may be far slower than the increasing ability of those countries to conduct, and benefit from, such efforts. That paper does not consider what was termed the "strategic counterfactual" as technology development in the general introduction (i.e., technological development that may have taken place under an alternative strategy towards TNCs). At that time, evidence on the technological capabilities of the newly industrialized countries of East Asia was still slim, and the relevant concepts have still not developed. None the less, the arguments in the Lall paper are leading up to the ideas suggested in the introduction.

Larry Willmore's comparison of foreign and domestic private firms in Brazil is one of the more careful studies of that genre. The 282 pairs of firms sampled are matched by sales and specialization, to minimize differences caused by size and technology. Willmore finds that, after those adjustments, significant differences persist between firms of local and foreign ownership. Among those, the more interesting ones are that TNCs utilize more capital-intensive techniques than local counterparts and achieve higher value-added as a proportion of sales; TNCs have higher advertising expenditures and export more of their output; they also achieve higher labour productivity and pay more for foreign technology. While some of those results are at variance with those of studies in other countries, they confirm that TNCs are efficient transmitters of know-how. They are interesting particularly because Brazil has been the largest single destination for TNC investments in the developing world. However, to what extent Willmore's findings reflect the inward-looking bias of the Brazilian trade regime, and the likelihood that the Brazilian private sector has remained relatively weak because of the overwhelming foreign presence, are difficult to say.

Blomström's study of foreign presence and productive efficiency in Mexico is a prelude to his volume on the spillover benefits of TNCs. He finds that foreign presence is positively correlated with structural efficiency (i.e., the presence of large, modern firms), with industries with foreign domination being closer to the "best practice" frontier than others. Such industries also display higher levels of concentration. Blomström finds that over time foreign entry speeds up productivity change in the modern sector while leaving the traditional sector unchanged. Those structural effects of TNCs are of great interest, and are hardly explored in the literature.

Foreign direct investment does not speed up the transfer of technologies to Mexico in Blomström's study, presumably as compared to other modes of technology transfer. The competitive pressures exerted by foreign affiliates, however, do seem to increase efficiency in local firms. All those findings are compatible with Willmore's study of Brazil; it may be worth-while to bear in mind the similarities in the economic environments of the two countries.

The next two chapters deal with different contexts: the most dynamic and export-oriented countries in the developing world, the Republic of Korea and Taiwan, Province of China. Koo's study of the Republic of Korea traces the evolution of industrial structure and trade patterns. The strongly selective strategy of the Government of the Republic of Korea towards foreign investors is outlined, with foreign presence having a marginal impact on the country's economic structure and comparative advantage (at a time when both were changing rapidly). A rough comparison of the capital and skill intensities of local and foreign firms fails to show any consistent pattern over different industries. Koo goes on to examine overseas investment by firms from the Republic of Korea. Koo does not, however, draw out the inferences of the strategy of the Republic of Korea for the development of indigenous firms, technological capabilities and dynamic comparative advantage. As suggested in the general introduction, those are some of the most interesting lessons to be drawn from its Japanese-style approach to TNCs and that strategic counterfactual deserves more analysis.

Chi Schive's study provides a detailed analysis of the patterns of foreign direct investment in Taiwan, Province of China. He draws attention to an interesting feature which is investment by overseas Chinese, largely from Hong Kong and South-East Asia. Foreign investors contributed about 20 per cent of exports from Taiwan, Province of China and 15 per cent of manufacturing employment in 1974–82, a significant, but not major role. The data suggest that foreign firms' technologies were, on average, more labour intensive than those of local firms, but the pattern varied by industry; that domestic-market oriented firms were generally more capital-intensive than export-oriented ones; and that foreign equity participation seemed to promote the rapid introduction of foreign technologies. Schive then describes overseas investments by Taiwan, Province of China until 1981 (but one has to bear in mind that those have really taken off in a major way since 1987, and now approach $8–10 billion per annum).

The strategy of Taiwan, Province of China with respect to foreign direct investment has certain similarities to strategy of the Republic of Korea, but there are also important differences, arising from the less controlled nature of industrial development in Taiwan, Province of China. Nevertheless, both countries display a sustained coherent and remarkably successful, effort to build up national capabilities and indigenous enterprise, while achieving dynamic growth and structural change. TNCs have played a marginal or subsidiary role in that process, while government interventions have been critical. The case studies fit in nicely with Dunning's "investment development cycle" but, as noted above, the causal connections between indigenous development and selectivity to foreign entry need further analysis.

9

Multinationals and Technology Development in Host Countries[1]*

Sanjaya Lall

*Source: S. Lall, *Multinationals, Technology and Exports* (London, Macmillan, 1985), pp. 114–130.

I Introduction

The promotion of domestic technological capabilities is becoming a growing concern for the more industrialised of the developing countries (LDCs). Among the many issues that have arisen in this area, some of the most complex and controversial have concerned the proper balance and the nature of the interaction between foreign and indigenous technologies.[2] In an activity like technological development, where dynamic learning effects and externalities are rife, many analysts have argued that there is a strong need for government intervention: untrammelled market forces by themselves would not lead to the optimal level of technological development in LDCs, and some deliberate exclusion of foreign technologies may be necessary to protect the learning process there.[3]

Multinational corporations (MNCs) for the developed world appear as an important topic in this debate. In many developing countries, MNCs are major producers of advanced industrial products and among the most important conduits for the transfer of modern technologies from abroad. They are often in the forefront of export activity and, in larger countries with relatively developed industrial structures, of local technological activity. It is the very fact of their technological strength, based upon 'frontier' innovation in the industrialised countries, and their competitive prowess in host LDCs which raises fears that they may stifle indigenous capabilities. In the language of the more polemical critics of MNCs, they act as 'agents of technological dependence' of host LDCs.

The case against MNCs in this guise is, however, neither coherent nor well articulated. There are different versions of the criticisms, some of which contradict the others. This paper is an attempt to separate out some of the strands of the arguments advanced and to evaluate them against some (regrettably scanty) evidence. It will focus on the experience of India, where I have been conducting some research on the process of techno-logical development. It may be said, with some justice, that India is an inappropriate example. It has severely restricted the inflow of foreign direct investment in the last two decades and has sought, behind formidable protective barriers and with widespread inefficiences, to promote not just self-reliance in production but also self-reliance in technology.[4] Existing foreign investments in the country have been forced to dilute the extent of foreign ownership, and their growth and diversification in response to their competitive strengths in open markets have been tightly controlled. Never-theless, most of the world's leading MNCs still operate in India, and are particularly active in high-technology industries.[5] India's attempt to develop its technological capabilities itself makes the role of MNCs an interesting one. Thus, the use of Indian examples is still of relevance to this discussion.

A primary source of confusion in this area is the lack of a clear defi-nition of what 'technology development' means. Part II of this chapter discusses this problem. Another source of confusion is that the impact of MNCs on different levels of technology development can be assessed in several different contexts: technology development *within* the LDC affiliate of the MNC; technology development of the affillitate *relative to* similar local firms in the host country; and the *direct or indirect effects* of the activities of MNC affiliates upon technology development in related (vertically linked or competitive) firms in the host country. Parts III–IV of the chapter deal with these questions in turn. The main conclusions are drawn in part VI.

Two other introductory points: first, this chapter does not deal with such difficult issues as the 'appropriateness' of products or processes transferred to host countries by MNCs, and, second, it does not define MNC presence *per se* as a bad thing (because it 'denationalises' industry) or as a symptom of indigenous technological 'dependence'. On the first point, it is assumed that these are broader questions of distribution and factor-pricing policy which have to be taken as given, and that foreign and local firms in similar activities do not differ much in their behaviour once the larger parameters are set. On the second, it is assumed that the same technological activity undertaken in a host country yields the same benefit whether it is by a foreign affiliate or a local firm: benefits differ only if behaviour patterns are different.

II What is 'Technology Development'?

This chapter is concerned only with manufacturing industry. In industry, technology development can be defined to encompass an enormous variety of activities.[6] We can simplify these into four categories.

In the sense that technology is simply the knowledge of how to carry out manufacturing activity, even the setting-up of a new assembly activity in a developing country can be said to transfer some new knowledge and so contribute to the technology of the host country. From this elementary stage, technology development can progress to the knowledge of operating imported technologies in increasingly sophisticated industries. The gaining of such operating knowledge – for which we use the convenient label of '*know-how*' – will include not only the assimilation of imported techniques (which can itself be a lengthy and active learning process) but also quality control (which also involves active technical effort), improved plant layout and production practices, slight modifications to equipment and tooling, trouble-shooting, the use of different raw materials, and so on. It is well accepted now that the acquisition of know-how, even in the context of imported technologies, is a real and significant source of technological progress in LDCs.[7]

The next stage of technology development involves the understanding of the nature of the underlying process and product technologies, and leads to their substantial adaptation, improvement and even replacement by new processes or products. We may call this the development of '*know-why*' capabilities. Such technology development arises partly as a natural extension and deepening of know-how capabilities, and partly as a result of conscious efforts to develop design, testing, pilot-plant and similar activities (the 'development' part of research and development, R & D, in industrial enterprises).

Know-why development may be followed by *applied research*, the application of given scientific knowledge to the process of commercial innovation. Again, the line between the acquisition of know-why and its extension into genuine innovation is very unclear, but we mention it because of the possibility (real in many LDCs) that the understanding of why technologies work the way they do may not lead on to risky and costly efforts to undertake innovation. The final stage of technology development within industry comprises the ability to undertake *basic scientific research*, pushing back the frontiers of knowledge without regard to specific commercial application.

The contribution of MNCs to technology development in host LDCs can take place at any or all of these levels. A positive effect at one level may co-exist with a negative effect at another. Moreover, at any given level, a positive contribution to technology development within the MNC affiliate may be associated with a negative effect on such development in other enterprises in the host country. The range of potential permutations is enormous, and we clearly cannot analyse them in any detail here. Certainly the lack of sufficient empirical evidence limits the scope for meaningful discussion. For this reason, we will simplify further and refer in the following analysis *only to know-how and know-why development* (the latter comprising all the advanced stages of technological activity from design and development onwards).

A very important point to bear in mind about the different levels of technology development in LDCs concerns its *net social value.* All technology development entails a cost, and each successive stage probably entails higher costs. The development of indigenous technological capability is not an end in itself: technology is simply one input into the process of industrial production, and the efficiency of the production process which results from the application of technology is the 'bottom line' which the country is concerned with. True, technology development has various cumulative dynamic and external effects, but the social cost entailed must always be compared with the cost of importing it from abroad.

These points are relevant here because India seems to have pushed technological self-reliance almost as hard as inward-looking industrialisation. Of all the industrially advanced LDCs, it is the one with the least relative reliance on foreign technology in any form (MNCs, capital goods imports, licensing, foreign engineering) in the past two decades. As I have argued elsewhere (my paper in Fransman and King), this policy has been pushed to counter-productive extremes, reinforcing the inefficiencies engendered by industrial policy. Not only is the extent of local technology generation by MNC affiliates and local firms highly conditioned by this framework, the broader economic implications of the efforts also have to be borne in mind.

Let us now turn to the three forms in which the effects of MNCs on technology development are evaluated.

III Technology Development within MNC Affiliates

There is a widespread, but mistaken, impression that technologies developed by MNCs in their home countries are transferred costlessly and without adaptation to affiliates in LDCs. Teece (1976) shows in great detail that the transfer of any technology to a new location – developed or less-developed – entails substantial transfer and assimilation costs. These costs arise, of course, whether the recipient is an affiliate or an independent firm, and range from pre-transfer engineering, equipment specification, adaptive R & D (most of these are undertaken in the technology exporting country) to detailed engineering, local design adaptation, start-up, trouble-shooting, and training (which are mostly undertaken in the recipient). After a plant is running, subsequent technology creation in the form of know-how (production engineering and minor adaptation) occurs over time, reaching a peak soon after technology introduction and tailing off gradually until a new technology is transferred or new problems encountered (Davies, 1979).

In the know-how phase, there seems no *a priori* reason to differentiate between the performance of foreign and local firms. As noted earlier, know-how accumulates as a result of problem-solving, and foreign and local firms encounter identical problems in given locations. Katz's (1978) studies show that foreign affiliates undertake minor innovation-type engineering just as successfully as local firms, while in terms of adaptation to local factor prices there is no sustained difference between the two groups (Lall, 1978). It is sometimes suggested that MNCs may perform better because of their higher-quality technical manpower, or because of their ready access to the accumulated know-how of the parent company. In India, there is little evidence to support or refute this at the level of production engineering.

It is when we come to the know-why and more advanced research phases that the literature leads us to expect MNCs to be relatively backward in local technology development. The economics of R & D location (see Lall, 1979, and Hirschey and Caves, 1981) dictate that the bulk of basic design and development work by MNCs be highly centralised; the need for high-level scientific manpower of several kinds and a highly developed technological infrastructure dictates that this centralisation occur in the developed world; and the need for close interaction, especially in engineering industries, between innovation, management and production entails that R & D be placed near the head office or the largest markets.

This does not mean that MNC affiliates do not perform basic design or development work in host LDCs. There has been a growing tendency among MNCs (if US data can be extrapolated to other home countries) to place R & D facilities in *some* LDCs. These are the larger, industrially more advanced and technically better endowed host countries. There are several sound economic reasons why R & D facilities are set up there: first, the transfer of increasingly more complex know-how is itself facilitated by the existence of local know-why capabilities (Teece, 1976); second, in certain products the needs of the local market differ from those of developed countries (e.g. automobiles, food products, toiletries) and large local markets justify the investment in R & D facilities; third, the use of some LDC facilities for export to the rest of the Third World leads both to long production runs and the need for product adaptation, strengthening the previous tendency (e.g. VW in Brazil); fourth, the use of local raw materials or the need to test certain products locally induces local investigative R & D activity (pharmaceuticals and food products); and, finally, in exceptional cases LDC R & D facilities can be utilised for the MNCs' global needs of innovation (but this generally occurs *after* local R & D is well established).

Thus, the facts that a relatively small proportion of MNCs' total R & D spending is allocated to the Third World and that most LDCs host no R & D by MNCs are quite compatible with the fact that large countries like

Brazil or India today support very active R & D by MNCs. In India there are some 500 officially recognised R & D establishments in private manufacturing industry. Firms with foreign equity (including those which have diluted the foreign share to 40 per cent because of government policy) account for over half these firms; in fact, nearly all foreign affiliates of any size have set up recognised R & D facilities (the next section will present an explicit comparison of R & D by local and foreign firms). Some of these, like the one set up by the Unilever affiliate, have gone in for basic scientific research, contributed major product innovations and led to the utilisation and export of formerly unused local materials.[8] A number of affiliates earn royalties and technical fees from abroad by the export of their know-how. It is often suggested that their access to the parent company enables them to utilise 'frontier' technology to enhance the value of their Indian R & D.

All this suggests that, *up to a certain level*, MNCs do not lag in innovative activity in large LDCs with a pool of skilled manpower. The question then arises: is this level the socially optimal one? Clearly, local R & D in LDCs is much smaller, more application-oriented and less 'deep' than R & D in the home countries of MNCs.[9] To a large extent this is inevitable, given the relative sizes of operations, the level of technological sophistication and the competitive needs of the two locations. However, many host countries (including relatively advanced ones like Canada) feel that MNC R & D is 'truncated' to an undesirable extent, with the truly innovative functions kept at home even when they could be efficiently located abroad.[10] The allegation is difficult to prove or disprove empirically: the social and private perceptions of the net long-term benefits of establishing R & D in a newly industrialising country can be widely different, depending upon the relative assessments of research capabilities, minimum scale requirements of research, dynamic learning effects and externalities. In their survey of the literature, Kamien and Schwartz (1982) demonstrate clearly how fragile is the empirical basis for generalising about the determinants of innovation even in the highly industrialised countries. In LDCs, where much less is known on the economics of industrial progress, the area of ignorance is far larger. Non-quantifiable and dynamic factors further compound the analytical difficulties.

Since firm conclusions are not feasible, let me round off this section with my own impressions on technology development within MNCs. First, to the extent that MNCs are the most efficient international transmitters of industrial know-how, their presence in LDCs promotes technology development *at the production level* in those sectors where the speed of technical change and the complexity of technology makes other methods of transfer relatively inefficient or costly.[11] By implication, their direct participation may be less necessary in activities with 'lower' or more stable technologies. It may be argued that newly industrialising countries have their comparative advantage in acquiring know-how, rather than spreading their limited technological resources thinly over 'deeper' technical learning. Certainly the most successful NICs, the Gang of Four in East Asia, have benefited enormously from this strategy of efficiently utilising imported technologies without forcing the pace of know-why accumulation. Judged by this criterion, the extent of technology development by MNCs is probably optimal.

Second, to the extent that countries wish to go beyond the know-how stage into *know-why and basic research*, and have the wherewithal to do so efficiently, MNCs may go to the desired extent only in a few instances. Some government intervention may then be necessary to bring private costs and benefits of local R & D into line with social ones. Two outcomes are possible: the MNC is induced to launch local R & D to the extent desired (and is able to do it very efficiently because of the backing of the parent company), or it refuses to undertake 'deeper' R & D in the given host country (or conducts it inefficiently), and the latter's objectives are only achieved by setting up independent R & D facilities. I suspect the actual outcome lies somewhere between these extremes. A case may then be made that in some cases MNCs do retard 'deep' technology learning. But it is a qualified case, and not as obvious as may appear at first sight.

IV Technology Development in MNCs Relative to Local Firms

An earlier survey of the literature (Lall, 1978) had suggested that there was no marked or consistent difference between MNCs and local firms as far as the adaptation of imported technologies was concerned. Given the specific needs of the host country, its technical capabilities and the inherent adaptability of the technologies in question, both sets of firms seemed to respond similarly to the economic environment. The available evidence on the relative efficiency of their responses is very mixed and of uneven quality, so we can deduce little from it.

What, then, of their relative propensities to undertake 'deeper' technological effort? Since no detailed empirical studies exist on the issue of successful innovation by foreign and local firms in LDCs, we may resort to two sets of rather crude indicators: exports of technology by foreign and local firms, and formal R & D spending by them.

Exports of technology have been used as a rough indicator of the level of technological competence reached by a developing country (Lall, 1982). The available evidence suggests that the bulk of technology export activity is undertaken by local firms in LDCs.[12] If this is an indicator of 'deeper' technological learning, we may infer that MNCs lag in the accumulation of know-why in these countries.

We must, however, note two important qualifications. First, many important forms of innovation do not show up in the foreign activities of industrial enterprises, and, if they do, they tend to affect the export of products rather than the export of technologies. Second, MNC affiliates may transfer their technology abroad *via* the parent company network (for royalties or in exchange for other technologies[13]) rather than in contractual forms which are caught by the data. In the Indian case, we have already noted that MNC affiliates are actively selling technologies in return for royalties. The Unilever affiliate exchanges technical information freely with its related firms overseas, and also exports its expertise by posting Indian engineers in other LDCs. Many of the innovations made in India are utilised in affiliates in S.E. Asia and Brazil. Certainly its impressive export effort (Hindustan Lever is the largest single private sector exporter in India) is based partly on the exploitation of its local research effort. Moreover, given the very restricted scope permitted to MNCs in Indian industry, it would be premature to infer from technology export data that foreign affiliates are less capable of know-why accumulation than local firms.

The use of R & D data may appear to be more reliable in this context. There are, however, problems here also. A number of other factors which influence firm-level R & D performance (see Kamien and Schwartz, 1982) must be controlled for before the influence of foreign ownership is assessed; R & D expenditures are an indicator of research input, not its output (innovation or learning); different firms may define it differently, and the composition of R & D between basic research, applied research and imitation may differ;[14] and a comparison of firms in different industries may be misleading if the inherent research-intensity of the industry is not taken into account. Some data I have analysed on the R & D performance in India, which deal with some of these problems, may be instructive.[15]

These data pertain to 145 firms in only two sectors, engineering and chemicals, minimising the differences in 'technological opportunity' which crucially affect R & D performance. The 100 engineering firms are also assigned a dummy variable distinguishing those engaged in complex (machine building) activities from those in simpler metal shaping activities. The two sectors chosen account for 80 per cent of India's foreign collaborations, so are a fair representation of MNC activity there. A number of control variables are included besides the degree of foreign ownership. The shortage of space precludes a detailed analysis of their rationale and expected signs. Some of the results for each of the sectors – we did not aggregate them for this exercise because of the differences in their technological characteristics – are shown in the Appendix Table.

As far as the impact of foreign ownership (variable x_1) is concerned, the two sectors show different tendencies. Taking a large number of regressions (not shown in the table) into account, engineering has a positive and consistently significant sign, while chemicals has a negative and only occasionally significant sign.[16] The two sectors also show interesting differences in the impact on R & D of firm size, age, export performance, and the proportion of highly paid employees: clearly, generalisations across different sectors cannot be drawn. Foreign ownership has a positive relationship with R & D in one major sector. *There is no support for the case that MNCs in general are less R & D intensive than local firms.*

In sum, these two indicators do not, in the final analysis, enable us to conclude that there are significant differences between the relative technological performance of foreign and local firms in India. Given the stringent controls on MNCs in India and the consequent low appropriability of the returns from their research, it is perhaps surprising that the evidence does not show a more negative result for foreign affiliates. A truer test would ideally cover a more open economy with a more competitive industrial structure: but we have to make do with the little information that we do possess.

V Effects of MNCs on Related Firms' Technology Department

There are two sets of firms 'related' to MNCs: those that supply inputs to MNC affiliates and those that compete with them in their product markets.

As far as vertically linked firms are concerned, the limited Indian evidence suggests that MNCs are as active in transferring skills, know-how and product design to suppliers as local firms.[17] The exact pattern of inter-firm linkages depends upon the technical characteristics of the products and the relative sizes of the firms concerned. The highly inward-looking Indian regime has induced all firms, regardless of ownership, to set up extensive local linkages: many of these linkages may, however, be socially inefficient and the resulting production facilities internationally uncompetitive. However, it is likely that the basic propensities to create linkages remains the same in more dynamic and efficient economies.

As far as competing firms are concerned, the debate is still conducted at a very general level. It is argued, on the one hand, that competition from technologically efficient MNCs induces local firms to improve their own technology,[18] and that the presence of MNCs leads to much more rapid diffusion of technology by imitation and 'contagion'.[19] On the other, it is argued that a strong foreign presence inhibits local firms from undertaking risky and costly research activity.[20] The two apparently contradictory views can be reconciled, of course: local firms may well be induced to upgrade their production technology by a greater reliance on licensing when faced with competition from MNCs operating with 'frontier' technologies, and, in the process, their independent know-why development may suffer. A strong MNC presence may, in other words, be associated both with better local know-how and 'shallower' local know-why (needless to say, this is on the assumption that the indigenous industrial sector survives MNC competition on the basis of licensed technology – the phenomenon of 'denationalisation' is assumed to be contained within socially acceptable limits).

We should, however, note some important qualifications to the argument that MNCs inhibit know-why development in competing firms. First, it assumes a specific relationship between licensing and in-house research, treating them as substitutes at 'deeper' levels of R & D; this may not be the case as firms grow more sophisticated and larger. Thus, licensing may become a *necessary input* into in-house technological development;[21] this is certainly the case with Japan, which for decades was the world's largest importer of licensed technology. If local enterprises in the NICs have reached this stage (and I believe many have), increased MNC competition will have net technological benefits. Second, we must be careful not to generalise to all industries: a number of basic sectors (textiles, steel, cement, machine tools) are not important stamping-ground for MNCs, and in these the inhibiting effects do not really arise. Third, the Indian case illustrates the dangers of closing the economy too much to foreign competition. Not only has industrial efficiency suffered and damaging technological lags developed (it is becoming increasingly apparent that independent R & D efforts in LDCs simply cannot keep up with world frontiers in many industries, even if they are mere imitators), but a great deal of technological effort has gone into socially unproductive uses like finding high-cost local substitutes for imported materials and equipment. Finally, some advanced technologies may be available *only* via MNC entry, so the question of inhibition is redundant.

These qualifications still leave a grey area where genuine concern can be voiced about the effects of MNCs on firms in lesser industrialised countries. Moreover, to the extent that know-why development does require large, sheltered markets in the initial, high-risk phases, a powerful foreign presence may increase the risk to unacceptable levels. The Japanese experience lies behind many arguments that local technology development can proceed very successfully without direct MNC participation. Unfortunately, it is not clear how far Japan can be emulated by the LDCs of today; and, given Japan's human resources, its actual experience does not prove that it may not have done *even better* with a more liberal policy on MNC entry.

VI Conclusions

The analysis of the nature and determinants of technology development in LDCs is in its infancy. We know little about its different phases and about the true comparative advantage of LDCs in the scale of technology 'deepening'. Not surprisingly, therefore, the relationship between MNCs and local technology development is fraught with confusion and needless polemic.

This chapter has sought to clarify some of the elementary concepts and separate out the different strands of the debate. It has distinguished between various sequential stages of technology development, concentrating on the basic categories of 'know-how' and 'know-why' acquisition. For each of these, it has discussed the impact of MNCs on technology development within the firm, in relation to local firms and in linkage or competition with local firms.

It would appear that the effect of MNCs on know-how development is positive in all its manifestations. Given their undoubted technological superiority in most areas of modern industry, and given also the inherent need to adapt technology to each particular host environment, MNCs contribute to know-how acquisition within their affiliates and, by linkages and competition, to related local firms. As far as know-why development is concerned, the picture is more mixed. MNCs have good economic reasons to keep basic innovative effort centralised in the developed world (though exceptions exist), and generally transfer less to LDCs than many host countries would like. Their presence may also inhibit local firms investing in their own know-why development.

These conclusions need two major qualifications. First, the comparative advantage of LDCs may in fact lie in know-how development, and the correct strategy for them may be to efficiently exploit imported know-why. If know-why develops naturally over time with increased sophistication of production, a reliance on MNCs (in sectors where they are predominant) may well be the best long-term policy. Second, even the development of know-why capabilities in competiting local firms may be stimulated by MNC competition once these firms have a certain size and competence. Thus, MNC entry would hasten the technological maturity of 'infant' industries which may otherwise simply grow into slothful, uncompetitive adolescents.

Notes

1. This paper was presented at the Seventh World Congress of the International Economics Association held at Madrid in September 1983.

2. For concise statements see Katz (1982) and Blumenthal (1979). Also see the various papers in Fransman and King (1984), and in particular the introductory chapter by Fransman.

3. See ibid, Dahlman and Westphal (1982) and Lall (1982).

4. See my paper in Fransman and King (1984).

5. For a statistical analysis of the industrial characteristics of MNC investment in India, see Lall and Mohammad (1983).

6. The typology set out below draws upon, but is not identical to, that of Dahlman and Westphal (1982). Also see the classification in my 1982 book, pp. 66–8.

7. For a survey of the results of pioneering research in Latin America into

plant-level development of know-how capabilities, see Katz (1978).

8. I am grateful to the executives of Hindustan Lever for providing me with detailed information on their R & D in India. This was used for a case study prepared for the ILO on technological change and employment generation by MNCs in developing countries (Lall, 1983a).

9. For a review of the literature see Caves (1982).

10. On Canada, conflicting views on 'truncation' are presented by McFetridge (1977) and Globerman (1976), the former suggesting that truncation presents real problems for Canada, the latter that it is the small scale of protected Canadian operations which restricts the generation of technology and also its efficient application (by licensing). Globerman concludes that economic nationalism has led to a misallocation of scientific resources in Canada.

11 On this point see Casson (1979).

12. This is the finding of an inter-country study of technology exports by the World Bank and the Inter-American Development Bank in which I am participating.

13. In Australia, for instance, Parry and Watson (1979) show that MNC affiliates often have technology swap arrangements with the parent companies.

14. For an examination of the impact of firm size and market structure on the composition of R & D expenditures, see Mansfield (1981).

15. I am very grateful to Mohammad Saqib for his help in collecting and processing this data. Some of the findings, pertaining to the engineering industry, are discussed in Lall (1983b).

16. In a similar exercise for Australia, Parry and Watson (1979) found a negative impact for the extent of foreign ownership on R & D within a sample of firms which all had some foreign shareholding.

17. See Lall (1980) for an empirical study of the truck manufacturing industry in India.

18. See Caves (1982), chapter 4.

19. The 'contagion' idea is developed by Findlay (1978), who argues, on this assumption, that LDCs' technical change is a direct function of the extent of foreign presence in the local economy.

20. See Lall (1982).

21. See Link (1983).

References

Blumenthal, T. (1979) 'A Note on the Relationship between Domestic Research and Development and Imports of Technology', *Economic Development and Cultural Change*, vol. 27, no. 2.

Casson, M. (1979) *Alternatives to the Multinational Enterprise* (London: Macmillan).

Caves, R. E. (1982) *Multinational Enterprise and Economic Analysis* (Cambridge: Cambridge University Press).

Dahlman, C. and Westphal, L. E. (1982) 'Technological Effort in Industrial Development – an Interpretative Survey of Recent Research', in F. Stewart and J. James (eds) *The Economics of New Technology in Developing Countries* (London: Frances Pinter).

Davies, S. (1979) *The Diffusion of Process Innovations* (Cambridge: Cambridge University Press).

Findlay, R. (1978) 'Relative Backwardness, Direct Foreign Investment, and the

Transfer of Technology: A simple Dynamic Model', *Quarterly Journal of Economics*, vol. XCII, no. 1.

Fransman, M. and King, K. (eds) (1984) *Technological Capability in the Third World* (London: Macmillan).

Globerman, S. (1976) 'Canadian Science Policy and Economic Nationalism', *Minerva*, vol. 14, no. 2.

Hirschey, R. C. and Caves, R. E. (1981) 'Internationalization of Research and Transfer of Technology by Multinational Enterprises', *Oxford Bulletin of Economics and Statistics*, vol. 43, no. 2.

Kamien, M. I. and Schwartz, N. L. (1982) *Market Structure and Innovation* (Cambridge: Cambridge University Press).

Katz, J. (1978) 'Technological Change, Economic Development and Intra and Extra Regional Relations in Latin America', Buenos Aires: IDB/ECLA, Working Paper no. 30.

Katz, J. (1982) 'Technological Change and Development in Latin America', in R. Ffrench-Davis and E. Tironi (eds) *Latin America and the New International Economic Order* (London: Macmillan).

Lall, S. (1978) 'Transnationals, Domestic Enterprises and Industrial Structure in Host LDCs: A Survey', *Oxford Economic Papers*, vol. 30, no. 2.

Lall, S. (1979) 'The International Allocation of Research Activity by U.S. Multinationals', *Oxford Bulletin of Economics and Statistics*, vol. 41, no. 4, and chapter 3 of this volume [*Multinationals, Technology and Exports*].

Lall, S. (1980) 'Vertical Inter-Firm Linkages in LDCs: An Empirical Study', *Oxford Bulletin of Economics and Statistics*, vol. 42, no. 3, and chapter 12 of this volume [*Multinationals, Technology and Exports*].

Lall, S. (1982) *Developing Countries as Exporters of Technology* (London: Macmillan).

Lall, S. (1983a) 'Technological Change, Employment Generation and Multinationals: A Case Study of a Foreign Firm and a Local Multinational in India', Geneva: International Labour Office, Multinational Enterprises Programme, Working Paper no. 27.

Lall, S. (1983b) 'Determinants of R & D in an LDC: The Indian Engineering Industry', *Economics Letters*, vol. 13, no. 4.

Lall, S. and Streeten, P. P. (1977) *Foreign Investment, Transnationals and Developing Countries* (London: Macmillan).

Lall, S. and Mohammad, S. (1983) 'Multinationals in Indian Big Business: Industrial Characteristics of Foreign Investment in a Heavily Regulated Economy', *Journal of Development Economics*, vol. 13, no. 1, and chapter 5 of this volume [*Multinationals, Technology and Exports*].

Link, A. N. (1983) 'Inter-Firm Technology Flows and Productivity Growth', *Economics Letters*, vol. 11, nos. 1–2.

McFetridge, D. G. (1977) *Government Support for Scientific Research and Development: An Economic Analysis* (Toronto: University of Toronto Press).

Mansfield, E. (1981) 'Composition of R & D Expenditures: Relationship to Size of Firm, Concentration and Innovative Output', *Review of Economics and Statistics*, vol. 63, no. 4.

Parry, T. G. and Watson, J. F. (1979) 'Technology Flows and Foreign Investment in the Australian Manufacturing Sector', *Australian Economic Papers*, vol. 18, no. 32.

Teece, D. J. (1976) *The Multinational Corporation and the Resource Cost of Technology Transfer* (Cambridge, Mass.: Ballinger).

Appendix Table Regression analysis (log linear) of determinants of R & D performance in India (1978–9)

Independent variables	Industry and Equation (Numbers)				
	Engineering (n = 100)			Chemicals (n = 45)	
	1	*2*	*3*	*4*	*5*
x_1		0.095^b (1.711)	-0.120^c (1.329)	-0.070 (0.701)	
x_2	0.903^b (2.661)		-0.017 (0.047)		0.287 (0.761)
x_3	0.574 (1.164)	0.694^c (1.359)			-1.810^b (2.456)
x_4	0.900 (0.815)	0.176^c (1.531)			0.207 (0.752)
x_5	0.369^a (2.811)		0.116 (0.616)		
x_6	-0.238^b (2.298)	-0.172^c (1.549)	0.605^a (3.879)	0.480^a (3.250)	
x_7	1.322^c (1.628)	1.596^b (1.853)		-0.086 (0.424)	
x_8				0.222^c (1.650)	0.300^b (2.231)
x_9	1.069^a (4.487)	1.061^a (4.133)			
x_{10}		-0.718 (1.202)			
R^2	0.414	0.356	0.268	0.279	0.208
F	8.79^a	5.95^a	3.168^b	3.407^b	2.821^b

Notes: t statistics in parentheses
Significance levels: a – 99%; b – 95%; c – 90%

Sources: Company balance sheets, Department of Science and Technology, Directorate General of Technical Development.

Symbols and definitions:
Dependent variable: R & D expenditures in 1978 as a percentage of sales in that year.

Independent variables:
x_1 – share of foreign equity in total equity
x_2 – size of firm as measured by sales
x_3 – age of firm in India
x_4 – number of foreign licensing agreements
x_5 – royalties paid as a percentage of sales
x_6 – exports as a percentage of sales, a measure of competitiveness
x_7 – percentage of total wages accounted for by highly paid technical and managerial employees, a measure of top-level skills
x_8 – selling expenses as percentage of sales
x_9 – dummy variable for engineering firms, with 1 = firms engaged in machinery manufacture and other sophisticated activities and 0 = others
x_{10} – average wage level, an index of general production skills

10

The Comparative Performance of Foreign and Domestic Firms in Brazil*

Larry N. Willmore[†]

*Source: *World Development*, 14 (1986), pp. 489–501.

Introduction

No author can hope to attract readers to yet another study of transnational firms unless some justification for the paper is provided at the outset. In this case, the inspiration arises from the fact that existing studies of the comparative performance of transnational firms in Brazil and elsewhere tend to be very aggregate and fail to control for differences in size or type of product. Studies based on data for individual firms or plants do exist, but they have few observations, cover very few industries, refer to only a few aspects of performance, or fail to control for size differences as well as industry (product mix) differences.

The present study represents an attempt to be both disaggregate and comprehensive. Detail and breadth are both necessary if we are to reach conclusions concerning the typical differences between local firms and their foreign counterparts operating in Brazil. The analysis is based on data for 282 pairs of foreign-owned and private Brazilian firms drawn from 80 manufacturing industries in the year 1978. The firms are matched by volume of sales, and in no case does the difference in sales exceed 10%. Average differences between the two sets of firms are measured, and their significance is tested, using various measures of size, value-added to output ratios, advertising expenditure, royalty payments, export performances, productivity, skill intensity and capital intensity.

An important caveat should be noted at this point: the paired firms in our sample interact in the same market, so it is possible that the behavior of local firms has been altered, through competitive and demonstration effects, by the very presence of foreign rivals. Foreign firms in developing countries are thought to introduce "inappropriate" (capital-intensive) technology and consumer goods that fail to meet the needs of the vast majority of the population (Stewart, 1979, pp. 78–100, and the references cited therein). If foreign firms, through advertising, create a demand for "inappropriate" products, this may induce local firms to satisfy the changed preferences of the population by producing the same type of products. Moreover, local firms may choose to follow the example of foreign firms and adopt the same "inappropriate" production techniques.[1] In short, our control group, which consists of local firms that survive and thrive in the face of foreign competition, may conceivably act as a mirror, reflecting characteristics of the comparison group of foreign firms.

The plan of the paper is as follows. The second section presents a brief review of the literature. The third section reports the results of tests for significant differences between matched pairs of firms in our data base. A concluding section summarizes the main empirical findings.

Review of the Literature

The purpose of this section is to provide a concise survey of previous studies of the comparative performance of transnational firms in Brazil's manufacturing sector. Selected references to studies of other countries are included to illustrate alternative methods of analysis. For a broad survey of the literature, see Lall (1978) and Caves (1982, Chapter 9).

Comprehensive data are not available, but foreign-controlled firms are believed to account for approximately a quarter of manufacturing employment, a third of the output, and more than a third of the sector's exports (Bonelli, 1980, p. 871; ECLAC, 1983, pp. 65–67; and ECLAC, 1985). Published estimates tend to vary not by year, but rather by sample size. Foreign-owned subsidiaries are much larger on average than local firms, so exclusion of small firms increases the foreign share. Von Doellinger and Cavalvanti (1975), for example, found foreign-controlled firms to account for 55% of the total sales in their sample of 318 large manufacturing enterprises.

Foreign direct investment is concentrated in the technologically "dynamic" industries which have shown rapid rates of growth. Nonetheless, despite fears of "denationalization," local firms and publicly-owned firms have grown at a faster pace than foreign subsidiaries in recent years. Moreover, there is little difference in the reported profitability of foreign compared to local private firms, but foreign firms are believed to remit profits by under-invoicing exports and over-invoicing imports despite the existence of a licensing system designed to prevent such practices (see Zini, 1984; Tyler, 1978, p. 361). Numerous studies have shown foreign firms to be characterized by higher export-sales ratios, greater labor productivity, greater capital intensity and higher wage levels compared to local firms in Brazil (von Doellinger and Cavalvanti, 1975; Meller and Mizala, 1982; Goncalves, 1982; Meller, 1984). These studies are quite aggregate, however, with disaggregation proceeding only to 21 subsectors – the two-digit level. The observed differences between foreign and local firms could be due to the fact that foreign firms are larger and operate in different industries rather than to the existence or nonexistence of foreign ownership in itself.

Case studies are a potentially rich source of information on differences between foreign and local firms, as well as their interaction over time. The collection of such data tends to be costly, however, and requires the co-operation of firms that are studied. As a result, researchers who analyze case studies find it difficult to control for differences in size and product mix, are tempted to generalize from an insufficient number of observations, and seldom report statistical tests of significance. The ambitious research program directed by Jorge Katz in Buenos Aires, for example, covers fewer than 60 firms drawn from a variety of industries in Brazil and five other countries of Latin America. Katz himself (1984, p. 15) notes that the case studies "make no claim to statistical representativeness"; the reader should bear this in mind when evaluating the research findings that he reports.[2]

Industry studies can also be used to investigate differences in the performance of local and foreign enterprise, with the advantage that research effort is concentrated on firms that produce similar products and compete in the same market. A number of studies of Brazilian industries do exist, of which a few outstanding examples are Evans (1979, Chapter 3) on textiles and pharmaceuticals and Newfarmer (1977 and 1979) on the electrical industry. These studies provide valuable analyses of changes in market structure, particularly concentration, foreign ownership and state participation, but they neglect the topic that is the subject of this paper, namely the comparative performance of foreign and domestic firms. Evans (pp. 136–138) does, however, make the interesting point that the nature of technological change may explain why foreign firms were much more successful in their penetration of the pharmaceutical industry than they were in competing with local firms in textiles. Textile technology tends to be embodied in capital goods which are available to all firms, domestic or foreign, for the price of new machinery, whereas pharmaceutical technology generally takes the form of patented products. New pharmaceutical products are developed by transnational corporations in developed countries, and produced by subsidiaries or licensees in developing countries. Locally-owned pharmaceutical firms, with no research facilities in advanced countries and a small volume of sales over which to amortize research and development costs, have a competitive disadvantage in new product development.[3]

In statistical analyses of the effect of foreign ownership and management on industrial performance, two basic approaches have been used. One approach is to collect information for pairs of firms — one foreign and one local — carefully matched by industry and size. Any observed difference between the two types of firms is then ascribed to the effect of ownership rather than the effect of industry or scale of production. This has the advantages of simplicity and weak assumptions. The difficulty is that the method does not make full use of available data: in many industries local firms comparable in size to foreign firms do not even exist. A second approach is to specify and estimate a regression model in which ownership characteristics are included as one of the explanatory variables. This makes better use of existing information — observations are not "wasted" for lack of a comparable local firm — but the method is quite demanding in terms of strong assumptions underlying a complicated theoretical model. If two categories of firms (foreign and local) are poorly matched by size or by industry, fitting a common regression model to the sample amounts to extrapolation beyond the range of the available data, with all the pitfalls inherent in such a procedure.

Matched Pairs of Firms

The "matched pairs" approach to control for size and industry mix, due to a dearth of adequate data, has been used very little in comparative studies of foreign and domestic firms. The few studies that do exist are based on a very small number of observations, which makes it difficult to reject the null hypothesis of no difference between the two types of firms at any reasonable level of statistical significance. Mason's (1973) data, for example, consist of 14 pairs of firms: five from Mexico and nine from the Philippines. The present author (1976) obtained information for a sample of 33 matched pairs of foreign and local firms operating in Costa Rica, while Chung and Lee (1980) were able to assemble data for only 17 matched pairs in South Korea.

In Brazil, ECLAC (1983, pp. 35–38) reports that for 65 matched pairs, foreign firms show lower export ratios than local firms, but the differences were not statistically significant. It is not clear, however, whether the firms were matched by size as well as by industry. If foreign firms are larger than local firms in the sample, this might account for the unexpected results since, among exporters, a very strong inverse relationship exists between firm size and export performance (see ECLAC, 1985, Chapters 3 and 5). In another study, Goncalves (1983a and b) analyzed 77 pairs of firms matched by four-digit industry and was unable to find significant differences in profit or growth rates in the 1968–80 period. This study suffers, however, from a failure to control for scale differences; the foreign firms are three times as large as the local firms in terms of average sales (see Goncalves, 1983a, Table 2 or 1983b, Table 2).

The best example of an application of the "matched pairs" approach to Brazilian data is Morley and Smith (1977, pp. 283–286), who test for significant differences between foreign establishments of differing national origin as well as differences between these establishments and their locally-owned counterparts. They argue that if the lack of competitive pressures allows foreign establishments to produce profitably without adapting their techniques of production to local conditions, then one should observe both (i) foreign plants utilizing more capital-intensive techniques of production than local plants and (ii) techniques of production varying by nationality among otherwise comparable foreign establishments. Matching establishments by scale (value-added) and by five-digit industry, they assembled a sample of 29 US–Brazilian pairs, 19 Western Europe–Brazil pairs, 29 US–West Germany pairs, and 24 US–other Western Europe pairs. Value-added per production worker was significantly higher for both groups of foreign establishments compared to their local counterparts, and the productivity of US plants was significantly higher than those owned by companies from West Germany or other countries of Westen Europe. These results are consistent with the existence of differences in techniques of production; nonetheless, a proxy measure of capital intensity — the value of electricity consumed per production worker — was significantly different only for the US–West Germany pairings, so their evidence on choice of technique is not conclusive.

Regression Models

The "regression" approach to the control of size, industry and other variables has been utilized quite widely in recent years by researchers in Brazil. Braga (1979), in a careful analysis of data for 267 local and foreign firms, regressed profit rates on firm size, market share, advertising, debt, a foreign ownership dummy and other variables. The foreign dummy has a positive coefficient in the regression equation, indicating that foreign firms are more profitable than local firms once the effect of other variables on profitability is accounted for, but the coefficient is significant only at the 20% level in a two-tailed test. Newfarmer and Marsh (1981, pp. 66–72) also failed to find a significant coefficient for an ownership dummy in a similar model estimated with data for over 150 electrical firms.

ECLAC (1985) estimated a nonlinear model of the probability of exporting with data for more than 12,000 firms and found the odds of exporting for a foreign firm to be double or triple that of a local firm once the effects of size, capital intensity, wage levels, product differentiation and other variables were accounted for. Among the subset of over 3,000 exporters, foreign firms had twice the export volume of local firms, holding constant the effect of differences in size, capital intensity, market structure and commercial policy.

No researcher has yet included a foreign ownership variable in a model of wage determination in Brazil. Lim, however, in a study of 141 local establishments and 159 foreign and "mixed" establishments in Malaysia found wages of the second group to be 3% higher on average than those of the first group after controlling for the effects of capital intensity, the proportion of employees paid with a fixed monthly salary, export/sales ratios and import competition. Surprisingly, variables for scale, trade unions and plant location were not significant. A shortcoming of the study is the incomplete control for inter-industry, as opposed to inter-firm, differences in wage levels. In any case, average wage differences, though statistically significant, were very small. Moreover, the absence of a variable for skill levels makes it impossible to conclude that foreign firms pay higher wages for labor of the same quality.

Small firms typically use less skilled labor, pay lower wages, use more labor-intensive techniques of production, operate fewer shifts and produce an output that is quite distinct from that of larger firms in the "same" industry. This dualism means that it is difficult to interpret the results of production functions estimated with cross-section data, especially in developing countries. Nonetheless, regression models are popular in cross-section analyses of productivity, and there have been several attempts in Brazil to measure the performance of foreign firms relative to local firms by including dummy variables in regression equations.

Tyler (1978) estimated an aggregate Cobb–Douglas production function for the entire manufacturing sector based on published fiscal 1971 balance sheet data for 850 local and foreign firms. He measured output by sales, the capital input by the inflation-adjusted book value of plant and equipment, and labor by the total number of employees. A foreign ownership dummy was positive and significant for the aggregate function, but when the same equation was fitted to each of the 21 two-digit subsectors, the foreign dummy was significantly greater than zero in only three equations. When Tyler estimated a more general Constant Elasticity of Substitution (CES) production function with the complete set of observations, the higher productivity of foreign firms appeared as greater returns to scale and a higher elasticity of substitution, but not as greater technical efficiency. Mascolo and Braga (1984) confirmed this result by estimating Variable Elasticity of Substitution (VES) production functions for 3,243 exporters at the three-digit industry level, dividing the sample into local and foreign-owned firms.

In another study Tyler (1979) assembled similar data for the years 1971–75 and estimated Cobb–Douglas production functions for two broadly defined industries: electrical machinery (75 firms) and domestic appliances and communication equipment (56 firms). A time variable captured Hicksian neutral technological change and a dummy variable for each firm captured differential efficiency. The coefficients of the technical efficiency dummies show a positive and significant correlation with foreign ownership, but not after controlling for size differences between foreign and domestic firms.

Tyler's research suggests that foreign firms tend to be no more productive than local firms once we control for differences in size (capital and labor) and industry. Unfortunately, the empirical results suffer from two serious biases. The first, which is noted by Tyler, is that by measuring output as sales "we are forced to implicitly assume that the ratio of value-added to total output is a random variable over the firm population" (1979, p. 117). If this ratio varies systematically by type of firm, statistical inferences are biased. It is shown below that in Brazil value-added/output ratios are significantly higher for foreign firms, so Tyler's results on this account are biased *against* the finding of a positive effect of foreign ownership on productivity. A second bias occurs because there is no provision for differences in the quality of labor hired by the two types of firms. If employees of foreign firms systematically have greater skills than employees of local firms, as is shown below to be the case, then the regression results are biased *in favor* of a positive relationship between foreign ownership and technical efficiency; output which should properly be ascribed to human capital — a purchased input — is credited to foreign ownership and management.

Morley and Smith (1977) overcome the first source of bias, but, by ignoring white-collar workers, aggravate the second source of bias in estimates of the relative efficiency of foreign firms. They obtained access to data at the establishment level from the 1969 Industrial Survey. In each of 17 four-digit industries, value-added per production worker was regressed on size, capital intensity and a dummy variable for foreign ownership. Size and capital intensity were not entered as continuous variables, but rather as a set of dummy variables denoting size classes and capital intensity classes. Size was measured by value-added and capital intensity by the cost of electricity consumption per production worker. the study lends some support to the thesis that foreign firms are more productive because they are more efficient than local firms, but the evidence is not overwhelming: at the 5% level, only 10 of the 17 regression equations are significant; in only seven equations is the coefficient of the foreign dummy significantly greater than zero.

Morley and Smith also regressed electricity consumption per production worker on size class dummies and a foreign ownership dummy. At the 5% level, nine of the 17 equations are significant and in five equations the coefficients of the foreign dummies are significantly greater than zero. They thus provide evidence that foreign firms tend to be characterized by higher capital/labor ratios than local firms in the same industry after controlling for differences in size. Newfarmer and Marsh (1981, pp. 57–61) reached similar results for their sample of electrical firms when they regressed the ratio of employment to fixed assets on ownership, firm size and other variables.

A New Test Using Matched Pairs

A microdata base utilized in a previous study (ECLAC, 1985) contains information from tax returns for the year 1978 for 12,435 firms, in 841 of which nonresidents hold more than 10% of the equity. It was possible to match 282 of the foreign firms to comparable local firms which appear to be owned solely by private Brazilian residents. Each pair was matched by sales volume and by the four-digit industry accounting for the largest proportion of total sales. The firms are not identified by name, and details concerning the product mix or conglomerate diversification are not known. No observations from industry 3099 — "other manufactured goods not elsewhere classified" — were used, since it is not likely that firms of a similar size in this "industry" will produce similar types of goods.

A major shortcoming of these data is that they fail to classify as "foreign" those firms which are controlled from abroad through holding companies or through other firms established in Brazil. Souza Cruz, the leading producer of cigarettes, for example, appears to be wholly-owned by residents of Brazil even though BAT Industries Ltd. of the United Kingdom holds three-quarters of the shares through its Rio de Janeiro holding company. Similarly, General Electric do Nordeste S.A. is misclassified as a local firm because its shares are held by General Electric do Brasil S.A., a corporation registered in Brazil but wholly-owned by its US parent. This underestimation of the number of foreign firms has affected previous research based on these data (*viz.* Braga, 1981; Mascolo and Braga, 1984; and ECLAC, 1985).[4] In the present study every attempt has been made to avoid matching foreign firms with "local" counterparts that are controlled indirectly by transnationals by crossing the data with those of "Quem e quem na economia brasileira" (VISAO, August 1978 and August 179) and Jean Bernet's *Interinvest Guide* (Rio de Janeiro: 4th edition, 1978 and 5th edition, 1983). Nonetheless, it is conceivable that some of the 282 pairs of local and foreign firms may in reality be pairs of foreign firms. If so, this will bias the observed differences between the two sets of firms toward zero.

It is worth emphasizing that this is not a random sample of foreign firms in Brazil. Many industries in which foreign firms are dominant, such as tobacco or rubber tires, are not represented at all due to the lack of locally-owned firms of comparable size. Volkswagen, Ford and General Motors are excluded from the study because no local automotive firm exists that is similar in size to these giants of the industry. On the other hand, 10 pairs of pharmaceutical firms are included, despite the predominance of foreign firms in that industry.

Since the matched pairs are drawn from diverse industries, comparison of the mean values for each type of firm or averages of simple differences can be misleading. Such comparisons inadvertently give a large weight, for example, to capital-intensive industries in measures of differences in capital intensity, or to export industries in measures of differences in export propensities. To avoid this, we follow Chung and Lee (1980) and calculate for each variable and each pair of firms the standardized difference, defined as the absolute difference expressed as a percentage of the average level for the two firms. Algebraically, if X_i represents the value of a variable for the ith foreign firm and Y_i the value for the local firm matched to it, then the standardized difference is

$$(100)(X_i - Y_i)/(X_i + Y_i)(1/2)$$

A negative difference indicates that the value for the local firm exceeds that registered by its foreign counterpart. Note that the standardized difference is bounded by +200% and −200%, values that result when one of the two firms of a matched pair registers a positive value and the other zero for a particular variable. When both X_i and Y_i are zero, as occurs frequently with some variables, the standardized difference is defined as zero.

Previous studies based on "matched pairs" have relied on nonparametric techniques to estimate the sign and significance of difference between the two sets of firms. Significant difference may be trivially small or very large, but nonparametric techniques do not provide us with information as to which might be the case. Fortunately, the large size of our sample permits us, by virtue of the Central Limit Theorem, to assume normality and use standard techniques of statistical inference which provide information on the size as well as the statistical significance of any observed differences.

Empirical Findings for the Full Sample

Table 1 reports mean values by type of firm for a number of variables, along with the mean standardized difference and its standard error. The large sample size means that it is relatively easy to reject the null hypothesis that average differences are zero even when differences between the two types of firms are quite small. The pairs are matched on the basis of sales volume, so the 282 foreign firms are only 0.6% smaller, on average, than domestic firms. Nonetheless, the standard error for this statistic is a low 0.2%, so the difference is statistically significant in a "t" test at the 1% level. The fact that the difference is significant at all reflects instructions given to the research assistant who assembled the matched pairs. Since foreign firms are larger than local firms, when confronted with a choice between a slightly larger or a slightly smaller local firm to match with the foreign firm, he was asked to favor the former.

The two sets of firms are closely matched by volume of sales, but in other measures of size they differ considerably. Foreign firms are 6% *larger*, on average, in terms of value-added, and 14% *smaller* in terms of employment. Value-added was estimated as total sales revenue plus change

Table 1 Test for significant differences between matched pairs of foreign and domestic firms (mean values for 282 firms unless otherwise indicated)

Variable	Foreign firm	Local firm	Standardized difference (%)	
Size of firm				
SALES – million cruzeiros	168.5	168.8	−0.6*	(0.2)
VA – value-added, million cruzeiros	102.5	96.4	6.2*	(2.3)
L – number of employees	338.5	416.5	−13.8*	(4.1)
EST – number of establishments	1.9	2.1	−7.8†	(3.7)
MULTI% – percentage of multi-establishment firms	45.0	51.8	–	
Value-added/Output				
VA/Q – value-added as a percentage of total output	58.3	55.1	5.9*	(2.2)
Product differentiation, Royalties				
ADV – advertising expenditures/domestic sales, percentage	1.2	0.9	20.3*	(7.9)
ROYTOT – total royalty payments, thousand cruzeiros	261.0	123.1	8.5	(5.7)
ROYTOT% – percentage of firms paying royalties	14.2	10.6	–	
ROYFOR – overseas royalty payments, thousand cruzeiros	126.3	45.8	9.0*	(3.7)
ROYFOR% – percentage of firms paying royalties abroad	7.4	3.5	–	
Export performance				
EXPORTS1 – exports of all firms, million cruzeiros	14.0	8.0	61.6*	(8.2)
EXPORT% – percentage of firms that export	68.1	48.6	–	
EXPORTS2 – exports (million cruzeiros) when both firms export (*n* = 111)	30.5	17.4	57.3*	(11.8)
XSUB – export subsidies as % of export sales (*n* = 111)	16.2	18.0	7.2	(10.8)

Labor productivity

VA/L – value-added per employee, thousand cruzeiros	374.3	295.2	19.9*	(3.8)
VA/LP – value-added per production worker, thousand cruzeiros ($n = 268$)	838.6	491.1	26.4*	(4.6)

Skill intensity

NONPL – non-production workers as a percentage of total employment ($n = 268$)	35.4	28.7	20.3*	(4.5)
W/L – annual wage per employee, thousand cruzeiros	91.6	65.4	30.5*	(3.1)
WNP/L – annual wage per non-production employee, thousand cruzeiros	133.1	106.1	26.6*	(3.4)
WP/L – annual wage per production worker, thousand cruzeiros ($n = 268$)	64.2	51.8	18.9*	(3.1)

Capital intensity

NWVA/L – nonwage value-added per employee (thousand cruzeiros)	252.2	206.5	12.8*	(4.7)
NWVA/LP – nonwage value-added per production worker, thousand cruzeiros	545.3	342.8	20.0*	(5.3)
ELEC/LP – electricity consumption per production worker, thousand cruzeiros ($n = 248$)	9.3	7.1	23.9*	(5.6)

Note: The numbers in parentheses are the standard errors of the mean of the standardized difference. *indicates statistical significance at the 0.01 level and † at the 0.05 level. All tests are one-tailed except those of firm size and VA/Q, which are two-tailed. Royalties include payments for technical assistance as well as payments for licensed technology and "brand names".

in inventories less purchases of raw materials, advertising, electricity, fuel and goods to be resold. In addition, only 45% of the foreign firms operate multiple plants or establishments, whereas 52% of the domestic firms own more than one establishment. As a consequence, the average number of plants operated by foreign firms is significantly lower than the average number operated by their local counterparts. These statistics illustrate the futility of matching foreign to local firms in terms of all aspects of size. The choice of sales as a variable to match the two sets of firms is unavoidably arbitrary.

Given that foreign firms are nearly the same size as their local counterparts in terms of sales, yet considerably larger in terms of value-added, it follows that they add more value per unit of output. The standardized difference of the ratio of value-added to output (sales plus inventory changes) averages 5.9% and is significantly different from zero at the 1% level in a two-tailed test. This result, in terms of sign though not significance, is similar to that found in an earlier study (Willmore, 1976, p. 512) for Costa Rica. The finding is consistent with the thesis that foreign firms are more vertically integrated, i.e. that they process more stages of manufacture within the firm, relying less on outside producers or imports for a supply of intermediate inputs. It lends no support to the belief expressed in early writings that transnational corporations "contribute less to domestic value-added than local firms,"[5] but a full study requires knowledge of the linkages of foreign and domestic firms with plants in local and overseas markets.

The higher value-added to output ratios observed for foreign firms may also be the result of specialization in higher-quality or more uniform-quality goods in addition to (or instead of) greater vertical integration. In other words, foreign firms may typically have higher ratios of value-added to output not because they produce more intermediate inputs in their Brazilian plants, but rather because the goods they produce command higher prices due to advertising, prestigious brand names, higher quality or greater quality control. The high advertising expenditure observed for foreign firms is consistent with this interpretation, as is the finding, reported below, that foreign firms employ techniques of production that are capital- and skill-intensive compared to those used by their local counterparts.

Foreign firms operating in Brazil are known to advertise heavily and to repatriate part of their profits as royalties and technical assistance payments which are claimed as costs and deducted from local income for tax purposes. Brazilian law, however, does not allow royalty payments when a nonresident owner holds 50% or more of the equity of a firm (see von Doellinger and Cavalvanti, 1975, pp. 88–96).

The statistics reported in Table 1 confirm that foreign firms do advertise much more heavily than comparable local firms. The fact that transnational subsidiaries account for a disproportionate share of advertising expenditures in Brazil (Newfarmer, 1977, pp. 205–214; ECLAC, 1983, pp. 78–80) is thus not attributable solely to their greater size or differences in product mix.

Only a tiny proportion of the firms in our sample registered any payments for royalty fees or technical assistance. This presumably reflects strict government control of such expenditures. Nonetheless, the average difference is positive for both total and overseas payments, and significant at the 1% level in the case of the latter.

The results for comparative export performance confirm those reported in ECLAC (1985). The exports of foreign firms are much higher, on average, than comparable local firms. Moreover, two-thirds of the foreign firms export at least part of their output whereas fewer than half the local firms are exporters. Restricting the sample to the 111 pairs in which each firm exports, the standardized difference between foreign and local firms averages 57% and is highly significant. These results are to be expected on *a priori* grounds, for the costs of exporting are much lower for foreign firms, which have access to market information and sales organizations through their parent companies overseas. The ECLAC (1985, Chapter 3) study reports first that a positive correlation exists between export volume and the rate of export subsidy and, secondly, that the foreign firms' share of subsidies tends to exceed their share of exports. The present study shows that the second finding may well be a spurious result stemming from the larger size of foreign exporters, for differences in the rate of subsidy for the 111 matched pairs of exporters are not significantly different from zero.

The results reported in Table 1 also reveal that foreign firms have much higher levels of labor productivity, even after controlling for scale and industry differences. The average difference is 26% in terms of value-added per production worker and 20% when productivity is measured as value-added per employee; both differences are significant at the 1% level. The division of employment between white-collar and blue-collar workers was not reported for all firms, so the number of matched pairs is reduced from 282 to 268 when this information is required.

Do foreign firms pay higher wages for the same quality of labor in Brazil? This question cannot be answered with the data available to us in this sample. What is evident is that foreign firms pay higher wages *and* employ higher quality labor compared to their local counterparts. The ratio of white-collar to blue-collar employees, a crude indicator of labor skills, is more than 20% higher for foreign firms. The average wage is also much higher for each category of employee: standardized differences are 26% in the case of white-collar employees and 19% in the case of production workers.[6] Disaggregate wage data are needed to reach definite conclusions, but it would be surprising if a major portion of such large wage differences were not attributable to differences in skill levels.

Table 2 Labor productivity, wages and capital intensity: Rank correlation between average levels and standardized differences

	Spearman rank correlation coefficient
Labor productivity	
VA/L ($n = 282$)	0.156
VA/LP ($n = 268$)	0.184
Wages	
W/L ($n = 282$)	0.180
WNP/L ($n = 268$)	−0.013
WP/L ($n = 268$)	0.176
Capital intensity	
NWVA/L ($n = 282$)	0.151
NWVA/LP ($n = 268$)	0.187
ELEC/LP ($n = 248$)	0.185

Note: Data for 248–282 matched pairs of firms ranked by average levels and by standardized differences (difference divided by average level). For definition of variables, see Table 1. All coefficients except −0.013 are statistically significant at the 0.01 level in a two-tailed test.

Transnational enterprises are often criticized for transferring capital-intensive technologies to less developed countries which require labor-intensive techniques if the manufacturing sector is to absorb their abundant supply of labor. The relevant question, however, is how well do foreign firms do, compared to similar local firms, in absorbing labor? The evidence from this sample of matched pairs of firms suggests that in Brazil they perform quite poorly.

Physical capital intensity has been measured by three different variables; nonwage value-added per employee, nonwage value-added per production worker, and electricity consumption per production worker. All three measures suggest that foreign firms utilize techniques of production that are significantly more capital-intensive than their local counterparts. This may be a result of the fact that they are accustomed to large-scale, capital-intensive production in their home countries and utilize similar techniques in their scaled-down Brazilian plants, or it may simply reflect the fact that foreign firms must pay higher wages and have access to less expensive credit compared to local firms. Our finding, because of a large sample size, differs from that reported by Morley and Smith (1977, pp. 283–286).

Not only do techniques of production differ markedly between foreign and local firms, there is also evidence that differences tend to be greater, the greater the skill- and capital-intensity of the industry. Table 2 reports the coefficients of rank correlation between standardized differences and the average levels of various measures of productivity, skills and capital

Table 3 Test for significant differences when multi-plant operation is similar or different (mean standardized differences of matched pairs)

Variable	Both single plants (n = 88)	Both multiple plants (n = 79)	For: Single Dom: Multiple (n = 67)	For: Multiple Dom: Single (n = 48)
EST	–	−8.5	–	–
		(6.6)		
VA/Q	6.0	10.8*	0.4	5.6
(F = 0.98)	(3.4)	(4.3)	(4.5)	(6.0)
ADV	18.4	23.1	10.8	32.2
(F = 0.26)	(14.7)	(14.4)	(15.9)	(19.6)
EXPORTS1	66.5†	46.4†	64.7†	73.1†
(F = 0.48)	(14.3)	(16.5)	(16.9)	(18.3)
VA/L	21.0†	29.2†	18.0*	4.9
(F = 1.48)	(7.0)	(7.1)	(8.1)	(8.3)
W/L	37.1†	32.6†	26.0†	21.4†
(F = 1.21)	(5.2)	(5.5)	(6.6)	(7.9)
NWVA/L	13.1	27.9†	5.5	−2.2
(F = 1.73)	(8.7)	(8.8)	(9.3)	(11.3)

Note: The numbers in parentheses are the standard errors of the mean. *indicates statistical significance at the 0.05 level and † at the 0.01 level. All tests are one-tailed except those for EST and VA/Q, which are two-tailed. '*n*' refers to the number of matched pairs in the sample. The *F* statistics report the results of an analysis of variance (ANOVA) test for heterogeneity of the mean standardized differences.

intensity. The coefficients are not very large, but, with the exception of the correlation between differences in wages of white-collar employees (WNP/ L) and average wages of white-collar employees, all coefficients are positive and statistically significant at the 0.01 level. In other words, techniques of production show some tendency to differ more by type of ownership in industries characterized by high skills, high capital intensity and high productivity.

Empirical Findings for Subsets of the Sample

The large sample of 564 foreign and local firms affords us the luxury of calculating statistics for subsets of the data. Results are reported below for two distinct divisions of the sample: (i) combinations of single and multi-plant operations, and (ii) manufacturing subsectors. It would also have been interesting to divide the sample by the nationality of the foreign owners, but this information was not available.

Since foreign firms tend to operate fewer plants than their local counterparts, some of the differences reported in Table 1 might arise from differences in multi-plant operations rather than foreign or local ownership *per se.* To test this possibility, the sample was divided into four groups: 88 matched pairs which only operate single plants, 79 which only operate more than one plant, 67 for which the foreign firm operates a single plant and its local counterpart multiple plants, and 48 for which the converse is true. As can be seen in Table 3, calculated differences do not vary significantly between the four possible combinations of multiple and single plant operations. The highest value the *F* statistic attains in analysis of variance (ANOVA) tests is 1.73, which does not allow one to reject, even at the 10% level of confidence, the null hypothesis that the four standardized differences are equal. Therefore, it would appear that observed differences in the performance of foreign and domestic firms are not the result of differences in the extent of multi-plant operations.

In addition, average differences between foreign and local firms were calculated for each of the 20 subsectors (two-digit industries) covered by the sample. The significant results of these calculations, along with the standard errors and the *F* statistics of the ANOVA tests, are reported in Table 4. There is surprisingly little evidence of subsector heterogeneity in the results. In only one case — wages — is it possible, at the 5% level, to reject the null hypothesis that differences between the two types of firms do not vary by subsector. Greater heterogeneity might have been expected, given the existence of a significant, positive relationship between the standardized differences and average levels of these variables (see Table 2). Apparently the subsectors are themselves too heterogeneous to reveal these potential inter-industry differences.

In sum, the findings reported in Table 1 appear to be applicable throughout Brazil's manufacturing sector. Nonetheless, it is worthy of note that some of the variables achieve statistical significance in a large number of subsectors, whereas others do so in very few. Wages, for example, are significantly higher for foreign firms at the 5% level in 11 industries. In contrast, differences in advertising intensity attain statistical significance in only three subsectors. Advertising differences also show the least significant variations from subsector to subsector ($F = 0.93$), whereas variations in wage differences are statistically significant ($F = 1.70$).

Summary and Conclusions

The empirical analysis of the previous section leaves us with a number of definite conclusions as well as some unanswered questions concerning the typical characteristics of a foreign firm compared to its local counterpart of the same size operating in the same industry.

One finding of interest is that foreign firms in Brazil operate significantly fewer plants than their local counterparts. The difference is not large because single plant operations are common for both types of firms.

Though unexpected, this finding seems reasonable for two reasons. First, foreign firms operate plants of a much larger scale in their countries of origin than they do in Brazil. Therefore, they can be expected to be less prone than local firms to divide their output among several plants in the smaller Brazilian market. Second, we found that foreign firms utilize quite capital-intensive techniques of production compared to their local counterparts, and capital intensity tends to increase the importance of scale economies.

Foreign firms also have significantly higher ratios of value-added to output, but it is not clear why this occurs. To what extent does this reflect greater vertical integration of production and to what extent does it reflect higher quality goods sold at higher prices? This is a point that requires further research and could profitably be included in detailed case studies of firms and industries. Chudnovsky (1979, p. 54), in his study of the Argentine pharmaceutical industry, actually found foreign firms to charge considerably lower prices than their local rivals, but this is not likely to be true for all industries and all developing countries.

Advertising expenditures and remittances for royalties and technical assistance are both significantly higher for foreign firms, and the evidence is overwhelming that foreign-owned firms export a much larger proportion of their output than do comparable local firms despite the fact that they do not benefit from a significantly higher rate of export subsidy. All these results are to be expected, since the advantages of the transnational corporation often stem from its possession of "brand names," proprietary technology, and links to overseas markets.

There is no doubt that foreign firms in Brazil typically have high levels of labor productivity compared to local firms of a similar size operating in the same industry. This could result from any one of a number of factors: (i) employees which have greater skills and training, (ii) more machinery and equipment per worker, (iii) greater technical efficiency, in the sense that the same output is produced with fewer inputs, or (iv) some combination of these three possibilities. The results of this study show very clearly that the first two factors play an important role in accounting for observed productivity. It is not possible, in the absence of a clearly specified production function, to measure differences in technical efficiency, so nothing can be inferred regarding the possible importance of this factor.

The fact that foreign firms utilize more capital- and skill-intensive techniques of production implies that they make less use of unskilled labor, the abundant factor of production in Brazil. This may be because they have to pay higher wages for labor of the same quality, or because quality controls for internationally known products impose rigidities in the production process to an extent unknown by local firms. Or it may simply reflect the absence of competitive pressures, permitting what Morley and Smith refer to as a "limited search" for more labor-intensive techniques of production.

Table 4 Test by subsector for significant differences between matched pairs of foreign and domestic firms (means standardized differences in percent)

Subsector	VA/Q	ADV	EXPORT1	VA/L	W/L	NWVA/L
Non-metallic min.	–	–	–	47.9*	40.5*	45.5*
(*n* = 12)				(13.8)	(13.5)	(16.4)
Basic metals	18.0*	20.9	80.8*	25.8*	41.0*	18.9†
(*n* = 46)	(6.2)	(16.3)	(18.7)	(7.2)	(5.8)	(10.0)
Machinery	–	45.8*	52.4†	18.2†	32.5*	–
(*n* = 44)		(17.1)	(22.3)	(10.2)	(7.7)	
Electrical equip.	9.2†	–	91.3*	–	23.6†	–
(*n* = 23)	(3.6)		(25.6)		(11.4)	
Transport equip.	–	–	52.0	23.1†	29.3*	25.9†
(*n* = 16)			(38.7)	(9.8)	(8.8)	(13.5)
Wood (*n* = 3)	–	–	136.5	–	–	–
			(62.2)			
Furniture	–	–	–	–	–	–
(*n* = 2)						
Pulp and paper	–	–	137.12*	–	45.6*	–
(*n* = 10)			(42.3)		(13.5)	
Rubber	14.3	–	–	33.0*	–	37.1†
(*n* = 3)	(7.6)			(1.3)		(11.0)
Leather	–	–	129.6†	–	–	–
(*n* = 2)			(13.1)			
Chemicals	–	–	83.5*	23.8	27.5*	–
(*n* = 27)			(21.8)	(14.3)	(10.9)	
Pharmaceutical	–	–	–	–	37.1†	–
(*n* = 10)					(16.0)	
Perfumes, soap	–	–	–	–	88.9	–
(*n* = 3)					(47.6)	
Plastics	–	141.8*	102.5†	65.7†	76.8*	64.2
(*n* = 8)		(39.1)	(51.7)	(30.6)	(17.4)	(35.6)
Textiles	–	–	77.3*	–	–	–
(*n* = 32)			(24.9)			
Clothing, footwear	–	–	–	–	–	–
(*n* = 8)						
Processed food	22.3	83.5†	–	–	41.8*	–
(*n* = 13)	(13.9)	(37.1)			(11.7)	
Beverages	−21.0	–	53.7	–	–	–
(*n* = 7)	(10.7)		(34.8)			
Printing	34.9†	–	–	62.5†	–	66.4†
(*n* = 6)	(9.3)			(21.7)		(32.2)
Other manufactures	–	–	–	–	48.6†	–
(*n* = 5)					(15.8)	
F statistic	1.59	0.93	1.31	0.94	1.70†	1.08

Note: The numbers in parentheses are the standard errors of the mean. *indicates statistical significance at the 0.01 level and † at the 0.05 level. All test are one-tailed except those for VA/Q, which are two-tailed. Statistics not shown were not significantly different from zero at the 0.10 level. "*n*" refers to the number of matched pairs in the sample. The *F* statistics refer to the results of an analysis of variance (ANOVA) test of the null hypothesis that the mean differences do not vary by subsector.

This study has benefited from access to an exceptionally large data base. As a result, in contrast to previous studies in Brazil and elsewhere employing the "matched pairs" approach, we have found quite large and significant differences between local and foreign firms. If local firms imitate their foreign rivals, this imitation is far from perfect. Ownership ties do make a difference. The implementation of policies which encourage or restrict foreign ownership can thus be expected to have direct effects on industry performance, quite apart from any indirect effects that result from modification of the behavior of locally-owned firms or changes in the size distribution of firms.

The finding that foreign firms differ from domestic firms should not come as a surprise, for subsidiaries of transnational corporations form part of a much larger organization. Von Doellinger and Cavalvanti (1975, pp. 42–46) estimated that foreign subsidiaries operating in Brazil account for only 2% of the global sales of the respective transnational enterprises and less than 1% of their global assets. In a broad sense, foreign-owned firms are thus much larger in size than any privately-owned Brazilian firm. Indeed, it is the ties to a parent company that give the foreign firm its advantage over local firms in export markets, enable it to attract and retain highly-skilled employees, and may explain its preference for capital-intensive and skill-intensive techniques of production.

Notes

† The views expressed are those of the author and do not necessarily reflect those of the United Nations Economic Commission for Latin America and the Caribbean. The author wishes to thank Decio Fialho Filho for competent and careful research assistance, Helson Braga for making the data available, and an anonymous referee for helpful comments on an earlier draft of the paper.

1. Blomström and Persson (1983) present evidence for Mexico that could be interpreted as support for such a "spillover" of technology from foreign to local firms. They report a positive coefficient of partial correlation between foreign presence in an industry and labor productivity of locally-owned plants, but their control for inter-industry variations in capital- and skill-intensity is very imperfect. For this reason, their finding may simply reflect the tendency of foreign firms to dominate industries characterized by high capital and skill requirements, hence high output per employee.

2. Katz (1984, p. 24) cites a comparison between "a locally-owned machine tool firm" and a "subsidiary of a British firm producing combustion engines" in support of the generalization that "subsidiaries of [transnational corporations] tend to develop stronger domestic technological capabilities in process engineering areas as well as in production planning and organization, rather than in aspects of new product design." (Katz, 1984, p. 24.) This may be true. But differences between the two types of products, namely rapid technological change in machine tools compared to internal combustion engines, might also explain the observed differences in research and development effort. Similarly, the (opposite?) conclusion that

270   *United Nations Library on Transnational Corporations*

large locally-owned firms can "as far as technological behavior is concerned," be grouped with "domestic subsidiaries of foreign firms" (p. 25) is based on very few observations, with insufficient control for other factors that might account for this result.

3. On the other hand, students of the pharmaceutical industry in Argentina (Chudnovsky, 1979, cited in Katz, 1984, p. 24) have concluded that domestic firms have a competitive edge over foreign subsidiaries that rely on parent companies for the development of new products.

4. The ECLAC 1983 study is based on published balance-sheet data, so does not underestimate the number of foreign-owned firms.

5. The quote is from Lim and Fong (1982, p. 582). See also Caves (1971, p. 13) and Newfarmer (1977, pp. 367–369). Lim and Fong in their article also present evidence in conflict with this belief. Lall, in his 1978 survey article, notes that the entire area of linkages and the creation of domestic value-added by foreign firms "cries out for detailed empirical research."

6. The wage and labor data reported in this study were taken from returns filed for payment of the industrial product tax (IPI) in calendar 1978. Wage data from corporate income tax returns for fiscal 1978 were also analyzed, but the results are not reported here, for they replicate those produced with the IPI data.

References

Blomström, Magnus, and Hakan Persson, "Foreign investment and spillover efficiency in an under-developed economy: Evidence from the Mexican manufacturing industry," *World Development,* Vol. 11, No. 6 (June 1983), pp. 493–501.

Bonelli, Regis, "Concentracao industrial no Brasil: Indicadores da evolucao recente," *Pesquisa e Planejamento Economico,* Vol. 10, No. 3 (December 1980), 851–884.

Braga, Helson, "Determinantes do desempenho da industria brasileira: Uma investigacao econometrica," *Revista Brasileira de Economia,* Vol. 33, No. 4 (October, 1979), pp. 501–570.

Braga, Helson, "Aspectos distributivos do esquema de subsidios fiscais a exportacao de manufaturados," *Pesquisa e Planejamento Economico,* Vol. 11, No. 3 (December 1981), pp. 783–802.

Caves, Richard E., "International corporations: The industrial economics of foreign investment," *Economica,* Vol. 38 (February 1971), pp. 1–27.

Caves, Richard E., *Multinational Enterprise and Economic Analysis* (Cambridge, U.K.: Cambridge University Press, 1982).

Chudnovsky, Daniel, "The challenge by domestic enterprise to the transnational corporation's domination: A case study of the Argentine pharmaceutical industry," *World Development,* Vol. 7, No. 1 (January 1979), pp. 45–58.

Chung, Byung Soo, and Chung H. Lee, "The choice of production techniques by foreign and local firms in Korea," *Economic Development and Cultural Change,* Vol. 29, No. 1 (October 1980), pp. 135–140.

Doellinger, Carlos von, and Leonardo C. Cavalvanti, *Empresas Multinacionais na Industria Brasileira* (Rio de Janeiro: IPEA/INPES Relatorio de Pesquisa No. 29, 1975).

ECLAC (United Nations Economic Commission for Latin America and the Caribbean), "Dos estudios sobre empresas transnacionales en Brasil," *Estudios e Informes de la CEPAL,* No. 31, E/CEPAL/G.1259 (Santiago: 1983).

ECLAC, "Market structure, firm size and Brazilian exports," *Estudios e Informes de la CEPAL,* No. 44, LC/G.1335 (Brasilia: 1985).

Evans, Peter, *Dependent Development: The Alliance of Multinational, State, and Local Capital in Brazil* (Princeton, NJ: Princeton University Press, 1979).

Goncalves, Reinaldo, "Proporcao de fatores, escolha de tecnicas e empresas multi-nacionais na industria de transformacao no Brasil," *Revista Brasileira de Economia*, Vol. 36 No. 2 (April 1982), pp. 161–181.

Goncalves, Reinaldo, "O crescimento de empresas multinacionais e nacionais privadas na industria de transformacao: 1968/80," *Pesquisa e Planejamento Economico*, Vol. 13, No. 1 (April 1983a), pp. 181–206.

Goncalves, Reinaldo, "Lucratividade na industria de transformacao: Empresas multinacionais versus nacionais privadas," *Revista Brasileira de Economia*, Vol. 37, No. 2 (April 1983b), pp. 207–224.

Katz, Jorge M., "Domestic technological innovations and dynamic comparative advantage: Further reflections on a comparative case-study programme," *Journal of Development Economics*, Vol. 16, Nos. 1/2 (September 1984), pp. 13–37.

Lall, Sanjaya, "Transnationals, domestic enterprises, and industrial structure in host LDCs: A survey," *Oxford Economic Papers*, Vol. 30, No. 2 (July 1978), pp. 217–248.

Lall, Sanjaya, and Sharif Mohammad, "Foreign ownership and export performance in the large corporate sector of India," *Journal of Development Studies*, Vol. 20, No. 1 (October 1983), pp. 56–67.

Lim, David, "Do foreign companies pay higher wages than their local counterparts in Malaysian manufacturing?" *Journal of Development Economics*, Vol. 4, No. 1 (1977), pp. 55–66.

Lim, Linda Y. C., and Pan Eng Fong, "Vertical linkages and multinational enterprises in developing countries," *World Development*, Vol. 10, No. 7 (July 1982), pp. 585–595.

Mascolo, Joao Luiz, and Helson C. Braga, "Caracteristicas tecnologicas do setor industrial exportador," in *VI Encontro Brasileiro de Econometria* (São Paulo: Sociedade Brasileira de Econometria, 1984), pp. 245–289.

Mason, R. Hal, "Some observations on the choice of technology by multinational firms in developing countries," *Review of Economics and Statistics*, Vol. 55 (August 1973), pp. 349–355.

Meller, Patricio, "Remuneracao e emprego das filiais manufactureiras na America Latina," *Revista Brasileira de Economia*, Vol. 38, No. 3 (July 1984), pp. 253–274.

Meller, Patricio, and Alejandra Mizala, "US multinationals and Latin American manufacturing employment absorption," *World Development*, Vol. 10, No. 2 (February 1982), pp. 115–126.

Morley, Samuel A., and Gordon W. Smith, "Limited search and the technology choices of multinational firms in Brazil," *Quarterly Journal of Economics*, Vol. 91, No. 2 (May 1977), pp. 263–287.

Newfarmer, Richard S. "Multinational conglomerates and the economics of dependent development: A case study of the international electrical oligopoly and Brazil's electrical industry," PhD thesis (Madison: University of Wisconsin, 1977).

Newfarmer, Richard S., "TNC takeovers in Brazil: The uneven distribution of benefits in the market for firms," *World Development*, Vol. 7, No. 1 (January 1979), pp. 25–43.

Newfarmer, Richard S., and L. C. Marsh, "Foreign ownership, market structure and industrial performance: Brazil's electrical industry," *Journal of Development Economics*, Vol. 8, No. 1 (February 1981), pp. 47–75.

Stewart, Frances, "International technology transfer: Issues and policy options," *World Bank Staff Working Paper* No. 344 (Washington, D.C.: July 1979).

Tyler, Willam G., "Technical efficiency and ownership characteristics of manufacturing firms in a developing country: A Brazilian case study," *Weltwirtschaftliches Archiv*, Vol. 114, No. 2 (1978), pp. 360–379.

Tyler, William G., "On using analysis of covariance to estimate a Cobb–Douglas production function: An empirical illustration with data from the Brazilian electrical machinery industry," in *I Encontro Brasileiro de Econometria* (São Paulo: Sociedade Brasileira de Econometria, 1979), pp. 109–127.

Willmore, Larry N., "Direct foreign investment in Central American manufacturing," *World Development*, Vol. 4, No. 6 (June 1976), pp. 499–517.

Zini, Alvaro A. Jr., "Evolucao da estrutura financeira das empresas no Brasil, 1969/1977," *Estudos Economicos*, Vol. 14, No. 1 (January 1984), pp. 83–105.

11

Foreign Investment and Productive Efficiency: The Case of Mexico*†

Magnus Blomström

*Source: *Journal of Industrial Economics*, XXXV (1986), pp. 97–110.

I Introduction

A widely held view among economists studying foreign investment is that one of the important contributions to the host country is likely to stem from external effects or spillovers. The spillovers can be of different kinds. The foreign firms may influence the productivity and growth of the domestically owned firm; they may change the nature and evolution of concentration; they may alter financing, marketing, and technological and managerial practices in the industries that they enter, *et cetera*. Because of great methodological difficulties in investigating these effects empirically in addition to lack of data, few empirical investigations appear in the literature. Three available econometric studies deal with the influence of foreign investment on the technical efficiency of host country firms. One focuses on Australia (Caves [1974]), one on Canada (Globerman [1979]), and one on Mexico (Blomström and Persson [1983]). All three find some support for the spillover benefit hypothesis, but none of the studies analyzes the nature of spillover efficiency in depth.

The present paper is an attempt to identify through what mechanisms the spillover efficiency of foreign investment takes place by analyzing the effects of foreign investment on the productive efficiency of the industrial structure in Mexico. We will examine whether the relative performance of firms within an industry varies systematically with the presence of foreign subsidiaries. We will also analyze the impact of foreign investment on structural change, that is how foreign entry influences the technological structure in host country industries.

The exposition of the paper is as follows. In section II causes and measures of differences in productive efficiency are discussed. Section III contains the hypotheses of what structural effects foreign investment has on domestic industry in an underdeveloped economy. Section IV gives the data and definitions used, and in section V the empirical results are presented. Finally, section VI draws the main conclusions.

II Causes and Measures of Differences in Productive Efficiency

An industry may be viewed as a number of establishments embodying techniques ranging from the most modern one, using the current best-practice technique, to the oldest operating establishment incorporating the best-practice technique of an earlier age (see for example Johansen [1972] and Salter [1960]). The technological structure of this industry can be described by the relative performance of the establishments within the industry, and an efficiency index, measuring the potential for an increase in the industry's production (or for input saving) by employing resources in establishments using the current best-practice technique, can be constructed.

Analyses of productive efficiency levels of industrial plants are often based on Farrell's efficiency frontier approach (Farrell [1957]). His approach is to compare the performance of actual establishments with the best-practice techniques observed in reality, instead of taking ideal combinations of inputs as the point of reference. He starts out by constructing an envelope including the minimum combinations of necessary inputs for producing one unit of output. Productive (or technical) efficiency is then measured by comparing observed input coefficient points for an establishment with the input coefficients on the efficiency frontier for the same factor proportions. Productive efficiency may thus be viewed as how closely the establishment attains the lowest possible real cost for the output it produces.

Closely related to Farrell's approach are studies based on Salter's approach focusing on the range between best-practice and "worse"-practice labor productivity and studies focusing on the distance between best-practice and average practice productivity. Salter's approach may, in fact, be regarded as a special case of Farrell's approach limited to a partial analysis of one input (labor).

One established measure of productive efficiency for an entire industry is the difference in efficiency between the best-practice technique and the industry average (see for example Carlsson [1972] and Førsund and Hjalmarsson [1974a]). This is a measure of structural efficiency. Such an efficiency index can be related to various explanatory variables, but there is no generally accepted theory of what determines technical efficiency at an industry level. Førsund and Hjalmarsson [1974b], however, emphasize the importance of both technological factors and relative price movements. The empirical results in Førsund and Hjalmarsson [1979] also indicate the importance of managerial factors. On *a priori* grounds we may thus identify at least four factors that influence the technological structure of an industry:

Rate of technical progress. It is an empirical question whether technical progress increases or decreases structural efficiency. A rapid technological progress may increase the dispersion between the best-practice firm and the industry average, since it can be perfectly efficient from an economic point of view to continue production in firms using capital equipment of old vintages even if more technically efficient techniques are available (see Johansen [1972]). If, however, the new technology results in a rapid structural change, the structural efficiency may increase.

Competitive pressure. Another explanatory factor of industry structure is the competitive pressure. It is assumed that greater competition, both domestic and international, results in a more efficient structure (see Carlsson [1972]). Both the level of concentration (which is commonly used as a measure of the degree of competition) and the rate of protection are therefore expected to be important determinants of the technological structure.

Market growth. A third hypothesis is that rapidly growing demand for an industry's output increases the dispersion in industry structure. Growing demand implies better possibilities for firms using capital equipment of older vintages to survive and for new firms (investing in best-practice) to enter. It is also reasonable to assume that falling or stagnating demand decreases the dispersion. Strömqvist [1983] shows that when the demand falls, an increasing share of investment goes to remedy old plants, while the investment share in new techniques decreases. The rate of market growth is therefore expected to be positively related to the dispersion between the best-practice firm and the industry average. Also, business cycles should be of importance here. In times of booms more firms can survive, while in recession many firms may be wiped out.

Ownership structure. It is further suggested that ownership structure has an influence on relative performance of the plants or firms within an industry. Multinational corporations (MNCs) are usually held to represent advanced technologies, and may therefore be an important source of structural change. Since the main purpose of this study is to analyze precisely this, we shall examine in more detail what structural effects are to be expected. In doing this we shall draw to a large extent on the existing body of literature on MNCs.

III MNCs and the Efficiency of Host Country Industry Structure

The standard theory claims that "for direct investment to thrive there must be some imperfection in markets for goods or factors, including among the latter technology, or some interference in competition by government or by firms, which separates markets" (Kindleberger [1969], p. 13). To be able to invest in production in foreign markets a firm must thus possess some asset in the form of knowledge of a public-goods character (for example product and process technology and management).

The monopolistic advantage which is a necessary precondition for foreign direct investment can obviously be of different kinds, and depending on which is the most crucial one, it may have different effects on the structure of the host country market. It is often claimed that MNCs have advantages due to the possession of proprietary technology (see for example Hufbauer and Nunns [1975]). If this technology is being transferred to the subsidiaries we may expect the rate of technical progress in industry in the host country to be affected by the MNC entry. Furthermore, if this technology "leaks out" more rapidly than it otherwise would have done, the host country can derive a spillover benefit through this channel. MNCs may, for instance, stimulate domestic firms to hasten their access to a specific technology, either because they would not have been aware of the existence of the technology, or because they would not have felt it profitable to try to obtain it in this manner.

Other studies suggest that the MNCs' advantages in possessing superior technology of production are overemphasized. The apparent differences between multinationals and host country firms reflect rather a movement along a fixed isoquant than a shift, and stem from differing factor prices faced by the two types of firms (see for example Mason [1973]). If this is the case, MNC entry need not have any significant influence on the technological frontier. It may nevertheless influence the technological structure because independently of what the monopolistic advantage consists of (process or product technology, special skills, cheaper capital, *et cetera*), it may provide a competitive edge for the foreign investors. MNC entry may therefore force existing firms exhibiting technical or allocative inefficiency (either because they operate on an inefficient scale or because they produce their output with inefficient combinations of inputs) to adopt more efficient methods. Particularly for concentrated industries this consideration should be relevant.

If MNCs' advantage lies in the fact that these firms apply modern management techniques, we may identify another possible source of structural change in the professional training that takes place within the foreign subsidiaries. If local managerial people who have been trained in such an environment move to a domestically owned firm, management practices in this firm may be substantially improved, and the firm may move closer to the efficiency frontier. This is a type of spillover efficiency that we would expect to be most important in underdeveloped countries, where the supply of managerial talent is in short supply.[1]

The fact that a MNC possesses different monopolistic advantages may also result in a specific conduct on the part of this firm. For example, since

short-term losses should not be too serious a problem for a foreign subsidiary, local competitors may be driven out of business by entering into
price-cutting wars. Or, as Newfarmer [1980] notes for the Brazilian electrical industry, MNCs may purchase domestic firms on especially favorable
terms because of their strong hold over technology and input markets. If a
MNC has a different type of conduct, this may also influence the technological structure.

To illuminate what characterizes multinational corporations in Mexican
manufacturing industry, and examine what impact they exert on productive
efficiency and structural change there, we proceed in two steps. The first is
to analyze whether deviation in efficiency varies systematically with the
presence of foreign subsidiaries in an industry, that is whether a MNC has
any independent influence on the technological structure. For this purpose
cross-section data on industry efficiency for the year 1975 will be used.
Secondly, we will analyze the impact of multinational investment on structural change, that is in what way foreign *entry* influences the deviation in
efficiency. For this purpose we will relate different aspects of structural
change between two years (1970 and 1975) to changes in foreign participation during this five-year period.

IV Data and Definitions

In this study a partial measure based on labor productivity is used in the
analysis of structural efficiency. In order to obtain the best-practice technique for each industry we do not employ individual plants or firms as our
observations. Instead we use size groupings of plants. Obviously this is not
the best solution but it can be justified by the data available. It has,
however, been shown that this is an efficient approach if the size and the
technique of a plant are strongly correlated.[2]

An advantage with our approach is that it needs only statistical information that is published and easily available even for other countries than
Mexico. This approach should therefore be useful also for other problems
related to productive efficiency.

The data sources used are the Mexican Census of Manufactures 1970
and 1975, supplemented by unpublished data broken down by ownership
in different industries.[3] The level of aggregation is the four-digit level and
the data are gathered at plant level. There are 230 individual four-digit
industries, but 85 had to be discarded because of data imperfections.[4]

The Census gives information on different sizes of plants within each
four-digit industry. Size is there defined in terms of employment, fixed
capital and gross production. All these measures have important weaknesses. For instance, two plants in an industry showing similarities in size in
terms of capital may be very different in terms of employment if they use

different capital intensities. However, the different measures of size turned out to be highly correlated, and a test showed that the results reported below were not significantly different whichever measure we used. In the regressions, fixed capital is used as the size measure.

When size is defined in terms of fixed capital there are 13 size classes. In order to maintain confidentiality, however, there are no data published on classes containing less than three plants. In such cases, two (or more) classes are aggregated into one. On average there are 6.5 size classes in each industry and the class averages are thus treated as our "plants".

The efficiency index is calculated in the following way. First the efficiency frontier is obtained by choosing the size class within each four-digit industry showing the highest value-added per employee. Value-added per employee in this size class is denoted y^+. Then the industry average (denoted $\bar{y}$) is calculated as the ratio of total value-added in each industry to the total number of employees. The efficiency index, e, for each industry, i, we then define as:

$$e_i = \frac{\bar{y}_i}{y_i^+}$$

The closer this efficiency index is to unity, the more equal is the actual output to the potential one.

V Empirical Analysis

MNCs and Technological Structure

The previous discussion on the determinants of productive efficiency may now be used to build a cross-section model that relates the deviations from the frontier 1975 to various explanatory variables. As was indicated, the rate of technical progress may have an influence on structural efficiency. Technical progress can be studied by observing changes in the best-practice technology between two periods. The more rapid the technical progress has been, the faster the frontier has moved. In this study we use the relative changes in labor productivity in the best-practice plants within each industry between 1970 and 1975 as a proxy for the rate of technical progress. This variable, denoted Δy^+, is thus defined as the ratio of y^+ (1975) to y^+ (1970).

The deviation from the frontier is also expected to be influenced by the degree of competition. There is no generally accepted theory of how competition should be measured, but in studies of industrial economics the concept of concentration is clearly associated with three factors that are all considered to be important determinants of competition. The factors are the number of firms in an industry, the inequality of market shares and the coalition potential. In their comparison of eleven different measures of industrial concentration, Vanlommel *et al.* [1977] find that the Herfindahl index is the best individual concentration index to capture these three factors. We will therefore use this index (denoted H) as an independent variable in our regressions.[5] Since the concentration index does not take foreign competition into account, we should also need a variable that takes care of this. Unfortunately, since no data on protection are available for 1975, we have to ignore it.[6]

Market growth may also influence the dispersion between the best-practice firm and the industry average. We define the market growth variable (MG) as the relative growth of employment of each industry in the period 1970–1975.[7] It is, however, not possible to capture the conceivable effects on the technological structure of business cycles since we have no data to take care of this.

Finally, the variable that we are most interested in: the foreign share variable (FS). In our statistical material a plant is defined as "foreign" if at least 15 percent of the shares are foreign owned. Foreign participation in an industry we define as the share of employees in an industry employed in foreign plants.[8]

We can now summarize the preceding discussion as follows:

$$e = f(\Delta y^+, H, MG, FS)$$

where e is our efficiency measure for productive efficiency for each industry. The statistical method employed is ordinary least-squares regression analysis. Since economic theory does not provide us with any guide as to what functional form to choose when specifying the econometric model, we have tested two forms; one linear and one log-linear. The results obtained from using the former are shown in equations (1) and (2) in Table I, while the results from the latter specification are shown in equations (3) and (4).[9] The different specifications of the model do not seem to influence the efficiency of the independent variables, but the log-linear estimations provided a somewhat lower R^2 value.

With the assumption of normally distributed errors, the impact of the Δy^+ variable is generally negative and significantly different from zero at the 0.01 level. It seems, thus, that a rapid technical progress increases the dispersion between the frontier and the industry average.

The Herfindahl index also turns out to be a significant explanatory variable but with a positive effect. Carlsson [1972], using the four-firm concentration ratio, finds the same. His interpretation of this is that in small, open economies (like Sweden) the concentration ratio reflects economies of scale and specialization rather than the market power of the largest firms. Due to underdevelopment, Mexico is also a relatively small economy, but a highly protected one. Carlsson's interpretation may therefore be valid even for small economies with little international competition.[10] However, one should also remember that our Herfindahl index is based on plant level

Table 1 Regression results for the determinants of structural efficiency: 145 industries

Equations	Constant	Δy^+	H	MG	FS	R^2
(1)*	0.6359 (0.0344)	−0.0716 (0.0142)	0.2333 (0.0672)	–	0.1820 (0.0569)	0.2889
(2)*	0.6396 (0.0388)	−0.0714 (0.0143)	0.2341 (0.0675)	−0.0044 (0.0211)	0.1866 (0.0612)	0.2891
(3)†	−0.1572 (0.0581)	−0.2221 (0.0427)	0.1201 (0.0528)	–	0.0650 (0.0181)	0.2724
(4)†	−0.1853 (0.0612)	−0.2293 (0.0429)	0.1182 (0.0527)	−0.0801 (0.0569)	0.0566 (0.0190)	0.2530

Standard error in parentheses.
*Lin.
†Log-lin.

data (see note 5). Such a concentration ratio may be a poor measure of a firm's market power and may well say more about scale economies. (It is not known how many plants the largest Mexican firms operate in each industry.)

When we use size groupings of plants in order to obtain the best-practice techniques, we get systematically higher structural efficiency, since the best-practice technique is always underestimated. This is thus due to the aggregation over plants when forming size groups. Furthermore, when the number of size classes decreases, this measurement error increases. One way of correction for this is to include the number of size classes among the independent variables, but this did not change the results in any significant degree, except for one thing: the Herfindahl index lost its efficiency as an influential variable. This is explained by the construction of this variable. Its magnitude is dependent on the number of plants in an industry. The simple correlation between the Herfindahl index and the number of size classes was −0.65 (for both lin and log).

The market growth (*MG*) variable seems to exert an insignificant influence, although this coefficient has the expected sign in all cases. Since it is not specifically highly correlated with any of the other independent variables, we thus conclude that market growth does not have any influence on structural efficiency.

The foreign share variable (*FS*) turns out to have a positive influence on structural efficiency. In all the regressions *FS* carries a positive coefficient that is significant at the 0.01 level. This result thus suggests, that MNCs have a positive independent influence on structure, so that industries dominated by foreign firms tend to be more efficient than others in the sense that the average firm is closer to the frontier. Furthermore, evidence from

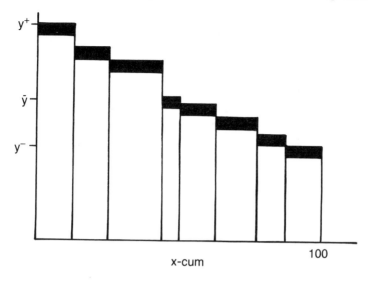

Figure 1 The range and shape of the efficiency distribution in an industry

Blomström and Persson [1983] indicates that technical efficiency of Mexican plants is positively related to foreign participation of various industries. This suggests that the influence of *FS* on the efficiency index *e* is not completely internal to the MNC.

So far we have analyzed whether deviation in efficiency varies systematically with the presence of foreign subsidiaries in an industry, but we have not been in the position to say anything about the way in which MNCs influence the technological structure. To be able to do that we will now relate different aspects of structural change between 1970 and 1975 to changes in foreign participation during this period.

MNCs and Structural Change

To illustrate the problem at hand we may look at Figure 1, where the "plants" in each industry are arranged in decreasing order of their efficiency value. Each rectangle or step in the diagram represents a "plant". Efficiency is measured along the ordinate axis and the share of employment (accumulated) along the abscissa axis.

The question is what part of the structure is influenced by MNC entry. Is for instance the rate of technical progress related to changes in foreign participation? To see this we tested the correlation between the relative changes in labor productivity in the best-practice plants within each industry between 1970 and 1975 (that is, Δy^+) and changes in foreign participation during this period (that is, $FS(1975) - FS(1970) = \Delta FS$).[11] This correlation turned out to be statistically insignificant which may be

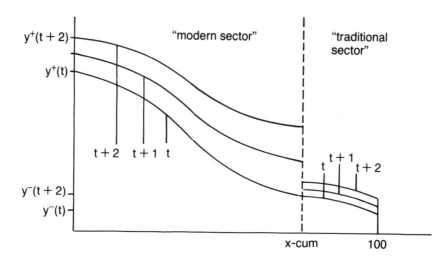

Figure 2 Illustration of structural change between period *t* and *t* + 2 as a result of foreign entry into an underdeveloped economy

interpreted that MNC entry does not have any influence on the rate of change of the technological frontier in different industries in Mexico.

Next the relationship between the relative change in labor productivity in the least efficient plants (Δy^-) within each industry between 1970 and 1975 (that is relative changes in the "tail" in Figure 1) and changes in foreign participation during this period was investigated. No correlation between the two variables was found. This seems to suggest that foreign entry has no specific tendency to "kick out" the least efficient firms in an industry, since if it had, foreign entry would result in higher increases in productivity here.

Finally, a test was made whether ΔFS was correlated with relative productivity changes in the industry average, $\Delta \bar{y}$ (defined as the ratio of $\bar{y}(1975)$ to $\bar{y}(1970)$). The simple correlation coefficient turned out to be 0.16 and we cannot reject the hypothesis that this variable is different from zero at the 0.05 level.

The results derived so far seem not to be totally consistent. Industries dominated by foreign firms tend to be more efficient than others in the sense that the average firms become closer to the frontier. At the same time, foreign entry turns out to be uncorrelated both with changes in the frontier and in the "tail". The explanation to the "inconsistency" may be found in the dual production structure in Mexico.

Most of the industrial output within each four-digit industry is produced by a small number of large firms using "modern" technology. The rest of the output is produced by a large number of small firms using different techniques. The markets in such economies are strongly segregated. Large, capital-intensive ("modern") firms producing high-grade goods are in general not directly competing with small, less capital-intensive ("traditional") firms producing low-grade goods, although these firms belong to the same industry according to the statistical classification.

The foreign firms naturally enter into the "modern" sector, and since the "tail" in nearly all of the industries is equivalent to the "traditional" sector, foreign entry seems to increase structural efficiency in the "modern" sector, leaving the firms in the "traditional" sector as they were.[12] The point can be illustrated in Figure 2. This is to say that foreign entry will increase the dual characteristic of the production structure.[13]

VI Conclusions

The empirical evidence from this study shows that foreign presence is positively correlated with structural efficiency in Mexican manufacturing industries. Industries dominated by foreign firms tend to be more efficient than others in the sense that the average firms come closer to the best-practice firm. The productive efficiency of the industrial structure is also found to be positively related to a Herfindahl index and negatively related to the rate of technical progress, while a variable for market growth does not have any significant influence on structural efficiency.

The finding that the Herfindahl index is positively correlated with the productive efficiency of the industrial structure is noteworthy. While there are statistical problems, one interpretation of this is that this index of plant concentration reflects economies of scale and specialization rather than the market power of large firms.

By relating changes in foreign participation during 1970 and 1975 to different aspects of structural change during this period it is found that foreign entry is uncorrelated both with changes in the technological frontier and changes in labor productivity in the least efficient plants. However, foreign entry is positively related to productivity changes in the industry average. One possible explanation of this finding is to be found in the dual production structure in underdeveloped countries. Foreign firms entering the "modern" sector may increase structural efficiency there, leaving the firms in the "traditional" sector as they were. We believe that this is a working hypothesis worth a more detailed study, since if it is correct, foreign entry will increase the dualism of the production structure in host underdeveloped countries.

Regarding the possible sources of spillover efficiency our results do not support the hypothesis that foreign investment speeds up the transfer of any specific technology to Mexico, not available also to domestic competitors. If that had been the case, the rate of technical progress in host country industries should have been related to MNC entry. Instead they indicate that the competitive pressure induced by the MNCs may be of importance. Considering the finding in Blomström and Persson [1983], that labor productivity in domestically owned plants in Mexican industries is associated with the presence of foreign firms, it is not inappropriate to assume that MNC entry increases efficiency in Mexican firms through competitive pressure. If, for instance, the impact of barriers to entry and the incentives to entry for foreign and domestic entrants are substantially different, so that entry becomes easier for the MNCs,[14] foreign investment may promote greater efficiency by increasing competition. Furthermore, the finding that foreign presence is positively correlated with structural efficiency may be a result of the fact that input markets start to operate better because of foreign entry. However, whether or not the training of labor and management within MNCs is a source of spillover efficiency cannot be judged by means of our results.[15]

In this study we have restricted ourselves to intraindustry effects of foreign investment. Naturally, interindustry influences should also be taken into account, but such influences are more difficult to measure in statistical material like ours. The impact made by foreign firms in the host economy on its suppliers in different industries, by insisting that they meet standards of quality control, may for instance be important. Brash [1966] provided an early discussion on this when he studied the impact made by General Motors in Australia on its suppliers. This subject is especially important in larger and more industrialized LDCs like Mexico because of their legislation requiring domestic content, but here we are left with very little empirical work.

Notes

†I am indebted to Richard E. Caves, Lennart Hjalmarsson, Robert E. Lipsey, Peter Svedberg and an anonymous referee for helpful comments. Financial support by Jacob Wallenbergs Fond and HSFR is gratefully acknowledged.

1. A study of the yoghurt industry in Mexico finds that the difference in performance between joint ventures and their Mexican competitors lies, not in the capital's origin, but much more in the management methods with which this capital is linked (Montavon [1979]).

2. For a general analysis of criteria with regard to grouping plants, see Johansson and Marksjö [1983].

3. Data specified for different ownership categories has been provided by la Dirección Estadística de la Secretaría de Industria y Comercio in Mexico.

4. The number of industries was reduced mainly because of changes in the classification system between 1970 and 1975. All four-digit industries 1970 that were divided into two or more industry classes 1975 were excluded. A few industries were also excluded because of missing information on some important variables.

5. The Herfindahl index has been calculated in the following way:

$$H = \sum_{i=1}^{n} \left(\frac{x_i}{X} \right)^2$$

where x_i represents the employment of the n individual plants and X represents the total employment of the industry.

6. Data on the rate of effective protection for 93 four-digit industries 1970 were, however, available. To get an idea of whether protection is an important determinant of structural efficiency we calculated the simple correlation coefficient between this rate of protection and $e(1970)$ (the efficiency index calculated on 1970's data). The coefficient turned out to be zero. This result suggests that the omission of a variable that takes care of protection in our regressions should not be too serious a problem.

7. An alternative measure of market growth defined as the relative real growth of gross production in each industry was also tried, but it did not change the results in any significant way.

8. An alternative measure for foreign participation defined in terms of gross production only had the effect that it lowered marginally the R^2 values in the regressions.

9. See Appendix for correlation matrices.

10. As was indicated in footnote 6, the rate of effective protection seems not to be an important determinant of structural efficiency.

11. We did not use the relative change in foreign participation since we want to capture the effects of foreign investment (and disinvestment) regardless of the degree of foreign participation in the initial period.

12. We arbitrarily use the size group containing the smallest plants (fixed capital stock less than 25 000 pesos) as our definition of the "traditional" sector. This definition is very simple and can be further sophisticated. In 1975, 56 percent of the total number of plants in the Mexican manufacturing industry belonged to this size group. Together these plants produced 1.4 percent of the total manufacturing output and employed 8 percent of the work force.

Of the total 145 industries used in this study, 101 have a "traditional" sector according to our definition, and this sector was always the least efficient one. Of the remaining 44 industries with no plants (or no information on plants) with capital stock of less than 25 000 pesos, the smallest size group anyway turned out to be the least efficient in 34 industries.

13. An alternative explanation of the set of results in this paper is that foreign firms, for some reason, tend to enter industries with a high e. For instance, they may be more prevalent in newer industries (for example chemicals and cars) which do not have a traditional sector. If this is true, multinationals have no independent influence on efficiency in Mexico. However, this contrasts with the findings in Blomström and Persson [1983].

14. For affirmative evidence on this point, see Gorecki [1976].

15. One way of penetrating deeper into the questions of spillover efficiency would be to analyze what effects entry of domestic firms of the same size as the MNCs would have on structure and structural change. The available data, however, precludes such an analysis.

Appendix Simple correlation coefficients for independent l in variables

	Δy^+	H	MG	FS	FS_A
Δy^+	1.00				
H	0.05	1.00			
MG	0.06	0.18	1.00		
FS	0.00	0.36	0.38	1.00	
FS_A^*	−0.04	0.34	0.33	0.94	1.00

Simple correlation coefficients for independent log-l in variables

	Δy^+	H	MG	FS	FS_A
Δy^+	1.00				
H	0.05	1.00			
MG	0.14	0.09	1.00		
FS	0.09	0.21	0.33	1.00	
FS_A^*	0.02	0.17	0.28	0.87	1.00

*FS_A is an alternative measure for foreign participation constructed as the foreign share of gross production in each industry.

References

Blomström, M. and Persson, H., 1983, 'Foreign Investment' and "Spillover" Efficiency in an Underdeveloped Economy. Evidence from the Mexican Manufacturing Industry", *World Development*, 11 (June), pp. 493–501.

Brash, D. T., 1966, *American Investment in Australian Industry* (Harvard University Press, Cambridge, Mass.).

Carlsson, B., 1972, 'The Measurement of Efficiency in Production: An Application to Swedish Manufacturing Industries 1968', *Swedish Journal of Economics*, 74 (December), pp. 468–485.

Caves, R. E., 1974, 'Multinational Firms, Competition and Productivity in Host-country Markets', *Economica*, 41 (May), pp. 176–193.

Farrell, M. J., 1957, 'The Measurement of Productive Efficiency', *Journal of the Royal Statistical Society*, A 120, Part III, pp. 253–290.

Førsund, F. and Hjalmarsson, L., 1974a, 'On the Measurement of Productive Efficiency', *Swedish Journal of Economics*, 76 (June), pp. 141–154.

Førsund, F. and Hjalmarsson, L., 1974b, 'Comment on Bo Carlsson's The Measurement of Efficiency in Production: An Application to Swedish Manufacturing Industries 1968', *Swedish Journal of Economics*, 76 (June), pp. 251–254.

Førsund, F. and Hjalmarsson, L., 1979, 'Generalised Farrell Measures of Efficiency: An Application to Milk Processing in Swedish Dairy Plants', *Economic Journal*, 89 (June), pp. 294–315.

Globerman, S., 1979, 'Foreign Direct Investment and "Spillover" Efficiency

Benefits in Canadian Manufacturing Industries', *Canadian Journal of Economics*, 12 (February), pp. 42–56.

Gorecki, P. K., 1976, 'The Determinants of Entry by Domestic and Foreign Enterprises in Canadian Manufacturing Industries: Some Comments and Empirical Results', *Review of Economics and Statistics*, 58 (November), pp. 485–488.

Hufbauer, G. C. and Nunns, J. R., 1975, 'Tax Payments and Tax Expenditures on International Investment and Employment', *Columbia Journal of World Business*, 10(2), pp. 12–10.

Johansen, L., 1972, *Production Functions* (North-Holland, Amsterdam).

Johannson, B. and Marksjö, B., 1983, 'An Interactive System Analysis of Industrial Sectors', *IIASA WP-83-00*, International Institute of Applied Systems Analysis, Laxenburg, Austria.

Kindleberger, C. P., 1969, *American Business Abroad* (Yale University Press, New Haven).

Mason, R. H., 1973, 'Some Observations on the Choice of Technology by Multinational Firms in Developing Countries', *Review of Economics and Statistics*, 55 (August), pp. 349–355.

Montavon, R., 1979, *The Role of Multinational Companies in Latin America. A Case Study in Mexico* (Saxon House, Hampshire).

Newfarmer, R., 1980, *Transnational Conglomerates and the Economics of Dependent Development: A Case Study of the International Oligopoly and Brazil's Electrical Industry* (Jai Press, Greenwich, CT.).

Salter, W. E. G., 1960, *Productivity and Technical Change* (Cambridge University Press, London).

Strömqvist, U., 1983, *Profit Structure and Patterns of Investment*, SIND 1983: 1 (Liber Förlag, Stockholm) (in Swedish).

Vanlommel, E., de Brabander, B. and Liebaers, D., 1977, 'Industrial Concentration in Belgium: Empirical Comparison of Alternative Seller Concentration Measures', *Journal of Industrial Economics*, 26 (September), pp. 1–20.

12

Foreign Investment and Economic Performance in Korea*

Bohn-Young Koo

*Source: J.H. Dunning, ed., *Multinational Enterprises, Economic Structure and International Competitiveness* (Chichester, Wiley, 1985), pp. 281–307.

Introduction

Korea has achieved remarkable economic progress during the past two decades (1962–82), registering over 8% real GNP growth per annum. With this high growth, the nation's industrial structure has undergone significant changes, transforming Korea from a backward agricultural nation to a semi-industrial modern state.

The purpose of this chapter is to examime the role foreign direct investment (FDI) has played in bringing about the marked changes in Korea's economic structure.[1] Although the pattern of out-going investment by Korean firms is also briefly surveyed, its effects on changes in Korea's economic structure are not comprehensively analysed, as the scale of Korean multinational activity is still very small, particularly in the manufacturing sector, which is the main object of our study.

The next section will briefly summarize the changes in Korea's economic and industrial structure during the past two decades and discuss the major industrial policies followed by the government during the period. This is followed by an analysis of the relationship between changes in the industrial structure and changes in trade patterns.

The fourth section will review the patterns of FDI and discuss foreign investment policies followed by the Korean government during the period. The fifth section will then critically examine the interrelationship between industrial structure, comparative advantage, and foreign investment, so as to gain further insight into the causes and the nature of FDI in Korea and to investigate the effects of the operation of the affiliates of foreign MNEs on allocative efficiency in Korea.

The sixth section will analyse various behavioural differences between Korean and foreign affiliates in order to draw some implications concerning the effect of FDI on sectoral or technical efficiency in Korea.

The seventh section will test Dunning's hypothesis on the relationship between net outward foreign investment and stages of development (Dunning, 1981) and then briefly examine the characteristics of outward investments made by Korean firms. The final section concludes the chapter with some policy observations.

Overview of the Changes in Korea's Economic and Industrial Structure

In 1962 Korea was still in the process of recovering from the Korean War, and was heavily dependent on foreign aid for its survival. The domestic savings ratio, savings to gross national product (GNP), was only 3.3%, while the ratio of foreign savings, which was mostly in the form of US aid, was 10.7%. Per capita GNP stood at only $87.

The economic structure was naturally very much underdeveloped, with the primary sector accounting for 36.6% of GNP, and the manufacturing sector for only 14.2%. Exports were negligible, amounting to only $55 million in 1962, and more than two-thirds of these were primary products.

Since then, Korea's economic structure has undergone immense changes, owing mainly to the government's consistent outward-oriented economic policies of the past two decades. Exports increased at the remarkable rate of 35% per annum during the period (in value terms), reaching $21.9 billion in 1982, while per capita GNP increased to $1,678.

Table 1 General economic indicators of Korea: 1962 and 1982

	Unit	*1962*	*1983*
GNP	$ billion	2.3	66.0
Per Capita GNP	$	87	1,678
Merchandise exports	$ billion	0.05	21.9
Merchandise imports	$ billion	0.4	24.3
Total exports to GNP[a]	%	5.1	40.3
Total imports to GNP[a]	%	16.6	41.2
Domestic savings to GNP	%	3.3	22.0
Foreign savings to GNP	%	10.7	4.6
Industrial Structure[b]	%		
Primary		36.6	16.9
Mining and Manufacturing		16.2	30.0
(Manufacturing)		(14.2)	(28.5)
Services		47.1	53.1

[a]Includes commodity and services.
[b]Based on the distribution of the value added.
Source: Economic Planning Board, *Major Statistics of Korean Economy*, 1983.

Accordingly, the share of exports increased from only 5.1% of GNP in 1962 to 40.3% in 1982. Over the same period the share of imports also increased form 16.6% of GNP to 41.2% (Table 1).

The industrial structure underwent significant changes during the period. The share of the primary sector decreased from 36.6% of GNP in 1962 to 16.9% in 1982, while the share of the manufacturing sector increased from 14.2% to 28.5%. Thus, the manufacturing sector came to far outweigh the primary sector in importance, when viewed in terms of their respective contributions to the nation's value added.

These changes in the pattern of Korea's economy were brought about mainly by changes in her trade patterns. Particularly fast growth in exports of manufactured goods was one of the key factors behind the striking changes in Korea's industrial structure. The share of manufacturing goods in total exports increased from 27% in 1962 to 94% in 1982; and the share of exports in total sales of manufactured goods increased from a mere 1.2% to over 29% over the same period. As a result, the manufacturing sector grew rapidly in importance and, within this sector, trade-related industries grew much faster than one-trade-related industries.

The Role of Government Policies

What were the government policies which brought about the changes just described? A review of the role of the government is essential, not only to understand how changes in Korea's industrial structure were brought about, but also to analyse their effects on the patterns of FDI which appeared later in Korea.

In 1962, the Korean government consciously embraced an outward-looking industrialization strategy and has pursued this strategy consistently for the past two decades. Adoption of an outward-looking strategy was perhaps inevitable for Korea, as the country was deficient in most natural resources and had only human resources in abundance. In order to promote industrialization, the government has wielded a comprehensive influence on the economy through various regulations and incentives. Although we do not propose to give details of all the industrial policies adopted by the Korean government, at least three important policy lines, which were generally maintained throughout the period, should be noted.[2]

First, in order to promote exports, various incentives were introduced, including income tax reductions for export-related earnings (abolished in 1973), free imports of export-related raw materials or equipment, preferential financing for export-related activities (abolished in 1982), and generous wastage allowances for imported raw materials (reduced in 1973). Above all, except in the late 1970s, reasonable exchange rate adjustments were made throughout the period.

Until the end of the 1970s, export promotion was the government's top priority. Export targets were set up for each year and regular monthly export-promotion meetings chaired by the President of the Republic were held to maintain the export orientation of private entrepreneurs.

Second, to encourage inflows of foreign capital, the Foreign Capital Inducement Act was introduced in 1960. Since Korea lacked the necessary domestic savings, she had to finance her investment by borrowing from foreign countries. Based on the Act, the government guaranteed the repayment of foreign loans and provided tax and other incentives to foreign investors and licensors of foreign technologies. Sometimes, explicit guarantees of profits or markets were made to large foreign investors to attract them to Korea. At the same time, two free export zones were established in 1970 and 1974. However, for most of the period the Korean government maintained relatively restrictive foreign investment policies, so most foreign capital came in the form of loans rather than direct investment.

Third, to facilitate the modernization of Korea's industrial structure, the government provided various tax and financial incentives for investments in industries deemed important by the government. Promotional laws were introduced, which specified the incentives and eligible products in such industries as electronics, shipbuilding, steel, machinery, and petrochemicals.

Many industrial parks were set up to help the growth of these industries, and for major projects the government sometimes intervened directly in the planning of individual plants, selection of plant operators (owners), and in the operation of the plants.

In summary, the pattern of industrialization which has emerged in Korea over the past two decades has been strongly influenced by government policies, although these policies have been influenced by (as well as influencing) changes in the nation's comparative advantage position and the level and structure of markets.

More recently, there has been a fundamental change in the way the government manages the economy. Realizing that heavy-handed government intervention had introduced many undesirable biases in the economy, the government began to reduce its intervention in the early 1980s and to introduce more competition in the economy through liberalization of imports and direct foreign investment and through abolition of government subsidies or incentives. The effects of these changes have not yet become apparent; we shall therefore only allude to them again in the final section of the chapter.

Industrial Structure and Trade Patterns in Korea

The industrial structure of an economy changes as its level of income grows. Usually, as per capita income rises, the importance of the primary sector decreases, while that of the industrial sector increases. However, depending on the character of the industrialization strategies adopted, considerable differences in the speed and pattern of industrial changes are likely to be observed.

In the case of Korea, the outward-oriented industrialization strategy adopted in the early 1960s brought about rapid changes in the nation's industrial structure. Therefore, we need to look at the changes in Korea's export and import patterns more closely before we analyse the effects of FDI on structural change.

Korea's export growth began with exports of simple labour-intensive products like garments, plywood, footwear, and wigs. However, the proportion of most of these products reached its peak in the early 1970s, and since then exports of more capital- and skill-intensive products such as cement, tyres, steel, electronics, and fabricated metal products have began to grow faster.

By 1980, exports of simple labour-intensive products had declined further in importance, and the heavy and chemical industries came to account for almost half of all merchandise exports. Among others, steel, ships, electronic products, and fabricated metal products became Korea's newest major export items. The textile industry still claimed 21% of total exports (or 27% of total merchandise exports) in 1980, but, due to a considerable decline in the contribution of clothing in total textile exports, the product mix of the textile exports had changed significantly from that of the early 1970s.

The share of primary goods in total exports declined sharply and consistently during the period, as a result of much faster growth of exports of manufactured goods. By 1980, primary goods accounted for less than 4% of total exports. Similarly, the share of the services sector in total exports declined considerably during the period, although it tended to rise again during the late 1970s, because of an increase in the value of sea and air transportation activities.[3]

Thus, since the early 1970s Korea's export pattern has been characterized by a steady increase in the proportion of exports of manufactured goods; and among manufactured goods, a marked shift from labour-intensive to more skill-intensive products.

Unlike exports, imports into Korea were tightly controlled by the government throughout the period. In consequence, for the most part only raw materials to be used in producing export goods, or materials that were in short supply domestically, and capital goods which could not be supplied by domestic producers were allowed to be imported.

Even by 1980, when significant import substitution had been accomplished in Korea, the chemical, metal, and machinery industries still accounted for 78% of imports of total manufactured goods, although structural changes had occured within each industry in accordance with their growth.

The share of primary goods in total imports fluctuated during the period, depending on the annual rice harvest and the price of oil. Recently, however, due to the rapid rise of oil prices, the share of primary goods has increased again, reaching 36% in 1980. But generally, imports of services have remained small throughout the period.

Changes in Korea's industrial structure were the inevitable consequence of these changes in her export and import patterns and the concurrent changes in her domestic demand pattern, which occurred as a result of increasing income levels.[4] For example, the growth of the fabricated textile products industry up to 1973 and its subsequent stagnation were the direct result of changes in the export volume of textiles; the same appears to have been true of the wood products industry (due to stagnation of plywood exports at a later stage). The consistent growth of the rubber products, fabricated metal products, and electronics industries also came mainly from continued export growth in these industries.

For some sectors, growth both of exports and of domestic demand has increased their relative importance. Examples are the basic chemicals, plastic products, and steel industries, while for other industries expansion in domestic demand has been the main reason for growth. Examples are the synthetic resins and rubber, petroleum refining, non-ferrous metal, and the business services industries.

Overall, import substitution appears to have had considerably less influence than either domestic demand or exports on changes in industrial structure. The growth of industries like chemical yarns (particularly between 1963 and 1980), chemical fertilizers, and petroleum (particularly between 1963 and 1973) has been the result of import substitution, but for many other industries import substitution was not directly related to the relative growth of the industry for three main reasons.

First, although import substitution occurred for some products, in any one industry, often imports had to be continued or even increased for other products of the same industry. This resulted in the growth of the industry, but caused no decrease in the industry's share in total imports. Examples are basic chemicals, steel, general machinery, electrical machinery, and precision equipment.

Second, for some industries import substitution resulted in an increase in imports of parts and components. Again, although the industry grew there was no decrease in import share. Examples again are general machinery, electrical machinery, and precision equipment.

Third, for some other industries, import substitution did not result in the relative growth of the industry, because either the speed of growth in the industry's exports or domestic demand was below that of the whole economy. Examples of this situation are fabrics (between 1973 and 1980), and drugs and cosmetics.

Basically, if imports had not been strictly controlled by the government, there might have been a closer negative relationship between changes in

Table 2 Industrial distribution of cumulative foreign direct investment in Korea
(in %)

	1963	1968	1973	1978	1980
Agriculture, fishery, and mining	0.0	0.8	0.5	0.6	0.6
Manufacturing	100.0	88.8	91.8	80.8	73.5
Food Processing	0.0	0.4	1.7	1.2	2.1
Beverages	0.0	0.0	0.0	0.1	0.1
Tobacco	0.0	0.0	0.0	0.0	0.0
Chemical fibre and yarns	7.7	8.4	3.8	3.0	2.7
Other fibre yarns	0.0	1.2	19.8	9.9	0.3
Fabrics	0.0	0.6	2.6	1.3	1.2
Fabricated textile products	0.0	0.0	2.2	1.5	1.4
Leather and leather products	0.0	0.0	0.4	0.4	0.4
Wood and wood products	0.0	0.2	0.4	0.2	0.2
Paper and paper products	0.0	0.0	1.1	0.6	0.6
Printing and publishing	0.0	0.0	0.1	0.1	0.1
Basic chemicals	0.0	0.0	1.7	7.7	11.3
Chemical fertilizers	0.0	40.8	6.0	4.9	4.5
Drugs and cosmetics	0.0	0.5	0.4	0.6	0.6
Plastics products	0.0	0.0	1.1	0.7	0.6
Synthetic resins, rubber and other chemical products	0.0	1.1	4.0	7.8	7.6
Petroleum products	91.3	25.2	10.4	7.9	4.2
Coal products	0.0	0.0	0.0	0.0	0.0
Rubber products	0.0	0.0	0.2	0.4	0.5
Non-metallic mineral products	0.0	6.8	4.4	2.0	1.9
Basic metal products	0.0	0.0	2.7	2.7	3.4
(Steel products)	(0.0)	(0.0)	(1.7)	(1.7)	(2.4)
Fabricated metal products	0.0	0.1	2.2	2.9	4.4
General machinery	0.0	0.5	3.5	3.9	4.1
Electrical machinery	0.0	0.0	1.4	1.8	2.5
Electronic and communication equipment	0.0	1.1	11.5	12.0	12.2
Transportation equipment	0.0	0.0	7.7	4.9	4.4
(Shipbuilding)	(0.0)	(0.0)	(0.3)	(1.0)	(1.0)
(Automobiles)	(0.0)	(0.0)	(7.4)	(3.5)	(3.4)
Precision equipment	0.0	1.1	1.1	1.1	1.3
Other manufacturing	1.0	0.8	1.4	1.1	1.0
Services	0.0	10.4	7.7	18.6	25.9
Hotel	0.0	4.3	3.5	12.0	13.5
Transportation and warehousing	0.0	0.0	0.6	0.1	1.7
Finance	0.0	5.2	1.7	4.1	4.7
Business services	0.0	0.9	1.8	2.4	6.0
Other services	0.0	0.0	0.0	0.0	0.0
Total	100.0	100.0	100.0	100.0	100.0
($ millions)	(7.5)	(50.2)	(339.0)	(879.6)	(980.0)

Note: The distribution has been based on the remaining balance of FDI in the year.
Source: Ministry of Finance.

imports and changes in industrial production. However, as noted earlier, imports were tightly controlled; in consequence, their patterns did not closely reflect the comparative advantage position of Korean industries.

Our conclusions regarding the relative influence of exports, imports, and domestic demand on changes in domestic industrial structure have already been confirmed by Kim (1980) in his comprehensive study on the sources of industrial growth in Korea. As the purpose of this chapter is not so much to examine the relationship between industrial structure and trade patterns as that between economic structure and direct foreign investment, we have not carried out any further statistical analysis here.

Industrial Pattern of FDI in Korea

In order to analyse the effects of FDI on Korea's industrial structure, we must first examine its changing level and composition over the past two decades. The relevant details are set out in Table 2.

FDI in Korea first began in the area of import substitution of key raw materials. The first foreign affiliate was set up in 1962 by an American textile firm named Chemtex, to produce nylon filaments. It was soon followed by investments in petroleum refining and chemical fertilizers. Until 1968, FDI in those three import-substitution industries (chemical yarns, chemical fertilizers, and petroleum products) explained 74.4% of all FDI in Korea. Other foreign subsidiaries were established in the non-metallic mineral products, hotels, and finance sectors. The period between 1963 and 1968 was a period of first-stage import substitution and the beginning of export-led growth in Korea.

Import-substituting FDI continued into the early 1970s in other areas such as non-synthetic yarns, basic metals, and petrochemicals. At the same time, some foreign investments were allowed in some basically domestic-market-oriented industries, such as food processing, paper products, pharmaceuticals, and automobiles.

However, as Korea's political and social stability became established and her location-specific advantage as a site for sourcing-type investments became better known, foreign firms began to set up processing plants to exploit Korea's low-cost and highly productive labour. Investments in electronics explained the bulk of such investment, but there were also export-platform-type investments in areas like cotton yarns, garments, plastic products, and some machine parts.

Thus by 1973 the foreign investment pattern in Korea had already become quite diversified. The share of chemical yarns, fertilizer, and petroleum-refining industries in total FDI declined sharply from 74.4% in 1968 to only 20.2% in 1973. On the other hand, the electronics industry came to account for 11.5% of total FDI; the non-synthetic yarns industry for 19.8%; the chemical industry (basic chemicals, drugs and cosmetics, synthetic resins and rubbers, plastics products and other chemical products, but excluding fertilizers) for 7.3%; and the broadly-defined machinery industry (including fabricated metal products, electrical and non-electrical machinery, transport equipment, and precision equipment, but excluding electronics) for 15.9%. This period from 1968 to 1973 was a period of continuous import substitution and export growth in Korea.

During the middle and latter part of the 1970s, foreign firms were more attracted to the heavy and chemical industries. By 1980, the chemical industry (excluding fertilizers) claimed 20.1% of all FDI, the broadly-defined machinery industry, 16.7%, and the electronics industry, 12.2%. The share of synthetic yarns, chemical fertilizers and petroleum products, which were the major areas for FDI, continued to decline during this period, reaching 11.3% by 1980.

At the same time, Korea witnessed increased FDI in the services area; indeed its share of all FDI rose sharply from 7.7% in 1973 to 25.9% in 1980. Investments in hotels accounted for more than half of this, followed by those in business services and finance.

Government Policy Towards FDI

The foreign investment policies followed by the government up to 1980 were generally restrictive. Although it offered tax and other incentives for approved foreign investors, the approval procedures were tightly controlled.

Basically, FDI was permitted only where the entry of foreign firms was considered compatible with the development strategies the government was following. For example, as export promotion was the major policy objective during the whole period, export-oriented affiliates were allowed almost without restriction. For many large-scale import-substituting projects, the government often directly intervened in their planning and operation through public corporations, as noted earlier. FDIs were not allowed in most domestic consumer goods industries, particularly in cases where the government believed that a viable indigenous producer existed.[5]

One means used to control the inflow of foreign investment has been the placement of restrictions on the extent of foreign ownership. Especially since about 1973, majority foreign ownership has been allowed only in special cases, such as for export-oriented or highly technology-intensive projects or for projects by Korean residents abroad or located in free export zones.[6]

These restrictions have been more rigidly applied in the case of FDI in the services sector, than in the manufacturing sector. Exceptions include FDI for building large-scale hotels to promote tourism. Some joint-venture merchant banks were also allowed, as a means to promote the inflow of foreign capital; while in some specialized business service areas such as computer or machinery leasing FDI was valued as a means of gaining information technology. Except for these areas, however, FDI has been rarely allowed in service industries.

Since restrictions on the inflow of foreign investment were widespread in Korea, it is natural that a good economic theory to explain satisfactorily the overall pattern of FDI in Korea is hard to find. Indeed most theories of FDI implicitly assume a non-interventionist government policy. However, since this frequently is not the case, particularly in developing countries, it is not surprising that these explanations are found wanting.

In the case of Korea, for example, as the consumer durable goods market was mostly closed to foreign investors, and since the market for labour-saving producer goods has been relatively small, there have been few instances of FDI, which could be explained by Vernon's product cycle model (Vernon, 1966, 1971). Radios, TVs, refrigerators, washing machines, elevators, and tyres are all being produced by domestic firms in Korea, and even the automobile market has been dominated by a domestic firm, rather than by a joint venture with a multinational car manufacturer.

Of course, some sourcing-type investments in the field of electronics may be considered as examples of Vernon's model, but in his study, income-elastic and labour-saving consumer or producer goods, not their parts, are the chief objects of explanation. Furthermore, the product cycle model cannot explain the bulk of other import-substituting investments in Korea.

Similarly, Caves' (1971, 1974) explanation of the causes of horizontal FDI is also only of limited validity in the case of Korea. Caves, adopting the industrial-organization approach, argued that direct foreign investments are likely to be found most frequently in differentiated oligopolistic industries. In Korea, however, because of government restrictions, FDI in industries where the market structures are differentiated oligopolies has been the exception rather than the rule. Food processing (2.1%), beverages (0.1%), paper products (0.6%), drugs and cosmetics (0.6%), and automobiles (3.4%) fall into this category; but FDI in these industries explained only 6.8% of total cumulative foreign investments at the end of 1980.[7]

Therefore, we can say that basically only two types of direct FDIs existed in Korea, one of which substituted for imports of raw materials and the other which exported most of its products. In the latter case, since the main purpose of the FDI was to exploit Korea's relatively low labour cost, inputs were imported in many cases.

Lastly, we have made a comparison of US and Japanese investment patterns in Korea, in order to examine Kojima's hypothesis (Kojima, 1978) regarding differences in behaviour between American and Japanese foreign investors. Kojima argued that most Japanese manufacturing investments in developing countries were made in industries where Japan was losing its comparative advantage, while most American investments were made in

Table 3 Percentage industrial distribution of cumulative American and Japanese investment in Korea (end 1980)

	US (%)	Japan (%)
Agriculture, fishery, and mining	0.7	0.4
Manufacturing	81.5	72.5
Food processing	1.0	3.1
Beverages	0.3	0.0
Tobacco	0.0	0.0
Chemical fibre and yarns	0.0	4.5
Other fibre yarns	0.0	0.2
Fabrics	0.1	2.2
Fabricated textile products	0.2	2.0
Leather and leather products	0.0	0.6
Wood and wood products	0.0	0.4
Paper and paper products	0.4	0.8
Printing and publishing	0.0	0.1
Basic chemicals	24.6	5.7
Chemical fertilizers	13.3	0.4
Drugs and cosmetics	0.4	0.2
Plastics products	0.0	1.1
Synthetic resins, rubber and other chemical products	8.4	8.7
Petroleum products	8.6	0.0
Coal products	0.0	0.0
Rubber products	0.1	0.8
Non-metallic mineral products	0.7	2.5
Basic metal products	0.7	2.7
(Steel products)	(0.5)	(2.3)
Fabricated metal products	3.1	5.1
General machinery	1.8	5.7
Electrical machinery	0.6	3.2
Electronic and communication equipment	8.1	16.2
Transportation equipment	8.0	2.9
(Shipbuilding)	(0.2)	(1.7)
(Automobiles)	(7.7)	(1.2)
Precision equipment	0.6	1.7
Other manufacturing	0.1	1.7
Services	17.9	27.1
Hotel	1.9	22.6
Transportation and warehousing	3.4	0.8
Finance	1.4	0.3
Business services	11.2	3.4
Other services		0.0
Total	100.0	100.0

Note and Source: same as in Table 2.

the highly technology-intensive and oligopolistic industries where the US had a comparative advantage.

As such, Japanese FDIs facilitated the restructuring of the Japanese economy, while at the same time helping the host countries to develop industries in which they have comparative advantage. On the other hand, American FDIs tended to increase the balance of payments difficulties and unemployment problems in the US, by reducing American exports to the host countries, while providing little help to the host countries in the exploitation of their potential comparative advantages.

A cursory examination of Japanese and American investment patterns in Korea, set out in Table 3, generally confirms Kojima's hypothesis. US investments have been relatively more concentrated in such Korean industries as basic chemicals, chemical fertilizers, petroleum products, automobiles and business services. These are all industries in which Korea does not enjoy a comparative advantage at this stage. On the other hand, Japanese investments have been relatively more concentrated in textiles, metal products, machinery, electronics, and hotels. Most of these are industries in which Korea currently enjoys or is expected to enjoy a comparative advantage in the near future. Therefore, in general, Kojima's argument seems valid in the case of Korea.

Nevertheless, his generalization appears to be a little too sweeping. First, there have been many cases of Japanese investment in technically advanced industries. Secondly, much of American investment in Korea has been made in the essential import-substituting industries, rather than in differentiated oligopolistic (consumer goods) industries; thus they have had little adverse effect on resource allocation. Thirdly, for a rapidly growing economy like Korea, the scope of so-called complementary investments becomes limited, as the nation's comparative advantage position changes so rapidly.

For example, Korea's comparative advantage has moved from simple labour-intensive products like wigs, plywood, garments, and consumer electronics (assembly) to more capital- and skill-intensive products like steel, ships, electronic parts, and fabricated metal products. For many of these skill-intensive products, the Korean products compete directly with Japanese products in the world market. Thus the so-called complementary investment by Japense producers argued by Kojima becomes less likely. The recent relative decline of Japanese investment in Korea appears to have been partly the result of this changing nature of the comparative advantage between the two countries.

Industrial Structure, Comparative Advantage, and Foreign Investment

Now that we have reviewed the changes in the patterns of industrial structure, trade, and direct foreign investment in Korea, we are ready to examine more systematically the interrelationship among them.

First, let us re-examine the relationship between trade patterns and patterns of FDI. According to our cursory examination of FDI patterns in Korea, it first began in import-substituting industries and then gradually moved to export industries. However, at a later stage, it moved back to (second stage) import-substituting industries like chemicals and machinery.

Table 4 clearly shows the changing industrial distribution of FDI in Korea, through examining the propensity to export by foreign affiliates. Although FDI in export-oriented industries was marginal until 1968, it grew rapidly between 1968 and 1973. However, since 1973 FDI in import-substituting industries has grown faster than that in export-oriented industries. In 1973 FDI's export orientation was even stronger than domestic firms when viewed in terms of its industrial distribution. However, for other years, the national average has been always higher than the FDI-weighted average.

This structure of FDI has been a direct result of the Korean government's foreign investment policy. As stated earlier, the Korean government has tried to maximize the contribution of foreign affiliates to Korea's economic growth by only allowing them to operate where their expected contribution was compatible with the development objectives the government was pursuing. Therefore, the pattern of FDI in Korea has closely followed the character of industrialization strategies being followed.

1973 was a turning point in Korea's industrialization process, because in that year the government began to pursue actively the development of import-substitution in the heavy and chemical industries. Consequently, the growth of export-oriented FDI has been relatively stagnant since then.

What is the meaning of the pattern of FDI paralleling Korea's industrialization strategy? Does it imply a closer relationship between the pattern of FDI and Korea's comparative advantage? The answer is a definite no.

Although export-oriented foreign affiliates were allowed to produce in Korea almost without restriction, it does not follow that the pattern of FDI will necessarily have a close relationship with the patterns of either exports

Table 4 Export/sales ratios in industries where FDI occurred 1963–80

	Average export/sales ratios	
	FDI weighted	*Total average*
1963	0.3	3.8
1968	4.3	8.6
1973	24.3	22.5
1978	19.3	23.6
1980	18.5	23.4

Table 5 Relationship between FDI and trade patterns[a]

| | Correlation coefficients between FDI and: | | |
	Exports	Imports	RCA[b]
1968	0.0957	0.0320	0.2070
1973	0.0003	0.2725	0.0079
1978	0.0437	0.3214*	0.1524
1980	0.1951	0.5129**	0.2706

[a]Patterns of FDI, exports and imports refer to industrial percentage distribution.
[b]RCA, defined as (exports − imports)/(exports + imports).
Notes: The year 1963 has been omitted because there was FDI only in three industries.
* and ** denote that the relationship is significant at 10% and 1%.

or comparative advantage in Korea. In order to invest in a foreign country, foreign firms need to be tempted not only by that country's location-specific advantages, but also to enjoy ownership and specific advantages over local producers.

For many export-oriented industries in Korea, foreign firms did not possess even the basic ownership advantages. Even for the consumer electronics, steel and shipbuilding industries, which have become Korea's major exporting industries at a later stage, foreign firms' ownership advantages were limited to certain lines of products in the industry or certain processes in production.

Therefore, foreign firms' export-oriented investments had to be limited to certain offshore export-platform-type industries, where they enjoyed favoured access to inputs or markets, and this is why, in Table 4, FDI firms appear less export-oriented than domestic firms (except for 1973), although their propensity to export in individual industries has been generally higher.[8]

By contrast it is evident that foreign firms possessed substantial ownership-specific advantages in most import-substituting industries. But here the restrictions imposed by the Korean government greatly reduced the possibility of internationalization of these advantages. The result then

Table 6 Relationship between foreign affiliates' share of total sales and skill ratios, 1980

	Propensity to export	RCA	Skill ratio
Foreign affiliates share in sales	0.0416	0.0836	0.1791

was less FDI than might otherwise have been the case in such industries as computers, consumer electronics, industrial machinery, automobiles, and precision equipment.

When foreign firms had strong ownership-specific advantages such as technical or managerial superiority, or favoured access to inputs or markets, they were either allowed majority foreign ownership or they came in without majority ownership with the conviction that they could still appropriate some economic rent from their advantages. Examples include FDI in industries like petroleum refining and fertilizers in the early stages of Korea's development and in petro- and fine chemicals, and some heavy machinery in recent years. As noted earlier, FDI was not allowed in most domestic-market-oriented consumer goods industries.

What then might we conclude about the effects of FDI on changes in Korea's industrial structure? We noted earlier that Korea's industrial structure has been strongly affected by changes in the patterns of exports and domestic demand and hardly touched by changes in the patterns of imports. We have noted also that because of constraints placed on it by the Korean government FDI had little to do with the patterns of either Korean demand or its comparative trading advantage. There is thus the strong implication that the influence of FDI on changes in Korea's economic structure has been very marginal.

Although the data are very limited we attempted some statistical exercises to check the validity of the preceding arguments. First, we ran a correlation analysis between the patterns of FDI in manufacturing industry and the patterns of exports, imports, and revealed comparative advantage (RCA) for four different years (cf. Table 5).

As earlier hypothesized, patterns of FDI had no close correlation with patterns of either exports or RCA. All the relationships were statistically not significant even at the 10% level. At the same time the data do suggest that over time the negative correlation between patterns of FDI and RCA has tended to increase. We believe that this reflects the move away from export-oriented towards import-substituting type FDI since 1973. This trend is also confirmed by the growing positive relationship between the pattern of FDI and that of imports over the last 8 years. However, as import substitution gains momentum and imports into Korea become more liberalized in future, this relationship between imports and FDI is likely to be weakened.

Another test of the relationship between patterns of FDI and trade used the market share of foreign affiliates, in individual industries as the dependent variable. Our results are set out in Table 6.

As would be expected, the share of foreign affiliates in the total sales for the industry was not related at all to propensity to export, RCA, or indeed in this case to the skill ratio (here represented by the proportion of administrative and technical workers to total workers), which has been used as an indicator of the technological intensity of a particular industry.

In summary then, the relationship between patterns of FDI and exports or comparative advantage in Korea has not been significant. On the other hand, due to an increase of FDI in large importing sectors, some significant positive correlation existed between patterns of FDI and imports, although this relationship is expected to become less significant in the future. We would emphasize, however, that the reasons for these findings have as much to do with government policy towards inward direct investment as with allocative efficiency of foreign affiliates in Korea. Given a different or non-interventionist policy on the government's part the impact of FDI on resource disposition may have been quite different.

Comparative Performance of Foreign and Domestic Firms

Some Statistical Findings

The participation of foreign-owned firms in an economy may not only affect allocative efficiency through altering the distribution of industrial investment, but also affect technical or sectoral efficiency, both directly through their own activities and indirectly through the spillover effects on indigenous firms in the host country. Both data and conceptual problems, however, make examining sectoral efficiency much more difficult than examining allocative efficiency.

Data on the performance of foreign firms are scarce in most countries, and particularly so in developing countries. In the case of Korea, however, some data are available on the performance of foreign affiliates from a survey carried out by the government in 1979.[9] These include the capital/labour ratios, financial structures, profitability, and value-added ratios of foreign firms from 1974 to 1978. Since similar data are available on all domestic firms it is possible to make some assessment on the distinctive character of FDI in these years.

Table 7 compares the average performance of all firms existing in Korea with that of foreign affiliates in 1978. The table shows that the latter, on average, were more capital-intensive, more skill-intensive (higher wages), less profitable, less debt-ridden, and produced more value added.

However, as the relative importance of direct foreign investments differed among industries, the differences in performance may have been the result of different weight of FDI by industries. But to what extent are these differences due to a different industrial distribution between foreign and all Korean firms? In order to examine whether any systematic differences in the performance of foreign and domestic firms existed, we examined the statistical significance of the average performance of foreign and domestic firms for each of 27 manufacturing industries.[10]

Table 8 sets out the number of industries where the relationship in

Table 7 Comparative performance of domestic and foreign firms (1978)[a]

	All firms[b]	Foreign firms	Statistical significance of difference[c]
Total assets per capita (W million)	9.0	23.3	P. > 99
Wage rate (W '000 per year)	1420	2319	P. > 99
Value added to net sales (%)	24.6	36.3	P. > 99
Value added per capita (W million)	2.8	3.0	P. > 50
Net profit to total assets (%)	4.98	3.64	P. > 95
Total debt to net worth (%)	366.8	97.6	P. > 99

[a] Comparison has been restricted to the manufacturing sector only.
[b] As all firms include foreign firms, their performances do not refer to the performances of domestic firms proper. However, as the proportion of foreign firms had been small (particularly in terms of number), bias due to this misrepresentation should be negligible.
[c] P. > 99 means that the difference in the performance of foreign and domestic firms was statistically significant at 1% level. The formula used to check the statistical significance of difference was $z = (\bar{X}f - \bar{X}a)/(sf/\sqrt{n})$, where $\bar{X}f$ and $\bar{X}a$ refer to the average performance of foreign and all firms, sf is standard deviation of performance of foreign firms and n is sample number of foreign firms.

performance between the foreign and domestic firms was in the same direction as in Table 7 and the number of industries where such relationships were statistically significant.

In the case of capital intensity, although there were some industries where foreign firms had a much higher capital intensity than domestic firms (e.g. beverages, basic chemicals, chemical fertilizers, synthetic rubbers and resins), there were others where the reverse held true.[11] Thus it could not be argued that, in general, foreign affiliates used more capital-intensive methods of production than their domestic counterparts.

In the case of wage rates, foreign firms' remuneration per worker was higher than that of domestic firms in almost all industries, and for most of them the difference was statistically significant. However, this appears to be because of the relatively larger average size of foreign firms, and the fact that foreign affiliates tend to produce the relatively more skill-intensive product lines within an industry.

Turning next to value-added ratios, the ratios were generally higher for foreign affiliates than for domestic firms. However, the differences were significant in only 13 out of 27 industries. In the case of value added per capita and profitability, there were very few statistically significant differences in the performance of foreign and domestic firms. In the case of total debt to net worth too, although in the majority of cases foreign firms had lower debt ratios, there were many industries where the differences were not statistically significant.

Table 8 Distribution of the relationship in the performance of foreign and domestic firms

	Total number of industries	With the same sign as in Table 7	Statistically significant among those with the same sign[a]
Total assets per capita	27	14	3
Wage rate	27	25	19
Value added to net sales	27	23	13
Value added per capita	27	12	3
Net profit to total assets	27	17	4
Total debt to net worth	27	19	14

[a]Significance level used was 5%, and the formula used to check the significance was the same as in Table 7.

Some Qualitative Observations

Due to a scarcity of good statistical data, our examination of foreign firms' influence on sectoral efficiency had to depend to a great extent on qualitative conjectures, and observation has to be limited to a few major sectors.

Let us begin with the textile industry. In the case of chemical fibres, foreign firms have certainly contributed to the growth and prosperity of the industry both through competition among themselves and competition with foreign products in the world market through exporting activities. In consequence the productivity of the industry has improved markedly during the past two decades.

In the basic chemicals, synthetic resins, and rubber sectors, most foreign subsidiaries enjoy monopolistic positions in the domestic market and protection from imports. Therefore the direct contribution to sectoral efficiency is likely to have been small. However, as producers of raw materials for Korea's major export industries (textiles, footwear, tyres, and plastics products), they would appear to have made some contribution to stabilizing the supply of raw materials and thus to the growth of these export industries.

Foreign investments in the petroleum refining and chemical fertilizer industries have made some indirect contribution to the growth of these sectors by providing the engineers and technicians necessary to operate the chemical plants. In addition, they have helped develop the engineering industry in Korea by providing engineers with learning experiences.

In the case of the electronics industry, it is a mixed picture. Most of the export-platform-type foreign investments have had only a marginal effect on sectoral efficiency in Korea. They have helped train some labour but this training has been mostly limited to simple assembly jobs. However, it does appear that they have passed on new knowledge and helped to improve the quality and output of their sub-contractors and hence of the final products. This is particularly noticeable in the case of the Japanese affiliates.

It is too early to determine the effects of the participation of foreign firms on the machinery industry. Major investments in this area began only in the late 1970s. There was some earlier investment in the automobile industry, but, as noted previously, the foreign firm was out-competed by the local firm.

In general, the effects of foreign firms in improving sectoral efficiency in Korea during the past two decades appear to have been positive, but not significant. Export-platform-type investments did not require much local input other than labour, and import-substituting foreign investments were heavily protected from imports. Also, as would be expected, research and development activities by subsidiaries of foreign firms were almost non-existent in all industries.

The above findings seem to be supported by a World Bank study (Westphal, Rhee, and Pursell, 1981). In discussing how Korea has established an independent base of technological knowhow and marketing expertise in many sectors, the authors concluded that FDI had played a very minor role in enhancing Korea's ability in these areas and that Korea's industrialization had been directed and controlled almost entirely by Korean nationals.

Outward Investment by Korean Firms

A Test of Dunning's Hypothesis for Korea

Before we conclude the paper, we will examine Dunning's (1981) hypothesis regarding the relationship between the levels of net outward investment (outward investment minus inward investment) and stages of development, and review the character of outward investment by Korean firms.

Professor Dunning, applying his eclectic theory of international producing, argues that the level of net outward investment in a country is related to its per capita GNP and development pattern in the following way. In Stage I, there is no outward investment by the country, primarily because the country's own enterprises possess few advantages over firms from other countries. At the same time, there is little incoming investment by foreign firms, as there are insufficient location-specific advantages offered by the host country.

In Stage II, inward investment begins to increase as the domestic market grows and infrastructure develops. Import-substituting investments will be attracted first, followed by export-platform-type investments. At this stage,

Table 9 Korea's international direct investment position 1962/82 ($ millions)

	Outward direct investment (I_0)	Inward direct investment (I_i)	Net outward investment $(I_0 - I_i)$
1962		0.6	− 0.6
1963		2.1	− 2.1
1964		3.1	− 3.1
1965		10.7	− 10.7
1966		4.8	− 4.8
1967		12.7	− 12.7
1968		14.7	− 14.7
1969		7.0	− 7.0
1970	7.5	25.3	− 17.8
1971	6.9	36.7	− 29.8
1972	5.1	61.2	− 56.1
1973	3.9	158.4	−154.5
1974	23.1	162.6	−139.5
1975	9.2	69.2	− 60.0
1976	8.2	105.6	− 97.4
1977	17.8	102.3	− 84.5
1978	43.4	100.5	− 57.1
1979	22.8	127.0	−104.2
1980	21.1	96.6	− 75.5
1981	40.1	105.4	− 65.3
1982	129.4	100.6	28.8

Source: Ministry of Finance. Investment is defined as capital flows plus reinvested profits of existing firms.

outward investment remains small, except in some neighbouring areas, as indigenous enterprises have not yet generated sufficient ownership advantages of their own.

In Stage III, outward investment by nationals begins to increase, as indigenous firms improve their competitive capacity and develop their own country-specific ownership advantages. On the other hand, as the ownership advantages of foreign firms in the mature or standard technology sectors become eroded, incoming investment begins to stabilize. As a result, per capita inward investment starts to fall, and outward investment begins to rise.

In Stage IV, a country becomes a net outward investor, as the ownership advantages of its firms increase and the propensity to exploit these advantages in a foreign location grows.

We would like to test this hypothesis against time-series data on Korea for the period from 1962 to 1982. Dunning has designated Korea a newly industrializing country to fall in Stage III. Table 9 shows Korea's inward, outward, and net outward investment position by year over the past two decades. According to the table, there was a tendency in Korea towards growing negative net outgoing investment up until 1973 and towards declining but still negative net outgoing investment after then. In 1982, however, for the first time, Korean firms invested more abroad than foreign firms invested in Korea.

In broad terms, Dunning's characterization of the relationship between a country's position of net outward investment and the level of development fits the Korean case quite well. However, there are a couple of important qualifications which should be added to this observation.

As pointed out by Dunning himself, much depends on the nature of the government's FDI and industrialization policies. In Korea, as pointed out earlier, procedures for the entry of foreign firms have become more restrictive since 1973. Therefore, much of the stagnant level of incoming foreign investment since then has been more a result of restrictive foreign investment policy in Korea than of declining investment opportunities in Korea or waning ownership advantages for foreign firms.

At the same time, depending on the character of the industrialization strategy adopted, different countries will show wide differences. For example, if a country runs a surplus in its current account balance, as in Singapore or Taiwan, outward investment will be encouraged. On the other hand, if the country runs consistent deficits in its current account, its ability to invest abroad will be severely limited.

As these differences in environment, system, and policy (ESP) variables will strongly influence the speed and character of changes in investment patterns described by Dunning, we believe that a very strong or precise hypothesis about the form of the development cycle may be difficult to make.

Status of Outward Direct Investment by Korean Firms

Outward direct investment (ODI) by Korean firms began as early as 1968, but ODI at the early stages was small in scale and limited mainly to forestry development in Indonesia (to provide logs to the Korean plywood industry) and construction activities in Indonesia and Guam. There were also several investments in high-seas fishing bases and trade agencies.

During the early 1970s, some additional ODIs were made in areas of forestry development, fishing, construction, and trade agencies. The first manufacturing ODI occurred during this period to produce food seasonings in Indonesia.

After 1975, as Korean exports continued to increase, many Korean firms began to set up trade agencies in various countries. The number of trading agents reached 194 and the amount of their investment $36.7 million by the end of 1982. Thus, in terms of the number of investments, these trade agencies accounted for 56.6% of the stock of Korea's ODI (at the end of 1982), although in value terms they accounted for only 13.6%.

Table 10 Industrial distribution of outward direct investment ($'000s)

	1968–72	1973–77	1978–82	Total	%
Agriculture			893	893	0.3
Fishery	552	5,493	3,168	9,213	3.5
Forestry	9,032	10,335	17,785	37,152	13.8
Mining			103,007	103,007	38.2
Manufacturing		7,578	25,873	33,451	12.4
Food Processing		1,600		1,600	0.6
Other fibre yarns			630	630	0.2
Fabricated textile products			923	923	0.4
Wood and wood products			7,234	7,234	2.7
Paper and paper products		1,348		1,348	0.5
Printing and publishing		60		60	
Synthetic resins, rubber and					
other chemical products		541	464	1,005	0.4
Rubber products			8,200	8,200	3.0
Non-metallic mineral products		1,761	4,110	5,871	2.2
Basic metal products		1,220	2,401	3,621	1.4
(Steel products)		1,220	2,401	3,621	1.4
Fabricated metal products			100	100	
General machinery			551	551	0.2
Electrical machinery			278	278	0.1
Electronic and communication					
equipment			819	819	0.3
Other manufacturing		1,048	163	1,211	0.4
Services	4,199	37,202	44,340	85,741	31.8
Construction	2,750	1,697	25,985	30,432	11.3
Transportation and ware-					
housing		1,700	1,042	2,742	1.0
Trade	1,050	20,562	15,045	36,657	13.6
Other services	399	13,243	2,268	15,910	5.9
Total	13,783	60,608	195,066	269,457	100

Source: Ministry of Finance.

In the late 1970s, mining began to emerge as another major area[12] of ODI, while Korean firms also began to invest in overseas transportation and warehousing activities. In addition, ODI continued in the areas of forestry, construction, and trade.

Table 10 shows the industrial distribution of Korea's ODI by period. Like Japanese ODI in the early days, Korea's ODI was relatively concentrated in overseas resource development. ODI in agriculture, fisheries, forestry, and mining all fall into this category, and together they accounted for 56% of all ODI by Korean firms through the end of 1982.

The other two major areas of foreign activity by Korean MNEs were in the fields of construction and trade. To support construction activities, mainly in the Middle East and more recently in South East Asia, many Korean construction firms set up subsidiaries in those countries. By 1982, several of the 50 largest international construction firms in the world were Korean. Clearly Korean firms seem to have established a country-specific ownership advantage in this sector of activity. In addition, as noted earlier, many trade agencies were established in trading-partner countries to promote sales in those countries.

Manufacturing investments by Korean firms have been relatively small, accounting for only 12.4% of total ODI. The major manufacturing investments so far have been in the fields of plywood, tyres, cement, and steel pipes. These are products in which Korea currently enjoys a country-specific advantage but that comparative advantage is eroding. In the future, as Korea's wage rates continue to rise, and as Korean firms search for new ways of entering protected industrial markets, ODI in manufacturing is expected to rise, both in developing and industrial countries. This predicted pattern is certainly consistent with Dunning's investment development cycle.

A review of the characteristics of Korea's ODI tells us that its effects on changes in Korea's industrial structure should have been minimal in the past. Most of the commodities which Korean firms developed abroad were available in the international market, some (in the mining area) have just begun their operation, and fish caught in the high seas were sold directly in the international market. Therefore the foreign activities by Korean firms in resource development do not appear to have made any significant contribution to the development of industries in Korea which use the resources domestically.

Neither is it obvious that the overseas activities of the Korean construction companies directly affected domestic economic structure, although indirectly, by increasing foreign exchange earnings, they have affected growth. The expansion of overseas construction activities may have marginally helped the growth of domestic construction-material-production industries and the heavy equipment industry, but here again the effect appears to have been minimal, as the proportion of materials or equipment supplied by domestic Korean firms has been small. Furthermore, the expansion of overseas construction activities has not been so much a result of ODI in the field, rather it has been the cause.

ODI in trade activities, although it may have helped the growth of Korean exports in general, has not been related to any changes in the activities of any specific industry. In one or two manufacturing sectors, however, ODI does seem to have had some impact on the restructuring of the Korean economy. Two industries may be noted for special reference. Hurt by the deep recession in the US construction market, Korea's plywood industry began to shrink rapidly in the early 1980s. The industry also began to lose its competitiveness, as Korean wage rates rose and as resource nationalism in forest-rich countries strengthened. The response to these events was for two Korean companies to set up plants in Indonesia to manufacture plywood. These appear to have been the first true cases of relocation of production facilities by Korean firms.

The second case is that of the fabricated metal and machinery industry. There is some suggestion that ODI has enabled Korean machine-makers to export manufacturing plants. In the future, as the foreign manufacturing activities of Korean firms increase, the growth of the fabricated metal and machine industry may be facilitated.

Overall, however, the ODI by Korean firms appears to have exerted very marginal influence on changes in Korea's industrial structure, at least up to the end of the 1970s.

Summary and Conclusions

This chapter has examined the relationship between direct foreign investment, trade, and industrial structure in Korea. We have found that the pattern of foreign direct investment in Korea has been strongly influenced by Korean government policy, which has been as much directed to changing the economic structure as exploiting its current advantages. In addition, we have found that foreign firms' influence on sectoral efficiency in Korea has been positive but marginal. The impact of the foreign activities of Korean firms on Korea's industrialization process also seems to have been very small, although it is expected to become stronger in the future.

The Korean case-study confirms that the effects of foreign direct investment depend on the environment, system, and policies (ESP) of the host countries as much as on the strategy and behaviour of foreign investors themselves. If the absorptive capacity of domestic businessmen, technicians, engineers, and labourers is underdeveloped, transfers of technology or skills cannot be effectively realized. Similarly, if the economic system of the host country is full of inefficiencies or biases, only those foreign firms who would enjoy special benefits from the biases in the system would come in. The same holds true for irrelevant policies. Thus any examination of the effects of foreign investment must take into consideration the underlying ESP status in the host country.

In the case of Korea, it seems that the absorptive capacity of the nation's labour force has been high due to the relatively high level of education and the good work ethic. Also, the economic system has not been excessively biased. Therefore industrial policies and foreign investment policies followed by the government have been important factors in determining the effects of foreign investment in Korea.

In general, it can be said that when the government followed an export-oriented industrialization strategy (1962–73), the effects of FDI on allocative and sectoral efficiency were positive. FDI in exporting industries contributed to allocative efficiency in Korea, while most FDI in import-substituting industries provided essential raw materials for exporting industries or for domestic consumption. On the other hand, when the government pursued an overly ambitious import-substituting industrialization strategy (1973–80) with heavy import protection, the positive effects of FDI may well have been much less. Inefficiency was inevitable for many new industries, particularly at their early stage of development, and resource allocation became biased as the government sought to over-develop some industries into exporting industries with the help from foreign investors.

In conclusion, then, changes in Korea's economic structure have been pretty much determined by the Koreans themselves, rather than by the activities of foreign-based MNEs. Foreign investors have had some influence in industries like electronics through their exporting activities, but their effects on both allocative and sectoral efficiency appear to have been marginal in determining the overall pattern of industrial development in Korea.

However, as the Korean government plans to open up the opportunities for both inward and outward investment in the future, its role in determining industrial development of Korea may become more important.

Notes

1. For a more comprehensive analysis of the role of FDI in Korea's recent economic growth, refer to Koo (1983).

2. For a comprehensive discussion on industrial policies followed by Korea, see Westphal and Kim (1977).

3. The relative growth of transportation activities in 1980 seems to have occurred both because of the second oil shock which sharply increased the cost of transportation services and of the rapid growth of shipping and airline companies.

4. Domestic demand structure is influenced by the changes in income, which in turn are influenced by exports. Therefore, in the case of Korea, total effects of exports on changes in industrial structure should have been much greater, although this cannot be shown statistically.

5. However, coming into the 1980s, a fundamental change also occurred in the policies on foreign investment. With the realization that the restriction of FDI in some key industries like consumer electronics and computers had resulted in under-development of these industries in Korea, and that the FDI is one of the most effective or indeed the only instrument for efficient technology transfer, particularly for highly advanced industries, the government reversed its position and began to liberalize the inflow of direct foreign investment.

6. As regards the changing form of foreign investment in Korea, refer to the author's study (1982), 'New Forms of Foreign Investment in Korea', KDI Working Paper Series 82–02. In this study, the author showed that in Korea the incidence of less-than-foreign-majority-owned investment increased considerably from about 1973, relative to that of majority-foreign-owned investments.

7. Consumer electronics is another field where the market structure had been differentiated oligopoly. However, most FDI in the field of electronics was either to produce parts and components or, in the case of final consumer goods, to export their entire products.

8. Refer to Koo (1983).

9. The government carried out another survey in 1983 regarding the performance of foreign firms during 1978 to 1982. However, most of the results were not available when the author was writing this chapter.

10. Several industries had to be omitted because either there was no foreign investment, or only a single foreign investment, or no domestic producers.

11. The higher capital intensity of foreign firms in Table 7 appears to have been the result of high (in absolute amount) capital intensity of foreign firms in some industries where the general level of capital intensity was very high.

12. This was because of three large investments amounting to a total of $93 million by the semi-state-run steel company in Korea (POSCO) in Australia, Canada, and the Antilles to develop bituminous coal.

References

Caves, R. E. (1971). International corporations: the industrial economics of foreign investment, *Economica*, **38**, February

Caves, R. E. (1974). *International Trade, International Investment, and Imperfect Markets*, Special Papers in International Economics, No. 10, November, Princeton University

Dunning, J. H. (1981). *International Production and the Multinational Enterprise*, London: Allen and Unwin

Kim, K. (1980). *Patterns of Industrialization and Their Causes in Korea*, Korea Development Institute (in Korean)

Kojima, K. (1973). *Direct Foreign Investment*, London: Croom Helm

Koo, Bohn-Young, (1982). *New Forms of Foreign Investment in Korea*, Working Paper 82–02, Korea Development Institute

Koo, Bohn-Young, (1983). *Role of Foreign Direct Investment in Korea's Recent Economic Growth*, Working Paper 81–04. Revised Korea Development Institute

Vernon, R. (1966). International investment and international trade in the product cycle, *Quarterly Journal of Economics*, **80**, May

Vernon, R. (1971). *Sovereignty at Bay*, New York: Basic Books

Westphal, L. and Kim, K. (1977). *Industrial Policy and Development in Korea*, World Bank Staff Working Paper No. 263, Washington DC

Westphal, L., Rhee, Y. W., and Pursell, G. (1981). *Korean Industrial Competence: Where It Came From*, World Bank Staff Working Paper No. 469

13

Foreign Investment and Technology Transfer in Taiwan*

Chi Schive

*Source: *Industry of Free China*, LXX, 2 and 3 (August/September 1988), pp. 13–23, 13–30.

Introduction

Direct Foreign Investment (DFI) can serve as an important channel for the introduction of foreign technology to the developing world, and its impact may be far-reaching and multifaceted. The purpose of this paper is to examine the relationship between DFI and economic development in Taiwan, with special reference to the role of DFI in introducing foreign technology.

The paper begins by presenting the patterns of DFI inflows into Taiwan since the 1950s, by source, capital composition, and industrial distribution. It next analyzes the contributions of DFI to Taiwan's economy, GNP, exports and employment. The core of the paper is devoted to examining the impact of the technology brought in by foreign investors on Taiwan's exports and employment. For example, have local companies receiving DFI ultimately developed into native multinationals? And what, if any, are the motivations and competitiveness in the world market? The conclusions reached at the end may be useful for other countries attempting to formulate their own DFI policies.

Profile of Direct Foreign Investment Inflows, 1952–86

Though the inflow of both private and non-private foreign capital into Taiwan can be traced back to its colonial period[1] (Rains and Schive, 1985, pp. 87–9), this section focuses on the trends and composition of DFI inflow in the process of Taiwan's modern economic development. By composition we mean the sources, industrial distribution, capital formation, and ownership structure of that investment.

The Trend of DFI Inflows into Taiwan

In 1952, the Chinese government on Taiwan promulgated two ad hoc regulations to guide overseas Chinese investment.[2] However, before the laws became effective, the first overseas Chinese investor, a Hong-Kong based paint manufacturer, had already brought in a total of H.K.$46,900 in 1951. Westinghouse, the first non-Chinese investor, put US$1.88 million into equipment for Taiwan Power Co. in 1953, which was also before the promulgation of the Statute for Investment by Non-Chinese Foreigners. A year later, a similar law, the Statute for Investment by overseas Chinese, became effective. Both statutes took a quite liberal stance with regard to foreign investment. There were no restrictions on foreign ownership in general, and a broadly-defined range of industries were to be opened to foreign investors. Used machinery and materials could also be converted into capital. The only major difference between these two Statutes was that overseas Chinese were allowed to invest in any industry—real estate and the service industries in particular—provided they waived the privilege of foreign-exchange settlement. Overall, a hospitable environment for DFI has existed since the early 1950s.

Figure 1 shows the trend of DFI arrivals between 1960 and 1986, as reflected in the balance of payments. Data for arrivals, not approvals, are used in this analysis because the arrived capital amounted to around 45% of that approved during the period observed. There are two reasons for this. First, the data for approvals refer to total capital committed, but paid-up capital is allowed to arrive any time within three to five years after approval; therefore, there is always a lag between the two figures. Second, and probably more important, many approved investment plans never materialized, including some multi-million dollar projects like the proposed Swedish investment in the China Shipbuilding Company, the Austrian investment in China Steel, and the deferred and reduced investment by Toyota.[3] The significant difference between these two sets of data argues against the use of approval data to assess DFI activity in Taiwan, unless some structural analyses are conducted to compensate for insufficiently detailed data on arrived investment.

The trend of DFI reveals several interesting points. First, there seems to have been a clearly increasing trend in arrived DFI since 1966. What made that year significant was the establishment of two export-processing zones (EPZs) in the vicinity of Kaohsiung, Taiwan's largest port. Between 1966 and 1970, these two EPZs attracted a total of $32.7 million in DFI, constituting 80 percent of total capital arrivals in EPZs and 23 percent of total arrived DFI. Another policy which has had the same effect in attracting export-oriented DFI calls for setting up bonded factories. In both cases import duties are waived, provided all products are exported. Both policies have given a significant push to the inflow of DFI, particularly that geared toward exports.

US$ mil.

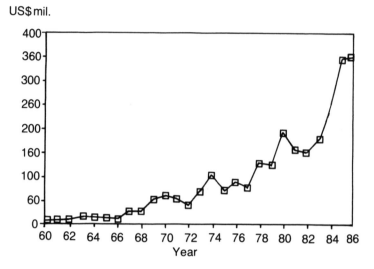

Figure 1 Arrived DFI, 1960–86

Second, the post-1966 increasing trend seems to have faltered in 1972, 1975, and 1982. The first drop could have been due to international political changes unfavorable to Taiwan. In 1972, The Republic of China lost her seat in the United Nations to Mainland China. As to 1975 and 1982, both were recession years in Taiwan, with economic growth rates dropping to as low as 4.3 and 3.3 percent, respectively. Both political stability and domestic economic conditions, therefore, have had a great bearing on DFI arrivals.

The political factor, which can affect Taiwan's ability to attract DFI in both ways, has received wide attention. Back in the 1960s Jacoby noted that "only after 1958, ... when the Republic of China had demonstrated its defensive strength against Communist China in the Formosa Strait, did foreign private capital expand" (Jacoby, 1968, p. 100). In the 1960s, Schreiber compared Taiwan's political stability with that of six other countries, and concluded that Taiwan was ahead of Mexico, Brazil, and Nigeria in that regard, but, as expected, behind the U.K. and Japan (Schreiber, 1970, p. 85). In his study of Asian LDCs, Koh asked American export-oriented companies with subsidiaries in Singapore, Taiwan, or Hong Kong to indicate the most favorable factors in their decisions to locate there. For Taiwan, political stability was the third most important reason, after only low labor costs and tax incentives (Koh, 1973). In brief, Taiwan's internal political stability may have helped lure foreign investors in the 1960s and after.

In December 1978, another significant political event, the breaking off of formal diplomatic relations between the ROC and the U.S., took place.

The dramatic change in the ROC's position in the international political arena could, obviously, have had far-reaching effects on the inflow of DFI into Taiwan. The uncertainty caused by the derecognition move has, however, been reduced by follow-up arrangements between the two countries, including the U.S. Congress' passage of the Taiwan Relations Act, which provides a limited guarantee of Taiwan's security, as well as the setting up of quasi-official agencies in both countries to facilitate a wide range of relationships between them. An economic factor proved equally important in offsetting a negative impact on DFI in Taiwan during that period. Taiwan's business situation in 1978 and 1979 was extremely positive, with the country experiencing its highest growth rate ever—13.9 percent—in 1978. Because DFI—both investment targeting the domestic market and that represented by the retained earnings of existing firms, with the latter constituting an increasing share of total arrived DFI (see pp. 320–2)—responded positively to Taiwan's domestic economic conditions, the immediate impact on DFI of the unfavourable political changes in 1979 was held to a minimum, as Figure 1 attests.

Sources of DFI in Taiwan

A quarter of the total DFI in Taiwan during the period 1952–84 came from overseas Chinese. During the 1980s, however, that share dropped significantly, to only 10 percent. Among non-Chinese investment, U.S. capital was in the lead with 31 percent of the total, followed by that from Japan (22 percent), others (12 percent), and Europe (10 percent). As regards trends in the sources of DFI, U.S. capital's share declined through the latest subperiod, 1981–84, while the shares of Japan and others increased. European investment rose through the 1960s and 1970s, but has remained at a plateau of 10 percent since then.

In interpreting sources of DFI, it may be noted that several U.S. investments were made through U.S. subsidiaries in other countries. Ford's Taiwan venture was in association with Ford Canada. Gulf's investment was linked with that of Bermuda Gulf, and part of Singer's investment was financed by Swedish Singer. A rough estimate of the data bias against U.S. investment would be around 4 percent, which is not enough to alter the above observations.

Size and Ownership of DFI

By 1987, a total of 1,944 applications by overseas Chinese investors and 2,303 applications by non-Chinese foreigners had been approved. Among non-Chinese foreigners, U.S. investors accounted for 15 percent of the investment projects, or 635 projects; Japan, with the largest share, accounted for 28 percent, or 1,195 cases. (See Table 1.)

The sizes of investments varied with their sources. As of 1987, the average non-Chinese investment was $2.56 million, much larger than the

Table 1 Approved DFI by source, 1952–84   Units: $ million, cases

Source	1952–60		1961–70		1971–80		1981–87		1952–87	
	Amount	Cases	Amount	Cases	Amount	Cases	Amount	Cases	Amount	Cases
Overseas Chinese	10(30)	54(70)	153(29)	647(53)	801(37)	774(53)	471(10)	469(31)	1,435(20)	1,944(46)
Foreigners	23(70)	23(30)	373(71)	564(47)	1,358(63)	675(47)	4,160(90)	1,041(69)	5,914(80)	2,303(54)
U.S.	21(62)	12(15)	221(42)	144(12)	534(25)	173(12)	1,492(32)	306(20)	2,268(31)	635(15)
Japan	2(8)	10(13)	87(16)	376(31)	369(17)	370(26)	1,325(29)	439(29)	1,783(24)	1,195(28)
Europe	–(–)	0(0)	36(7)	16(1)	225(10)	46(3)	683(15)	112(8)	944(13)	174(4)
Others	0(0)	1(1)	29(6)	28(2)	230(11)	86(6)	660(14)	184(12)	919(12)	299(7)
Total	33(100)	78(100)	526(100)	1,211(100)	2,159(100)	1,449(100)	4,631(100)	1,510(100)	7,349(100)	4,247(100)

Source: Investment Commission, Ministry of Economic Affairs, Statistics on Overseas Chinese and Foreign Investment, Technical Cooperation, Outward Investment, Outward Technical Cooperation.

average overseas Chinese investment of $0.74 million. Among non-Chinese investors, European investments were the largest, averaging $5.43 million; followed by U.S. investments ($3.57 million) and others ($3.07 million). The smallest non-Chinese investments, averaging $1.49 million, were from Japan.

The variations in investment size reflect the relationships between the investors and the host country. It is to be expected that overseas Chinese investments would be the smallest, because, to a large extent, those investors are not "foreigners" and are not treated as such. Their great familiarity with Taiwan's economy and their close connection with the local people facilitate their participation, so that even a relatively small investment can achieve its goals. Another relevant factor in this regard is that most of the overseas Chinese investors are from Hong Kong or Southeast Asian countries.

Japanese investors share many of the same characteristics as overseas Chinese. During their fifty-year colonial period, the Japanese not only learned a great deal about Taiwan's economy, language, and culture, but also built up a cordial relationship with the natives. This unique relationship, based largely on personal contact, helps reduce both risk and investment size.

Europeans, on the other hand, have no such connections, and their investments tend to be much larger, as a result. The average investment sizes for Americans and others lie somewhere between those for Japanese and Europeans.

Turning to the ownership structure of DFI, Americans and Europeans in particular clearly preferred majority control, or even wholly owned ventures. Investors from other regions also showed the same tendency toward majority ownership, according to the 1985 data, but their rate of participation in companies of which they owned no more than 60 percent tended to be higher than that by U.S. and European ventures.

Table 2 Ownership structure of foreign enterprises, 1985   Units: %

Investment Source	39%	40–59%	60–99%	100%
Overseas Chinese	23.3	13.7	34.7	28.3
Foreigners	18.9	28.5	19.1	33.5
U.S.	13.4	21.5	14.1	51.0
Japanese	21.2	34.2	21.4	23.2
European	15.8	15.8	23.7	44.7
Others	20.8	22.1	15.6	41.5

Source: Investment Commission, Ministry of Economic Affairs, *An Analysis of the Operations and Economic Impact of Foreign Enterprises*, 1975, 1985.

Table 3 Capital composition of DFI, 1965–1986   Units: %

Year	Imports				Technical know-how	Reinvested earnings
	Currency	Machinery	Materials	Total		
1965	28.6	50.0	21.4	71.4	0.0	–
1969	84.9	8.8	2.1	10.8	–	4.2
1972	87.9	4.3	0.5	4.8	–	7.3
1975	63.2	2.0	0.2	2.2	–	34.6
1979	81.6	1.1	0.2	1.3	–	17.1
1981	–	–	–	–	–	35.2
1983	–	–	–	–	–	26.5
1984	–	–	–	–	–	38.1
1985	–	–	–	–	–	19.5
1986	–	–	–	–	–	15.5

Note: No breakdown of DFI capital is available for 1978–1986.

Source: Data for 1965 from Liu, 1971, p.51. Other data from the Central Bank of China.

Japanese investors, on the other hand, preferred joint ventures, especially those with near-equal ownership (foreign ownership between 40 and 59 percent). Although overseas Chinese showed no strong preference for equal ownership, their ownership behavior was otherwise similar to that of Japanese investors.

The same explanations for investment-size variation by investor region can be applied here. In fact, a positive correlation between those two findings exists: i.e., a majority-owned foreign firm tends to commit more capital than a minority-owned firm does, given identical company size and financial structure. This helps explain why non-Japanese and non-Chinese foreigners tend to make larger investments than overseas Chinese and Japanese.

The Capital Composition of DFI in Taiwan

According to Article 3 of the Statute, foreign capital may include: (1) foreign currency; (2) permissible imports of domestically needed machinery, equipment and materials; and (3) reinvested earnings. In 1965, imports of machinery and materials accounted for a large share of foreign capital, but that share has declined significantly since 1969. Machinery and materials investments were at first replaced by an increase in current imports, which have in turn been supplanted by reinvested earnings. These changes have a wide range of implications.

First, 50 percent of the DFI capital brought into Taiwan in 1965 in the form of machinery may have been used equipment. Strassman's study of DFI in Latin America in the 1960s found that "among American subsidiaries, 79 percent of those in Mexico and 57 percent of those in Puerto Rico used second-hand machines" (Strassman 1968 p. 211). He showed, furthermore, that about three-fifths of foreign firms used second-hand machinery, while only about one-third of national firms did so. Taiwan's case may well be the same as that of the Latin American countries in the 1960s.

There are several advantages to using old machinery. The most obvious consideration is the difference in cost between old and new equipment. One potential advantage to indigenous investors is that they can exploit that equipment by selling it to their subsidiaries at higher prices, given the imperfect market for used machinery (James 1974). On the other hand, while smaller in size, older machines might be easier to operate and main- tain, which again suits foreign investors, given the small scale of their oper- ations and the lack of skilled labor in the developing host countries. These factors help explain why second-hand machinery was widely used in general, and by foreign investors in particular, in LDCs, including Taiwan.

By 1969, however, imported machinery accounted for only 8.8 percent of DFI capital, and that share became negligible in the 1970s. This decline could indicate that foreign investors arriving between 1965 and 1969 used less and less old machinery, which could have happened if a large portion of DFI after 1965 was primarily export-oriented. In point of fact, DFI in Taiwan did become very export-oriented after 1965, which caused a sharp change in capital composition.

Second, the increasing share of reinvested earnings as a source of DFI capital reveals several important points. First, the increasing trend of that share implies the success of existing investments. More significantly, as that share has increased to around 30 percent of the total investment since 1975, local economic conditions will have a direct bearing on the inflow of further DFI. Judging from the experience of developed countries like the U.S., whereby around 50 percent of DFI capital has come from retained earnings (Wichard and Freidlin, 1976, p. 41), this trend of self-financing is expected to increase.

Third, the law allows a foreign investor either to treat the technology brought in as part of the capital, or to license it to its subsidiary. Appar- ently investors prefer the latter, because of two possible advantages: (1) In licensing, a royalty is collected from the subsidiary, to which it is con- sidered a cost; thus, except during the tax-holiday period, that is an obvious tax incentive to licensing. (2) In a licensing situation, returns far outweigh risks.

Investor preference for licensing arrangements may change soon, however, because of the surge in high-tech industry and the establishment of a science-based industrial park in Hsinchu, where a few famous high- tech companies have begun operations, with no cash commitment, but by capitalizing their technical know-how up to a maximum of 20 percent of the total capital (Simon and Schive, 1986).

Table 4 DFI by industry, 1987   Unit: %

Industry	Overseas Chinese		Non-Chinese		Total	
	Approval	Arrival	Approval	Arrival	Approval	Arrival
Primary	2.10	–	0.19	–	0.55	–
Manufacturing	60.20	72.52	83.61	93.84	79.04	89.83
Textiles	6.20	15.47	0.81	1.22	1.86	3.90
Chemicals	4.07	17.44	17.35	17.51	14.76	17.49
Basic metals						
& products	2.66	7.18	8.09	8.41	7.03	8.18
Machinery	2.34	5.24	11.09	10.23	9.38	9.29
Electrical &						
electronics	3.40	5.77	35.19	43.74	28.98	36.60
Services	37.70	27.48	16.20	6.16	20.41	10.17
Total	100.00	100.00	100.00	100.00	100.00	100.00

Sources: 1. Investment Commission, Ministry of Economic Affairs, *Statistics on Overseas Chinese and Foreign Investment, Technical Cooperation, Outward Investment, Outward Technical Cooperation,* 1982.
2. Investment Commission, Ministry of Economic Affairs, *An Analysis of Operations and Economic Effects of Foreign Enterprises in Taiwan,* 1983.

Industrial Structure of DFI in Taiwan

According to both approval and survey data, DFI has been concentrated heavily in the manufacturing sector. As of 1987, 89.83 percent of existing DFI was in the manufacturing sector. The electrical and electronics industry took the lion's share, with 36.60 percent of the total investment. Chemicals took the second-largest share, 17.49 percent, followed by machinery (9.29 percent) and basic metals and products (8.18 percent). The other industries (garments; wood, bamboo and rattan products; and paper products) accounted for a total of 14.37 percent. The service sector took only 10.17 percent of total DFI, and almost no investment took place in the primary sector.

Because DFI in Tawian has been dominated by non-Chinese foreigners, their industrial structure should also be expected to dominate DFI. In fact, non-Chinese investors have concentrated more in the manufacturing sector and the electrical and electronics industry than have overseas Chinese, while the latter have shown a much greater tendency to invest in the service sector and textile industry. The approval data show that 20.41 percent of total overseas Chinese investment has been in the service sector.

The differences in the industrial structures of overseas Chinese and foreigners' investments are attributable to the different natures of those investors. First, most overseas Chinese investors were from Hong Kong

Table 5 DFI Contribution to Taiwan's capital formation, 1965–83
Units: $ million and %

Period	Arrived DFI		DFI as percentage of domestic capital formation		
	Manufacturing	*Total*	*Country, Total*	*Manufacturing*	*Private, Total*
1965–68	60.6	75.8	2.20	4.70	3.31
1969–72	161.9	202.4	4.32	7.33	5.47
1973–76	266.8	333.5	1.74	4.25	3.27
1977–80	414.3	517.9	1.37	4.27	2.50
1981–83	384.8	481.0	1.35	3.86	2.79
1984–86	740.4	925.5	2.51	5.77	4.46

Note: DFI in manufacturing is estimated as 80 percent of total arrived DFI.

Source: Appendix Table 1.

and Southeast Asia. The technological level there, except in Hong Kong, could not have been higher than that in Taiwan. As a result, their investment would naturally be concentrated in the mature or light industries, such as textiles and non-metallic products, and cement. Overseas Chinese also showed a great interest in the service sector, the construction and hotel industries in particular. These two industries were generally not open to investment by foreigners, but many overseas Chinese were allowed to invest in them after they abandoned their claim to exchange settlement. In short, overseas Chinese DFI represents a "neighboring" investment which differs from the more traditional, more "distant" non-Chinese DFI.

DFI's Contribution to Taiwan's Economy

DFI's Contribution to Taiwan's Capital Formation

Since DFI represents resources of additional capital to the host country, its contribution to the receiving country's capital formation should receive priority concern. However, in the case of Taiwan, when DFI started picking up in the mid-1960s, its proportional contribution to the country's total capital formation ranged from insignificant to modest—from 1.37 to 4.32 percent during 1965–85, with a declining trend in the 1970s. Because DFI came from private investors and was concentrated in the manufacturing sector, the share of DFI in private capital formation was higher, between 2.50 and 5.47 percent during the same period, but this share also declined during the 1970s. The contribution of DFI to the manufacturing total was even higher, ranging from 7.33 percent at its peak in 1969–72, to 3.86 percent in the subperiod 1981–83. As these figures show, DFI has not made a significant contribution to Taiwan's total capital formation, except modestly in the manufacturing sector.

DFI's Contribution to Taiwan's Exports and Employment

Though DFI has not been a major source of Taiwan's capital formation, looking at foreign firms, defined as local companies with any amount of foreign capital, the results are quite different. For example, a total of 795 foreign firms contributed 8.34 percent of Taiwan's total GNP in 1979. While many foreign firms are joint ventures, and our definition of DFI tends to overestimate its role in the economy, the weighted figure for foreign ownership still amounts to about half the unweighted figure.

Other indicators, either weighted or unweighted, are more significant. For example, exports of foreign firms accounted for around 20 percent (with a definite declining trend) of the country's total exports between 1974 and 1982; weighted figures for the same period range from 9.1 to 15.5 percent. Foreign firms' contributions to manufacturing employment was around 15 percent, with the weighted figures running from 10.33 percent at the peak in 1977 to 8.48 percent at the low point in 1982 (Table 6). These data reveal unmistakably that DFI has played an active and important role in Taiwan's development, particularly in the areas of employment and exports. How were these results achieved?

Foreign Firms' Technology, Employment and Exports

When introducing a new technology—whether for a new product, new process, improved equipment, of different organizational structure—a foreign firm must carefully evaluate the different aspects of that technology in order to ensure the best results from it. In the neoclassical framework, the issue is how, or to what extent, imported technology affects the efficiency of resource allocation. Given the abundance of labor and the shortage of capital in an LDC, "appropriate" technology will be labor-intensive—employment as a function of capital committed will be maximized—as a response to either the low cost of labor or the high cost of capital. The essential question remains, however, whether the technology brought into an LDC economy through DFI will be "appropriate."

There have been two alternative hypotheses regarding the technology issue. The first states that, if foreign firms apply the same technology as their parent companies (presumably capital-intensive, given the relatively low capital cost and relatively high wages in DCs as compared to LDCs), then DFI will decrease the efficiency of resource allocation.

The second hypothesis says that, because of foreign firms' advantages in technology, access to information, or simply experience, they may have more options in choosing technologies or in adapting them to their host countries' needs. Thus they will improve resource allocation in their host countries by applying more suitable technologies than their counterparts. Our empirical findings must seek to determine which of these conflicting

Table 6 DFI Contribution of Taiwan's GNP, exports and employment, 1974–85 Units: $ million, %

GNP due to foreign firms

Year	No. of foreign firms	Unweighted			Weighted by foreign ownership		
		Total	% of nat'l total	% of mfg.	Total	% of nat'l total	% of mfg.
1974	723	882	6.20	21.37	–	–	–
1977	747	1,492	7.66	24.31	–	–	–
1979	795	2,696	8.34	28.00	1,328	4.27	14.3
1982	847	2,570	5.62	19.09	1,253	2.74	9.3
1985	618	3,546	6.00	13.02	1,476	2.50	5.46

Exports due to foreign firms

Year	Unweighted		Weighted	
	Total	% of nat'l	Total	% of nat'l
1974	1,196	21.8	854	15.5
1977	1,960	20.9	1,269	12.1
1979	3,284	20.4	2,030	10.8
1982	4,275	19.7	2,572	9.1
1985	4,862	15.84	3,386	11.04

Employment due to foreign firms (1,000 persons)

Year	Unweighted			Weighted		
	Total	% of nat'l	% of mfg.	Total	% of nat'l	% of mfg.
1974	245	4.46	15.78	–	–	–
1977	298	4.98	16.28	189	3.16	10.33
1979	357	5.55	16.65	210	3.26	9.79
1982	326	4.78	14.63	189	2.77	8.48
1985	234	3.09	8.79	148	1.96	8.96

Source: Investment Commission, Ministry of Economic Affairs, *An Analysis of the Operation and Impacts of Foreign Enterprises*, various issues.

hypotheses—whether DFI will help or hinder the efficiency of resource allocation in LDCs—is correct.

An Overall Comparison between Foreign and National Firms' Factor Intensities

Table 7 shows that in 1976 foreign firms, on the whole, used an average of $6,490 in fixed assets per employee, compared with $7,150 for national firms. Foreign firms used more labor-intensive technologies than national firms in producing foods and beverages, apparel, wood, bamboo and rattan products, leather products, rubber and plastic products, chemicals, and electrical products and electronics. In the textile, paper products, non-metallic products, and machinery industries, however, foreign firms used more capital-intensive technologies than their local counterparts. The non-metallic products industry is an extreme case in which foreign firms had a very high capital-labor ratio, compared not only with national firms in the same industry but also with foreign firms in other industries. A careful examination of foreign firms in the non-metallic industry reveals that a few large minority-owned foreign cement factories accounted for that high capital-labor ratio. Indeed, foreign firms' capital intensities varied among industries, and did not exhibit any consistent pattern vis-à-vis the capital intensities of local firms in the same industries.

The above findings suggest that, in order to explain the differences in factor intensity between national and foreign firms, the industrial structures of both types of investment should be taken into account. Since the average capital-labor ratio (k) is an average of each individual industry's capital-labor ratio (k^i) weighted by employment (w^i), the difference between the average k^f, representing foreign firms, and the average k^n, representing national firms, can be decomposed into two parts: one attributable to the difference in k^i (the ith industry's capital-labor ratio) between foreign and national firms; and the other attributable to the difference in w^i (the industrial structure measured by employment) between foreign and national firms. The first part of the deviation is due to intra-industry differences in k, while the second part is due to inter-industry distribution differences. In other words, the use by foreign firms, as a whole, of more (or less) capital-intensive technology may have been due to one or both of two factors: (1) On an individual industrial basis, foreign firms used more (or less) capital-intensive technology than did their national counterparts; and (2) Foreign firms were more (or less) concentrated in capital-intensive industries. It is not necessary for these two factors to have the same direction of influence.

The results in Table 8 indicate that, on the basis of the employment structures of national and foreign firms, foreign firms used more capital-intensive technology than did national ones, on the average. However, because DFI has tended to be concentrated in more labor-intensive indus-

Table 7 Fixed assets per employee of national and foreign manufacturing firms, by industry, 1976[1]   Unit: $1,000

| Industry | Foreign firms | | | National firms |
	Overseas Chinese	Non-Chinese	Total	
Foods and beverages	4.32	6.13	5.10	11.68
Textiles	10.29	25.66	17.74	7.61
Apparel	1.32	1.13	1.24	1.53
Wood, bamboo, and rattan products	3.79	1.87	2.79	3.87
Paper and products	12.13	9.58	10.92	6.89
Leather and leather products	1.63	0.97	1.32	1.74
Rubber and plastic products	2.29	2.05	2.13	3.58
Chemicals	15.05	11.66	13.32	21.84
Non-metallic products	33.13	22.21	27.53	7.39
Basic metals and products	1.74	4.42	3.79	9.42
Machinery	1.74	17.32	16.32	6.87
Electrical and electronics	2.58	2.60	2.60	4.55
Manufacturing, total[2]	8.20	5.77	6.49	7.15

Notes: 1. Figures were weighted averages.
2. The figure for the national manufacturing total – including some industries with no DFI, such as the refinery and miscellaneous industries – was $8,390.

Sources: 1. *An Analysis of Operations and Economic Effects of Foreign Enterprise* (Taipei: Investment Commission, 1977).
2. *The Report of 1976, the Committee on Industrial and Commercial Censuses of the Taiwan-Fukien District of the Republic of China* (Taipei: The Committee on Industrial and Commercial Censuses of the Taiwan-Fukien District, 1978).

tries, foreign firms, on the whole, have tended to use more labor-intensive technology. Thus it is not the intra-industry difference in factor intensity but the difference in investment structure, between national and foreign firms, that explains the overall difference in factor intensities between these two groups.

Factor Intensity of Foreign Firms with Different Market Orientation

Although direct comparison of national and foreign firms' technologies within the same industry shows no significant differences, similar studies of foreign firms with respect to their different market orientations may show different results. The method applied here is: each firm's capital-labor ratio was weighted by its exports and domestic sales in order to take into account

Table 8 Differences in factor intensity between national and foreign firms due to intra- and inter-industry differences   Unit: $1,000 per employee

	Total difference of k (national firms' minus foreign firms')	Intra-industry difference	Inter-industry difference
Based on national firms' employment structure	0.66	−2.41 (−365.15)	3.07 (465.15)
Based on foreign firms' employment structure	0.66	−0.16 (−24.24)	0.82 (124.24)

Notes: Decomposing formula derived as follows:

$$k^N - k^f = \Sigma k_i^N w_i^N - \Sigma k_i^f w_i^f$$
$$= \Sigma(k_i^N - k_i^f)w_i^N + \Sigma(w_i^N - w_i^f)k_i^f$$
$$= \Sigma(k_i^N - k_i^f)w_i^f + \Sigma(w_i^N - w_i^f)k_i^N$$

N: national; f: foreign; k: fixed assets per employee; w: employment share; i: ith industry.

Source: Ibid.

the degree of its export activity; for this purpose, it was assumed that each firm used identical technology for its export and domestic sales. Two measures of capital intensity (machinery and equipment per unit of direct labor, and fixed assets per employee) are presented in Table 9.

On average, foreign manufacturing firms used $7,600 worth of machinery and equipment per unit of labor in export activities, but $15,500 in production for the domestic market. As to the value of fixed assets per employee, foreign firms used half as much capital per unit of labor in export-oriented production as they did in production for the local market. Apparently, foreign firms as a whole tended to use different technologies for different markets.

On an industry basis, foreign firms producing foods and beverages, apparel, plastic and products, non-metallic products, and machinery used much more capital-intensive technology for domestic sales than for exports. Foreign firms producing wood, bamboo and rattan products, and paper and products applied much the same technology for both markets. The only exception is the textile industry, in which firms used more capital-intensive technology for exports than for the domestic market. Examining the data closely by industry, foreign firms in the wood, bamboo, and rattan industry had a very high export ratio for that year (93.89 percent), while those in the paper and products industry exported only 16.69 percent of

Table 9 Capital–labor ratios of foreign firms, weighted by exports and domestic sales, by industry, 1975   Unit: $1,000

Industry	Machinery and equip. per direct labor		Fixed assets per employee		Exports/ sales (%)
	Exports	Domestic sales	Exports	Domestic sales	
Foods and beverages	1.92	8.45	3.11	12.26	20.77
Textiles	21.24	14.34	26.84	19.95	77.61
Apparel	0.63	1.47	1.26	2.34	96.84
Wood, bamboo, and rattan products	1.18	1.37	1.92	2.74	93.89
Paper and products	8.74	8.87	12.00	11.42	16.69
Leather and products	0.66	1.63	1.61	2.76	99.96
Plastic and rubber products	1.42	13.03	2.29	10.76	85.29
Chemicals	17.55	19.61	16.24	17.61	43.17
Non-metallic products	28.71	42.97	24.58	50.79	8.58
Basic metals and products	2.42	4.08	3.89	5.24	50.13
Machinery	2.08	9.45	3.32	10.47	35.67
Electrical and electronics	2.05	1.95	2.89	3.95	63.56
Total	7.55	15.47	9.00	18.18	57.96

Source: Primary data from foreign firm survey by the Investment Commission, Ministry of Economic Affairs, 1975.

their production. The former industry, therefore, was highly export-oriented, while the latter targeted the local market. There may have been a correlation between the market orientations and technologies used by foreign firms in these two industries. The case of the textile industry can be explained by the outward orientation of a few large foreign firms which produced artificial fibers.

The finding for the electrical and electronics industry is unusual: Foreign firms' exporting activities used slightly more capital-intensive technology than did their activities aimed at the local market, in terms of machinery and equipment per unit of direct labor. That situation is reversed, however, when we measure the capital-labor ratio in terms of fixed assets per employee. This disparity may stem from two factors. First, this industry has a very broad scope of production, ranging from heavy electrical equipment to home appliances to electronics and parts. The manufacture of some products (e.g., electrical equipment and electronic parts) requires a heavy capital commitment. Many parts producers came to Taiwan expressly because of the strong local demand which exports had created, as evidenced by the high proportion of indirect exports to total sales.[4] Thus, some of the exports in this industry may be capital-intensive by nature.

The second factor relates to an assumption we made at the beginning: the technologies for the export and domestic markets may, in fact, not be identical. Nonetheless, product mixes tend to average out the different characteristics of the technologies associated with different products.

The examination from the same data source of a group of foreign firms which were located in EPZs, which exported all their production, and which seemed not to have a broad scope of production, sheds some light on the above arguments. Foreign electrical and electronics producers in EPZs had only $789 worth of machinery per unit of labor—38.46 percent of the overall average for that industry.[5] Thus, the highly exported-oriented foreign firms, as represented by foreign firms in EPZs, used even more labor-intensive technology than did firms producing for mixed markets.

Effect of Technology Differences on Employment

Returning to the resource-allocation issue, foreign firms which apply labor-intensive technology in their export production must have a significant effect on local employment. Two indicators will illustrate this impact clearly. First, assuming identical employment per dollar of sales, we may separate employment due to export production from that for local sales, by using the sales data for the two markets. Summing these figures for each industry and dividing by the industry's total employment will indicate the industry-level employment effects attributable to domestic sales.

If the total percentage of employment due to exports is larger than the average export ratio, then we can conclude that production for export tends to create more jobs than does production for domestic sales. This result is soundly confirmed by Table 10. In manufacturing, exports accounted for 56.09 percent of total sales, but contributed 75.57 percent of total employment. The same finding holds true for all other industries except textiles; in some industries (apparel, wood, bamboo, and leather and products) both figures are very high and quite close.

The same data permit us to calculate the number of employees per million dollars of either exports or domestic sales for foreign firms. The results, shown in Table 11, indicate that the overall employment effect per million dollars' worth of exports is 120 persons, compared to 50 persons per million dollars of domestic sales. With the exception of textiles, for the same reasons given above, domestic sales in all industries always created less employment per dollar of sales than did exports.

Foreign Firms and Export Marketing

Since foreign firms have exported 57% of their total production, did foreign investors participate actively in their subsidiaries' export marketing? Foreign investors with a competitive advantage in marketing (Caves, 1971) do tend to play an active role in the export marketing of their subsidiaries. And the empirical results should validate this inference firmly.

Table 12 provides information on exporting firms' various marketing

Table 10 Export ratios and employment due to exports of foreign firms, by industry, 1975 Unit: %

Industry	Employment due to exports	Average export ratios
Foods and beverages	46.87	20.77
Textiles	75.51	77.61
Apparel	97.38	96.84
Wood, bamboo, and rattan products	94.75	93.89
Paper and products	22.90	16.69
Leather and products	99.99	99.96
Plastic and rubber products	94.42	85.29
Chemicals	54.70	43.17
Non-metallic products	32.60	8.58
Basic metals and products	62.92	50.13
Machinery	64.60	35.67
Electrical and electronics	77.08	63.56
Total	75.57	56.09

Note: Exports include indirect exports, which are defined as sales to exporting firms used in exports.

Source: Foreign Firm Survey, Investment Commission, Ministry of Economic Affairs, 1975.

channels. Each firm was asked about its sources of foreign marketing information, including: (1) its parent company, (2) foreign agents, (3) foreign customers, (4) government agents or industrial associations, (5) trading companies, and (6) international fairs. The results are presented in Table 12.

Of a total of 127 foreign exporting firms, 95 (74.8 percent) utilized their parent companies' export marketing facilities, either exclusively or in conjunction with other marketing methods. The proportion of majority-owned foreign firms whose marketing was handled by parents was as high as 80 percent. Further examination of the data shows that 26 (20.5 percent) of the foreign firms relied completely on this marketing method available only to foreign firms. Of those 26 foreign firms, 25 were majority-owned, and 11 were in the electrical and electronics industry. In general, marketing through foreign firms was the most popular of the six export-marketing methods available to foreign firms. We can thus conclude that, in addition to introducing the appropriate technology favoring exports, DFI has alleviated Taiwan's export-marketing problems at large.

In regard to the technology transfer in general, without specifying the content of technology transferred from multinationals to their local subsidiaries, two surveys conducted in 1973 and 1987, respectively, produced similar conclusions. First, foreign firms, defined as local companies with

Table 11 Number of people employed by foreign firms per million dollars of exports and domestic sales, by industry, 1975   Unit: person

Industry	Exports	Domestic sales
Foods and beverages	87.4	25.8
Textiles	77.1	86.6
Apparel	184.7	152.4
Wood, bamboo and rattan products	185.8	158.8
Paper and products	112.9	76.0
Leather and products	264.1	42.0
Plastic and rubber products	198.0	68.0
Chemicals	57.8	36.5
Non-metallic products	125.0	24.3
Basic metals and products	145.5	86.3
Machinery	120.0	36.5
Electrical and electronics	126.9	65.7
Total	120.8	49.8

Source: Foreign Firm Survey, Investment Commission, Ministry of Economic Affairs, 1975.

any proportion of foreign capital participating in their capital structures, were much more likely to apply foreign technology than national ones (Schive, 1979; San, 1988). Moreover, the majority-owned foreign firms had an even higher propensity to introduce foreign technology than the minority-owned ones. Thus DFI did serve as an effective channel for international technology transfer, and the degree of foreign capital involvement in a local company had a positive impact upon the company's behavior in adopting foreign technology.

Taiwan's Outward Investment: Native Multinationals

Taiwanese companies began to go abroad at a significant level only in the 1970s, about ten years after the surge of DFI into Taiwan. By 1986, the total outward investment remitted was $391 million[6]—76 percent of the approved amount, of 14.9 percent of the arrived DFI up to that time. Outward investment as measured by official data, however, is seriously underestimated. For example, one source shows that Taiwan's DFI in Thailand amounted to $52 million in 1970–75 alone (Edwards, 1977, p. 42); the official figure is $2.2 million. Vernon's study indicates that there were a total of 178 Taiwanese MNCs in Thailand by 1978; official statistics show 23 investment projects approved and 14 having begun operations, with five surviving as of 1981 (Vernon, 1977, p. 27). Under these circumstances, the quality, not the quantity, of data should be emphasized.

Table 12 Export-marketing methods of Taiwan's exporting foreign and national firms, by industry   Unit: %

Industry	Number of firms	Foreign agents	Inter-national fairs	Foreign customers	Foreign partners	Trade associ-ations	Trading co's
Textiles							
(1) National firms	76	22.4	7.9	85.5	–	46.1	19.7
(2) Foreign firms	17	53.0	17.6	52.9	47.1	35.5	5.9
(3) Majority owned foreign firms	10	40.0	30.0	40.0	50.0	40.0	–
(4) Minority owned foreign firms	7	71.4	–	71.4	42.9	28.6	14.3
Apparel							
(1)	49	32.7	12.2	87.8	–	26.5	14.3
(2)	22	40.9	9.1	72.7	81.8	4.5	9.1
(3)	18	44.4	5.6	66.7	88.9	5.6	5.6
(4)	4	25.0	25.0	100.0	50.0	–	25.0
Plastic and plastic products							
(1)	34	35.3	11.8	94.1	–	26.5	8.8
(2)	27	37.0	14.8	70.4	74.1	18.5	7.4
(3)	24	33.3	12.5	70.8	75.0	16.7	4.2
(4)	3	66.7	33.3	66.7	66.7	33.3	33.3
Metal products							
(1)	11	54.5	27.3	81.8	–	36.4	9.1
(2)	15	6.7	–	80.0	80.0	–	–
(3)	13	7.7	–	76.9	84.6	–	–
(4)	2	–	–	100.0	50.0	–	–
Electrical and electronics							
(1)	17	29.4	17.6	76.5	–	47.1	–
(2)	46	50.0	15.2	63.0	80.4	19.6	–
(3)	39	51.3	12.8	56.4	87.2	17.9	–
(4)	7	42.9	28.6	100.0	42.9	28.6	–
All industries							
(1)	187	29.9	11.8	86.6	–	36.9	13.9
(2)	127	40.9	12.6	66.9	74.8	16.5	3.9
(3)	104	39.4	11.5	62.5	80.8	15.4	1.9
(4)	23	47.8	17.4	87.0	47.8	21.7	13.0

Note: Each firm may use more than one marketing method at any given time.

Source: Data were provided by Professors Yen Hwa and Yung-sun Lee, based on a fall 1972 survey of the manufacturing exporting firms in Taiwan conducted and sponsored jointly by the Graduate Institute of Economics, National Taiwan University, and the Kiel Institute for World Economics, West Germany.

The Trend of Taiwan's Outward Investment

Officially, the first Taiwanese outward investment was made in 1959, when a local firm invested $100,000 worth of machinery in a Malaysian cement plant. After a lull of two years, a jute-bag manufacturer restarted Taiwan's capital outflow in 1962 by setting up a plant in Thailand. Throughout the

1960s, Taiwan's direct foreign investment hovered around $800,000 annually. However, outward investment has been increasing at an annual rate of 23.78 percent since the early 1970s.

By the end of 1981, the government had approved a total of 163 investment applications; of all the firms, which had made such applications, 48 (29 percent) were no longer in existence (Schive, 1982). Of these defunct ventures, 35 had actually gone into operation but had withdrawn, due the failure of the business or to the outcome of the Vietnam War. Formosa Plastics, the largest manufacturing concern among the 54 local companies with at least one subsidiary by the end of 1981, has applied for twelve foreign ventures, only four of which were in operation at that time. Since then, a series of investments in the U.S. petrochemicals industry has been initiated, with a total capital commitment of $43 million by 1986. Taiwan's second-largest manufacturing MNC, Tatung, had eight projects approved and in operation by 1981. Since then, Tatung has added an Irish TV plant to its worldwide network. Pacific Wire and Cable Co., the third largest Taiwanese MNC in manufacturing, had five projects approved, but dropped one of them by 1981. This company began a new trend in Taiwan's outward investment by setting up a high-tech joint venture, Mosel, in Silicon Valley. In the trade industry, a semi-governmental trading company set up a worldwide network of twelve overseas subsidiaries.

In general, the U.S. received the lion's share, of Taiwan's outward investment approved by 1981, 40.7 percent, and 54.7 percent by 1985, with five ASEAN countries accounting for another 32.6 percent and 28.9 percent by 1981 and 1985, respectively. The remaining investment was distributed mainly in Latin America and Africa. (See Table 13) As regards the industrial structure of Taiwan's outward investment, 24.1 percent of the remitted capital went to the electrical and electronics industry by 1981, and 34.0 percent of the approved capital by 1986. Chemicals, the second-largest industry for Taiwan's outward investment fund, attracted 15.7 percent of the total outward DFI by 1986. (See Table 14)

Motives for Outward Investment

Taiwan's investors went abroad for four primary reasons: (1) to secure supplies of raw materials; (2) to pursue profits by supplying host-country markets; (3) to facilitate exports; and (4) to gain access to technology in its country of origin. The first category of investors included plywood makers, a fishing company, a pineapple canner, and petrochemical producers. Thailand, Malaysia, Indonesia, and Costa Rica were the host countries to primary resource-oriented ventures, and the U.S. for industrial resource-oriented ones. Formosa Plastics, a good example of the second type, initiated a $24 million series of investments in the U.S. with its 1983 acquisition of a vinylchloride monomer (VCM) plant. Part of the VCM produced was shipped back home. This investment, therefore, can be

Table 13 Approved and remitted outward investment, 1959–85, by country   Units: $ million, cases

Outward investment	Total	ASEAN Countries						U.S.	Others
		Thailand	Malaysia	Singapore	Philippines	Indonesia	Total		
Approved by 1981									
Amount	112.1	4.9	3.1	7.8	9.8	10.9	36.5	45.6	29.9
Cases	163	23	18	20	8	10	79	28	56
Approved by 1985									
Amount	214.2	9.5	7.3	9.3	10.1	25.8	62.0	117.2	35.8
Cases	219	26	19	23	9	12	89	60	70
Remitted by 1981									
Amount	59.9	2.6	2.9	7.5	0.7	5.4	19.1	27.1	13.7
Cases	114	14	12	16	6	4	52	26	39

Source: 1. Schive (1982), P.10.
2. Investment Commission, Ministry of Economic Affairs, Statistics of Approved Overseas Chinese and Foreign Investment, Republic of China, 1985.

regarded as one taking advantage of low materials costs (i.e., the low prices of ethylene and energy).

Firms in the foods and beverages, textiles, plastic and plastic products, and non-metallic materials industries were motivated to invest overseas by the desire to supply the domestic markets of the host countries. The major investors in the foods and beverages industry were monosodium glutamate (MSG) producers, while the leaders in the textile industry were processors of synthetic fibers. Several investors in the plastics industry were also interested in foreign subsidiaries. Most of the firms in the non-metallic materials industry were cement manufacturers.

To make this type of investment, a parent firm must have sufficient experience and technology to compete with local firms and other MNC subsidiaries. The Taiwanese investors in these four industries share the common characteristic of a long period of development and experience in their areas. For example, the MSG and cement industries were established by the 1950s, and the PVC and PE plastics industries were well-developed by the late 1950s and late 1960s, respectively. The synthetic fiber industry has experienced rapid growth since the 1960s. Thus, investors in the four industries were equipped with the necessary technology and experience before they ventured into the relatively risky foreign market.

The third type of outward investment is aimed at facilitating exports of Taiwanese goods. DFI in the electrical and electronics industry and the trade industry can be classified in this category. As Table 14 indicates, the United States attracted 53 percent of Taiwan's outward investment in the electrical and electronics industry, and 81 percent in trading by 1981. With the U.S. market absorbing around 40 percent of Taiwan's total exports in 1970, it was seen that the imposition of import quotas on Taiwanese goods would impede that country's trade. As a result, trading partners established subsidiaries to bring in semi-finished products, which are not as tightly restricted, and thereby to penetrate trade barriers. Taiwan's three largest electrical and electronics producers all have ventures in the U.S., and other large exporting manufacturers are eager to set up trading offices in their major export markets.

Another way to penetrate the fenced markets of major trading partners, particularly those with quota systems, is "quota hopping": Taiwanese exporting companies may set up offshore production in other countries to bypass quota restrictions. This has been the case for Taiwan's footwear industry in Latin America and, more recently, the Caribbean, and for textile ventures established in Singapore and in some French colonies, aiming at the EEC market. This type of export-promoting investment relies upon materials from the parent company or from Taiwan.

The final type of motivation to become an MNC is often seen in the recently developed high-tech industries. In 1979 a private firm, United Microelectronics Co. (UMC), was organized to commercialize several

Table 14 Taiwan's outward investment remitted 1959–81, by industry and by country   Units: $ million, %

Industry	Total ($ mil.)	ASEAN countries (%)						U.S.	Others	Approved by 1986 ($ mil.)
		Thailand	Malaysia	Singapore	Philippines	Indonesia	Total			
Foods and beverages	0.933	63	–	–	–	–	63	25	12	9.79
Textiles	0.337	–	28	–	–	–	28	65	7	11.05
Garments and footwear	0.256	–	–	77	23	–	100	–	–	2.38
Wood, bamboo, and rattan products	2,041	5	87	3	–	–	95	–	5	4.00
Paper	1,960	–	–	–	–	100	100	–	–	20.26
Leather and leather products										0.86
Plastic products	6,566	–	–	11	1	4	16	84	–	12.77
Chemicals	8,343	–	–	5	–	–	5	95	–	42.81
Non-metallic products	6,977	–	–	20	–	–	20	7	73	13.57
Primary metals and products	1,013	–	–	52	–	29	81	19	–	7.17
Machinery	0.050	–	–	–	–	–	–	100	–	1.62
Electrical and electronics	12,339	2	1	16	1	–	20	53	27	92.38
Trade	7,383	–	–	3	1	–	4	81	15	14.91
Construction, finance, services and others	3,058	–	–	–	–	–	–	2	98	32.95
Total	51,256									271.83

innovations developed in Taiwan's government-funded research institute, the Industrial Technology and Research Institution (ITRI). To ensure the continuous inflow of advanced technology, UMC set up a subsidiary, Unicorn, in Silicon Valley, and maintained close relations with three other R&D-based overseas Chinese-operated companies, Mosel, Qusel, and Vitelic. Each of these three companies operates both in Taiwan's science-based industrial park and in Silicon Valley, and each uses domestic capital. All of these companies have successfully turned out a great number of patents for the design and manufacturing of very-large-scale integrated circuits (VLSIs) (Schive, forthcoming). This newly emerging type of outward investment can be explained only by the desire to gain access to the U.S. technology market.

Competition and Technology Transfer: Taiwan's MNCs in ASEAN Countries

Taiwanese firms in ASEAN countries face competition both from indigenous firms and from the multinationals of other countries. Intuitively, these firms would seem to be at an advantage when competing with DC multinationals in LDC host economies because of: (1) lower managerial costs; (2) better understanding of the host country; (3) more appropriate technology; and (4) better connections with local and world market distribution channels (Chen, 1983, p. 194). Tables 15 and 16 present TMNCs' motives for investing in ASEAN countries, and their competitive edge over MNCs from developed countries, respectively.

The first, second, and fourth most important reasons for investing in ASEAN countries related to the market factor. Investors were motivated largely by the need to create a new market or to use the host country as a base for exporting to a third country. A third motive was that protectionism in the host countries created pressure for original suppliers to maintain factories there. Taiwanese firms must be encouraged to go multinational by finding buyers for their used or depreciated machinery. (See also pp. 320–2 on the capital composition of DFI in Taiwan). Surprisingly, Taiwan's MNCs rank consideration of the costs of labor and materials very low. That finding, however, is in line with Hymer's industrial organization approach to DFI, which de-emphasizes cost factors.

The main competitive advantages TMNs had over their DC rivals are in marketing factors: products better suited to host markets, lower prices, and better marketing channels. These are exactly what Lall asserted were the "marketing advantages" of MNCs from LDCs (Lall, 1982, p. 37). Factors linked to operation and management style, which were considered of moderate importance, favor the more appropriate technology of MNCs from LDCs and their greater familiarity with the host countries. As has frequently been pointed out, these factors are, in fact, the weakest points of MNCs from DCs (Lall, 1978, p. 238; Wells, 1983, p. 22).

Table 15 Motives for Taiwanese investment in ASEAN countries

Motives	Weighted rating
Opening a new market	0.09
Promoting exports to a third country	0.81
Exporting machinery	0.78
Host country market threatening protectionism	0.72
Improving image in home market	0.55
Competition from already internationalized firms from home country	0.51
Access to cheap raw materials	0.43
Access to cheap labor	0.26
Diversification of business risks	0.11

Note: The questionnaire allowed three rankings: high (2 points), medium (1 point), and low (ϕ points). Weighted-average figures are simple averages of these points.

Source: Schive (1982).

If the large-scale production techniques which MNCs from DCs always employ in their own countries mean the full utilization of scale economies, then their adaptation to the smaller markets of host countries destroys this advantage and increases production costs. Furthermore, highly capital-intensive and automated production techniques may not be employed effectively in many host countries, because local labor markets cannot furnish either the advanced technology or the skilled labor required. Thus, when DC multinationals use the same technology in their overseas operations as they use at home, the result is often lower productivity, in terms of both labor and capital (Marsden, 1970, p. 478). In this environment, it

Table 16 Competitive advantages of Taiwanese MNCs vis-à-vis DC MNCs in host countries

Advantages	Weighted rating
Product better suited to host market	1.15
Lower price of product	1.06
Better marketing channels	0.94
Equipment easier to operate	0.70
Lower operating costs	0.70
More appropriate management style	0.67
Lower salary for managers from parent firm	0.15

Note: Ibid.

Source: Ibid.

Table 17 Factor intensity of Taiwanese subsidiaries in ASEAN countries
Units: No. of firms and %

	In comparison with	
Taiwanese subsidiaries	*Home plants*	*Local firms*
More labor-intensive	9(40.9)	2 (9.1)
Similar	10(45.5)	14(63.6)
More capital-intensive	3(13.6)	6(27.3)

Source: Schive (1982).

is argued, smaller-scale, more labor-intensive technology ("intermediate technology") is more appropriate (Schumacher, 1973). In other words, what the host country needs is technology that can be easily operated and is inexpensive, even though it is not necessarily the most advanced.

Assuming that the value of equipment per worker (the capital-labor ratio) represents the degree of technological sophistication and the scale of operation, the data in Table 17 support the "appropriate technology" argument. These figures indicate that fourteen (63.6 percent) of Taiwan's 24 subsidiaries in ASEAN countries applied a technology similar to that used by their local counterparts, while six companies (27.3 percent) used more capital per worker than local companies did. Compared to their home plants in Taiwan, however, only three subsidiaries (13.6 percent) had a higher capital-labor ratio. Thus, half of the six Taiwanese subsidiaries with higher capital-labor ratios than their local counterparts had to use a more labor-intensive technology than they would have in Taiwan.

Thus, Taiwan's investors in ASEAN countries tended to use technology which was either similar to or more labor-intensive than what they used at home. In both cases, the technology transferred is smaller in scale and easier to operate than the technology of DCs.

Summary and Conclusions

DFI in Taiwan has shown an increasing trend since 1960, with one-fifth of that investment coming from overseas Chinese and the balance from the U.S. (31 percent), Japan (24 percent), and Europe (13 percent). Among these different investors, the U.S. and European firms tended to be larger in size and to have majority-owned capital structures; Japanese investors, on the other hand, preferred joint ventures, especially those in which equity ownership was more equally shared with the natives.

Pre-1965 DFI brought in 50 percent of its capital in the form of machinery, much of it very likely second-hand. Since 1965, as DFI has become more export-oriented and well-established, a growing proportion of capital has taken the form of foreign exchange and retained earnings. Given the growing importance of the last source of DFI, local economic conditions have become more relevant to future DFI.

As regards the industrial structure, non-Chinese investors have concentrated on the manufacturing sector, and on the electrical and electronics industry in particular. Overseas Chinese have focused on mature industries or the service sector.

DFI has never contributed more than 5 percent to Taiwan's gross capital formation since 1965, though its contribution to the total investment of the manufacturing sector rose to 7.33 percent between 1969 and 1972. Nonetheless, around 20 percent of the country's total exports were attributable to foreign firms, which generated 15 to 17 percent of the total employment in the manufacturing sector during the period 1974 to 1982. Here lie the major contributions of DFI to Taiwan's economy.

A study of foreign firms' technology shows that these firms used more labor-intensive technology than national ones, mainly because they were more heavily concentrated in the labor-intensive industries than the latter. A further study of foreign firms' technology in relation to their market orientations indicates that foreign exporting firms used a much more labor-intensive technology than those supplying the domestic market. Thus, market orientation is a crucial factor in determining the "appropriate" technology used by foreign firms, and the orientation of foreign firms helped improve resource-allocation efficiency in Taiwan in the 1960s and 1970s. The export-marketing assistance provided by foreign parent firms to their local subsidiaries also had an important role to play in this regard.

Taiwan's outward investment has grown substantially since the 1970s, and the official statistics show only the tip of the iceberg. The main competitive advantages of Taiwanese MNCs are their small-scale production techniques and their superior marketing and technological skills, which allow them to introduce and develop products which are welcome in the host markets. Because the technology brought in by Taiwanese MNCs is not as capital intensive as that used by MNCs from DCs, it is better suited to the basic conditions and comparative advantages of the host countries.

In spite of the complexities and difficulties involved in analyzing DFI's functions in a country's development, the above findings suggest that Taiwan has used DFI successfully for promoting its growth and development. In certain specific areas, Taiwan's experience provides several lessons. First, among these factors facilitating the inflow and effective utilization of capital, a positive attitude and favorable policies toward DFI are probably the most important. Second, foreign firms' market orientation is the most important factor in determining the "appropriate" technology used. Third, the importation of used machinery by foreign investors has posed no problem at all for the users or the economy.

Looking toward the future, capital inflows into and outflows from Taiwan are expected to increase for the following reasons. First, the country's domestic market will expand as a result of economic growth in general and a more liberal policy toward DFI. Second, Taiwan is currently undergoing an industrial restructuring as a result of a rising domestic wage level and the spread of international protectionism. The development of high-tech industries and the revitalization of existing industries are vital to continued economic growth, as is high-tech oriented DFI in both directions. Finally, as it moves toward a more advanced industrial structure, Taiwan will have to abandon those of its traditional industries which are losing comparative advantage. That is, Taiwan will become more active in searching for investment opportunities in other countries and even in mainland China.

Notes

1. In 1939, for instance, the Japanese owned 18.4 percent of all companies with more than five employees, and in 1941 they controlled 91 percent of all paid-up capital in private business. The colonial government also raised funds from Japan and the New York stock market to finance its public investment projects (Chang, 1980).

2. They are: Regulations for the Encouragement of Investment in Productive Enterprises by Overseas Chinese and Chinese Residents in Hong Kong and Macao; and Regulations Governing the Importation of Commodities with Self-Provided Exchange by Overseas Chinese for the Purpose of Making Investments in Productive Enterprises.

3. Toyota's initial investment had anticipated a plant assembling 200,000 cars per year in 1983 and a total capital of $500 million. The project was dropped because of disputes over export requirements. A much smaller proposal was submitted two years later, this time with a total capital commitment of $6.3 million.

4. Indirect exports are products sold to local downstream producers which end up as reexports. The ratio of indirect exports to total sales varied from 16.8% in 1966 to 9.2% in 1985. (See *An Analysis of Operations and Economic Effects of Foreign Enterprises*, Taipei: Investment Commission, 1987.)

5. Primary data from the 1975 survey of foreign enterprises, Investment Commission, Ministry of Economic Affairs.

6. Including the trust fund of $246 million established in 1986.

References

Caves, R. E. (1971), "International Corporations: The Industrial Economics of Foreign Investment," *Economica* 149 (Feb.): 1–27.

—— (1974), "Industrial Organization," in *Economic Analysis and the Multinational Enterprise*, ed. J. H. Dunning (London: George Allen & Unwin).

Chang, C. H. (1980), *Industrialization in Taiwan During the Colonial Period* (Taipei: United Economic) (in Chinese).

Chen, E. K. Y. (1983), *Multinational Corporations, Technology, and Employment* (London: Macmillan).

Hymer, S. (1976), *The International Operation of Nation Firms: A Study of Direct Foreign Investment* (Cambridge, Mass.: MIT Press).

James, D. D. (1974), *Used Machinery and Economic Development* (Michigan: Michigan State University, International Business and Economic Studies).

Jacoby, N. H. (1966), *U.S. Aid to Taiwan: A Study of Foreign Aid, Self-Help, and Development* (N.Y.: Praeger).

Koh, K. H. (1973), *Factors Influencing U.S. International Firms in Locating Export Oriented Manufacturing Facilities in Singapore, Taiwan and Hong Kong* (Unpublished dissertation, Indiana University).

Lall, S. (1978), "Transnationals, Domestic Enterprises, and Industrial Structure in Host LDCs: A Survey," *Oxford Economic Papers* 30 (July): 217–48.

—— (1982), *Developing Countries as Exporters of Technology* (London: Macmillan).

Lecraw, D. J. (1981), "Internationalization of Firms from LDCs: Evidence from the ASEAN Region," in *Multinationals from Developing Countries*, ed. K. Kumar and M. G. McLeod (Lexington, Mass.: Lexington Books): 37–52.

Marsden, K. (1970), "Progressive Technologies for Developing Countries," *International Labor Review* 101 (May): 475–502.

Ranis, G. and C. Schive (1985), "Direct Foreign Investment in Taiwan's Development," *Foreign Trade and Investment*, ed., W. Galenson (Madison, Wisconsin: University of Wisconsin Press).

Rhee, Y. W. and L. E. Westphal (1978), "A Note on Exports of Technology from the Republic of China and Korea," *World Bank*, mimeo paper.

San Gee (1988), "Direct Foreign Investment and Technology Transfer in Seoul, the ROK, *1988 Conference on the Industrial Policies of ROC and ROK* (KDI).

Denis Simon and Chi Schive, (1985), "The Development of the Informatics Industry in Taiwan: the Role of Government in High-Tech Industry," *Economic Essays* 13, P. 153–80; also in *National Policy for Developing High Technology Industry*, ed., Francis W. Rushing and Carole Ctanz Brown (Boulder: Westview, 1986): pp. 201–226.

Schive, C. "Direct Foreign Investment and Transfer of Technology: Theories and Taiwan's Evidence," *Proceedings of the National Science Council* 3, No. 4:455–8.

—— (1982), *A Report on Private Outward Investment* (Investment Commission, MOEA) (in Chinese).

—— (1987), "Trade Patterns and Trends of Taiwan," *Trade and Structural Changes in Pacific Asia* (Chicago: University of Chicago Press, NBER series).

—— (forthcoming), "The Next Stage of Industrialization in Taiwan & Korea," in *Development Strategies in Latin American and East Asian Countries*, ed. G. Gereffi and D. Wyman (Princeton: University of Princeton Press).

—— and K. T. Hsueh (1987), "The Experience and Prospects of High-Tech Industrial Development in Taiwan, R.O.C.—The Case of the Information Industry," *1987 Joint Conference on the Industrial Policies of the Republic of China and the Republic of Korea* (Taipei: Chung-Hua Institution for Economic Research).

Schumacher, E. F. (1973), *Small is Beautiful: A Study of Economics as if People Mattered* (London: Blond & Briggs).

Schreiber, J. G. (1970), *U.S. Corporate Investment in Taiwan* (Cambridge, Mass.: Harvard University Press).

Strassman, W. P. (1968), *Technological Change and Economic Development: The Manufacturing Experience of Mexico and Puerto Rico* (Ithaca: Cornell University Press).

Ting, W. L. and C. Schive (1981), "Direct Investment and Technology Transfer from Taiwan," in *Multinationals from Developing Countries*, ed. K. Kumar and M. G. McLeod (Lexington, Mass.: Lexington Books): 101–14.

Well, L. T., Jr. (1983), *Third World Multinationals* (Cambridge, Mass.: MIT Press).

Appendix Table 1 Approved and arrived DFI, US $ million, 1952–86

Year	Inward DFI			Outward DFI
	Approved amount	Arrived amount	Repatriated amount	Remitted amount
1952–60	35.65[1]	41.47(116.32)[2]	–	–
1961–70	523.58	241.59(46.14)	–	4.05
1971–80	2,159.17	940.05(43.54)	182.40(19.40)[3]	69.42
1981	395.76	156.50(39.54)	21.01(13.42)	58.08
1982	380.01	149.18(39.26)	50.43(33.80)	21.84
1983	404.47	175.40(43.36)	39.33(22.42)	16.49
1984	558.74	231.59(41.45)	80.99(34.97)	70.32
1985	702.46	343.68(48.93)	55.73(16.22)	82.65
1986	770.38	350.22(49.64)	69.22(19.76)	68.50

Notes: 1. Arived DFI before 1958 included imports financed with foreign exchange provided by overseas Chinese investors.
2. Percentages of approved amount.
3. Percentages of arrived amount.

Source: Investment Commission, Ministry of Economic Affairs, *Statistics of Approved Overseas Chinese and Foreign Investment, Republic of China*, various issues.

PART FOUR: Policies Towards Transnational Corporations

The previous parts have shown that TNCs have a broad range of effects on developing economies, and it is not easy to draw up a simple, consistent set of policy measures for host governments. Paul Streeten's chapter is a typically clear, penetrating and challenging analysis of the problems facing policy makers in that field. He notes the various contributions that TNCs may make to host countries, but concludes that "far from being able to quantify precisely these effects, we do not even know, in general, their direction" (p. 351). The problems of specifying counterfactuals are described, and traditional approaches to measuring welfare effects evaluated. Streeten goes on to analyse the problems of bargaining with TNCs, an analysis that still offers many valuable insights, some two decades after it was written. The peculiarities of the international technology market and the contribution of TNCs to regional integration are the subjects of the final parts of that chapter.

Lecraw provides an empirical examination of the bargaining process between TNCs and developing host countries. He analyses the sources of bargaining power of a TNC, focusing on the level of equity participation in, and control over, the subsidiary as the critical variables to be studied. A careful examination of evidence collected from 153 subsidiaries (largely domestic-market oriented) suggests that the percentage of equity ownership and effective control over the subsidiary are not closely related, but seemed to be J-shaped, with high and low levels of control associated with high levels of success (as viewed by the TNCs). The percentage of equity participation is strongly influenced by bargaining between TNCs and host governments, but clearly there are limits to the extent to which TNCs can be pushed. The availability of non-equity means of control, on the other hand, reduces the value of equity ownership *per se* to the TNC. Those findings have useful implications for policy formulation.

The chapter by Stephen Guisinger analyses the vexed question of incentives to attract TNCs. He starts with the definition of incentives, and finds that there are six different aspects of incentives that influence the investment decision. His definition is much broader than the conventional one of tax holidays and other such direct fiscal policies: he includes protection, price controls, performance requirements, labour legislation, credit provision and so on, as incentives that affect the firm's bottom line in decision making. In that broad sense, incentives do affect a TNC's investment decisions, particularly the levels of effective protection provided to the affiliate. However, developing countries often compete among themselves by offering incentives, cancelling out the total benefits expected from raising incentive levels. The many attempts that have been made to curtail incentive wars have not been successful because of the existence of the prisoner's dilemma: it always pays an individual country to break the agreement in order to attract more investment at the cost of its partners.

That paper provides a useful comprehensive framework for governments of the developing countries to rationalize the battery of policy instruments at their disposal in dealing with TNCs. The process of negotiation usually tends to be ad hoc and haphazard, and a clearly set-out approach of that type could yield significant benefits, especially by forcing host governments to look beyond direct fiscal measures to attract foreign investors.

14

The Multinational Enterprise and The Theory of Development Policy[1]*

Paul Streeten

*Source: J.H. Dunning, ed., *Economic Analysis and Multinational Enterprise* (London, Allen and Unwin, 1974), pp. 252–279.

Introduction

In the early phase of the theory of development policy in the Fifties it was capital that was stressed as the strategic factor in development. Foreign investment by the multinational enterprise (MNE) was therefore regarded mainly as a source of foreign funds which supplemented domestic savings efforts. Nurkse's thesis that countries are poor because they are poor and needed large injections of foreign capital became widely accepted.[2] According to this view, a poor country could not raise its low ratio of savings to national income very quickly or very easily. A low savings and investment rate led to a low rate of capital accumulation. This, in turn, implied that workers were endowed with relatively little capital: this kept their productivity low. Low productivity per worker perpetuated low income per head. The low investment ratio was both cause and effect of poverty. In order to break out of this vicious circle of poverty, massive injections of capital from abroad would be necessary. Foreign investment could contribute to pulling poor countries out of this low equilibrium trap.

The experience of the last 20 years has shown that capital was considerably less scarce, and that capital/output ratios were lower, than this doctrine has postulated. Capital was more abundant, partly because more foreign aid and private foreign capital were available, and partly because, in spite of their low incomes, many countries achieved quite high domestic savings ratios. During the Sixties, the share of gross investment in the GNP of developing countries was nearly 20 per cent and the share of savings in GNP over 15 per cent, substantially higher than either the early writers had anticipated or countries industrialising earlier had achieved at a corresponding stage. Rostow had reasoned that the ratio of investment to income would have to rise from 5 to 10 per cent in order to achieve 'take-off'. England had a savings ratio of only 5 per cent in the eighteenth century, during her industrial revolution, and achieved 10 per cent not until the 1840s.[3] It is, of course, true that the savings ratio of 16.6 per cent in 1970 for all developing countries is lower than the 22.9 per cent achieved by the industrialised countries in the same year. But by historical standards domestic savings ratios were unprecedently high and by the standards of the early writers they were unexpectedly high. In addition, there is now much evidence that the capital in existence was underutilised. The under-utilisation of labour had, of course, been a common theme from the beginning of the study of development policy, but the emphasis on capital underutilisation, often substantially greater than in developed countries, is relatively recent.[4]

The absence of a severe bottleneck in capital was confirmed by certain *a priori* considerations. It was found that there was no reason why the savings ratio out of low incomes should be smaller than that out of high incomes. It was also argued that savings and capital are not so much a factor of production with which countries are 'endowed' and which causes development to proceed, as the *result* of the adoption of new technologies and of development. The identification of investment opportunities tends to generate the necessary savings.

High growth rates were associated with relatively high savings ratios and low capital/output ratios. Capital/output ratios were low, partly because the adoption of existing Western techniques of production economised in the use of capital to invent new techniques, thus avoiding the waste of trials and errors, partly because some countries spent relatively little on capital-intensive overhead facilities, and partly because in countries where land was abundant a high rate of growth of the labour force yielded considerable extra agricultural output with relatively little extra capital, even if non-monetary investment, such as land-clearing, is properly accounted for. For these reasons capital turned out to be not such a severe constraint as had been thought.[5]

Another strand of thinking stressed the contribution that foreign capital could make to scarce foreign exchange. Foreign exchange scarcity was derived from the trade pessimism that prevailed in the Fifties and from doctrines of structural imbalance. While foreign exchange clearly was a serious bottleneck in the progress of many countries, others achieved remarkably high growth rates of exports in the Sixties.

The contribution of private overseas investment tended to be seen in the framework of a Harrod–Domar model, linking growth rates with either savings or foreign exchange receipts. But it soon became evident that many activities of the MNE brought with them relatively little capital or foreign exchange, but a good many other things instead.[6] Direct foreign investment in developing countries, including reinvested earnings, rose to $4000 m annually at the end of the Sixties, compared with total capital formation in the developing countries of about $40000 m and the total external flow of financial resources of nearly $16000 m.

Later writers stressed training and the transfer and local creation of skills (investment in human capital), management, entrepreneurship (i.e. innovative rather than administrative management), science and technology, and research and development (R & D). As it became increasingly clear that development involves also social, cultural and political change, interacting in a complex manner with economic factors, and as the definition and objectives of development shifted from accelerated aggregate economic growth to social objectives such as equality and, above all, jobs, livelihoods and generally meeting the needs of the masses of poor people, the contribution of the MNE came to be judged by its effects upon these objectives rather than by the contribution of savings or foreign exchange to economic growth.

The relation between the MNE and these social objectives will, to a large extent, depend upon the ability and willingness of the host government to pursue the 'right' policies. A view focusing only on the contribution of the MNE to resources generally available for development is justified if the government pursues appropriate policies with respect to distribution and employment, through science policy, land reform, foreign exchange rates, etc. If, on the other hand, such policies are absent or defective, the MNE may be judged by its impact on variables normally regarded as proper direct objectives of government policies.

Thus, with an efficient fiscal system and an honest administrative service, the MNE can be encouraged to pursue efficiency and high profits. Through tax collection, these profits will then make a contribution to the attainment of the social objectives. But if the fiscal and administrative system is defective, the direct contribution of the MNE towards the social objectives will have to be taken into account. Efficiency and profit criteria will then have to be supplemented by criteria of social justice, regional development, employment creation, environmental protection, etc.

The change in thinking reflected earlier changes in the nature of private overseas investment. The most important of these is the shift from nineteenth century portfolio to direct foreign investment, often accompanied by the MNE's efforts to raise capital locally. There was also the growing importance of new technologies, some of them embodied in capital equipment, others independent of specific pieces of equipment but related to organisation, marketing and the commercial use of scientific knowledge. The growing size of the multinational firm and the tendency to horizontal, vertical and, much more rarely, lateral integration of the operations of the firm meant that monopoly or oligopoly power played an increasing role. The shift of analytical emphasis from capital goods and financial flows to technology, advertising and bargaining reflects these changes in the system of international production.

The Operations of the MNE and their Implications for Policy Objectives

The difference between targets, needs or requirements and domestically mobilisable resources has been identified or measured by a variety of 'gaps'—gaps in savings, foreign exchange, skills. While such aggregation has serious weaknesses and has recently been replaced by much greater emphasis on detailed project by project appraisal, it can serve as a very rough first approximation. The impact of MNEs on national development policies can then be listed under their contribution to filling these various gaps and by their effects on other variables relevant to the development objectives.

(1) The contribution to filling the resource gap between desired investment and locally mobilised savings.
(2) The contribution to filling the foreign exchange or trade gap between foreign exchange requirements and foreign exchange earnings plus official net aid. While this gap is *ex post* always identical with the savings gap, requirements or targets for foreign exchange are not identical with those for savings if there is a structural balance of payments problem.
(3) The contribution to filling the budgetary gap between target revenue and locally raised taxes.
(4) The contribution to filling the management and skill gap by providing foreign management and training local managers and workers.

The analytical value of looking at the contribution in terms of one or more of these gaps is that the value to the economy may exceed the value accruing from a particular project. Gap analysis brings out the multiplier effect of the foreign contribution. If domestic resources are underutilised because some crucial component is missing (e.g. foreign exchange or a particular kind of skill), the breaking of this bottleneck has a magnifying effect upon resource mobilisation in the rest of the economy. Unless such externalities are properly allowed for in project appraisal, they will get left out.

In addition, the contribution of the MNE may be judged by the following criteria.

(5) Technology is very poorly developed in many developing countries. The MNE may either transfer foreign and often inappropriate technology or, by adaptation or new invention, generate a more appropriate technology. It is in the market for knowledge that some of the most interesting problems arise.
(6) Entrepreneurship is something different from a skill that can be taught and learned. The MNE may contribute to the growth of indigenous entrepreneurs by subcontracting to ancillary industries, repair shops,

component makers, etc. It may be in its interest to stimulate such growth among its suppliers or buyers or those performing intermediate tasks between inputs and outputs of the firm.

(7) The MNE may, through its own actions, shift the balance of bargaining power in negotiating and renegotiating contracts. Most obviously, the balance of power will be quite different at the time before an investment is made and after money has been sunk. Less obviously, negotiation will itself improve the skills in negotiation and will contribute to the stock of useful knowledge for later negotiations.

(8) An important contribution often quoted is the ability of the MNE to establish contact with overseas banks, market outlets, sources of supply and other institutions, which would otherwise remain unknown to the indigenous firms.

Finally, there are the contributions to macroeconomic policy objectives. Among these the following may be singled out.

(9) The MNE may make a contribution to creating jobs and thereby raising employment.

(10) It may improve a country's income terms of trade either by lowering costs more than export prices or by reducing dependence on foreign products.

(11) It may contribute to a more efficient market structure or reduce the type of monopoly profits that are enjoyed in the form of inefficiency and a 'quiet life'.

A major difficulty in assessing these contributions is that far from being able to quantify precisely these effects, we do not even know, in general, their direction. MNEs provide capital, but also may reduce domestic savings (e.g. if saving is limited by investment opportunities and these themselves are limited, or foreign investment leads to a shift to wages with a lower savings propensity) and impose capital servicing costs upon the host country. They may improve its foreign exchange position but equally may reduce foreign exchange earnings and may impose a primary and secondary foreign exchange burden, depending on the relation between retained profits and new investment on the one hand and remittances on the other.[7] They may contribute to public revenue, but frequently tax concessions, investment grants, the provision of factory sites and tariff policy erode this contribution. They may transfer and adapt technology, but it may be inappropriate for the available factors or social and physical conditions of the country, not just in some abstract, irrelevant sense but inappropriate in relation to the cost that the country has to pay for it. They may provide foreign management and train local managers, but, like engineering technology, the management techniques may be inappropriate, because they economise in the use of uneducated, diseased, ill-nourished and undisciplined labour, the employment of which would yield social but not equivalent private benefits. They may encourage local entrepreneurs, but again they may stifle the growth of indigenous entrepreneurship in weak and rudimentary markets. They may provide training in the skills of negotiation by producing managers and officials who put their experience to work in negotiating for their countries, but they may also reinforce the uneven initial balance of power.

They open up a society to world influences and thereby enable it to draw on resources and skills on a world-wide scale, but they also destroy local activities by exposing them to these influences. They may reduce unemployment or they may raise it by increasing wage costs and destroying traditional crafts. They may improve or worsen the terms of trade according to the direction of their activities and their foreign trade bias. They may make local industry more competitive or more monopolistic. Politically, they may introduce benefits by wider contacts, but may also create unrest and, by buying up politicians and officials who should be controlling them, spread corruption. Socially and culturally, they may increase inequalities between income groups, sectors and regions, may Westernise attitudes, on the one hand imposing a sophisticated, high income, consumption pattern, on the other, possibly leading to high turnover, low-mark-up methods of business. They often use capital-intensive techniques to produce capital-intensive products for a small, relatively well-off élite, including the aristocracy of workers fortunate enough to hold jobs. On the other hand, they may identify processes or components in a set of vertically integrated operations which are labour-intensive and locate these in low-income countries, exporting the semi-finished products and then reimporting them to the parent country. They may bring traditional societies into the twentieth century or they may reduce them to 'dependence', imposing technical, managerial and cultural subservience on the host country.

Another theoretical difficulty in analysing the contribution to development of the MNE is the problem of attribution. The MNE may, in particular circumstances, do things that (*a*) are not essential attributes of the MNE but might be peculiar to particular individuals responsible for its affairs, or to the policies of host governments,[8] or to a specific locality or to history; or (*b*) could have been done equally well or better in other ways than through the MNE. Ideally one would wish to identify those features that are peculiar to *all* (or a group of) MNEs and *only* to MNEs.

Amongst the most common charges raised by developing host countries against the MNE are the following. Some of them raise the problem of attribution, especially to government policy. Some of them were mentioned as the reverse side of the positive effects but it is worth bringing them together.

(i) Its impact on development is very uneven and it therefore creates or reinforces dualism and inequality. This inequality may apply to income by size (employed workers *versus* the rest), by sector (manufacturing, mining, plantation *versus* food for domestic consumption) and by region (urban, industrial *versus* rural).

(ii) It introduces inappropriate products, which are normally closely linked to the technology and inappropriate consumption patterns. This point is related to the previous one, for inequality of income distribution gives rise to a fragmented consumption pattern and to a small market for sophisticated consumer goods.[9] These are the goods produced by the sophisticated technology in the rich industrial countries for their high-income markets, in which the monopolistic advantage of the MNE lies.

(iii) A consequence of the previous two points is that the *local* investment funds on which the MNE draws and which have an opportunity cost are wrongly allocated and not in accordance with the social priorities of the country.

(iv) The MNE is also charged with influencing government policy in directions unfavourable to development. It may secure excessive protection, tax concessions, subsidies to inputs or provision of factory sites or other services of infrastructure. As a result substantial private profits may be consistent with low or negative social returns.

(v) It is said to stifle private enterprise, because its superior know-how and management prevent indigenous entrepreneurs from initiating enterprises.

(vi) Finally it is accused of causing political friction by the suspicion that foreign interests control assets and jobs.

The above approach of listing under various headings the merits and drawbacks of the MNE (which might be described as the laundry list approach) is common but unsatisfactory. What would be more satisfactory is an analytical framework in which these various possibilities are accommodated, possibly classified according to relevant criteria, and then filled with empirical, quantitative content.

In the first place, one would seek criteria by which the importance of the different headings can be distinguished. These might be found in the nature of the MNE's operations: are they conducting vertically integrated activities, beginning with extraction and ending with the final processed product? Or are they market-orientated manufacturing subsidiaries drawing on the brand name or the research of the parent company? Distinctions by type of product or by type of process may be useful here.

Next, it is important to identify the cause leading to the various possible outcomes: are they government policies and, if so, are these themselves autonomous or exogenous variables or are they the result of the firms' pressure, persuasion or bribery? Are they the result of the transfer of existing but inappropriate technologies? Are they the result of the use of bargaining power by large, well-informed companies confronting small, weak, ignorant, fragmented and competing governments?

Research on the MNE

Much of the research on the MNE has been in the neo-classical tradition. Sir Donald MacDougall analysed foreign investment as a flow of additional capital into a country, while everything else is held constant. The static effects of marginal investments can be analysed according to marginal productivity theory.[10] This approach can then be enlarged by gradually relaxing the restrictive assumptions and tracing the implications of increasing returns, indivisibilities, imperfect competition, learning by doing, etc. Much of this was done by Sir Donald MacDougall. It is also possible to assume that the foreign firms shift or twist the production function in various ways with varying results on marginal returns, intra-marginal returns and the distribution of profits between domestic and foreign capitalists and workers. As restrictive assumptions are relaxed, the range of possible conclusions is enlarged and it is then quite possible to construct cases where the introduction or enlargement of privately profitable foreign investment detracts from the host country's real income. MacDougall concluded that the most important direct gains from more rather than less foreign private investment 'seem likely to come through higher tax revenue from foreign profits (at least if the higher investment is not induced by lower tax rates), through economies of scale and through external economies generally, especially where ... firms acquire "know-how" or are forced by foreign competition to adopt more efficient methods'.[11]

Some of the limitations of this approach were pointed out by Balogh and Streeten,[12] although not with specific reference to developing countries. MacDougall himself had reasoned that the host country might lose if the foreign investment used strongly labour-saving techniques or if the foreign firms used their monopoly power to exploit local buyers.[13] These objections were elaborated by subsequent writers.

Most of the writings on the MNE had, of course, to abandon the assumption of perfect competition on which much of MacDougall's analysis was based. Kindleberger, Caves and Díaz-Alejandro[14] specifically build their analysis on the assumptions of imperfect competition, oligopoly with interdependence recognised or monopoly power.

Even in the case of developed countries, where markets are less imperfect, the widely observed fact of two-way investment in the same industry is inconsistent with the assumption of perfect competition. In developing countries competition is notoriously imperfect or absent in sectors and industries in which the MNE operates.

Awareness that oligopoly is in the nature of the MNE has led to an approach that has combined the theory of industrial organisation as applied to the relations between oligopolies and the theory of international trade and investment.[15] This approach identifies a special advantage of the firm (e.g. superior knowledge or goodwill acquired by the use of a brand name) that enables it to produce abroad in spite of the inferiority of local knowledge and connections, combined with an advantage in producing near the place of sales or the source of supply. In this way the superiority of producing abroad over exporting from a home base or licensing the right to make use of the special advantage, are explained. Tariffs and other protectionist devices, often cited as the main cause of the establishment of local subsidiaries, will tend to raise profits of the subsidiary but are neither a necessary nor a sufficient condition; not necessary, because even without protection the special advantage may be exploited; not sufficient, because where the special advantage is absent, no amount of protection will lead to the establishment of a subsidiary.[16] The proprietary knowledge or the goodwill possessed by the firm is an indivisibility, so that its use abroad involves low costs to the firm, and it tries, through patents or advertising, to prevent others from appropriating this advantage. The local knowledge acquired in the process, also, is indivisible and this will tend to make for a few large firms carrying out investment and setting up an oligopolistic structure.

A related approach, without, however, the rigorous framework of a theory, has become known as the doctrine of the product cycle. This doctrine[17] has emphasised *monopolistic* elements in investment, *technological innovation* with special rights in new discoveries and *uncertainty* about costs, demand and rival behaviour. The new theory (or 'model' or 'concept' or 'hypothesis', as Raymond Vernon prefers to call it) also emphasises the need for experiment and reconnaissance, the economies of scale to be reaped from research, marketing and management and the ability to routinise novel processes after a time. It is essentially a model of a succession of temporary monopolistic advantages, which are gradually eroded through diffusion and imitation. It is a model of a know-how treadmill.

According to this model, new products are first introduced by large firms with extensive research programmes in their established, wealthy domestic markets. Consumers' tastes are better known there, incomes are high and demand for the new product is price inelastic. If the product proves successful, output expands, costs per unit fall and the firm begins to export. In markets where exports are successful, they are backed at first by small foreign investments aimed at marketing and servicing the product. These are followed by assembly and local purchase of some components. If conditions are favourable or if exports are threatened by rivals, more processes are located abroad and foreign subsidiaries are established to make use of lower labour costs and proximity to the market. Ultimately, the product may be exported from the foreign subsidiary to the parent home market or to other markets abroad. This particular product cycle is closed, though new ones will meanwhile have started. On this view, exports serve as a feeler, a form of reconnaissance. They establish whether a market exists and whether it should be backed by investment. Diffusion may, however, take other forms than foreign investment. There may be licensing or imitation.

The model of the product cycle does not, however, account fully for a recent trend in foreign investment to which attention has now turned, viz. the location of low-income countries of low-skill, labour-intensive processes or the production of assembly of components or spare parts in a vertically integrated multinational firm. Above all, in electronics and electrical components, but also in the making of gloves, leather goods, luggage, baseballs, watches, motor car parts and other consumer goods, and in electrical machinery, machine tools, accounting machines, typewriters, cameras, etc., processes that require much labour and limited capital and skills (sewing, boring holes, assembling) have been located in South Korea, Taiwan, Mexico, Hong Kong, Singapore and the West Indian islands.[18]

In one sense, the doctrine of comparative advantage seems to be vindicated, though in a manner quite different from that normally envisaged. It is foreign, not domestic, capital, know-how and management that are highly mobile internationally and that are combined with plentiful, immobile, domestic semi-skilled labour. Specialisation between countries is not by commodities according to relative factor endowments, but by factors of production: the poor countries specialising in low-skilled labour, leaving the rewards for capital, management and know-how to the foreign owners of these scarce but internationally mobile factors. The situation is equivalent to one in which *labour itself* rather than the *product of labour* is exported. For the surplus of the product of labour over the wage, resulting from the co-operation of other factors in less elastic supply, accrues abroad. The differential international and internal elasticities of supply in response to differential rewards, and the differences in monopoly rents entering the rewards of these factors have important implications for the international distributions of gains from investment and trade.

Since the firms operate in oligopolistic and oligopsonistic markets, cost advantages are not necessarily passed on to consumers in lower prices or to workers in higher wages, and the profits then accrue to the parent firms. The continued operation of this type of international specialisation depends upon the continuation of substantial wage differentials (hence there must be weakness of trade union action to push up wages), continuing access to the markets of the parent companies (hence stronger pressure from importing interests than from domestic producers displaced by the low cost processes and components, including trade unions in the rich importing countries) and continuing permission or encouragement by host countries to operate with minimum taxes, tariffs and bureaucratic regulations.

The packaged nature of the contribution of the MNE, usually claimed as its characteristic blessing, is in this context the cause of the unequal international distribution of the gains from trade and investment. If the package broke or leaked, some of the rents and monopoly rewards would spill over into the host country. But if it is secured tightly, only the least scarce and weakest factor in the host country derives an income from the operations of the MNE, unless bargaining power is used to extract a share of these other incomes.[19]

The situation is aggravated if there is technical progress, so that the labour-intensive activity in the underdeveloped host country might be knocked out by an innovation using capital or technology in the parent country. Other processes or components will still be left to which the labour force could be switched. But such switching has its costs. Skills acquired are wasted and the bargaining power of the host country and its labour force is further reduced, unless retraining is short and its costs are carried by the MNE.

The bargaining power of host countries and of the plentiful factor—semi-skilled labour—in such a situation is likely to be weak and the question is whether such a division of gains between parent and host, between the foreign investment 'package' and domestic labour, remains acceptable. The gains to the host country are confined to the wages of those employed if the alternative is unemployment. The fact that these earnings are in foreign exchange may put them at a premium. There may, in addition, be linkages, but these may be positive or negative. While such investment has attractions for some countries faced with labour surpluses and foreign exchange shortages and poorly endowed with natural resources, the potential gains may not be considered worth the social risks and social costs, including a form of dependence and dualistic development of a new kind, different from that of the colonial mines or plantations economy, but similar in its distributional impact.

Transfer Pricing

One important reason why the MNE does not fit easily into the theory of comparative advantage and its normative conclusions is the phenomenon of transfer pricing. A large and growing volume of international trade today is conducted within the firm—between affiliates, subsidiaries, branches located in different countries—and not between independent firms. It has been estimated that one quarter to one third of world trade in manufactures (and possibly more) is intra-firm trade and therefore not at arm's-length. This proportion is likely to be even larger for LDCs. This fact has very important implications of which existing trade and investment theory has hardly begun to take note.

The reason why intra-firm trade raises entirely different issues from inter-firm trade is that the items entering such trade will be valued according to other considerations than those determining competitive market prices. The chief considerations relevant to the pricing of intra-firm transactions will be taxation (including allowances and loss offset provisions), tariffs, exchange rates (expected changes, multiple rates, restrictions on remissions), political and social pressures (trade unions, fear of potential competitors) and joint ventures with local share holders.[20] The phenomenon goes much deeper than 'fiddling' prices to evade tax payments. The allocation of the large overhead and joint costs, that give the MNE its special advantage, between firms, products and components is bound to be arbitrary within wide limits and a policy of maximising global post-tax profits from the world-wide system of operations of the firm will greatly reduce the significance of declared prices, capital values and rates of return for purposes of national policy.

It may, of course, remain true that the actual quantities traded will obey the principle of comparative advantage. Firms will presumably be guided by money costs and, to the extent that these reflect comparative costs, the principle will remain applicable. Those looking for the appropriate competitive prices would find them in the hypothetical or real second set of books kept by the companies for their accounting purposes. Indeed, the theory of transfer pricing presupposes that the firm has some idea of what it would charge in a competitive market. Other forces, such as oligopolistic market structures, bilateral monopoly and subjective risk premia will, of course, qualify or suspend the application of the doctrine of comparative advantage, but the transfer pricing mechanism by itself need not interfere with it as far as quantities traded are concerned.

But this is of little use to ignorant and weak host governments, concerned with framing policies with respect to taxation, tariffs, foreign exchange rates, foreign exchange restrictions and local participation in shareholding. Neither existing theory nor practice are equipped to deal with this new phenomenon and it presents an important agenda for future research.[21]

The implications for the theory of economic policy will become clearer only after considerably more work has been done on the range, scope and limits of transfer pricing. But it is plain that these are important implications for tax policy, tariff policy and setting other incentives for MNEs. The incentive and opportunity to overprice inputs in order to reduce declared profits can be mitigated or reversed by a state trading corporation trading in all imports or by local participation and control (though participation without control based on full information creates an incentive to over-invoice). These corrective measures, however, may create new difficulties.

Ultimately, the only proper response to an organisation that takes a global view will be global control. Thus, if companies had to be incorporated internationally and pay uniform internationally determined tax rates, one important incentive for transfer pricing would be removed. But until such de-nationalisation and internationalisation, national governments will have to find ways of counteracting some of the potential damage done to them by transfer pricing.

Problems of Bargaining

The oligopolistic structure and certain other features peculiar to the market for advanced technology limit the use of analysis in terms of smooth and continuous marginal productivity and demand functions and of project evaluation by means of shadow prices. The location of subsidiaries in developing countries normally draws on the R & D expenditure of the parent firm and on its technical know-how generally, or on exploration costs or on heavy advertising expenditure or on other overhead or joint costs. These expenditures precede and do not enter into the operating costs of the enterprises but they bestow a 'special advantage' on the enterprise. (Whether the advantage is real, because based on scientific knowledge, or imagined and 'artificial', because based on the exploitation of created fears and wants, is not relevant here, except in so far as the 'advantage' cannot be used to justify the activity.) The 'special advantage' of the MNE is an indivisibility of this type. Since the activities in low-income countries do not enter into the calculations when R & D expenditure (the Philips research centre near Eindhoven is an exception), exploration costs or administrative costs are decided upon at headquarters, the cost of using the results of these expenditures in LDCs is small, not only *ex post*, when only variable costs count, but also *ex ante* in relation to expected returns. In the extreme case, this cost is zero or even negative. Normally, there will be positive costs of administration and adaptation. There may also be opportunity costs of using the technology in low-income countries. Operations there may reduce profits on established lines in other countries. Asking for favourable terms by one country may also set a precedent for quotations in other countries, where the opportunity costs may be higher.

On the other hand, such opportunity costs may be negative. Operation by the subsidiary may raise profits, or may prevent a fall in profits, elsewhere. The possibility of such 'organic' interaction makes the bargaining process even more difficult for the host country, for it implies that entirely properly calculated local profits may be low, yet be of greater value to the company than is reflected in these profits, because of their contribution to the profits, or to the reduction of losses, of the whole system of the company's world-wide operations. The use of bargaining power in this situation would require knowledge of the world-wide operations, including the threats from competitors, not just of those in the country. So much for the cost to the MNE.

To the host country desiring to acquire the technology (or any other of the 'special advantages') on the other hand, the cost can be high. It is the cost of embarking itself on the research and independently evolving the know-how or of duplicating exploration. The existence of such large fixed and joint costs means that there is a large gap between the minimum 'returns' a MNE will accept and still find it worth while investing, and the maximum 'returns' the enterprise can enjoy and make it still worth while for the host to permit operations. In principle, it would be possible to determine this range for different acts of investment both by different firms and for different sizes of investment and different contracts of the same firm.

This large gap between marginal and average costs of the technology is only one of several factors making for monopoly power. Another arises from the fact that knowledge to buy knowledge is often the knowledge to be bought itself and from the fact that tie-in agreements make it possible to make the transfer of technical knowledge conditional on the purchase of certain pieces of equipment or other inputs. In these ways the MNE can extract a yield substantially above the marginal costs incurred by the transfer.[22] The only mitigating factor is the competition between several oligopolies in possession of competing know-how.

One source of monopoly power of the MNE therefore derives from the technological dependence of the developing host country. But there is a second quite distinct source, which also leads to a divergence between private profits and social benefits and establishes a range within which bargaining can take place. This source is the policy pursued by the government of the host country. Tariffs and non-tariff barriers on competing imports, taxes on the exports of necessary inputs, subsidies to inputs, overvaluation of exchange rates and tax concessions can lead to social losses. If imported inputs are overvalued, costs overstated and profits understated, an appearance of greater need for protection is created than is warranted.[23] While apparently no or low real profits are repatriated, repatriation takes place through transfer pricing or charges such as management fees, royalties or interest which accrue to the parent firm. The point is well made by Díaz-Alejandro: 'if foreign investors can borrow from host country's credit resources at interest rates which are often negative in real terms, make profits sheltered behind effective rates of protection which reach 100 per cent and above, benefit from holidays and exemptions from import duties on their raw materials, and remit profits abroad at overvalued exchange rates, there may be doubts as to the net benefits which the host country receives from such an activity.'[24]

It is often argued that governments have the remedy in their own hands. Let them reduce protection, liberalise trade, establish 'realistic' exchange rates, raise the price of capital, lower the cost of labour and thus align private costs to social costs. There is some evidence that, where the incentives are right (e.g. the relative price of capital is high), the MNE *does* adapt its techniques of production to local factor availabilities, using more capital-saving methods of production than domestic enterprises. But assuming the government believes that the investment is useful for the country, it is often the MNE that uses pressure on the government to introduce the 'distortions'. Ignorance about the value of the technology and the accounting methods induce the country to accept the terms of the MNE.

Policies themselves are influenced by the MNEs, both when negotiations are conducted about their establishment and, later, by their operations. The link between unequal distribution of income and wealth and the tendency of the MNE to cater for the needs of a relatively rich élite illustrates the point. While it is true that the MNE caters for the needs of an unequal income distribution, the profits and wages it generates reinforce this distribution. It is just as true to say that the income distribution elicits the product range and the processes employed by the MNE, as it is to say that the product range and the processes reinforce the income distribution.[25]

Similarly, protection is often treated as if it were autonomously determined by government policy. In fact, governments yield to the pressures of foreign companies documented by transfer prices. This is not to say that foreign companies welcome the complicated system of import controls, delays, red tape and corruption. But such a system is partly the result of the pressures of interest groups, including those of foreign companies.

The author has argued that continuous, smooth, marginal productivity curves are inappropriate in analysing the relations between host government and MNE. For the transfer of a certain 'package' of know-how, capital, management and inputs there is a range of values which would be acceptable to both sides but which both sides have an interest in concealing. The ability to conceal the relevant values is however much greater for the MNE than for the host country.

In settling the bargain and in drawing up the contract, a large number of items may be for negotiation, in addition to tax concessions and tariff and non-tariff protection of the product.[26] Among these are:

Specific allowances against tax liabilities, such as initial or investment allowance, depletion allowances, tax reporting techniques, loss offset provisions, etc.
Royalty payments, management fees and other fees.
Duty drawbacks on imported inputs for exports.

Content of local inputs.
Profit and capital repatriation.
Structure of ownership and degree and timing of local participation.
Local participation in management at board level.
Obligations to train local labour.
Transfer pricing.
Rules and requirements relating to exporting.
Degree of competition and forms of competition.
Credit policies (e.g. subsidised interest rates).
Extent of capitalisation of intangibles.
Revalorisation of assets due to currency devaluation.
Subsidies, e.g. to energy, rent, transport.
Place and party of jurisdiction and arbitration.
Time and right of termination or renegotiation.

A contract between the MNE and the host government will contain provisions under some of these headings.[27] Such possible contracts can be ranked in an order of preference by the MNE and by the government. If both the MNE and the government prefer a certain contract to another, the latter can be eliminated. The only complication here is that either party has an interest in concealing the fact that its interest coincides with that of the other party. For by appearing to make a concession, when in fact no concession is made, it may be spared having to make a concession on another front where interests conflict.

But leaving this complication aside, amongst the contracts that remain when those dominated by others have been eliminated, the order of preference for the MNE will be the reverse of that for the government. If the least attractive contract from the point of view of the MNE is outside the range of contracts acceptable to the government, no contract will be

Ranking of contracts in order of preference

MNE	Government
	F

MNE	Government	
A	C	↑
B	(E)	
C	(D)	Range of bargaining
(D)	B	
(E)	A	↓

(F)

E and D are ruled out because both the MNE and
the Government prefer C; F is ruled out because it
is unacceptable to the MNE.

concluded. But if there is some overlap, there is scope for bargaining. The precise contract on which the two partners will settle will be determined by relative bargaining strength.

At the same time, in determining the relative value of the different contracts, the host government will find cost-benefit analysis useful. By comparing the present value of the stream of benefits with that of the costs the disparate components in the bargain can, at least in principle, be made commensurable. Cost-benefit analysis and bargaining power analysis are not alternative methods of approach but are complementary. Cost-benefit analysis will not tell a government whether a particular project is acceptable or not, i.e. whether it falls within the bargaining range, but it will help it to rank those that are acceptable.

It has sometimes been argued that host countries are well advised to accept any project and contract that shows a rate of 'return'[28] to the foreign firm lower than the maximum that the country would find acceptable. (In terms of the table: the Government should accept A.) But this is clearly one-sided pleading. Vaitsos has compared this with advice given to workers to settle for a subsistence wage. It could equally well be said that the foreign company should be content with any 'returns' higher than the minimum acceptable to it (i.e. C).

A particular form *of this argument* is the often repeated attack on those who compare the inflow of new investment and retained profits with the profits remitted abroad and use the difference as an index of the gain to the host country. The attack usually takes the form that the effects of the foreign investment on real incomes in the economy and on exports and import substitution must be taken into account. The fault of this argument is that it neglects to compare the impact of the foreign investment with the best feasible alternative, such as domestic investment or borrowing and hiring the necessary factors. If the social opportunity costs of foreign investment were to include the benefits to be derived from the forgone next-best alternative, there would, for any specific project, be only one way of doing it that shows positive returns. The maximum returns forgone by choosing the foreign investment project must appear as a cost of this project. The appropriate shadow price is the benefit lost as a result of not adopting the best of the alternative projects rejected.

In cases where good, other-foreign, non-foreign or less-foreign feasible alternatives exist, the analysis should compare profit outflows with the opportunity cost of providing the same package from alternative sources. Only in cases where no alternative exists is the analysis that takes full credit for the foreign investment for all its indirect effects correct.[29]

The main forces determining where within this bargaining range a settlement is made are information, skill in negotiation and competition from other countries that have similar attractions for the MNE and from other firms wishing to enter. Information about some important aspects of cost and price determination is secret. Information about other aspects is hard to get. The market price of some imported component produced by the vertically integrated firm and not normally bought and sold is not easy to verify. As Vaitsos puts it, 'there is no price for Volkswagen doors'. Such transactions are essentially different from market transactions.

Another aspect of bargaining power arises from the threat that the firm will go to some other developing country if the terms of the contract are too hard. This raises the possibility of joint action by several LDCs, such as that displayed by OPEC. Such agreements suffer from the drawbacks of all cartel agreements: they face the Prisoner's Dilemma. The more successful the ring, the stronger the incentive for any member to break away and to underbid the ring. On the other hand, if others were to break away, the losses to those who adhere might be greater than if they had never joined an agreement. The situation is therefore highly unstable unless solidarity is strong or effective deterrents are applied. Cartel-like agreements on taxation also encourage the search for substitutes that reduce dependence on the host country.

There is almost universal evidence that foreign investors say that tax concessions and pioneer status play no or only an insignificant part in bringing them to the country.[30] This is entirely consistent with the rejection of a continuously downward-sloping marginal revenue function and the presence of a range of outcomes (a substantial element of rent or quasi-rent), all acceptable to the firm, which would induce the specific investment.

Since there are possibilities of trade-off between various items on the list on pp. 361–2, a proper evaluation would have to consider the whole set of conditions. Thus it might be possible to recoup some of the taxes lost by an understatement of profits resulting from transfer pricing by putting a tariff on intermediate inputs or capital goods. Or, for the firm, the removal of protection may be compensated by the provision of public services such as transport, power or training.

From the point of view of the host country, it is important to evolve a strategy that maximises the impact on domestic policy objectives subject to not deterring the company, assuming at least one contract has positive benefits. There may be a number of items on which negotiation will benefit both sides. There will be others, where changes in conditions will alter the types of MNEs attracted but not the total of foreign investment.

A specific choice arises as to whether to make *markets* more attractive by tariff and non-tariff barriers against competing products or whether to improve *resources* and *inputs* by providing better physical and social overhead facilities. The firms attracted will be those catering for import substitutes for the domestic market in the first case and those producing exports and re-exports in the second.

The second strategy of making resources and inputs more attractive implies:

(i) Fewer controls and greater administrative efficiency.
(ii) Greater security and less political uncertainty.
(iii) More investment in education, training, transport facilities and utilities.

Peculiarities in the Transfer of Technology

If, then, one of the specific contributions of the MNE is technical knowledge and if this knowledge bestows bargaining power, why has competition in the market not eroded this power? Why has the market system not provided incentives for the appropriate direction and utilisation of science and technology? Though underdeveloped countries are poor, they are potentially large and growing markets. Why have there been so few inventions of low-cost, simple, agricultural or industrial machinery? Why has there not been more progress in low-cost construction or transport? Why do those industrial countries that have a comparative advantage in manufacturing industry, protect, often at high cost to themselves, their agriculture, instead of exchanging low-cost machinery and durable consumer goods (say a £10 refrigerator) for the agricultural exports of underdeveloped countries? Henry Ford announced in 1909 that his aim was to produce and sell a cheap, reliable model 'for the great multitude' so that every man 'making a good salary' could 'enjoy with his family the blessing of hours of pleasure in God's great open space'. The mass production of the Model T Ford ushered in a major industrial and social revolution, the products of which have, incidentally, destroyed the 'great open space'. Why has no one initiated a corresponding revolution to raise and tap the purchasing power of the world's teeming millions? Insufficient foresight in the face of still small markets (small in terms of purchasing power) and overestimation of risks or a divergence between private (including political) and social risks may be part of explanation. Another part follows from the concept of the product cycle. The multinational enterprise is aware of its vulnerability. Concentration on sophisticated, high-income, high-technology products rather than simpler products is the result of wishing to maintain its monopoly advantages in technology. Simplicity is easier to imitate than complexity and the profits of the MNE derive from maintaining superiority in technology.

It is easier to see why the market in complex, specialised, often secret or patented, modern technology is different from the market for turnips or even for land. Technical and managerial knowledge and its commercial and industrial application cannot easily be assimilated to the treatment of the conventional factors of production: land, labour and capital, for at least five reasons.

In the first place, knowledge, although clearly not available in superabundance, is not scarce in the sense that the more it is used in one direction, the less is left over for use in another, or the more I use it, the less is left for you. The stock of knowledge is like an indivisible investment and average costs diverge widely from marginal costs. The result of this is that it is much cheaper for the MNE to use what it already has: the existing but 'inappropriate' technology developed in high-income, labour-scarce countries than to spend money on developing a new technology, more appropriate for the conditions of the developing countries.

Second, there is the well-known difficulty of appropriating the fruits of efforts devoted to increasing knowledge and the need either to treat it as a public good or to erect legal barriers to appropriation by others, in order to create and maintain incentives for research and invention. This leads to the divergence of social from private benefits and costs.

Third, knowledge is, in a sense, substitutable for other productive factors, so that an improvement in technical knowledge makes it possible to produce the same product with less land, labour or capital, or with more capital but a more than proportionate decrease of labour or land, or a better product with the same amount of other factors. But its costs fall under those of either labour (especially trained employees) or capital (purchase of patents or research laboratories or equipment or intermediate products or other assets embodying the knowledge). As a result, the market for knowledge is normally part of the market for these inputs. If the owners of the inputs that embody knowledge command monopoly power, they can exercise this power over the sale of the knowledge component of the whole package.

Fourth, the accumulation of knowledge is only tenuously related to expenditure on its acquisition. Indeed, useful knowledge can be accumulated without any identifiable allocation of resources for this purpose and, conversely and more obviously, large resources can be devoted to research without any productive results. There is, in the nature of discovery, uncertainty about the outcome of efforts devoted to inventions. This uncertainty cannot be removed by insurance, for insurance would also remove the incentive for research. A common way of reducing it is through diversification of research activities. Only large corporations are capable of this. In a private enterprise system the large MNE has an enormous advantage in reducing the risks attached to research.[31]

A fifth and even more fundamental difference lies in the absence of the justification of the common assumption about the 'informed' buyer. Where technology is bought and sold, as it often is, through the purchase of an asset (or through admitting direct private foreign investment), the under-developed recipient country as 'buyer' of the technology is, in the nature of things, very imperfectly informed about many features of the product that it buys. The common assumption about an informed buyer choosing what suits him best is even less justified here than is usual. In some case, if the country knew precisely what it was buying, there would be no need—or considerably less need—to buy it. Knowledge about knowledge is often the knowledge itself.[32] Part of what it buys is the information on which an informed purchase would be based. As a result, the recipient government will be in a weak position *vis-à-vis* the investing firm when it comes to laying down terms and conditions. Excessive 'prices' paid by recipient governments for capital equipment or imported components and technologies inappropriate from the country's point of view, or acceptance of excessively onerous conditions must therefore be the rule rather than the exception in a market where information embodied in equipment is bought by ignorant buyers.

The five features characteristic of the market for technical knowledge— (i) indivisibility, (ii) inappropriability, (iii) embodiment in other factors, (iv) uncertainty and (v) impossibility to know the value until the purchase is made—go some way towards explaining the absence of a free market in which the low-income countries could buy knowledge.

The situation is quite different from that of an 'equilibrium price' reached in a competitive market. It is more like that of a bilateral monopoly or oligopoly where bargaining theory applies. There is a gap between the incremental cost to the owner of the technology of parting with it and the value to the country or firm wishing to acquire it. The cost to the seller is either zero, since the investment has already taken place, or the small amount required to adapt it to the circumstances of the developing country. The value to the buyer is the large amount that he would have to spend to start inventing and developing from scratch and to 'go it alone'. The final figure in the range between these two limits is determined by bargaining strength, which is very unequally distributed.

International inequality and internal inequality in the poor countries reinforce one another. Unequal income distribution is both effect and cause of inappropriate technologies and products. It is an effect because capital-intensive methods and products raise the share of profits and of rewards for skills and reduce that of unskilled labour; and markets for sophisticated, differentiated products require a small élite with high incomes. And it is a cause, because the existence of a market for differentiated luxuries deprives enterprises of any incentive to produce for a mass market of low-cost, more appropriate products.[33] Henry Ford had the advantage not only of imagination but also of relatively high real wages.

Regional Integration and the MNE

Many developing countries are eager to promote regional integration and one of the questions they ask is what contribution the MNE can make to this. According to traditional theory, tariff reductions between a group of countries which maintain a common external tariff afford higher protection to investment within the protected area. The export opportunities of foreign firms to the region are reduced and therefore, if they wish to continue selling, their incentive to invest in the region is raised. We have seen that such tariff protection is neither a sufficient nor a necessary condition for the establishment of local subsidiaries by the MNE. It is not sufficient because, without the special advantage over indigenous enterprises discussed on p. 355, investment cannot take place; and it is not necessary because with that advantage investment may take place even without tariff protection, though protection may lead to establishment of a local subsidiary instead of exports to the country. But given the necessary and sufficient conditions, regional protection will raise the returns and strengthen the incentive to invest.

This incentive is further reinforced if, as a result of tariff reductions, the market is enlarged or its rate of growth accelerated, and if some firms, wishing to maintain market shares, fear that unless they invest, others will anticipate them, or if some firms see themselves forced to follow those that have gone ahead, in order to maintain their shares of the market.

It is, of course, true that such regional arrangements will tend to reduce profits and hence investment incentives for industries which are now prevented from purchasing lower-cost outside supplies required for their inputs and those hampered in selling to outside markets.

In addition, the risks of investment inside the region will be reduced and hence the incentive to invest strengthened. If each nation pursues its own commercial and monetary policy, markets may be suddenly cut off or precipitously reduced as a result of import or foreign exchange restrictions, exchange rate changes or other measures. Regional integration provides a degree of security of selling within the region, which will stimulate investment by the MNE. At the same time, the risks of trading with and investing in other regions may be raised.

Against these forces must be set the fact that real wages will tend to be raised as a result of integration. To that extent, the incentive to invest that resulted from low wage costs is reduced. While integration will tend to lead to greater efficiency, stronger competition and economies of scale, these same forces will tend to raise labour costs and to that extent reduce the otherwise stronger incentive of the MNE to operate.

Here again, the question of the distribution of the gains from integration arises: distribution between the MNE and integrated countries as a group, and distribution between different participating countries. In oligopolistic conditions, there are no forces making automatically for lower prices of products or higher rewards to indigenous factors. If the gains are wholly absorbed by higher profits, whether open or concealed, the host countries, which created the opportunities for these gains, will not find the arrangement acceptable. But even if the countries as a group benefit, difficult problems of the distribution of these gains between the more advanced countries, which will attract the firms, and the less advanced, will have to be resolved.

In analysing the effects upon the MNE, it is important to distinguish between the incentives of a larger and securer market and those of a more rapidly growing market. The former enables investing firms to exploit economies of scale and to set up larger plants; the latter makes for the more rapid introduction of up-to-date equipment, incorporating the latest technical knowledge. Both make for unit cost reductions, but the reasons are different in the two cases.

An important difference between regional integration between advanced industrial countries and that between developing countries is the emphasis on improved *trade* patterns for the former, and on improved *investment* planning for the latter. Obviously, both trade and investment are important for both groups of countries, and equally obviously there are causal links between international trade and investment. But when developing countries seek closer regional integration, trade between them is initially relatively small and, more important, it is neither always desirable nor politically feasible to permit the mechanism of 'trade creation' to work, according to which the established high-cost industries in normally already more industrialised member countries. Resources are not as shiftable as this doctrine supposes. Moreover, countries joining a union are not concerned with maximising intra-union production, but, at the cost of some union inefficiency, in securing for themselves some of the new industries, jobs and accompanying technology, that cater for the whole market. The criterion of comparative advantage may be politically unacceptable where the location of new firms is concerned just as much as in guiding trade from existing firms.

Another important difference between regional integration among advanced countries and developing countries is that in the former case the domestic economies are already integrated. Economic opportunities are open to all, factors of production are relatively mobile, agents respond to incentives and income differentials are not too large. This is not true of most developing countries. The domestic economies of these countries are 'dualistic'. A modern sector confronts a traditional one. While it is impossible to draw a sharp line between the two and while movements and transactions between them take place, they are not as fully integrated as the market in a rich economy. If such dualistic economies pursue regional integration with reliance on the MNE, there is a danger that only the small, modern sectors of the joining countries are integrated, while the rest remains in isolated poverty. One cannot rely on the automatic effects of market forces to spread the benefits widely. It is therefore important to bear in mind the need to promote measures of greater *national* integration, side by side with a move towards *regional* integration, if the dualistic division is not to be aggravated by the operations of MNEs.

Notes

1. The author is grateful to G. Helleiner, S. Lall, M. Sharpston and Frances Stewart for comments on an earlier draft.

2. Nurkse (1953).

3. Cameron (1967), Deane (1961), Deane & Cole (1962), and Deane (1965).

4. cf. Baer & Hervé (1966), Burton (1965), Islam (1967), Kabaj (1969), Lewis & Solige (1965), Meier (1969), National Council of Applied Economic Research, New Delhi (1966), Power (1963, 1966), Schydlowsky (1971), Steel (1971), Thomas (1966), United States Department of Commerce (1966–8), Williamson (1964), Winston (1968, 1970, 1971a–b).

5. Lewis (1965).

6. Behrman (1960).

7. See pp. 363–4.

8. For the problem as to what consequences are to be attributed to government policy and which to the MNE, see p. 361.

9. See pp.§361 and 367.

10. MacDougall (1960).

11. MacDougall (1960), p. 210. MacDougall wrote with special reference to Australia and assumed, *inter alia*, perfect competition.

12. Balogh & Streeten (1960).

13. MacDougall (1960), pp. 199, 203.

14. Kindleberger (1969), Caves (1971a, b) and Díaz-Alejandro (1971).

15. Caves (1971a). See also Dunning (1973).

16. See p. 364.

17. Among the contributors to this discussion are Hirsch (1967), Hufbauer (1965), Posner (1961), Linder (1961), Vernon (1966, 1971) and Wells (1969).

18. Helleiner (1973).

19. cf. Pazos (1967) writes: 'The main weakness of direct investment as a development agent is the consequence of the complete character of its contribution' (p. 196). Also Hirschman (1969). But Pazos and Hirschman emphasise the detrimental effect on the growth of indigenous factors, whereas the question treated here is the distribution of gains.

20. The argument is developed and documented in an interesting paper by Lall (1973) and by Vaitsos (mimeo, 1970a, b; 1973).

21. The literature on this subject is still somewhat thin. The main work has been done by Vaitsos (mimeo 1970a, b and mimeo 1973), Vernon (1971) and UNCTAD (1972). Tugendhat discusses the problem (1971) and refers to a Ph.D. thesis by Shulman. The firms have defended their policies in Green & Duerr (1968). The US tax authorities have done a good deal of work on the subject.

22. See below, pp. 365–7.

23. But understatement of profits will not normally occur if the country grants generous tax concessions. Although higher tax rates than in other countries are not the only reason for underdeclaration of profits, they, together with the desire to remit profits in the face of foreign exchange restrictions, are among the most important ones.

24. Díaz-Alejandro (1971).

25. Stewart (1973).

26. See Vaitsos (1973).

27. The treatment of the government as a guardian of the interests of the whole nation is, however, misleading. See Streeten (1971). A third force in the bargain may be the government of the parent company.

28. 'Return' is in quotation marks because it does not refer to the irrelevant ratio of declared profits to arbitrarily valued capital, but to the whole range of benefits over costs, some of which cannot readily or precisely be quantified.

29. As we have seen in the discussion of attribution, just as certain faults have to be attributed to government policies rather than the MNE, so certain virtues may be the result of combining capital, management and know-how, but not necessarily through the MNE. A host country has to ask itself the following questions:

(i)   is the MNE wanted at all?
(ii) if so, should the particular product that it produces be available?
(iii) if so, should it be imported or produced at home?
(vi) if produced at home, how is the package most effectively assembled?
(v)   if through a MNE, how can the best bargain be struck?

30. Hughes & Seng (1969) and UNCTAD Study (1969). There are several reasons for this e.g. firms tend to regard special incentives as liable to be soon removed.

31. cf. Arrow (1962b).

32. Vaitsos (1970a, b). Arrow (1962b) writes: '... there is a fundamental paradox in the determination of demand for information: its value for the purchaser is not known until he has the information, but then he has in effect acquired it without cost'.

33. Stewart (1973).

References

Arrow, K. (1962a), "The Economic Implications of Learning by Doing", *Review of Economic Studies*, 29, 80, pp. 155–73.

Arrow, K. (1962b), "Economic Welfare and the Allocation of Resources to Invention", *The Rate and Direction of Inventive Activity: Economic and Social Factors*, National Bureau of Economic Research, Princeton Univ. Press, pp. 609–26 (reprinted in D.M. Lamberton (ed.), *Economics of Information and Knowledge*, Penguin Modern Economics Readings).

Baer, W. and Herve, M. (1966), "Employment and Industrialisation in Developing Countries", *Quarterly Journal of Economics*, 80.

Balogh, T. and Streeten P.P. (1960), "Domestic versus Foreign Investment", *Bulletin of the Oxford University Institute of Statistics*, 22, pp. 213–24.

Behrman, J. (1960), "Promoting Free World Economic Development Through Direct Investment", *American Economic Review*, 50, pp. 271–81.

Burton, H.J. (1965), "On the Role of Import Substitution in Development Planning", *Philippine Economic Journal*, First Semester.

Cameron, R. (1967), "Some Lessons of History for Developing Nations", *American Economic Review, Papers and Proceedings*, S7, 2, p. 313.

Caves, R.E. (1971a), "International Corporations: the Industrial Economics of Foreign Investment", *Economica*, 38, 149, pp. 1–27.

Caves, R.E. (1971b), "Industrial Economics of Foreign Investment, The Case of the International Corporation", *Journal of World Trade Law*, 5, 3, pp. 303–14.

Deane, P. (1961), "Capital Formation in Britain Before the Railway Age", *Economic Development and Cultural Change*, No. 3.

Deane, P. (1965), *The First Industrial Revolution*, London, Cambridge University Press.

Deane, P. and Cole, W.A. (1962), *British Economic Growth, 1688–1959; Trends and Structure*, London, Cambridge University Press.

Díaz-Alejandro, C.F. (1971), "The Future of Direct Foreign Investment in Latin America", Yale Economic Growth Center Discussion Paper, No. 131.

Dunning, J.H. (1973), "The Determinants of International Production", Oxford Economic Papers, 25, 289–336.

Dunning, J.H. (1976), "The Determinants of International Production", *Oxford Economic Papers*, 25, 289–336.

Green, J. and Duerr, M.G. (1968), *Intercompany Transfers in Multinational Firms*, New York: The Conference Board.

Helleiner, G.K. (1973), "Manufactured Exports from Less Developed Countries and Multinational Firms", *Economic Journal*, March, pp. 21–47.

Hirsch, S. (1967), *Location of Industry and International Competitiveness*, London, Oxford University Press.

Hirschman, A.O. (1969), "How to Divest in Latin America and Why", Princeton Essays in International Finance, No. 76, November.

Hufbauer, G.C. (1965), *Synthetic Materials and the Theory of International Trade*, London, Duckworth.

Hughes, H. and Seng, Y.P. (1969), *Foreign Investment and Industrialization in Singapore*, Madison, University of Wisconsin Press.

Islam, N. (1967), "Comparative Costs, Factor Proportions and Industrial Efficiency in Pakistan", *Pakistan Development Review*, Summer.

Kabaj, M. (1969), *Problems of Shift Work as a Means of Improving Capacity Utilisation*, Vienna, United Nations Industrial Organisation.

Kindleberger, C.P. (1969), *American Business Abroad*, New Haven, Conn.: Yale University Press.

Lall, S. (1973), "Transfer Pricing by Multinational Manufacturing Firms", *Oxford Bulletin of Economics and Statistics*, 35, pp. 173–95.

Lewis, S. and Souge, R. (1965), "Growth and Structural Change in Pakistan Manufacturing Industry", *Pakistan Development Review*, Spring.

Lewis, W.A. (1965), "A Review of Economic Development", The Richard T. Ely Lecture, *American Economic Review*, 60, 2, pp. 1–4.

Linder, S.B. (1961), *An Essay on Trade and Transformation*, New York and Stockholm, Wiley and Almqvist and Wiksell.

MacDougall, G.D. (1960), "The Benefits and Costs of Private Investment from Abroad", *Economic Record*, pp. 13–35.

Meier, G. (1969), "Development Without Employment", *Banca Nazionale del Lavoro Quarterly Review*, 22, pp. 309–19.

National Council of Applied Economic Research (1966), *Underutilisation of Industrial Capacity, 1955–64*, New Delhi.

Nurkse, R. (1953), *Problems of Capital Formation in Underdeveloped Countries*, Oxford, Blackwell.

Pazos, F. (1967), "The Role of International Movements of Private Capital in Promoting Development", in J.H. Adler (ed.), *Capital Movements and Economic Development*, London, Macmillan.

Posner, M.V. (1961), "International Trade and Technical Change", *Oxford Economic Papers*, 13, pp. 323–41.

Power, J.H. (1963), "Industrialisation in Pakistan: A Case of Frustrated Take-off", *Pakistan Development Review*, Summer.

Power, J.H. (1966), "Import Substitution as an Industrialisation Strategy", *Philippine Economic Journal*, Second Semester.

Schydlowsky, D. (1971), "Fiscal Policy for Full Capacity Industrial Growth in Latin

America", Economic Development Report, No. 201, Development Advisory Service, Center for International Relations, Harvard University.

Steel, W. (1971), "Import Substitution and Excess Capacity in Ghana", Economic Development Report, No. 198, Development Advisory Center for International Relations, Harvard University Press.

Stewart, F. (1973), "Trade and Technology", in P. Streeten (ed.), *Trade Strategies for Development*, London, Macmillan.

Streeten, P. (1971), "Costs and Benefits of Multinational Enterprises in Less-Developed Countries", in J.H. Dunning (ed.), *The Multinational Enterprise*, London, Allen and Unwin.

Thomas, P. (1966), "Import Licencing and Import Liberalisation in Pakistan", *Pakistan Development Review*, 6.

Tugendhat, G. (1971), *The Multinationals*, London, Eyre and Spottiswoode.

UNCTAD(1969), "Queen Elizabeth House Study on Private Foreign Investment", Oxford (mimeo).

UNCTAD (1972), "Policies Relating to Technology in the Countries of the Andean Pact: Their Foundations", Santiago, TD/107.

US Department of Commerce (1966–68), *Overseas Business Reports* (May 1966– April 1968).

Vaitsos, C.V. (1970a), "Transfer of Resources and Preservation of Monopoly Rents", Economic Development Report, No. 168, Center of International Affairs, Harvard University (mimeo).

Vaitsos, C.V. (1970b), "Bargaining and the Distribution of Returns in the Purchase of Technology by Developing Countries", *Bulletin of the Institute of Development Studies*, 3, 1.

Vaitsos, C.V. (1973), *Income Generation and Income Distribution in the Foreign Investment Model*, Oxford University Press and Fondo de Cultura Economica.

Vernon, R. (1966), "International Investment and International Trade in the Product Cycle", *Quarterly Journal of Economics*, 80, pp. 190–207.

Vernon, R. (1971), *Sovereignty at Bay*, New York, Basic Books.

Wells, L.T. (1969), "Tests of a Product Cycle Model of International Trade: US Exports of Consumer Durables", *Quarterly Journal of Economics*, 83, pp. 152–63.

Williamson, O. (1964), *The Economics of Discretionary Behavior: Managerial Objectives in A Theory of the Firm*, Englewood Cliffs, Prentice-Hall.

Winston, G.C. (1968), *Excess Capacity in Underdeveloped Countries; The Pakistan Case*, Centre for Development Economics, Williams College.

Winston, G.C. (1970), "Overinvoicing, Underutilisation and Distorted Industrial Growth", *Pakistan Development Review*, Winter.

Winston, G.C. (1971a), "The Four Reasons for Idle Capital", Oxford (mimeo).

Winston, G.C. (1971b), "Capital Utilisation and Development: Physiological Costs and Preference for Shift Work" Williams College, February (mimeo).

15

Bargaining Power, Ownership, and Profitability of Transnational Corporations in Developing Countries*

Donald J. Lecraw[†]

*Source: *Journal of International Business Studies*, (Spring/Summer 1984), pp. 27–43.

Introduction

Over the past 20 years there has been continuing controversy over the determinants and effects of different patterns of ownership and control of the subsidiaries of transnational corporations (TNCs) in less developed countries (LDCs). Some countries such as Singapore and Hong Kong place virtually no restrictions on the percentage of equity ownership held by TNCs in most sectors of their economies; others place severe restrictions on equity ownership by TNCs and prohibit it outright in many sectors of their economy; others require that foreign ownership be reduced or phased out over time. One of the advantages of foreign direct investment (FDI) sometimes cited by TNCs based in Japan and in LDCs is the generally higher level of equity participation they have given to investors in the host country [Lecraw 1977, 1981; Wells 1983]. The reasons expressed by host governments for encouraging (or insisting on) local equity participation are complex and sometimes contradictory, ranging from better access to information, and control of payments for technology transfer and management fees, to control over pricing of output and intracompany trade, reinvestment, and remittance of profits and capital.[1] As importantly, a high level of foreign ownership may carry significant political costs for the host government quite apart from its economic impact.

Recently, Fagre and Wells [1982] have used a bargaining power framework to explore the relationship between the characteristics of a TNC (size, intrafirm transfers, advertising and R&D intensities, and product diversity) and the percent equity ownership position that TNCs achieved in their subsidiaries in the host country.[2] The first step of the analysis in this paper replicates this work using a different data set and extends the analysis to include additional characteristics of the host country and of TNCs that might influence their relative bargaining power.

Poynter [1982] has shown that a TNC may find it advantageous to bargain not for increased equity ownership, but for control over the variables critical to the success of the subsidiary from the TNC's viewpoint. The second step of the analysis relates the relative bargaining power of a TNC and of the host government (as proxied by their characteristics) to the degree of control the TNC exercised over its subsidiary in the host country.

Finally, Killing [1982] has shown that there is a link between the profitability (success) of a TNC's subsidiary and the division of overall control between the TNC and its local partners. The third step of the analysis of the paper examines the TNC's control over several of the functions within its subsidiary—marketing, finance, technology, production, imports, exports, and so on—evaluates the importance of control over these functions to the TNC, and analyzes the relationship between the TNC's control over these critical success variables and the success of the subsidiary from the TNC's viewpoint.

The research presented here links what had previously been 3 separate areas of analysis into a more unified framework, and tests hypotheses that are generated by this framework on a common data set. In this way, this research both supports and extends the work of Fagre and Wells, Killing, and Poynter.

The conclusions in this paper are based on data gathered from 153 subsidiaries of TNCs that operated in 6 manufacturing industries in the 5 countries of the ASEAN region: Thailand, Malaysia, Singapore, Indonesia, and the Philippines. These countries vary greatly in income levels, size of the domestic market, resource base, development strategies, and policies toward FDI. The TNCs in the sample were based in the United States, Europe, Japan, and several LDCs. The sample then may give a good basis on which to reach generalizations concerning the determinants of ownership and control of the subsidiaries of TNCs in LDCs, and concerning the effects of ownership and control on the success of these investments.

The next section sets out the theoretical framework for the analysis. The third section describes the methodology and tests the hypotheses generated from the theory. The fourth section draws some implications from the analysis for policy of both TNCs and host governments.

Theoretical Framework

In the pioneering work of Vernon [1971], Stopford and Wells [1972], and Franko [1971], 4 factors were seen as major determinants of the level of equity ownership of TNCs in their subsidiaries: the desired ownership level of the TNC; the bargaining power of the TNC; the desired level of local equity participation of the host country: and the bargaining power of the host government (including the bargaining power of locally-owned firms in the host country). Analysis of the determinants of equity participation in terms of the relative bargaining power and the equity ownership policies of the TNC and the host country governments has proved to be a fruitful approach and will be used in the first part of the analysis of this paper.

Over the past 10 years several authors have developed a comprehensive theory of the international activities of firms that can be used to analyze the decision of a firm on the mode of its international activity: exports, licensing, or FDI.[3] In order to operate internationally, a firm must possess firm-specific (ownership) advantages in technology, production, marketing, finance, and management that allow it to compete with firms in the market for goods and services abroad. These firm-specific advantages are often due to the country-specific advantages of the firm's home country: natural resources, market size, income level, and factor costs. The host country possesses advantages in location as well as in its natural resources, markets, and factor costs.

A TNC will undertake FDI when 3 conditions are met: when its firm-specific advantages allow it to compete in the host country; when the host country has advantages that are attractive to the TNC; and when the advantages of internalizing the transaction within the firm by FDI are greater than the advantages of transferring the goods and services it possesses via the market for exports or licenses of its technology (broadly defined to include all forms of the firm's expertise, including brand names). The stronger the internalization advantages for the firm, the greater will be its desire to use FDI as the mode of its international activity and the greater its desire to retain ownership in its subsidiary abroad to appropriate the return earned on these advantages.

Placed into a bargaining framework, firm-specific advantages may give the TNC bargaining power over the host country: internalization advantages influence its desire to retain ownership and control over the appropriation of the returns of its subsidiary.[4] The desired ownership structure of a TNC for its subsidiaries in LDCs is then a function of its firm-specific advantages, internalization advantages, and host country advantages. Several of these factors have been described at length elsewhere and will be only briefly outlined here.[5]

Internalization advantages for an R&D-intensive TNC may be great if, as is often the case, the market for its technology is not perfect due to asymmetric information [Killing 1980]. R&D-intensive TNCs, therefore, often prefer to exploit their firm-specific advantages by internalizing the transaction through FDI in wholly-owned subsidiaries rather than via the market for technology. Possession of a proprietary product or technology may also increase the bargaining position of a TNC over the host government, particularly if other TNCs or local investors cannot supply technology of the same type or level of advancement.

As with technology, the external market for marketing skills and brand names is often imperfect. Faced with these imperfections, marketing-intensive TNCs often choose to exploit their firm-specific advantages by internalizing the transaction through FDI (again in wholly-owned subsidiaries in order to appropriate the return) rather than via the market for licensing brand names or products. Such firms may have the ability to develop a marketing package that is independent of the country in which they operate, may place little value on inputs from local partners in the form of marketing expertise and access to channels of distribution, and may fear loss of control over product quality [Horst 1974].

In the past, considerable emphasis has been placed on TNCs as providers of scarce capital resources at costs lower than those available to local investors in LDCs. Unless a TNC is willing to change its strategy to become a financial intermediary making portfolio loans or investments, it can only exploit this firm-specific advantage—access to relatively inexpensive capital—by internalizing the transaction via FDI.[6] The lower the cost of capital for the TNC relative to capital costs in the host country, the greater are the internalization advantages for the TNC. If capital is indeed a scarce resource that can best be provided by the TNC, its bargaining power and hence its level of equity participation might increase with the size of the investment (in terms of assets) and the investment's capital intensity.

Another source of bargaining power for the TNC may be its ability to sell the output of its subsidiary in the host country on export markets, either to other units of the TNC, to independent firms, or through its own channels of distribution in markets in other countries. The TNC's access to export markets may become an especially important bargaining chip if the host country is following a development strategy based on export-led growth. TNCs have the choice of exploiting their firm-specific advantage—access to export markets—via FDI or by serving as a trading company for exports of locally-owned firms in the host country. The decision whether to exploit proprietary expertise in international trade via the market as trading firms or to internalize it via FDI is a complex one, and not well understood. [See Moxon 1983; and Lecraw's comments on Moxon's paper, 1983b.] Moxon, writing about export platform FDI, concluded on theoretical grounds that firms will undertake FDI based on a firm-specific advantage in access to export markets "when the parent possesses a complete package of export marketing and technological advantage, and where the costs of operation and control of the subsidiary do not offset these advantages."

Management expertise is another firm-specific advantage which TNCs may provide to their subsidiaries in the host country and which may increase their bargaining power. Conversely, host governments may push for increased local equity participation in order to increase the management expertise of their entrepreneurs and managers. Quantifying the effect of "management expertise" on the bargaining power of TNCs is difficult. Host governments also have difficulty in assessing the value of this expertise for the local subsidiary and the host economy. As the complexity of the managerial technology increases, however, the advantages of internalizing the transfer via FDI may increase, thereby increasing the TNC's desire to exploit its firm-specific advantage via FDI and its desire for a high degree of equity ownership and control.

Finally, the desire of a TNC to exploit its firm-specific advantages via FDI may depend on the managerial (or other) resources the firm has available to commit to the subsidiary. For example, a small, fast-growing firm may not have excess managerial capacity or financial resources to use for the investment, operation, and control of a subsidiary in an LDC. In this case, it may find that licensing or exports are the most profitable means by which it can exploit its firm-specific advantages in proprietary technology, marketing, and management. By extension, such a firm may be more apt to be satisfied with minority equity participation rather than commit its scarce financial and managerial assets to acquire and control a higher percentage of the equity in its foreign subsidiaries.

The preceding analysis implicitly assumed that TNCs use their bargaining power to achieve their desired level of equity participation in their subsidiaries in LDCs in order to appropriate the highest possible share of the return on their firm-specific advantages by internalizing the transactions within the firm. [See Magee 1977.] There are 2 problems with this viewpoint.

First, there may be ways by which the TNC may appropriate the return on its foreign investment other than by equity participation—licensing and management fees paid by the subsidiary, sale of inputs to the subsidiary, sale of its output to other units of the TNC or on world markets, and interest on intracompany debt. The TNC may use its bargaining power not to increase its equity ownership, but to secure some other means by which to appropriate this return, possibly by manipulating the transfer price of these other payments. Despite the efforts of host governments and their local partners, control of these variables to reflect arm's-length, free-market values ("fair" values) has often been quite difficult [Lecraw 1984]. Through these and other means, the use of internalization to appropriate returns through equity ownership in a subsidiary may be reduced and the TNC may use its bargaining power to gain advantageous concessions other than equity participation if it can control the allocation of the returns from the subsidiary in other ways. The fewer the transactions between the parent TNC and its subsidiary, however, the fewer the possibilities for the TNC to appropriate the return on its firm-specific advantages except through equity participation.

Second, TNCs may bargain for increased equity participation in order to increase their control over the operations of their subsidiary, to try to ensure that the internalization advantages are in fact realized. The link between the level of equity participation and the TNC's control over its subsidiary, however, may not be straightforward. Depending on the type of technology transferred, the capabilities of the local partners, and host government policies, a TNC may be able to control the operations of its subsidiary that are critical from its viewpoint without majority ownership, or, conversely, may have little control over these operations despite majority (or even complete) ownership. A TNC may therefore be willing to trade reduced equity ownership for increased control of variables crucial to the success of the venture from its point of view, if such a trade-off is possible. In this way, TNCs have sometimes been able to reduce host-government intervention in the operations of their subsidiaries, while at the same time appropriating their desired share of the surplus generated by their firm-specific advantages.[7]

The link, therefore, between the bargaining power of the TNC, the level of its equity participation, its control of the subsidiary, and its perception of the success of the investment is complex and may be difficult to trace. One implication of this analysis, however, may be testable using the data in this study. All else being equal, the desire of the TNC for a high level of equity participation should increase as the economic ties between its subsidiary and the parent (through trade in inputs and outputs, machinery, and management and technology fees) decrease, because the potential of appropriating the profits of its investment, except through return on equity, has decreased.[8] The hypotheses concerning the relationship between TNC and host-country characteristics, the level of equity ownership desired by the TNC, and the bargaining power of the TNC and host country are displayed in Table 1.

To this point the analysis has sketched the often tangled relationship between the bargaining power of the TNC and its desired level of equity participation, the level of participation it achieves, and its control of its subsidiary, either as a whole, or over its critical strategic variables. The bargaining power of the host country also influences this relationship as the host country uses its bargaining power to appropriate a share of the profits earned by the TNC within its country.[9] The host country may possess scarce resources or control access to markets—either of which increases its bargaining power with the TNC. If the host government controls access to its markets through tariffs or nontariff barriers to trade and if the TNC investment is designed to serve the host-country market, the host government can bargain access to its domestic market to gain equity participation for host-country nationals. The more attractive the host-country's internal market, the less open it is to trade; and the more willing the host government is to forego the immediate gains that the TNC may be able to provide via FDI, the greater the bargaining power of the host country. Similarly, the greater the diffusion of the expertise that TNCs can provide, the greater is the opportunity for the host government to play TNCs against one another in bargaining over the level of equity ownership and the share of the

Table 1 Expected signs

Independent variables	Dependent variables		
	Actual equity ownership	S^{TNC}	Effective control
Technological leadership	+	+	+
Advertising intensity	+	+	+
Subsidiary assets	+	+	+
Capital/output	+	+	+
Exports/sales	+	+	+
TNC assets	+	?	+
TNC-subsidiary linkages	−	?	+
Host-country attractiveness	−	−	−
Potential TNC investors	−	−	−
Time (1960 = 1)	−	−	−
Dummy-Japanese TNC	−	?	−
Dummy-LDC TNC	−	?	−
Dummy variable European TNC	?	?	?
Constant term	+	?	+

surplus from the venture accruing to each partner. In general, the greater the country-specific advantages of the host country, the greater its bargaining power and the higher the level of local ownership it may gain for local investors.

Several researchers have recently analyzed the relationships between the level of a TNC's equity participation, its control of the operations of its subsidiary, the success of the investment, and the reasons for failure. [See Killing 1982; Schaan 1982; and Beamish and Lane 1982.] These researchers used intensive interviews with small samples of Canadian firms that formed joint ventures both in developed countries (the United States) and in LDCs (Mexico and Kenya). Their general conclusion was that the relationship between joint venture success and equity ownership was U-shaped, that is, joint ventures in which the TNC held a small minority share (control was with the local partner) or a large majority share (control was with the TNC) tended to be more successful than joint ventures in which the partners held roughly equal shares (control was split). Joint ventures in which control was roughly equal at the board level or divided along functional lines tended to experience splits between the TNC and its local partner when the joint venture was under pressure from its external political or economic environment. These splits between the partners often led to friction at the operating level, compromises with which neither partner was satisfied, reduced commitment to the venture, and unsatisfactory performance.[10]

Data collected as part of the present study, although considerably less detailed than those of Killing [1982] and Schaan [1982], can be used to analyze the relationship between equity ownership, the assets brought to the venture by the TNC and the local partner, the critical success variables of the venture, the division of control, and the success of the venture.[11]

The next section describes the data and methodology used to test some of these hypotheses on the determinants of the relative bargaining power of TNCs and host governments, equity ownership, control, and success of subsidiaries of TNCs in LDCs.

As part of this study, data were collected using a questionnaire during interviews with 153 subsidiaries of TNCs based in the United States (52 subsidiaries), Europe (35 subsidiaries), Japan (43), and other LDCs (23) located in the 5 ASEAN countries: Thailand (39 subsidiaries), Malaysia (31), Singapore (29), Indonesia (19) and the Philippines (35). The characteristics of the firms in the sample and the 6 light manufacturing industries in which they operated are described in Lecraw [1981, 1984]. In general, these industries were quite concentrated (average 4-firm concentration ratio of 71.2 percent), exported little of their output (exports/industry sales averaged 5.1 percent), imported a high percentage of their inputs (imports/total inputs averaged 41 percent) and operated behind high tariffs (nominal tariffs averaged 33.4 percent). In general, the TNCs in the sample had majority ownership in their subsidiaries (71 percent), the subsidiaries were quite small (assets averaged $4.1 million), and profits were high (19.8 percent on equity). The subsidiaries generally produced for the local market (export/sales averaged 7.1 percent) although a few subsidiaries exported more than 50 percent of their output.[12] [See Lecraw 1984, Tables 1–4.]

Methodology

The analysis in the previous section developed several hypotheses concerning the relationship between the relative bargaining power of the TNC and the host government, their desires for equity participation, the level of equity participation, the level of control achieved by the TNC in its subsidiary in the host country, and the success of the subsidiary. This analysis led to the hypotheses that the bargaining power of the TNC would increase with the level of the technology the TNC initially transferred to the venture, with the venture's on-going dependence on the TNC for technology in the future, with increasing advertising intensity of the TNC, with increasing dependence of the subsidiary on the TNC for export markets, and with increased size and capital intensity of the venture. The bargaining power of the host country would increase with increasing attractiveness of its local market and the degree it controlled market access through tariffs, and with increasing availability to the host country of the TNC's proprietary assets from other sources.

There was a problem in directly observing and measuring the 4 variables which jointly determine the actual level of equity ownership (EO) in this model: TNC bargaining power (BP^{TNC}), host country bargaining power (BP^{HC}), the TNC's desired level of equity ownership (DE^{TNC}), and the host country's desired level of equity ownership (DE^{HC}). The model has 5 structural equations:

$$EO = f(BP^{TNC}, BP^{HC}, DE^{TNC}, DE^{HC}). \quad (1)$$

$$BP^{TNC} = g(X). \quad (2)$$

$$BP^{HC} = h(X). \quad (3)$$

$$DE^{TNC} = l(X). \quad (4)$$

$$DE^{HC} = m(X). \quad (5)$$

where X is a vector of the TNC and host country characteristics. The BP^{TNC}, BP^{HC}, DE^{TNC}, and DE^{HC} are unobserved variables, but the X, and Equity Ownership are observable. This problem led to the construction of a reduced form equation:

$$EO = n(X) \quad (6)$$

If the reduced form (Equation 6) is estimated, it is incorrect to draw explicit conclusions on the link between the X, and bargaining power and desired equity ownership, or the link between bargaining power and desired equity ownership to actual equity ownership. This is a problem with drawing conclusions from the estimation of any reduced-form equation when the structural equations contain unobserved variables and hence cannot be estimated separately. It reduces the strength of the conclusions of the analysis of this paper about the usefulness of the bargaining power framework or, at best, conclusions are left to the interpretation of the reader.

Part of this problem can be circumvented if several assumptions are made. If the TNC's desired level of equity ownership does not vary between host countries and if the TNC achieved its desired level in at least one country, then the highest level of equity ownership of the TNC in any LDC can be used as a proxy for its desired level of ownership. If the host country's desired level of equity ownership does not vary among TNCs and if it achieved this level with a subsidiary of one TNC, then the lowest level of TNC equity (the highest level of host country equity) can be used as a proxy for the host country's desired level of equity ownership. Then, the differences between actual Equity Ownership and the TNC's desired ownership, and between actual Equity Ownership and the host country's desired ownership can be observed and the ratio of these differences related directly to the characteristics of the TNC and the host country. (If $DE^{TNC} = EO$, S^{TNC} was set equal to 1,000.)

$$S^{TNC} = \frac{EO - DE^{HC}}{DE^{TNC} - EO} = q(X) \qquad (7)$$

S^{TNC} might be considered the success of the TNC in bargaining with the host country. (See Figure 1.) S^{TNC} depends on the 2 sets of variables which have been identified with the relative bargaining power of the TNC and the host country. This methodology follows Fagre and Wells. S^{TNC} is a combination of their 2 variables, "Firm-Corrected Owership" and "Country-Corrected Ownership."[13] Data were collected for the firms in the sample on EO, the X, and they were used to construct S^{TNC} under the assumptions listed above.

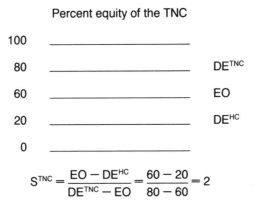

Percent equity of the TNC

$$S^{TNC} = \frac{EO - DE^{HC}}{DE^{TNC} - EO} = \frac{60 - 20}{80 - 60} = 2$$

Figure 1 The relationship between the actual level of equity ownership (EO), the desired level of ownership of the host country (DE^{HC}), and the TNC (DE^{TNC}), and bargaining success (S^{TNC})

The bargaining power of the TNC may increase as the technological intensity of the product and process technology it brings to the subsidiary increases. Three measures might be used as proxies for the intensity of the TNC's R&D. The most often used proxy for R&D intensity has been the R&D sales ratio of the parent TNC. The technology transferred to the subsidiary, however, may be older than the latest technology produced and used by the TNC at home. The R&D intensity of the subsidiary, as measured by local R&D/(subsidiary sales) is an even more unreliable measure since, typically, significant R&D is not performed at the subsidiary level. Licensing and technical service fees as a percent of sales is also not a satisfactory measure because the size of these fees often does not reflect the value of the technology transferred due to manipulation of transfer prices by the TNC and because some host governments control the level of these payments. A measure of technological intensity was used that might circumvent these problems. It ranked on a scale of 1 to 10 the technological leadership of the parent TNC as perceived by the firm's managers.

This measure embodies not only the technology that could have been transferred with the initial investment, but also the potential for further transfer in the future, another potential source of bargaining power for the TNC.

Finding a reasonable proxy for the advertising intensity of the firm also presented problems, although they were not as severe as those for technological intensity. The advertising to sales ratio of the subsidiary relative to other firms in the industry in the host country was used.

The bargaining power of the parent TNCs may have increased as the capital requirements of the subsidiary increased. The capital intensity and capital requirements variables were straightforward to measure: total assets/output and total assets. These 2 variables were correlated, however, so that when they were entered in the regression equation together, they were significant at only the 10 percent level.

Export intensity was measured as exports/sales. The higher the export/sales ratio, the greater the bargaining power of the TNC.

The size (assets) of the parent TNC relative to the other parent TNCs in the industry was included in the regression equation to test the hypothesis that for smaller firms capital and managerial resources were a binding constraint on their ability to undertake majority equity participation in their subsidiaries abroad.

As the economic linkages between the TNC and its subsidiary increase, the TNCs may have become less reliant on subsidiary profits for earning a return on their investment. The flow of resources between the TNC and its subsidiary as a percent of sales was used to proxy this linkage effect: inputs, interest on loans and intrafirm suppliers credit, intrafirm sales, management and technical service fees, and an imputed rental value on machinery and equipment supplied by the TNC.[14]

Finding a proxy for the "attractiveness" of the host country as a site for a subsidiary proved difficult because many variables could influence a TNC's perception of host country attractiveness. Moreover, the relative importance of the various factors could vary between TNCs and over time. The managers interviewed were asked to rank from low (1) to high (10) the attractiveness of the host country as an investment site at the time of the investment.

The number of TNCs that had already undertaken a FDI in the countries of the ASEAN region in the firm's industry at the time it made its investment was used as a proxy for the number of potential entrants into the industry in the host country. As this number increased, the relative bargaining power of the TNC should decrease.

"Time" was included as an explanatory variable because the TNCs in the sample had invested in different years. Host economics and government policies had changed over time and multinationals based in Japan and LDCs tended to be late entrants.

Finally, when the TNC was based in Europe, Japan, or an LDC, 3 dummy variables were used to pick up any residual difference between the percent ownership attained and the relative bargaining power of the TNC and the nationality of the parent TNC. These dummy variables test the hypothesis that TNCs based in different countries "give" local partners a greater share of the equity in their foreign subsidiaries. These dependent and independent variables are tabulated in Table 1 with their expected signs.

Results

Table 2 displays the regression results. For the regression on Actual Equity Ownership all the coefficients had the expected sign and most were significant at the 5 percent level. Note that, everything else being equal, the TNCs in the sample based in Japan and LDCs had a lower level of Actual Equity Ownership although only by 4 percent and 7 percent, respectively. U.S.-based and European TNCs had about the same propensity for equity participation given firm and country characteristics (their relative bargaining strengths). Smaller TNCs tended to take lower equity positions than did larger ones. The regression results lend some support to the hypotheses on the determinants of the relative bargaining power of TNCs and the host countries. Actual Equity Ownership increased as the technical leadership, the advertising intensity, and the export ratio increased, and decreased as host country attractiveness and the number of potential TNC investors increased, and with time. Although the coefficients of the variables representing the capital intensity and capital requirements had the expected sign, they were only significant at the 10 percent level.[15]

The regression on S^{TNC} supports these conclusions. Notice that the variables used to proxy a TNC's desire for equity ownership—TNC assets, TNC-subsidiary linkages, and the TNC home country dummy variables—were no longer significant because S^{TNC} factors the desired level of equity ownership out of the relationship. Time was significantly negative, indicating that the 5 host countries had become more successful in their bargaining with TNCs for equity ownership over time.

These results support and extend those of Fagre and Wells and give a more solid foundation to the hypothesis that the level of equity participation of TNCs is influenced by their relative bargaining position with host country governments.

Control Over the Subsidiary

The next issue to be considered is that of control over the operations of the subsidiary in the host country.[16] There may often be no straightforward relationship between the percentage of equity ownership of the TNC and

Table 2 Regression results

Independent variables	Dependent variables		
	Actual equity ownership, EO	TNC bargaining success (×100), S^TNC	Effective control
Constant	50.3***	5.3	6.2***
	(5.70)	(.84)	(4.13)
Technological leadership	1.32**	2.4***	.21***
	(2.12)	(2.37)	(3.21)
Advertising intensity	1.20**	.87*	.12**
	(1.98)	(1.76)	(2.13)
Subsidiary assets	.35*	.72*	−.10*
	(1.67)	(1.72)	(1.66)
Capital/output	.42	.17	.07
	(1.37)	(1.43)	(1.10)
Exports/sales	3.12***	5.5***	.37***
	(2.91)	(3.25)	(2.97)
TNC assets	.63***	1.1	.10**
	(2.50)	(.73)	(1.98)
TNC-subsidiary linkages	−5.14**	−2.3	.30***
	(2.23)	(1.24)	(2.75)
Host-country attractiveness	−2.15***	−3.6***	−.14
	(3.01)	(3.12)	(1.15)
Potential TNC investors	−2.77***	−2.7**	−.12**
	(2.63)	(2.11)	(1.98)
Time (1960 = 1)	−.52**	−.74**	−.05**
	(2.55)	(2.20)	(2.02)
Dummy-Japanese TNC	−.04***	−.17	+.07**
	(3.50)	(.84)	(2.10)
Dummy-LDC TNC	−.07**	.32	−.03*
	(2.91)	(.15)	(1.92)
European TNC	+.02	+.87*	.02
	(1.10)	(1.67)	(1.61)
$\bar{R}^2$	.63	.47	.55

The t statistics are in parentheses

*** significant at the 1 percent level
** significant at the 5 percent level
* significant at the 10 percent level

control over its subsidiary. "Control" was broken down into 18 areas in production, finance, marketing, exports, and imports, including overall management control. (See the Appendix for a list of these areas.) The managers of the 153 subsidiaries rated the importance of control over each of these factors for the success of the investment from the parent TNC's viewpoint (1 = no importance; 10 = critical importance), and the degree of control that the TNC had over each factor (1 = no control; 10 = complete control). These data were used to construct a composite measure of the

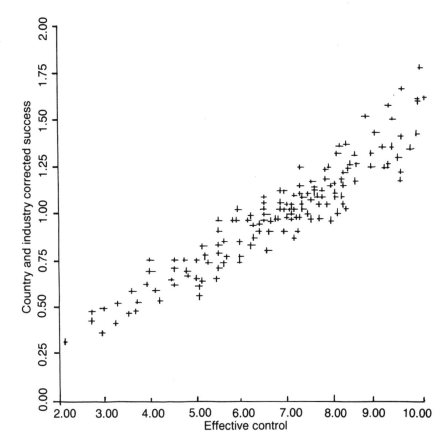

Figure 2 The relationship between country and industry corrected success and effective control

TNC's control over its subsidiary. "Effective Control." (Details of how this measure was calculated are in the Appendix.) Effective Control essentially was a measure of the degree of control that the TNC had over the 18 variables weighted by their importance for the success of the investment from the TNC's viewpoint. Put another way, Effective Control measured the degree of control over the critical success variables retained within the TNC compared to the control lost to those outside the TNC, such as local partners or the host government. Effective Control was scaled from 1 (no effective control) to 10 (complete effective control). For the firms in the sample, the correlation between the TNC's percent equity ownership in its subsidiary and its Effective Control over its subsidiary was .57, far from a 1 to 1 correspondence.

The next step in the analysis was to examine the relationship between Effective Control as a dependent variable and the factors that may have

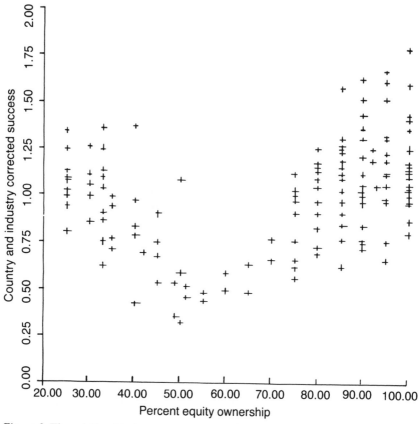

Figure 3 The relationship between country and industry corrected success and equity ownership

determined the relative bargaining power and desires for equity ownership of the TNCs and the host countries as independent variables using linear multiple regression. The expected signs of the coefficients are displayed in Table 1 based on the theory presented in the previous section. Notice that the expected signs are the same (except for "TNC-subsidiary linkages") for Effective Control as for Actual Equity Ownership since the factors that influenced Actual Ownership and Effective Control were the same. A higher degree of linkages between TNC and subsidiary may reduce the TNC's desire for equity ownership (because it can take its profits in other forms besides on its equity), but should increase its level of effective control.

The results of the regression analysis generally supported the hypotheses, although there were a few surprises (Table 2). First, although TNCs based in Japan and LDCs had generally lower actual equity ownership than U.S. and Europe-based TNCs, Japanese TNCs seem to have retained a

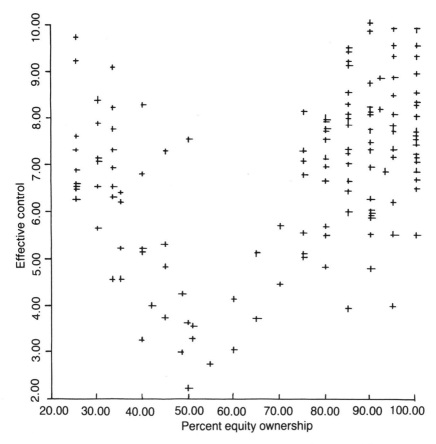

Figure 4 The relationship between effective control and equity ownership

slightly higher degree of Effective Control within the TNC (significant at the 5 percent level), given their relative bargaining power. This result may have some interesting policy implications, since one of the reasons given by host-country governments for an increased level of local equity partici- pation has been to retain control of the activities of the subsidiaries of TNCs.[17]

The relationship between Effective Control of a TNC over its subsidiary and the success of the investment was tested using 3 measures of success: the profitability of the subsidiary; the success of the subsidiary as rated by the TNC (1 = unsuccessful; 10 = very successful); and the "corrected" success where the success rating of an individual subsidiary was scaled in relation to the average success rating of the firms in the sample in the same industry in the same country, that is, country and industry corrected success (CICS). The TNCs were asked to rate the success of their invest- ment because profitability was not the only component of success for the

TNCs in the sample, and because the reported profitability fo the subsidiaries of TNCs has been found to differ from actual profitability.[18] The CICS rating was used to try to isolate the relationship between Effective Control and the success of the subsidiary independent of industry and country effects. The scatter diagram plotting CICS against Effective Control is in Figure 2. The relationship was roughly linear: the greater the Effective Control, the greater the CICS of the subsidiary from the TNCs' viewpoint. This relationship also held when success and profitability were plotted against Effective Control, although there was a much wider scatter about the trend, as expected.

The relationship between Percent Equity Ownership and CICS is displayed in Figure 3. Note that the relationship was roughly J-shaped. The lowest level of CICS occurred when equity ownership was roughly split between the TNC and its local partners. When equity ownership clearly resided with one partner or the other, the subsidiary tended to be more successful from the TNC's point of view. This J-shaped relationship also held between Overall Management Control and CICS, not surprising in light of the high correlation (.63) between Percent Equity Ownership and Overall Management Control. These results support the research of Killing [1982] and Schaan [1982] and provide it with statistical support drawn from a large sample of firms based in different home countries, operating in several industries, and investing in several host countries.

Conclusions and Implications

The theoretical and statistical analyses of this paper have traced the relationships between the characteristics of TNCs and host developing countries, their desired equity ownership in the subsidiary, control over the subsidiary, and the success of the TNCs in attaining their goals using a bargaining power framework of analysis. There was not a close relationship between Percent Equity Ownership and Effective Control. Some TNCs with a low percent of the equity in their subsidiaries had a high degree of control over the critical success variables in their subsidiaries. Conversely, some TNCs with a high level of equity ownership had a low degree of control over these variables. Some TNCs were able to control their subsidiaries in LDCs by means other than through their share of the equity of the subsidiary. There was a close linear relationship between the level of control a TNC had over the areas of operation of its subsidiaries that were critical to success, and the success of the investment from the TNC's viewpoint. The relationship between the TNC's overall management control and its equity ownership position in its subsidiary and the success of the subsidiary from its viewpoint was roughly J-shaped. Low success occurred when ownership and overall control were roughly equally divided between the TNC and its local partner. These conclusions have several implications for TNCs and host countries alike.

First, the relative bargaining power of TNCs and host LDCs, as proxied by the variables in Table 1, had a strong influence on the percent equity participation the TNCs in the sample attained in the ASEAN Region. Before investing in the LDC, TNCs might do well to assess their relative bargaining power so that they do not set unreasonable target levels of equity participation in negotiations with investors and host governments in LDCs. If the relative bargaining power of a TNC and the host government changes over time, negotiations may be initiated by either party to change the level of equity participation to reflect these changed conditions. Conversely, if a host government sets mandatory minimum levels of equity participation by its nationals, it may either discourage FDI (if the levels are higher than warranted by its relative bargaining power) or give up potential benefits of increased local ownership (if the levels set are too low).

Second, because the relationship between equity participation and effective control was not close, a TNC may be able to retain control over the factors of the operation of its subsidiary that are important to it, even though it has a low level of equity participation. A TNC may therefore be able to reduce the level of its equity participation in response to host country demands while retaining control over the factors that are critical to the success of its investment. If the TNC has significant linkages to its subsidiary in the LDC, it may be able to appropriate a satisfactory share of the profits earned on its firm-specific advantages in ways other than through its share of the dividends from its equity investment.

In its drive for increased equity ownership, a TNC may cause the host government to react in such a way as to reduce the TNC's control over these key factors in spite of its higher equity position, or, conversely, the TNC may not invest in a country that does not allow it its desired level of equity participation even though the TNC may be able to appropriate a satisfactory share of profits despite a reduced level of equity ownership. This trade-off between equity and control may be particularly important in countries where the host government perceives a high economic and political cost associated with foreign ownership. Conversely, host governments may have placed undue emphasis on the level of equity participation of TNCs in their economies in their desire to appropriate a share of the profits earned by TNCs operating in their economies, rather than focusing on the level of effective control and the linkages between TNCs and their local subsidiaries.

Third, there was a strong relationship between effective control and the success of the investment from the TNC's viewpoint. The relationship between Overall Management Control (and percent equity participation) and success was J-shaped: high and low levels of Overall Management Control (and high and low levels of equity participation) led to greater success than when ownership and management control were split roughly equally. These results reinforce the previous conclusions that it may be to the TNC's advantage to trade off reduced equity participation for increased effective control, a trade-off that may be available if increased equity participation (because it is highly visible) carries a high perceived cost to the host government, but effective control does not (because it is more difficult to discern, monitor, and regulate). TNCs should be careful about reaching a situation in which the level of equity ownership and control is roughly equal between the partners. On the other hand, host governments might gain more benefits for their countries if they bargained over increased local control rather than for increased local equity participation if they are concerned about losing control over their economies to TNCs and about the effects of transfer pricing on the flow of net benefits to their economies.

Fourth, although TNCs based in Japan have typically taken a lower level of equity ownership in LDCs than U.S. or European TNCs, they managed to retain a higher level of effective control over their subsidiaries, even when the relative bargaining power (as proxied by firm and country characteristics) of the 3 groups of firms is taken into account.

Notes

†Donald J. Lecraw has published books and articles on industrial organization, choice of technology, economic development, and international trade.

This research was partially funded by the United Nations Centre on Transnational Corporations and the Centre for International Business Studies, The University of Western Ontario. The author is also grateful to Paul Beamish for suggesting that the data base that the author compiled could be used to test several of the hypotheses presented in this paper.

1. Ironically, one of the persistent problems in joint ventures in LDCs is often the desire of local partners for a quick payback at the expense of the continued reinvestment desired by the TNCs.

2. In this paper the term "subsidiary" is used rather loosely to refer to a direct investment by a TNC in the host country regardless of the extent of the TNC's equity position in that subsidiary.

3. See Dunning [1979], Casson [1979], Buckley and Casson [1976], Rugman [1980], and Buckley [1981].

4. The greater the advantages of internalizing the international activity via FDI relative to licensing or export, the lower the relative returns to these activities and the more the firm will strive to retain a high share of the profits of the venture abroad by a high level of equity position in its subsidiary in the host country.

5. See Stopford and Wells [1972, Chapter 8] and Fagre and Wells [1982].

6. Conglomerate diversification, especially if the parent firms acts as a holding company, may be one form of externalizing the TNC's proprietary asset of access to relatively inexpensive capital. Conglomerate diversification usually occurs within national boundaries, although with a few notable exceptions (for example, Seagrams attempt to take over Conoco).

7. See Poynter [1982] and Bradley [1977] for analyses of the determinants of

host government intervention against TNCs and the strategic alternatives available to TNCs to reduce this intervention.

8. This effect may be decreased somewhat if the TNC is concerned about the price at which intrafirm goods and services are transferred and if there is a potential conflict over transfer prices with its local partner.

9. See Stern and Tims [1975], de la Torre [1981], and Streeten [1976] for analyses of the relative bargaining power of host countries.

10. In a preliminary draft of their paper, Fagre and Wells [1982] wrote, "As a practical matter, we had to use the degree of control (as measured by equity ownership) to indicate bargaining success." But further on they wrote, "Developing nations, just as many multinational corporations, generally equate equity ownership with control. In reality, ownership and control may not be perfectly related.... However, there is probably a reasonable correspondence between the percentage of equity ownership held by a parent corporation and the actual degree of control exercised over the affiliates in most cases." Fagre and Wells cited previous work by several authors to support this statement.

11. See Lecraw [1981, Table 3.4] and Kumar and Kim [1982].

12. There were wide variations about these averages. See Lecraw [1983a] for further data on the firms in the sample.

13. This measure may be better than that used by Fagre and Wells in that the comparison is for subsidiaries in LDCs, not to the ownership level of the TNCs' European subsidiaries where business conditions may be radically different from those in the host LDC.

14. See Vaitsos [1974, Chapter 5] for an analysis of transfer pricing by TNCs.

15. The correlation between capital intensity and capital requirements was .43.

16. See Hayashi [1978], Puxty [1979], Sim [1977] and Welge [1980] for analyses of comparative management and control systems among U.S., British, German, and Japanese TNCs.

17. This statement makes the assumption that local joint venture partners will act in the interest of the nation in exercising their control over the subsidiary. Even if this is not true, however, at least they will use their control for their own benefit and, to the extent they are part of the nation, the nations gains. This argument is roughly similar to "I'd rather be had by someone within my group than by a stranger."

18. See Vaitsos [1974, Chapter 5].

References

Beamish, P., and Lane, H. "Joint Venture Performance in Developing Countries." London, Canada; University of Western Ontario, 1982. Mimeo.

Bradley, D. G. "Management Against Expropriation." *Harvard Business Review*, July-August 1977, pp. 75–83.

Buckley, P. J., and Casson, M. "The Optimal Timing of a Foreign Direct Investment." *The Economic Journal*, March 1981, pp. 75–87.

———, *The Future of the Multinational Enterprise*. London: Macmillan, 1976.

Casson, M. *Alternatives to the Multinational Enterprise*. London: Macmillan, 1979.

de la Torre, J. "Foreign Investment and Economic Development, Conflict and Negotiation." *Journal of International Business Studies*, Fall, 1981, pp. 9–32.

Dunning, J. "Explaining Changing Patterns of International Production: In Defense of the Eclectic Theory," *Oxford Bulletin of Economics and Statistics*, November 1979, pp. 269–295.

Fagre, N., and Wells, L. T. Jr. "Bargaining Power of Multinationals and Host

Governments." *Journal of International Business Studies,* Fall 1982, pp. 9–24.

Franko, L.G. *Joint Venture Survival in Multinational Corporations.* New York: Praeger, 1971.

Hayashi, K. "Japanese Management of Multinational Operations: Sources and Means of Control." *Management International Review,* 18, No. 4 (1978), pp. 47–57.

Horst, T. *At Home Abroad: A Study of the Domestic and Foreign Operations of the American Food-Processing Industry.* Cambridge, MA: Ballinger, 1974.

Killing, P. "Technology Acquisition: License Agreements or Joint Ventures." *Columbia Journal of World Business,* Fall 1980, pp. 38–46.

———, "How to Make a Global Joint Venture Work." *Harvard Business Review,* May/June 1982, pp. 120–127.

Kumar, K., and Kim, K. Y. "The Korean Manufacturing Multinationals." East-West Center, University of Hawaii, 1982. Mimeo.

Lecraw, D. J. "Direct investment by Firms from Less Developed Countries." *Oxford Economic Papers,* November 1977, pp. 442–457.

———, "Internationalization of Firms from LDCs: Evidence from the ASEAN Region." In *Multinationals from Developing Countries,* edited by K. Kumar and M. McLeod, Lexington, MA: D.C. Heath Lexington Books, 1981.

———, "Performance of Transnational Corporations in Less Developed Countries." *Journal of International Business Studies,* Spring-Summer 1983a, pp. 15–33.

———, "Comment on Moxon," *International Business Strategies in the Asia-Pacific Region,* edited by R. Moxon, T. Roehl, and F. Truitt. Vol. 4, Part 1. JAI Press, 1983b.

——— . "Evidence on Transfer Pricing by TNCs." In *Transfer Pricing and the MNE,* edited by Alan Rugman, Cambridge, MA: MIT Press, forthcoming, 1985.

Magee, S. "Technology and the Appropriability of the Multinational Corporation." In *The New International Economic Order.* Cambridge, MA: MIT Press, 1977.

Moxon, R. "Export Platform Investment in the Asia-Pacific Region." in *International Business Strategies in the Asia-Pacific Region,* edited by R. Moxon, T. Ruehl, and F. Truitt. JAI Press, 1983.

Poynter, T. A. "Government Intervention in Less Developed Countries: The Experience of Multinational Companies." *Journal of International Business Studies.* Spring-Summer 1982, pp. 9–25.

Puxty, A. G. "Some Evidence Concerning Cultural Differentials in Ownership Policies of Overseas Subsidiaries." *Management International Review* 19, No. 2 (1979), pp. 39–52.

Rugman, A. M. "Internalization as a General Theory of Foreign Direct Investment: A Re-Appraisal of the Literature." *Weltwirtschaftliches Archiv.* Band 116, Heft 2, 1980, pp. 365–379.

Schaan, J. L. "Joint Ventures in Mexico." Ph.D. proposal. Business School, The University of Western Ontario, London, Canada, 1982. Mimeo.

Sim, A. B. "Decentralized Management of Subsidiaries and Their Performance: A Comparative Study of American, British, and Japanese Subsidiaries in Malaysia." *Management International Review* 17, No. 2 (1977), pp. 45–51.

Stern, E., and Tims, W. "The Relative Bargaining Strengths of the Developing Countries." *American Journal of Agricultural Economics.* May 1975, pp. 225–236.

Stopford, J., and Wells, L. T. Jr. *Managing the Multinational Enterprise.* New York: Basic Books, 1972.

Streeten, P. "Bargaining with Multinationals." *World Development,* Vol. 4, No. 3, March 1976.

Vaitsos, C. V. *Intercountry Income Distribution and Transnational Enterprises.* Oxford: Oxford University Press, 1974.

Vernon, R. *Sovereignty at Bay.* New York: Basic Books, 1971.

Welge, M. K. "A Comparison of Managerial Structures in German Subsidiaries in France, India, and the United States." *Management International Review* 21, No. 2 (1980), pp. 5–21.

Wells, L. T. Jr. *Third World Multinationals: The Rise of Foreign Investment from Developing Countries,* Cambridge, MA: MIT Press, 1983.

Appendix

Calculation of effective control

Factors	Control(C) 1(no)–10(complete)	Importance(I) 1(none)–10(critical)
Output pricing	6	8
Output volume	4	9
Output quality	8	10
Technology transfer	10	10
Technology control	10	10
Capital expenditures	5	7
Financing source	1	2
Financing cost	2	2
Financing amount	1	1
Dividends timing	5	6
Dividends amount	7	6
Fees paid to the TNC	7	8
Advertising and marketing and expenditures	4	7
Channels of distribution	3	2
Import price	6	5
Import source	8	10
Import volume	4	3
Export price	9	3
Export destination	8	4
Export volume	7	2
Overall management	6	7

$$\text{Effective control} = \frac{\Sigma C\,1}{1} = \frac{801}{122} = 6.6$$

16

Host-country Policies to Attract and Control Foreign Investment*

Stephen Guisinger

*Source: T. Moran, ed., *Investing in Development: New Roles for Foreign Capital?* (New Brunswick, Transaction Books, 1986) pp. 157–172.

Policies that attract and control foreign direct investment have become the focus of considerable attention in both developed and developing countries in recent years, but for quite different reasons. For developing countries, the interest is prompted by the debt crisis: The poorer countries need additional foreign capital to fuel economic growth but cannot add more loans that call for fixed schedules of repayment. The flexibility inherent in dividend and capital repatriations makes foreign equity investment substantially more attractive than it has been in the past. Developing countries are eager to know what incentive policies can most efficiently attract the desired amount of capital and what controls on foreign investment can ensure that other national objectives—domestic ownership of key industries and balance-of-trade objectives, for example—are also attained.

The interest of the developed countries, which are primarily capital exporters, flows from a desire to have access to host-country markets. Increasingly, access is through local production rather than through exports. Investment controls that limit foreign participation in these markets can be as injurious as tariffs. Moreover, a number of developing countries impose restrictions that require firms to sell portions of their output in foreign markets and specify minimum amounts of inputs that the firms must buy in the host country. Some observers feel that these performance requirements, if left to multiply, could become a serious impediment to a liberal world trading environment.

Three basic questions lie behind this interest in investment incentives and performance: Do countries use investment incentives to compete for foreign investment capital? Do both incentives and performance requirements actually work? And if they do work, have they caused significant shifts in the international flow of trade and investment?

Do Countries Use Incentives to Compete for Foreign Investment?

If this question is interpreted as "Do countries have at least one policy instrument that raises the profit of foreign investors?," the answer seems to be a definite "yes." Every country has at least one instrument—whether it is a cash grant, a tax holiday, or a subsidized loan—that benefits both domestic and foreign investors.

The question can, however, be interpreted another way: Do countries have at least one incentive that discriminates in favor of foreign investors relative to domestic ones? Although many countries have on occasion granted foreign firms incentives that were denied local investors, few have done so on a systematic basis.

But the search for evidence of such incentives misses the point. The context in which the question is normally posed calls for evidence about the *overall* impact of investment policies: Do incentives, on balance, outweigh disincentives, and is this net balance more favorable in one country than in others? The question has to be answered in relative terms.

Getting an answer to this question is difficult for two reasons. First, where does one draw the line between investment policies and other policies? Second, how does one sum up the influence of the wide array of investment policies into a single measure of attraction or repulsion?

The distinction between investment and other policies is not clear-cut. The array of policies that affect investment profitability can best be described as a spectrum. At one end are policies, such as cash grants, that have an obvious, direct impact on the profitability of individual investments. At the other end are policies, such as monetary policy, that affect investment profitability only indirectly and clearly cannot be termed investment policies. In the middle are policies that are difficult to classify.

Table 1 lists the complete array of investment incentive and disincentive measures available to a country and places them in one of four categories:

(1) measures affecting the revenues of an investment project;
(2) measures affecting costs of inputs purchased by an investment project;
(3) measures affecting the value of factors of production used by an investment; and
(4) measures affecting investment profitability but not classifiable in the other three categories.

No government uses all of these measures to implement investment policy. Coordinating the more than forty measures on the list would result in an administrative nightmare. Yet governments generally do use more than one instrument. A recent study of the policies employed in ten developed and developing countries in 1982 found that the national inventories of these measures ranged from a low of twelve to a high of thirty-five, with the average country relying on twenty-two incentive and disincentive measures.[1]

Table 1 Classification of incentives and disincentives

Incentives/disincentives	Effect on after-tax return on owner's equity
Affecting Revenues	
Tariffs	+
Differential sales/excise taxes	+ or −
Export taxes/subsidies (including income tax credits)	+ or −
Quotas	+
Export minimums	−
Price controls (or relief from)	+ or −
Multiple exchange rates	+ or −
General overvaluation of currency	−
Government procurement preference	+
Production/capacity controls	+
Guarantees against government competition	+
Prior import deposits	+
Transfer price administration	−
Affecting Inputs	
Tariffs	−
Differential sales taxes (and exemptions therefrom)	+ or −
Export taxes/subsidies (including utilities)	+ or −
Quotas	−
Price controls	+
Multiple exchange rates	+ or −
Subsidy or tax for public-sector suppliers	+ or −
Domestic-content requirements (including R&D)	−
Prior import deposits	−
Transfer price administration	−
Limits on royalties, fees	−
Multiple deduction for tax purposes	+
Cash or in-kind grants for R&D	+
Affecting components of Value-added	
Capital	
Direct subsidy	
Cash grant	+
Tax credits/investment allowances } Specify if reduces book value: taxable or not	+
Subsidized leasing	+
Cost of capital goods	
Tariff/sales tax exemption on imported/domestic equipment	+
Prior import deposits	−
Local-content requirement for capital equipment	−
Limits on use of used equipment	−
Subsidized buildings	+
Subsidized cost of transportation	+

Table 1 continued

Incentives/disincentives	Effect on after-tax return on owner's equity
Affecting Components of Value-added, continued	
Cost of debt	
Subsidized loans	+
Loan guarantees	+
Covering of foreign exchange risks on foreign loans	+
Priority of access (including limitations on foreign firms)	+ or −
Cost of equity	
Subsidized equity through public investment agencies	+
Exemption from capital gains taxes/registration taxes	+
Dividend tax/waiver	+ or −
Guarantee against expropriation or differential treatment	+
Limitations on debt/equity ratio	−
Controls/taxes on remitted dividends	−
Minimum financial/in-kind ratio	−
Corporate tax	
Tax holiday/reduction	+
Accelerated depreciation	+
Special deductions and valuation practices (inflation adjustment; multiple plant consolidation)	+
Tax sparing and double-taxation agreements	+
Loss-carry-forward provision	+ or −
Contractual stabilization of rates	+
Labor	
Wage subsidies (including indirect, i.e., multiple deductions of wages for tax computations/reduction of taxes on labor)	+
Training grants	+
Minimum wage	−
Relaxation of industrial relations laws	+
Local labor requirements	−
Land	
Cash subsidy for purchase/rental	+
Exemption/rebate of taxes on land	+
Not classified	
Limitations on foreign ownership	
Free-trade zones	
General preinvestment assistance	
Countertrade requirements	
Foreign exchange balancing requirements	

How a government selects a particular set of instruments from a large array of possibilities is a tantalizing question not addressed here. National investment policy portfolios appear to be the product of a country's history, size, and government organization, to name just a few determining factors. The large number of instruments observed in many countries may stem from the fact that old policies are hard to terminate when new ones are added or that competition to attract foreign investment has caused governments to adopt policy instruments they would otherwise prefer to do without. It is unlikely that each policy instrument is allied with a specific objective; many seem to be substitutes for one another, and therefore redundant.

The issue at hand, however, is not why governments choose particular policies but rather whether investment policies, taken together, repel or attract foreign investment. Up to this point, an implicit assumption has been that the effects of investment policies can be measured along a single dimension—the cumulative value of incentives less the value of dis-incentives—similar to the way in which the rate of effective protection provides a cardinal scale for assessing the strength of tariff protection. Yet, it is possible that investment policies may have multiple attributes, with the net incentive being just one of several that affect investors. If this is true, it is unlikely that a single measure will capture the total impact of these multiple attributes.

Information collected from a variety of sources—including responses to survey questionnaires on investment location decisions, personal interviews with investors, and the literature on foreign direct investment—suggests that six principal attributes of investment policies influence the location decision: the net incentive, the variety of incentives, stability of incentives, timing of incentives, investment promotion activities, and government services.

The net incentive is the aspect of incentive policies on which most analysts focus. For a proposed investment project, it can be conceived of as the increase in profitability (internal rate of return or net present value) that is attributable to all the measures listed in Table 1. Tariffs are included in this definition because governments occasionally substitute factor-based incentives (such as cash grants and labor subsidies) for commodity-based ones.[2] For example, the Board of Investment in Thailand has the authority to increase the level of protection from competing imports (including a complete ban on imports) and to lower tariffs on imported inputs as part of a negotiated investment incentive package that includes a tax holiday, with Board discretion over its length (zero to eight years). The Board has several different combinations of tariff and tax concession measures that can yield the same after-tax rate of return for investors.

Variety of Incentives

The notion that the mix of incentive instruments, quite independently from the actual net incentive received, may influence investment behavior does not fit well into international economic theory, but it can be explained by theories of management, especially organizational behavior and marketing. Some instruments may have more appeal; for example, tax abatements may be more intrinsically attractive to corporate decision makers than labor training grants—even though the impact on the after-tax rate of return is identical. Investors may prefer certain incentive instruments because their effects are not transparent to competitors and the tax-paying public. A large menu of incentives also gives investors maximum flexibility to design their own package.

Stability of Incentives

The stability of investment policies over time is an important consideration for investors. Although most incentive policies are fixed contractually prior to investment, governments nevertheless control other policies that can increase or decrease profitability during the course of the investment's life. A country's reputation for "obsolescing bargains"—for progressively watering down initial incentives with subsequent disincentives—may deter investors.

On the other hand, another type of policy instability can sometimes be a positive factor. For example, one automobile manufacturer invested in a European country on the assumption that government policies would eventually change in the direction of restricting entry for the products the manufacturer was exporting to that country. When that day came, the manufacturer wanted to be well established. The manufacturer thought that both current market conditions and existing incentives were inadequate, but the possibility of increased incentives in the future prompted his positive decision.

Timing of Incentives

The benefits and costs associated with a country's incentive and disincentive instruments are not distributed uniformly over time. Cash grants are disbursed quickly, whereas tariff protection is spread over the life of a project. Cash is generally more certain to be realized by the investor than are the benefits of tariff protection, which depend on the stability of government policies and the commercial success of the venture. Some countries, for example, Belgium, provide incentives to new investments but impose disincentives (in the form of mandatory severance pay for employees) on investments at the end of their lifetime.

Investment Promotion Activities

Many governments spend large sums on investment promotion, including advertising, traveling delegations, and representative offices abroad. Ireland has more than ten offices in Europe, North America, and the Far East (including five in the United States), staffed with representatives that call on prospective investors. Like good marketers, these representatives "sell the sizzle, not the steak," and a full menu of incentives often provides the sizzle. Although promotion and incentives often appear as complements, they are ultimately substitutes, since governments must allocate funds between the two types of activities.

Government Services

For some projects, the provision of government services at less than full cost can be an important enticement. In many countries, buildings in industrial estates are provided at subsidized rates. Examples abound of governments building roads, bridges, ports, and housing projects to accommodate the plans of potential investors. In almost every case, these services have other users, so it is hard to identify the true subsidy element. Still, the capacity of a government not only to share the cost of infrastructure but also to see that services are delivered in the proper amounts and on time is regarded by investors as an important consideration in their investment location decision. The "one-stop shop" concept—the ability of one agency of government to negotiate and deliver incentives packages that include government services—is often attractive to prospective investors.

In summary, investment policies have at least six different aspects that appeal to investors. No single measure captures the impact of these six attributes on the potential investor. The relative strengths of these various elements are not known, making it difficult to analyze the effectiveness of any one element on investment flows. The impact of the net incentive must be analyzed by controlling for the effects of the other five elements. It is commonly assumed that the net incentive dominates these attributes, but to date no evidence exists to confirm or reject this assumption.

Do Incentives Work?

One often encounters the opinion, generally unencumbered by hard empirical data, that incentives do not work—or at least that certain incentives do not work. The arguments take various forms. One is that governments waste incentives on companies that were going to make an investment in the host country anyway. The cost of these windfall gains, so the argument goes, may exceed the benefits of any induced investment.

Another argument is that investors select host countries on the basis of real and enduring factors—such as market size and strength or labor and transport costs—rather than in response to artificial and fleeting factors, such as tax holidays and cash grants. One variation of this argument is that incentives may even be counterproductive, since the need to offer them is seen by investors as a sign of fundamental weakness in the host-country economy. Still another argument is that most non-tariff incentives—such as cash grants or tax holidays—are simply too small to matter much to investors.

The alleged insignificance of non-tariff incentives does not seem to be borne out in practice. Under reasonable assumptions, a one-time tax-free cash grant of 50 per cent of the value of an investment is tantamount, insofar as the investor is concerned, to a 30-per cent annual effective rate of protection over the lifetime of the investment.[3] This rate of effective protection means little unless it is put in perspective. The common external tariff of the European Economic Community provides Ireland, for example, with an average effective rate of 27 per cent. The 50-per cent grant that the Irish government provides to selected new investments effectively adds another layer of protection, equal to that already existing from tariffs.

Although only a few countries offer cash grants ranging up to 50 per cent, many countries offer an array of other non-tariff incentives that come close to this level. Mexico grants tax credits to investments in priority regions and priority industries that amount to as much as 30 per cent of the value of the investment. The value of these tax credits, combined with subsidized loans and other fiscal incentives, can exceed 40 per cent of the value of investments. Portugal recently proposed giving cash-grant equivalents of up to 40 per cent to help restructure its textile industry. France offers cash grants of more than 50 per cent to high-technology firms willing to locate in regions targeted for development.

Empirical Studies of Incentive Effectiveness

One difficulty in conducting empirical studies of the effectiveness of fiscal incentives is that no country keeps a good record of the incentive measures granted to new investors. Whereas tariff protection is often granted through one instrument by one agency and applied uniformly to all firms in an industry, fiscal incentives are spread over many instruments, administered by a variety of agencies, and often applied at different rates to firms in the same industry. Sometimes good information exists on the use of one particular incentive instrument. At other times, complete information is available on incentives in a few selected investments. But neither of these provides the type of data needed to test hypotheses about the impact of the net incentive on investment decisions. In a study that we recently conducted under World Bank auspices, my colleagues and I attempted to bridge the data gap by collecting detailed information on seventy-four foreign investment projects directly from multinational enterprises in four industries—food products, automobiles, computers, and petrochemicals.[4] Numerous problems were encountered in obtaining data. Firms do not maintain complete records on incentives received in the past, nor do managers always have a clear concept of what is meant by the term "incentives." Some managers, for example, regarded tax holidays as investment incentives but treated accelerated depreciation strictly as an accounting convention.

Another problem was the definition of effectiveness. When countries compete for foreign investment, several of them often offer more or less the same investment package. The slight advantage that the incentives of one country may have over another's package generally makes little difference in the site selected. In surveys of the importance that decision makers attach to various factors affecting the investment location, other considerations—the cost of labor, infrastructure availability, proximity to markets— frequently rank well above incentives.

Can we conclude from such surveys that incentives are not effective? The answer would certainly be in the affirmative if one country could eliminate its incentives with no loss of foreign investment. Whether this is true or not depends on what other countries do. If they maintain their incentives, it would seem likely that the country dropping such measures would lose foreign investors. If, on the other hand, other countries follow the first one's lead, each country would more than likely maintain its share of investors. This dependence of outcomes on the strategies of other participants in a particular process is characteristic of "the prisoner's dilemma." In the case of incentives, the prisoner's dilemma often leads to competitive bidding in which all participants are left worse off than if no bidding had occurred. But the fact that granting incentives is not effective for all countries involved in bidding wars does not imply that any one country can withdraw with no injury to itself. Incentives may be effective in an asymmetrically perverse way: An increase in incentives may produce no net gain in competitive situations, but unilateral withdrawal may be highly detrimental to a country's inflow of foreign capital.

Inquiries into the effectiveness of incentives thus always beg the question: What do other countries do when one country raises or lowers it incentives? In the World Bank study, we chose an admittedly extreme basis for measuring the effectiveness of incentives. Respondents were asked the following hypothetical question: Would your firm have located in a particular country (i.e., where the seventy-four cases were in fact located) if no incentives (including market protection through tariffs) had been offered to you *and* if competitor countries maintained their incentive packages at their traditional levels? With the question posed in this manner, many respondents indicated that, in this hypothetical case, the absence of incentives would have affected their decision even though, in the real instance,

Table 2 Dominant influence on location decision

Investment orientation	Non-policy influence	Policy-related influence		
		Policy stability	Commodity-based	Factor-based
Domestic market	8	3	23	2
Common market	9	6	0	11
Worldwide export market	7	0	1	4
Total	24	9	24	17

Source: Stephen Guisinger and Associates, *Investment Incentives and Performance Requirements* (New York: Praeger, 1985), p. 49.

the presence of incentives was not a major factor in their decision. In the absence of incentives, they would have chosen another location or would have served the host-country market through exports from existing production facilities in the home country or elsewhere.

Table 2 shows responses from the seventy-four projects surveyed. In twenty-four cases, respondents indicated that they would have stuck with their original decisions. Nine of the sixteen investments in food processing fell into this category, underscoring the importance of market or raw-materials proximity to the decision on location; for many firms in this industry, incentives are truly "icing on the cake." For the fifty cases in which incentive policies were decisive factors in the choice of investment location, twenty-four projects cited tariff and non-tariff barriers as important, and seventeen identified fiscal incentives as important.

In nine cases, firms indicated that it was the instability of investment policies, as described earlier, that motivated their investment location decision. Sometimes it was a threat—rarely made explicitly but frequently inferred from government behavior—that future import barriers would be coupled with restrictions on foreign investment; the clear implication was that a firm had best invest now or forfeit future opportunities. In other instances, governments hinted that new performance requirements would be imposed on existing foreign investments unless owners made additional investments in the host country. Studies using either survey techniques or data on existing incentive levels would not pick up these nine cases in which the government's power to vary incentives levels was the deciding factor.

Because the World Bank study did not follow stratified sampling procedures, few generalizations can be made about the comparative effectiveness of incentives among industries or across countries. Nor is it possible to conclude from the study that certain types of incentive instruments are more effective than others. This chapter already has emphasized the problems inherent in that line of inquiry. The study suggests, however, that the withdrawal of all incentives—an admittedly draconian step for most countries—would seriously impair the ability to attract new foreign investment, although this result depends on the assumption that the incentive policies of other competitor countries remain unchanged.

Do Performance Requirements Affect Trade and Investment?

The third question is by far the most difficult. The prevalence of performance requirements is not hard to document, but their influence on investment decisions and on the pattern of foreign purchases and sales by an investment project is far more difficult to discern. The World Bank found that among seventy-four cases, thirty-eight were subject to trade-related performance requirements (typically, to export a certain fraction of their output). Other performance requirements included domestic content and trade balancing—the foreign-exchange cost of imported inputs must be offset by export earnings. No standard definition of performance requirements exists. The narrow definition of trade-related performance requirements comprises only those government restrictions that seek to reduce foreign-exchange costs or to raise foreign-exchange earnings of investment projects. Broader definitions include almost every form of government restriction on an enterprise, but most typically those that stipulate specific proportional requirements for ownership and employment based on national origin.

One problem of measuring the incidence of performance requirements encountered in the World Bank study was the use of implicit performance requirements administered through discretionary incentives. Many countries have created investment promotion agencies empowered to grant incentives to projects meeting certain criteria. The Industrial Development Authority in Ireland and the Economic Development Board in Singapore are notable examples. In lieu of explicit performance requirements on all new investment projects, these agencies reward projects designed to meet trade performance criteria and withhold incentives from those projects that do not. The World Bank study found an inverse correlation between market size and the imposition of formal performance requirements. Large developing countries, such as Brazil, India, and Mexico, have not delegated investment review and promotion responsibilities to a single agency, relying on decentralized decisions based on formal, automatic performance criteria applied uniformly to all investment projects. Small countries, such as Ireland and Singapore, do not explicitly impose domestic-content and export-minimum requirements on investors but prefer to exercise leverage through discretionary incentive policies.

Performance requirements act as turbochargers for incentive instruments. They magnify and redirect the rents from incentive measures by linking the receipt of incentive benefits to the fulfilment of certain performance criteria. The World Bank study found no investments subject to performance requirements that did not also enjoy substantial incentives, and it would be difficult to envisage these investments ever having been made if the requirements were present but the incentives absent. Governments use these incentive-generated rents to promote balance-of-payments equilibrium and import substitution. By stipulating quantitative targets for exports or domestic content in individual investments, these objectives can be served more efficiently. Performance requirements sidestep some of the prohibitions of the General Agreement on Tariffs and Trade (GATT) on export subsidization. But as Hufbauer and Erb have argued: "Perhaps now the concept of export subsidies should extend even further to cover the provision of licensing rights conditioned on export performance, such as the right of establishment or the right to apply for fiscal incentives."[5]

Another feature of the more broadly defined performance requirements is that they are designed to keep the incentive-created rents at home. If rents were merely exchanged among nationals of a country, only the income redistributive effects and the real resource costs of rent-seeking would provide cause for concern. However, when foreign investors are introduced into the picture, part of repatriated profits due to rents represents real resource losses. Governments seek to block these losses by stipulating limitations on foreign equity ownership and imposing ceilings on repatriation.

The World Bank study found that, of the thirty-eight investments subject to performance requirements, only four would have been located elsewhere (or would not have been made) were it not for the requirements. In these four cases, all in the automobile industry, the investors already had a substantial stake in the host country's market either through domestic production or exports. The investments were necessitated by the decisions of the governments to require that imports be offset with exports.

The study did not attempt to address the issue of trade distortions brought on by performance requirements because of conceptual and information gaps. To isolate the independent effect of performance requirements on trade patterns, a series of assumptions must be strung together. For example, in the absence of performance requirements, would the investment have been made at all? If so, what type of project would have been built? What kind of incentive package would the government have granted if performance requirements were not permitted?

Assumptions about these issues are critical because they determine the costs that performance requirements impose on firms. At present, only information about the number and type of performance requirements, by country and industry, is available. These are useful data, but they say little about the changes in firms' behavior induced by performance requirements.

Performance requirements may, indeed, have little effect in practice for several reasons. First, investors may meet the performance criteria without the need for the explicit requirements. In this case, they are simply redundant. Second, governments have on occasion relaxed performance requirements previously imposed on an investment in response to worsening external market conditions or internal shortages of intermediate inputs. Finally, requirements may not be enforced. Although legally binding, performance requirements are often regarded by governments as little more than good faith agreements that firms should do their utmost to achieve.

Although some analysts exaggerate the potency of performance requirements, these measures—including the implicit variety described above—are widely used by countries that have both the level of domestic incentives and the bargaining strength to make them stick. The problem is that researchers have no convenient method of measuring their impact in the same way that effective rates of protection measure the significance of tariffs. The number of performance requirements found in an industry or a country is irrelevant; number has no bearing on their aggregate strength. Until thorough case studies are compiled that convincingly detail the incentives and investment projects that would occur in the absence of performance requirements, their influence will remain in the realm of anecdote and speculation.

Conclusion and Policy Implications

Investment incentives are a modern Hydra. The Herculean GATT severed the head of direct export subsidies, but not tax incentives, investment credits, and subsidized loans and performance requirements have sprung up to take their place. The number and complexity of investment incentives pose serious problems for anyone wishing to assess the importance of such measures.

Evidence of an indirect nature has been provided to show that the impact of investment incentives on the investor's rate of return may be quite important when compared with the levels of effective protection that many investors in both developed and developing countries enjoy. Thus, while any individual incentive measure may have a small effect, the cumulative effect of all incentive measures granted by a host country nevertheless may be substantial.

It also has been shown that out of a sample of seventy-four foreign investment projects undertaken by multinational enterprises in four industries (automobiles, chemicals, food products, and computers) fifty—or two of every three investments studied—would have been located in a different country if incentives had been withdrawn (provided that all other countries maintained their incentive systems at existing levels). This does not, however, suggest that countries can gain by increasing incentive levels, since their actions may be matched by other countries, canceling out any advantage that the increase momentarily gave the initiating country. The World Bank study, for which the survey was done, found substantial competition among some countries for foreign investment, suggesting that, at least for these nations, policy changes in one country more than likely stimulate changes in the policies of its competitors.

If a "prisoner's dilemma" situation exists—with rounds of competitive bidding leading to no net change in any one competitor's share of total foreign investment—each country has an interest in limiting the use of incentive instruments. Clearly, investment incentives may have a role in promoting a higher aggregate volume of investment worldwide; but once the appropriate volume of investment is attained, further incentives aimed at increasing one country's share may prove to be collectively futile. The Treaty of Rome attempted to limit the use of incentives to influence investment location by placing a ceiling on the cumulative value of incentive awards equal to 75 per cent of the value of the investment. This ceiling applied only to the least developed regions, and lower ceilings were imposed on more developed areas of the European Community. The Association of South East Asian Nations (ASEAN) also has attempted to limit the use of incentives among its members.

The principal problem in all of these efforts to curtail the use of incentives is one of negotiating enforceable agreements: The rewards from cheating can be substantial. The increased interest of multilateral institutions such as the GATT, the World Bank, and the recently proposed Multilateral Investment Guarantee Agency in the problems of incentive proliferation may bring their powers of enforcement to bear on the cheating problem. However, as this chapter has emphasized, many conceptual and informational gaps remain to be closed before any truly workable agreements can be reached.

Another policy implication is that performance requirements do not constitute a separate set of issues; rather, they determine how the rents created by investment incentives are directed to achieve social objectives. Performance requirements accelerate and redirect the rents generated by incentive policies. Any attempts to negotiate away performance requirements will very likely result in compensating changes in host-country incentive policies, possibly contributing further to distortions in trade and investment pattern.

Notes

1. Stephen Guisinger and Associates, *Investment Incentives and Performance Requirements* (New York: Praeger, 1985), pp. 5–8.

2. The substitution between factor-based and commodity-based measures is discussed in Eric Bond and Stephen Guisinger, "Investment Incentives as Tariff Substitutes: A Comprehensive Measure of Protection," *Review of Economics and Statistics*, Vol. LXVII, No. 1 (February 1985), pp. 91–97.

3. Stephen Guisinger, "Do Investment Incentives and Performance Requirements Work?," *The World Economy*, Vol. 9, No. 1 (March 1986), Footnote 7.

4. Guisinger and Associates, op. cit.

5. Gary Hufbauer and Joanna Erb, *Subsidies in International Trade* (Washington, D.C.: Institute for International Economics, 1984), p. 83.

Select Bibliography

Agmon, T. and C.P. Kindleberger, *Multinationals from Small Countries* (Cambridge, Mass., MIT Press, 1977).

Balasubramanyam, V.N., *Multinational Enterprises and the Third World* (London, Trade Policy Research Centre, 1980).

Baranson, Jack, "Technology transfer through the international firm", *American Economic Review*, 60 (1970), pp. 435–440.

Barnet, Richard J. and Ronald E. Müller, *Global Reach: The Power of the Multinational Corporations* (New York, Simon and Schuster, 1974).

Bergsman, Joel and Wayne Edisis, "Debt-equity swaps and foreign direct investment in Latin America" (Washington, D.C., International Finance Corporation, Discussion Paper No. 2, 1988), mimeo.

Biersteker, T.J., *Distortion or Development: Contending Perspectives on the Multinational Corporation* (Cambridge, Mass., MIT Press, 1978).

Blomström, Magnus, "Foreign investment and productive efficiency: the case of Mexico", *Journal of Industrial Economics*, XXXV (1986), pp. 97–110.

——, *Foreign Investment and Spillovers* (London, Routledge, 1989).

——, *Transnational Corporations and Manufacturing Exports from Developing Countries* (New York, United Nations Centre on Transnational Corporations, 1990).

Brooke, Michael Z. and H. Lee Remmers, *The Strategy of Multinational Enterprise* (London, Longman, 1970)

Buckley, Peter J. and Jeremy Clegg, eds., *Multinational Enterprises in Less Developed Countries* (London, Macmillan, 1991).

Buckley, Peter J. and Mark Casson, *The Future of the Multinational Enterprise* (London, Macmillan, 1979).

——, "Multinational enterprises in less-developed countries: cultural and economic interactions" (Reading, University of Reading Discussion Papers in International Investment and Business Studies, Series B, No. 126, January 1989), mimeo.

Cable, Vincent and Bishnodat Persaud, eds., *Developing with Foreign Investment* (London, Croom Helm, 1987).

Cantwell, John, *Technological Innovation and the Multinational Corporation* (Oxford, Basil Blackwell, 1989).

Cantwell, John and Paz Estrella Tolentino, "Technological accumulation and third world multinationals" (Reading, University of Reading Discussion Papers in International Investment and Business Studies, No. 139, 1990), mimeo.

Casson, Mark, *et al., Multinationals and World Trade: Vertical Integration and the Division of Labour in World Industries* (London, Allen and Unwin, 1986).

Casson, Mark and Robert Pearce, "Multinational enterprises in LDCs", in Norman Gemmell, ed., *Surveys in Development Economics* (Oxford, Basil Blackwell, 1987), pp. 90–132.

——, "Intra-firm trade and the developing countries", in D. Greenway, ed., *Economic Development and International Trade* (London, Macmillan, 1988), pp. 132–156.

Caves, Richard E., "Multinational firms, competition and productivity in host country markets", *Economica*, 41 (1974), pp. 176–193.

——, *Multinational Enterprise and Economic Analysis* (Cambridge, Cambridge University Press, 1982).

Caves, Richard E., Harold Crookel and Peter Killing, "The imperfect market for technology licences", *Oxford Bulletin of Economics and Statistics*, 43 (1983), pp. 249–267.

Chen, Edward K.Y., *Multinational Corporations, Technology and Employment* (London, Macmillan, 1983).

Chudnovsky, Daniel, "Regulating technology imports in some developing countries", *Trade and Development*, 3 (1981), pp. 133–150.

Cohen, Benjamin I., *Multinational Firms and Asian Exports* (New Haven, Yale University Press, 1975).

Connor, James M., *The Market Power of Multinationals: A Quantitative Analysis of U.S. Corporations in Brazil and Mexico* (New York, Praeger, 1977).

Contractor, Farok J., "Technology importation policies in developing countries", *The Journal of Developing Areas*, 17 (July 1983), pp. 499–520.

Courtney, William H. and Danny M. Leipziger, *Multinational Corporations in LDCs: The Choice of Technology* (Washington, D.C., U.S. AID, 1974).

De la Torre, José, "Foreign investment and export dependency", *Economic Development and Cultural Change*, 23 (1974), pp. 135–150.

Dunning, John H., *International Production and the Multinational Enterprise* (London, Allen and Unwin, 1981).

——, *Explaining International Production* (London, Unwin Hyman, 1988).

Dunning, John H., ed., *Economic Analysis and Multinational Enterprise* (London, Allen and Unwin, 1974).

——, ed., *Multinational Enterprises, Economic Structure and International Competitiveness* (Chichester, John Wiley and Sons, 1985).

Encarnation, Dennis J. and Louis T. Wells Jr., "Evaluating foreign investment", in Theodore Moran, ed., *Investing in Development: New Roles for Foreign Capital?* (Washington, D.C., Overseas Development Council, 1986), pp. 61–86.

Enos, John L., "Transfer of technology", *Asian-Pacific Economic Literature*, 3 (March 1989), pp. 3–37.

Ernst, Dieter and John O'Connor, *Technology and Global Competition: The Challenge Ahead for Newly Industrializing Economies* (Paris, OECD, 1989).

Evans, Peter B., "Direct investment and industrial concentration", *Journal of Development Studies*, 13 (1977), pp. 373–385.

——, *Dependent Development: The Alliance of Multinational State and Local Capital in Brazil* (Princeton, Princeton University Press, 1979).

Finger, James M., "Tariff provisions for offshore assembly and the exports of developing countries", *The Economic Journal*, 85 (1975), pp. 365–371.

Forsyth, David J.C. and Richard R. Solomon, "Choice of technology and nationality of ownership in a developing country", *Oxford Economic Papers*, 29 (1977), pp. 258–282.

Fröbel, Folker, Jürgen Heinrichs and Otto Kreye, *The New International Division of Labour* (London, Cambridge University Press, 1980).

Grunwald, Joseph and Kenneth Flamm. *The Global Factory: Foreign Assembly in International Trade* (Washington, D.C., The Brookings Institution, 1985).

Helleiner, Gerald K., "Manufactured exports from less-developed countries and multinational firms", *The Economic Journal*, 83 (March, 1973), pp. 21–47.

——, "The role of multinational corporations in less developed countries' trade in technology", *World Development*, 3 (1975), pp. 161–189.

——, *Intra-firm Trade and Developing Countries* (London, Macmillan, 1981).

——, "Transnational corporations and direct foreign investment", in Hollis B. Chenery and T.N. Srinivasan, eds., *Handbook of Development Economics* (Amsterdam, Elsevier Science Publishers, 1989), pp. 1442–1480.

Hill, Hal, "Foreign investment and East Asian economic development", *Asian-Pacific Economic Literature*, 4 (September 1990), pp. 21–58.

Hirschman, Albert O., "How to divest in Latin America and why", *Essays in International Finance* (Princeton, Princeton University Press, 1969).

Hood, Neil, M. and Stephen Y. Young, *The Economics of Multinational Enterprise* (London, Longman, 1979).

Hughes, Helen and Yoh Poh Seng, *Foreign Investment and Industrialization in Singapore* (Madison, University of Wisconsin Press, 1969).

Hymer, Stephen H., *The International Operation of National Firms: A Study of Direct Foreign Investment* (Cambridge, Mass., MIT Press, 1976).

ILO, *Employment Effects of Multinational Enterprises in Developing Countries* (Geneva, International Labour Office, 1981).

——, *Technology Choice and Employment Generation by Multinational Enterprises in Developing Countries* (Geneva, International Labour Office, 1984).

Jenkins, Rhys, *Transnational Corporations and Industrial Transformation in Latin America* (London, Macmillan, 1984).

——, *Transnational Corporations and Uneven Development* (London, Methuen, 1987).

——, "Comparing foreign subsidiaries and local firms in LDCs: theoretical issues and empirical evidence", *Journal of Development Studies*, 26 (January 1990), pp. 205–228.

Khan, Kushi M., ed., *Multinationals of the South* (New York, St. Martin's Press, 1986).

Kindleberger, Charles P., *American Business Abroad* (New Haven, Yale University Press, 1969).

Kopits, George F., "Intra-firm royalties crossing borders and transfer-pricing behaviour", *Economic Journal*, 86 (1976), pp. 781–805.

——, "Taxation and multinational firm behaviour: a critical survey", *IMF Staff Papers*, 23 (1976), pp. 624–673.

Kumar, Krishna and Maxwell G. McLeod, eds., *Multinationals from Developing Countries* (Lexington, D.C. Heath, 1981).

Lall, Sanjaya, "Transfer pricing by multinational manufacturing firms", *Oxford Bulletin of Economics and Statistics*, 35 (August 1973), pp. 173–193.

——, "Less developed countries and private foreign direct investment: a review article", *World Development*, 2 (1974), pp. 43–48.

——, "Transnational, domestic enterprises and industrial structure in host LDCs: a survey", *Oxford Economic Papers*, 30 (1978), pp. 217–248.

——, "Multinationals and market structure in an open developing economy: the case of Malaysia", *Weltwirtschaftliches Archiv*, 115 (1979), pp. 325–348.

——, "Vertical interfirm linkages in LDCs: an empirical study", *Oxford Bulletin of Economics and Statistics*, 42 (1980), pp. 203–228.

——, *Developing Countries as Exporters of Technology* (London, Macmillan, 1982).

——, *Multinationals, Technology and Exports* (London, Macmillan, 1985).

——, *Building Industrial Competitiveness in Developing Countries* (Paris, OECD, 1990).

Lall, Sanjaya, ed., "Exports of technology by newly-industrializing countries", *World Development*, Special Issue, 12 (1984), pp. 471–660.

Lall, Sanjaya and Paul Streeten, *Foreign Investment, Transnationals and Developing Countries* (London, Macmillan, 1977).

Lall, Sanjaya, in collaboration with Edward K.Y. Chen, Jorge M. Katz, Bernardo Kosacoff and Annibal Villela, *The New Multinationals: The Spread of Third World Enterprises* (Chichester, John Wiley and Sons, 1983).

Langdon, Stephen, *Multinational Corporations in the Political Economy of Kenya* (London, Macmillan, 1981).

Lecraw, Donald J., "Direct investment by firms from less developed countries", *Oxford Economic Papers*, 29 (1977), pp. 442–457.

——, "Performance of transnational corporations in less developed countries", *Journal of International Business Studies*, 14 (1983), pp. 15–33.

——, "Bargaining power, ownership, and profitability of transnational corporations in developing countries", *Journal of International Business Studies* (Spring/Summer 1984), pp. 27–43.

Lim, Linda Y.C. and Eng Fong Pang, "Vertical linkages and multinational enterprises in developing countries", *World Development*, 10 (1982), pp. 585–595.

Mason, Robert H., "Some observations on the choice of technology by multinational firms in developing countries", *Review of Economics and Statistics*, 55 (1973), pp. 349–355.

Moran, Theodore H., ed., *Investing in Development: New Roles for Foreign Capital?* (New Brunswick, Transaction Books, 1986).

Morley, Stan A. and George W. Smith, "Limited search and the technology choices of multinational firms in Brazil", *Quarterly Journal of Economics*, XCI (1977), pp. 263–287.

Nayyar, Deepak, "Transnational corporations and manufactured exports from poor countries", *The Economic Journal*, 88 (1978), pp. 59–84.

Newfarmer, Richard S., "TNC takeovers in Brazil: the uneven distribution of benefits in the market for firms", *World Development*, 7 (1979), pp. 25–43.

——, "International industrial organization and development: a survey", in Richard S. Newfarmer, ed., *Profits, Progress and Poverty* (Notre Dame, University of Notre Dame Press, 1985), pp. 13–62.

Newfarmer, Richard S. and William F. Mueller, *Multinational Corporations in Brazil and Mexico: Structural Sources of Economic and Non-Economic Power* (Washington, D.C., U.S. Government Printing Office, 1975).

Nixson, Frederick I., "Business behaviour in the private sector", in Colin H. Kirkpatrick, Nick Lee and Frederick Nixson, eds., *Industrial Structure and Policy in Less Developed Countries* (London, Allen and Unwin, 1984), pp. 86–149.

Oman, Charles, *New Forms of International Investment in Developing Countries* (Paris, OECD, 1984).

Parry, Tom G., "The multinational enterprise and two-stage technology transfer to developing nations", in Robert G. Hawkins and A.J. Prasad, eds., *Research in International Business and Finance*, vol. 2 (Greenwich, Conn., JAI Press, 1981), pp. 175–192.

Plasschaert, Sylvain R.F., *Transfer Pricing and Multinational Corporations* (Farnborough, Saxon House, 1979).

Porter, Michael, *The Competitive Advantage of Nations* (New York, Free Press, 1990).

Reuber, Grant L. *et al.*, *Private Foreign Investment in Development* (Oxford, Clarendon Press, 1973).

Riedel, James, "The nature and determinants of export-oriented direct foreign investment in a developing country: the case of Taiwan", *Weltwirtschaftliches Archiv*, 111 (1975), pp. 505–528.

Rugman, Alan M. and Lorraine Eden, *Multinationals and Transfer Pricing* (Beckenham, Croom Helm, 1985).

Schive, Chi, "Foreign investment and technology transfer in Taiwan", *Industry of Free China*, LXX, 2 and 3 (August/September 1988), pp. 13–23, 13–30.

Sharpston, Michael, "International subcontracting", *Oxford Economic Papers*, 27 (1975), pp. 94–135.

Singer, Hans W., "The distribution of gains between investing and borrowing countries", *American Economic Review*, 40 (1950), pp. 473–485.

Solomon, Richard F. and David J. Forsyth, "Substitution of labour for capital in the foreign sector: some further evidence", *Economic Journal*, 87 (1977), pp. 283–289.

Sosin, Kim and Loretta Fairchild, "Capital intensity and export propensity in some Latin American countries", *Oxford Bulletin of Economics and Statistics*, 49 (1987), pp. 191–208.

Streeten, Paul P., "The theory of development policy", in John H. Dunning, ed., *Economic Analysis and the Multinational Enterprise* (London, Allen and Unwin, 1974), pp. 252–279.

Teece, David J., "Technology transfer by multinational firms: the resource cost of transferring technological know how", *The Economic Journal*, 87 (1977), pp. 242–261.

Tolentino, Paz Estrella E., *Technological Innovation and Third World Multinationals* (London, Routledge, 1991).

Tyler, William G., "Technical efficiency and ownership characteristics of manufacturing firms in a developing country: a Brazilian case study", *Weltwirtschaftliches Archiv*, 114 (1978), pp. 360–379.

UNCTC, *Transnational Corporations in World Development: Trends and Prospects* (United Nations publication, Sales No. E.88.II.A.7).

——, "Recent developments related to transnational corporations and international economic relations: the triad in foreign direct investment", E/C.10/1991/2.

UNIDO, *Foreign Direct Investment Flows to Developing Countries; Recent Trends, Major Determinants and Policy Implications* (Vienna, United Nations Industrial Development Organization, 1990).

Vaitsos, Constantine V., "Power, knowledge and development policy", in Gerald K. Helleiner, ed., *A World Divided* (Cambridge, Cambridge University Press, 1976), pp. 113–146.

——, *Intercountry Income Distribution and Transnational Enterprises* (Oxford, Clarendon Press, 1974).

Vernon, Raymond, "International investment and international trade in the product cycle", *Quarterly Journal of Economics*, 80 (1966), pp. 190–207.

——, *Sovereignty at Bay* (New York, Basic Books, 1971).

——, *Storm over the Multinationals: The Real Issues* (London, Macmillan, 1977).

——, "The product cycle hypothesis in a new international environment", *Oxford Bulletin of Economics and Statistics*, 41 (1979), pp. 255–267.

Wells, Louis T. Jr., *Third World Multinationals* (Cambridge, Mass., MIT Press, 1983).

Westphal, Larry E., Yung W. Rhee and Gary Pursell, "Foreign influences on Korean industrial development", *Oxford Bulletin of Economics and Statistics*, 41 (November 1979), pp. 359–388.

Whitmore, Katherine, Sanjaya Lall and Jung-Taik Hyun, "Foreign direct investment from the newly industrialized economies" (Washington, D.C., World Bank Industry and Energy Department Working Paper, Industry Series Paper No. 22, 1989), mimeo.

Willmore, Larry, "Direct foreign investment in Central American manufacturing", *World Development*, 4 (1976), pp. 499–517.

——, "The comparative performance of foreign and domestic firms in Brazil", *World Development*, 14 (1986), pp. 489–501.

Name Index

Subject Index